THE TIBET GUIDE

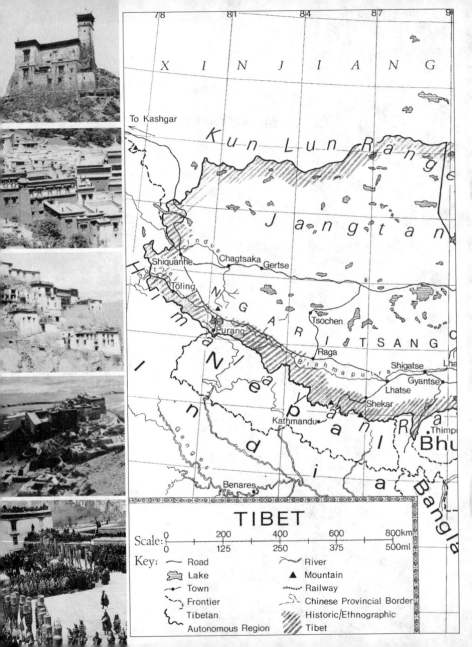

TIBET

Scale:
| 0 | 200 | 400 | 600 | 800km |
| 0 | 125 | 250 | 375 | 500ml |

Key:
- ⌇ Road
- 🌊 Lake
- •‑ Town
- ⌇ Frontier
- ⌇ Tibetan Autonomous Region
- 〜 River
- ▲ Mountain
- ⌇ Railway
- ⌇ Chinese Provincial Border
- ⧗ Historic/Ethnographic Tibet

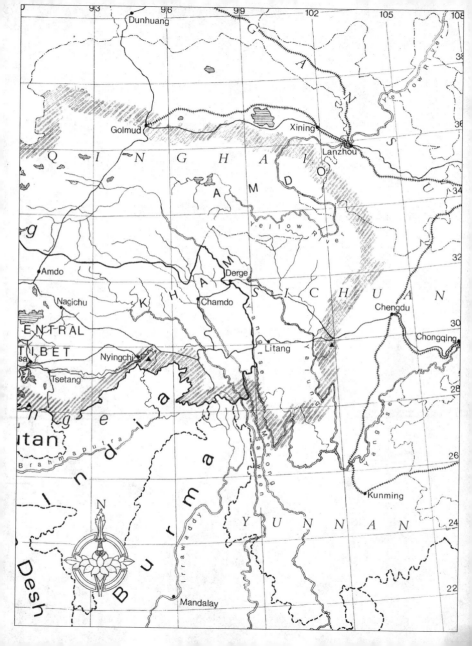

Revised Edition

THE TIBET GUIDE
Central and Western Tibet

STEPHEN BATCHELOR

with Brian Beresford and Sean Jones
and an Iconographical Guide by Robert Beer

Foreword by the Dalai Lama

Wisdom Publications · Boston

WISDOM PUBLICATIONS
199 ELM STREET
SOMERVILLE, MASSACHUSETTS 02144

© Wisdom Publications Inc. 1998

Maps of the Gyantse Kumbum are adapted with permission from Franco Ricca and Erberto Lo Bue, *The Great Stupa of Gyantse* (Serindia, 1993).

Library of Congress Cataloging-in-Publication Data

Batchelor, Stephen
    The Tibet guide : central and western Tibet / Stephen Batchelor ; foreword by Dalai Lama -- Rev. ed.
        p.   cm.
    Includes bibliographical references and index.
    ISBN 0-86171-134-3 (alk. paper)
    1. Tibet (China)--Description and travel--Guidebooks.   I. Title.
DS786.B35   1998
915.1 ' 50459--dc21   97-40033

ISBN 0-86171-134-3

03 02 01 00 99
   6   5   4   3   2

Book Design: L. J. Sawlit

Wisdom Publications' books are printed on acid-free paper and meet the guidelines for the permanence and durability of the Committee on Production Guidelines for Book Longevity of the Council on Library Resources.

Printed in the United States of America.

CONTENTS

PUBLISHER'S ACKNOWLEDGMENTS

The publisher wishes to express appreciation to Melissa Mathison and Harrison Ford and Richard Gere for their support of this book project as well as their generosity of spirit in reflecting the light of their celebrity on the cause of Tibet.

The publisher gratefully acknowledges the help of the Hershey Family Foundation in sponsoring this book. The Hersheys' generous ongoing support has been critical to the development of Wisdom.

Thanks also to Distant Horizons, Bindy Gross, Sandra Magnussen, Pamela Butler, as well as many others who contributed to the realization of this book. We offer our sincere gratitude for the donations they made in support of this new edition of *The Tibet Guide*.

THE DALAI LAMA

FOREWORD

The future of Tibet depends in part upon the actions of those of us who are outside of Tibet. Although we Tibetans must bear the primary responsibility for bringing change to our country, by ourselves we cannot make our voices heard effectively in the wider forum of the world community. Our struggle for freedom and preservation of the distinct Tibetan culture and way of life will largely remain obscured without the help of the outside world.

I am happy to hear about this new edition of *The Tibet Guide: Central and Western Tibet* by Stephen Batchelor. While the Chinese authorities have been allowing foreigners to visit occupied Tibet again for more than ten years, there is still a general lack of information concerning the true situation in Tibet. Many tourists enter the country unaware of the distinct culture and history of the Tibetan people. Seeing monks and nuns inside the monasteries, they may wrongly believe that religious freedom has been restored in Tibet as a whole.

The need for a balanced and accurate depiction of the state of affairs in Tibet is obvious. The present book presents the basic facts about Tibet in a manner that prepares tourists for what they will encounter when they reach the Land of the Snow. In this way, the book should help to fill the gap of knowledge about Tibet.

Although it is frequently not Tibetans who benefit financially from the tourist industry in Tibet, I nonetheless still encourage those who wish to travel there to go and see the situation for themselves. In addition, the interest that the outside world shows in Tibet gives hope to the Tibetan people, kindling their faith in the justice of their cause. It is my fervent prayer that all those who travel to Tibet will return with a renewed commitment to add their voice to the growing international concern and support for human rights and religious freedom in Tibet.

Tenzin Gyatso
His Holiness the 14th Dalai Lama
August 19, 1997

PREFACE

Tibet is simultaneously the most inspiring and the most tragic place I have been. The landscape, with its vast plains and soaring mountains sheltered beneath huge crystalline skies, is inspiring. So too are the noble, resilient, and warm-hearted people. The religious sites, which evoke the memory of the monks, nuns, yogis, and yoginis who practiced (and even today struggle to practice) there, are also inspiring.

At the same time Tibet is a land of tragedy. The scenes of utter destruction that greet you at the sites of many monasteries, the tales of imprisonment and torture you hear from the mouths of men and women subjected to these abuses since the Chinese occupation, and the ubiquitous reminders of the systematic attempt by a colonial power to impose its will on another people are all immensely tragic.

I do not intend to condone uncritically the former regime or to acquiesce in the Chinese occupation of Tibet as though it were an irreversible fact. Pre-1959 Tibet was neither the mystical paradise of certain romantic and nostalgic writers nor the medieval hell of Chinese propaganda. It was a land where a high degree of spiritual freedom coexisted with what for most people today would be an unacceptably backward and rigid feudal society.

Ultimately, the "Tibet Question" has nothing to do with a comparison of the relative merits and demerits of the past and present state of affairs. It is instead a question of the rights of an ethnically, linguistically, and culturally distinct people to political self-determination and religious freedom. The current Chinese policies of economic liberalization and respect for "ethnic minorities" and the cultural achievements of the past should not mislead us into thinking that the rulers in Beijing have budged an inch on the issue of Tibetan independence. China continues to be a repressive totalitarian state which tortures and imposes draconian prison sentences on those who challenge its authority. If anything, recent events suggest that the Chinese are more intent than ever on stamping out any suggestion of greater political autonomy for the Tibetan people.

The aim of *The Tibet Guide: Central and Western Tibet* is to provide a thorough background to the history and culture of Tibet as well as detailed descriptions of the major historical and religious sites of the central and western provinces of the country as they are today. The book should be of value to anyone intending to visit Central or Western Tibet as a tourist, a trekker, a pilgrim, or a scholar. At the same time, the book provides an informed and up-to-date picture of Tibet, which should be both informative and enjoyable for armchair-travelers as well as students of Tibetan religion and culture. At a future date, I hope to compile a companion volume to *The Tibet Guide: Central and Western Tibet*, which will cover the provinces of Kham and

Amdo in eastern and northeastern Tibet.

While the organization of the material, the maps, and the descriptions of routes enable a visitor to find his or her way around the country, the details that one expects to find in a conventional guidebook concerning hotels, restaurants, bus terminals, and so on have been somewhat reduced. My experience of traveling in Tibet has shown me that the country is very far from establishing a stable tourist infrastructure. If you are traveling with an organized group, such details will in any case be of little relevance. If you are traveling independently, the most reliable source of information on these matters will be the grapevine of current knowledge shared among fellow travelers. Nonetheless, to help you plan your trip and to assist you with the practicalities of the journey, important travel information—including information on visas, health, and air connections—has been included in the section called Travel in Central and Western Tibet.

Numerous people have been involved in helping me compile and edit the information contained in this book. I am particularly indebted to many Tibetans who guided me around the sites and shared the oral history of the places I have visited over the last twelve years. In addition, another rich source of information has been the *Bod rgya tshig mdzod chen mo*, an encyclopedic three volume Tibetan dictionary (with Chinese), published in the early 1980s in Lhasa and soon to be available in English translation.

This book would probably never have been written if it had not been for the initial encouragement and continued support of Dr. Nicholas Ribush, whose recent field trips to Tibet have provided detailed, updated descriptions of sites. Coupled with my own observations, Dr. Ribush's reports have enabled me to revise my earlier accounts and make the present edition of *The Tibet Guide* as accurate as possible.

I am likewise indebted to Robert Beer for the iconographical guide; Sean Jones and the late Brian Beresford for the section on Western Tibet; and Chris Shaw for the original maps and diagrams. Others who have contributed in various ways to this project over the years are: Bradley Rowe, Gyurme Dorje, Keith Dowman, Andre Alexander, John V. Bellezza, Janet Moore, Heather Campbell, and Sara McClintock. Thanks are also due to the photographers whose work is featured in this book, including Hugh Richardson, Robin Bath, Simon Chaput, Brian Kistler, Hamid Sardar, Amina Tirana, Trey Nicholson, and Vern Soni.

Finally, I must thank my wife, Martine, who accompanied me to Tibet on my first two visits and provided invaluable support throughout the entire project.

Stephen Batchelor
Sharpham College
July 1997

HOW TO USE THIS BOOK

The Tibet Guide: Central and Western Tibet has been written primarily to provide visitors to Central and Western Tibet with a comprehensive description and explanation of what they will see when they are there. All the major historical sites in Central and Western Tibet are covered, with special attention to their religious and cultural significance.

The book is divided into four main sections that correspond to the three main regions of Central and Western Tibet plus the capital city of Lhasa. Each of these sections is further divided into chapters that cover particular sites within the region. The chapters are organized in three parts: travel details, history, and a description of the site. The numbers on the maps refer to buildings that are included in the description of the site.

Technical Buddhist terms and names of important historical figures are listed in the glossary. The iconographical guide enables you to identify the most common deities and lamas depicted in Tibetan Buddhist paintings and statues.

A simplified and nonscholastic method of transcribing Tibetan words has been used; it does not differ greatly from the systems used in other books on Tibet. One of the most important things to remember about pronouncing Tibetan words is that if the word ends in *e*, that *e* is *always* accented. *Gyantse*, for example, is pronounced *Gyantsé (Gyantsay); Sera Me,*

Sera Mé (Sera May), and so forth. The section Useful Words and Phrases transcribes many common Tibetan words in a way designed to convey the approximate English sound equivalents.

Unless stated otherwise, the shrines, chapels, statues, paintings, and other objects mentioned at religious sites are always described in the order they are passed by a pilgrim circumambulating the site in a clockwise direction. In descriptive passages, *left* and *right* always refer to the viewer's left and right. To say, for example, that a particular chapel is to the left of a certain building means that it is to the left of the viewer when the viewer is facing the entrance of that building. In describing a room, the term *front wall* means the wall through which you enter the room; *back wall*, the wall you face from the entrance; *left-hand wall*, the wall to your left as you stand at the entrance; and *right-hand wall*, the wall to your right as you stand at the entrance. This can be confirmed by reference to the accompanying diagram.

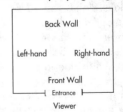

The terms "first floor" and "first story" indicate the ground floor of a building, while "second floor" or "second story" refer to the story that you reach after climbing one set of stairs. Note that this usage follows the American system.

INDEX OF MAPS AND DIAGRAMS

TABLES

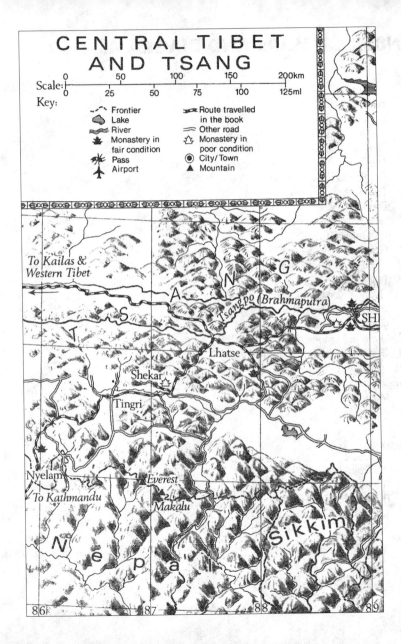

CENTRAL TIBET
AND TSANG

Scale:

| 0 | 50 | 100 | 150 | 200km |
| 0 | 25 | 50 | 75 | 100 | 125ml |

Key:

- ⌇ Frontier
- 🏔 Lake
- ∿ River
- ☗ Monastery in fair condition
- ☀ Pass
- ✈ Airport
- ⟫ Route travelled in the book
- ═ Other road
- ☆ Monastery in poor condition
- ◉ City/Town
- ▲ Mountain

To Kailas & Western Tibet

T S A N G

Tsangpo (Brahmaputra)

SH

Lhatse

Shekar

Tingri

Nyelam

To Kathmandu

Everest

Makalu

N e p a l

Sikkim

86

87

88

89

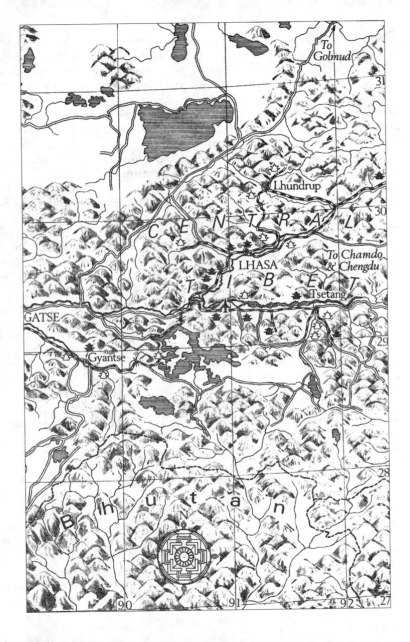

THE LAND & ITS PEOPLE

Three hundred million years ago what is now Tibet was covered by the Tethys Sea, a vast ocean that covered much of India and Asia. The Mediterranean is but Tethys's last remaining puddle. Forty million years ago immense pressure from the Indian land mass started to force the area to the north upward, resulting in the soaring Himalayan range and, swelling beyond it, the vast Central Asian plateau. The high open land of Tibet rests on this plateau and stretches for 2,000 km (1,250 miles) from India in the west to China in the east, and for over 1,000 km (600 miles) from Nepal in the south to the Chinese province of Xinjiang (Turkestan) in the north. Its average elevation is 4,000 m (13,000 feet) above sea level. On three sides it is bordered by some of the loftiest mountains in the world: to the south by the Himalayas, to the west by the peaks of the Karakoram and to the north by the Kunlun and Tangla ranges. The land gradually descends eastward, its vast barren spaces interrupted by subsidiary mountain ranges and deep gorges, until it meets the lowlands of China's westernmost provinces of Sichuan and Yunnan.

Some of Asia's greatest rivers have their sources on the Tibetan plateau. In the far west, near the sacred Mount Kailash, the Indus and Sutlej begin their long courses westward and join each other in the plains of Pakistan. Close by springs the Tsangpo (Brahmaputra), which flows eastward through Southern Tibet like a massive life-giving artery, finally breaking through the Himalayas in a series of dramatic gorges and emptying into the Bay of Bengal. In the far east of the country the Salween and Mekong Rivers begin their journeys into Southeast Asia, while the Yangtse flows due east as far as Shanghai and the Yellow River pours into the East China Sea south of Tianjin.

The altitude of Tibet ranges from semi-tropical, forested lowlands along the southern borders at around 1,000 m (3,200 feet) to some of the highest snow peaks in the world at 8,000 m (26,000 feet). In the lower regions, one finds monkeys, red pandas, and deer. As one rises to the grasslands one may see marmots, pikas, kyang (wild asses), wild yak, gazelles, and black-necked cranes. At the higher levels live ibex, brown bears, snow leopards, and snow grouse. Many of the larger mammals have been killed in recent years by Chinese hunters, and plans are underway to establish nature preserves to protect the most threatened species.

From the abundant lianas and bamboo that thrive in the lower forests, one moves upward through mixed forest of oak, ash, rhododendron, and other deciduous trees to the evergreen trees that reach to the broad open grasslands. Here grasses of various kinds are mixed with occasional shrubs and, on sheltered slopes, wind-resistant pines and other small trees. In the fertile valleys, poplar, willow, and similar trees line the fields and surround the villages. As one moves toward the snow line one finds lichens, mosses, and algae, with a variety of alpine flowers. In recent years, vast forested areas in the east of the country (Kham and Amdo) have been cut down and the timber taken to China. In Central Tibet the forested area begins east of Lhasa on the borders of Kongpo. This too is being systematically eroded for both fuel and construction.

The northern half of Tibet is a virtually uninhabited desert called the Jangtang (Northern Plain). Only occasional hunters and collectors of salt and borax roam this wasteland. The south reaches of this plain are an extensive area of mountainous grazing land inhabited by nomads and their herds of sheep, goats, and yaks. These people, wild and unkempt in appearance, live in black animal-hair tents, surviving on meat and dairy products. Even today they maintain their traditional lifestyles that may well date back over two thousand years. Periodically, they bring supplies of dried meat, wool, butter, and cheese down from the highlands into the towns and villages and trade them for *tsampa* (roasted barley flour), cloth, and simple manufactured goods.

The majority of Tibetans live in the southern part of the country in the area irrigated by the Tsangpo and its tributaries, and in the eastern provinces of Kham and Amdo. These more hospitable regions of gentle, protected valleys pro-

duce the crops on which the Tibetans depend: barley, wheat, and a small variety of vegetables and fruit. Animal husbandry is also practiced and on the farms you will find cows, goats, pigs, and horses. There are numerous scattered villages, many of which consist of only a couple of farming compounds. A typical compound is a single-story, whitewashed, quadrangular complex with an entrance leading into an open courtyard. Around the courtyard is the living area for the farmer's family and storage rooms and barns for their livestock. Flags, often shredded and faded by harsh winds, stream from masts erected from the flat roofs. These are replaced every new year as an auspicious sign to usher in the spring. Fuel, such as wood, brush, and dried dung, is often stored on the roofs.

The southern valleys are the places where Tibetan culture and civilization developed. Until the Chinese campaign of systematic destruction, monasteries, hermitages, and religious monuments dotted the landscape. These varied in size from small establishments with a single shrine room and quarters for a handful of monks or nuns, to vast institutes of learning with populations of up to several thousand monks. There are few towns of any size, Lhasa, Shigatse, Tsetang, Gyantse, and Chamdo being the largest. Traditionally, these were centers of trade and the seat of a regional governor.

The influence of Tibetan culture has spread beyond the borders of "political Tibet," that is, the area actually or nominally under the control of the Lhasa government. Bhutan, Nepal, Sikkim, Ladakh, and a few other areas in north India such as Spiti and Lahoul are still repositories of ancient Tibetan learning. Ethnically, too, it seems that many of the people living in these areas are descended from Tibetan stock.

It is believed that the Tibetans originated from non-Chinese nomadic tribes who wandered into the country from the northeast around two and a half to three thousand years ago. They are a hardy, independent people, whose natural warmth and good humor have been noted by most Western travelers who have ventured into Tibet since the seventeenth century. It is difficult to know the exact population of the country. The Dalai Lama's office claims that there are six million Tibetans in Tibet, whereas a Chinese survey conducted in 1982 puts the figure at 3.87 million Tibetans living within the People's Republic of China. The Dalai Lama's office further claims that 1.2 million Tibetans were killed during the Cultural Revolution. Hugh Richardson, the head of the British Mission in Lhasa in the forties, considered two million to three million to be an accurate estimate at that time. At present a further 100,000 or more Tibetans live as refugees in India, Nepal, Bhutan, Europe, and America.

Until the Chinese takeover beginning in 1950, this nation of nomads, farmers, and traders lived a simple but, according to most accounts, contented life. Most people readily accepted their place within a society consisting of aristocratic landowners, peasants, clergy, and merchants. The population was kept stable by as many as an estimated one-third of men living as monks. The agricultural resources of the land were sufficient to provide all with plenty to eat. Despite the number of monks, a system of polyandry—whereby one woman had more than one husband—existed. Compared with other Asian countries, there was a relatively high degree of literacy, and the majority were at least able to read and recite the commonest prayers. A simple code of law was devised in the seventh century and elaborated by subsequent rulers, but in practice local custom often determined the sometimes brutal punishments inflicted for crimes. Taxes were levied from all levels of society: landowners had to give a percentage of their income; peasants had to provide labor, army service, and travel assistance; and monks repaid their endowments with prayers and rituals. People journeyed either by foot, on horseback, or, where possible, in coracles. Except for a couple of cars owned by the Dalai Lama, there was no wheeled transport in the country until the 1950s.

Few of these traditional ways of life continue today. Nomads and farmers are still the mainstay of the economy, but many of the latter have been forced to become part of collective farms and work units. Apart from a few crafts centers, there is still virtually no manufacturing industry in Tibet. There is one factory, in Tolung, west of Lhasa, which makes cement.

The balance between population and agricultural resources was catastrophically upset by the massive influx of Han Chinese, resulting in famines from 1959–63 and 1968–73. While there have been some improvements in recent years in the material lot of Tibetans, the laws of Communist China make any expression of resistance to the system a crime. Schools have indeed been built, but the majority of high school classes are taught in Chinese. Tibetans who wish to receive the kind of further education that will allow them to enter professions or rise in the ranks of the civil service must pursue their studies in Chinese, usually in China itself. I was told that a university degree from Lhasa University is regarded as equivalent to a high school diploma from a Chinese school.

Hydroelectric plants have been installed that provide electricity for most townships. A network of roads and bridges is still being constructed to connect all major towns and roads, and the Chinese have declared their intention to build a rail link into Tibet. The "new" China is encouraging Western investment in Tibet and channeling increasing amounts of government funding into economic developments in the Lhasa area. Tourism is seen as a crucial element in the generation of wealth in Tibet.

Before traveling to Tibet, the foreign tourist may wish to contemplate the complex moral issues that surround tourism there. Some Tibetans have argued that tourism is nothing more than a means of subsidizing the Chinese occupation of the country. By visiting Tibet, tourists contribute much needed foreign exchange to the Chinese government, only a small percentage of which is likely to reach the local people. On the other hand, it is also true that worldwide awareness of and sympathy for the plight of Tibet has increased enormously ever since foreign visitors have been allowed freedom of access to the country. The Dalai Lama has personally encouraged people to go to Tibet and see the situation there for themselves. Moreover, the emergence over the last few years of an increasingly free-market economy in China and Tibet has meant that many Tibetans have been able to start companies and run their own (usually small-scale) businesses.

Although it may entail sacrificing comfort and convenience, if you stay in small Tibetan-run hotels, eat at Tibetan-run restaurants and shop in Tibetan stores, you can contribute directly to the local indigenous economy. At the same time, you will also be able to see firsthand some of the effects of the Chinese occupation of Tibet, including the widespread presence of Chinese military police throughout the country.

THE HISTORY OF TIBET

THE YARLUNG EMPIRE (629–842 C.E.)

Yumbulagang, 1950

The two great civilizations bordering Tibet—India and China—were at first barely aware of the movements of the people scattered over the high, inhospitable regions beyond their frontiers. They considered them unkempt, illiterate, barbarian tribes who occasionally had to be pushed back across the border where they belonged but for the most part could be ignored. This situation began to change in the seventh century C.E. when a mighty king called Songtsen Gampo suddenly made his presence felt in both countries with the threat of invasion by a powerful, swift, and well-organized army.

Tibetan historians regard Songtsen Gampo as the thirty-third king in a line that began with the magical descent from the skies of Nyatri Tsenpo. This man appeared on a mountain called Yarlha Zhampo at the head of the Yarlung Valley in Central Tibet. The people of the region declared him their chieftain and he built a palace called the Yumbulagang from which to rule. While allowing for the mythological aspects of this story, Nyatri Tsenpo can be dated at about 500 B.C.E. It is also possible that he was Indian in origin, since the Tibetans consider him to be related to one of the Indian dynasties contemporary with the historical Buddha. Although the significance of Nyatri Tsenpo and the early Yarlung kings has no doubt been embellished by later historians, his appearance probably coincides with the first stirring among the Tibetans of the notion of a social and political identity.

The first twenty-seven kings of the Yarlung dynasty adhered to the native Bön religion, an animistic cult governed by exorcists, shamans, and priests, the early nature of which remains veiled behind centuries of Buddhist antagonism and Bön's own self-imposed transformation as a means of keeping up with the Buddhists. During the reign of the twenty-eighth king, Lhatotori (fourth century C.E.), the first Buddhist scriptures appeared in Tibet. They also fell from the sky and had the good fortune to land on the Yumbulagang, where the king lived with his court. This event can be understood as the first acknowledgment of Buddhism among the ruling circles. Bön, however, was not to be easily swept aside, and conflicts between it and the imported Buddhist faith were eventually responsible for the collapse of the dynasty.

Songtsen Gampo

Songtsen Gampo was born in 617 C.E. and ascended the throne at the age of thirteen. He ruled for twenty years, during which time he established the borders of a powerful empire that extended far beyond the immediate area of the Yarlung Valley. Tibetan forces were active from the plains of Northern India to the Chinese frontiers in the east and the borders of the Turkish empire in the west. Songtsen Gampo established a summer capital in Lhasa and built a palace on the Red Hill (the site of the Potala). As a gesture of friendship toward their threatening neighbor, Nepal and China each offered the king a bride from their royal families.

In broadening his horizons, the king became aware of the Buddhist civilization prevailing not only in its country of origin, India, but also as the spiritual inspiration of the newly formed T'ang dynasty of China. The prestige and significance of Buddhism was further impressed upon him by his Nepalese and Chinese wives and the dowries they brought with them containing magnificent statues of the Buddha. Whether this warring man actually became the devout Buddhist king that popular tradition makes him out to be is open to question. But it is certain that he encouraged the building of temples to house the images brought by his wives and was probably responsible for the construction of several other religious shrines throughout the land. He also sent his minister Tönmi Sambhota to India to create a written script suitable for the transcription of Tibetan. This enabled the Tibetans to start translating the Sanskrit Buddhist scriptures into their own language.

Trisong Detsen

The second great ruler of the Yarlung dynasty, Trisong Detsen, did not begin his reign until 755, more than a hundred years after the death of Songtsen Gampo. He inherited a strong empire, consolidated by the four kings who had ruled since Songtsen Gampo, and launched further military expeditions into the heartland of China and India. Despite these political advances it seems that Buddhism had not progressed greatly and the country was still very much in the grip of the Bön tradition. In the face of considerable resistance from Bön factions in the court, Trisong Detsen started on a wide-scale restoration of the Buddhist temples erected by Songtsen Gampo and invited a number of notable Indian Buddhist masters to Tibet. Principal among these were Shantarakshita and Padmasambhava.

The monk-philosopher Shantarakshita, even today known to the Tibetans as the Great Abbot Bodhisattva, established the monastic order in Tibet and inspired the construction of the first major monastic institute of Samye. On his advice, the king invited Padmasambhava, an Indian tantric adept, to Tibet to help pacify the local demons who were still hindering the propagation of the new religion. Padmasambhava was able to beat the Bön priests at their own game and more than anyone else was responsible for turning the tide in favor of Buddhism. His charismatic personality lodged itself firmly in the Tibetan imagination and became a lasting symbol for the victory of the wisdom, compassion, and power of Buddhism over the more primitive and less universal beliefs of Bön. The king was also deeply impressed by Padmasambhava and even offered him his wife of two years, Yeshe Tsogyel, as a consort, an act that scandalized the Bön faction and forced Padmasambhava to flee into hiding.

Ralpachen

After the death of Trisong Detsen in 797, his sons, Mune Tsenpo and Tride Songtsen, continued the policy of disseminating Buddhism. Wars with China also continued. The third and last great king of the Yarlung period, Tri Ralpachen, came to power in 815. He made a treaty with the Chinese and established peaceful relations with them. He was also responsible for undertaking a new and more reliable set of translations of Buddhist writings from the Sanskrit. However, scandal, jealousy, and infighting between the different factions in his court resulted in his assassination in 838. His death sadly augured the breakup of the dynasty.

Ralpachen's elder brother Langdarma took the throne. This king was a support-er of the Bön faith and immediately set out on a violent persecution of Buddhism. Temples and monasteries were desecrated and monks forced to disrobe or flee. Within a few short years Buddhism was almost entirely suppressed in Central Tibet. The Buddhists, however, were to have the last word. In 842, during the performance of a play, a monk called Lhalungpa Pelgyi Dorje fatally wounded the king with a well-aimed arrow. Pelgyi Dorje escaped to the eastern district of Kham and joined the handful of monks and translators who had managed to find refuge there beyond the reach of the court's fury.

THE MIDDLE AGES (842–1642 c.e.)

After Langdarma's assassination the unified Tibetan kingdom broke up into a number of small principalities and fiefs ruled by diverse members of the previous aristocracy. One branch of the royal family settled in Western Tibet and established the prosperous kingdoms of Guge and Purang and continued to support Buddhism. In the others, though, support for Buddhism declined, and Central Tibet entered a spiritual dark age that lasted for nearly two hundred years. Various Tibetan clans still harassed the Chinese and Khotanese border areas, occasionally establishing small centers of power. But with the collapse of the T'ang dynasty in 907, China and Tibet drifted apart and had no formal relations with each other for another three hundred years.

The Buddhist Revival

A renewed interest in Buddhism started during the beginning of the eleventh century. Much of this was inspired by the arrival of the Indian master Atisha in the western kingdom of Guge in 1042. Atisha was invited by King Yeshe Ö and his grandnephew Jangchub Ö. Yeshe Ö was a devout ruler who was a supporter of another influential Buddhist figure of the time, the monk and translator Rinchen Zangpo. A famous story recounts how Yeshe Ö was captured by a Turkic army and held for ransom, the sum for his release being the weight of his body in gold. Although most of this sum was raised, the king forbade it to be used for his release and insisted instead that it be spent on inviting Atisha to Tibet. As a result of this act of self-sacrifice, Atisha spent the remaining twelve years of his life in Tibet, traveling from Guge to Central Tibet, where he spent his last years in Netang, near Lhasa. Atisha's disciples founded the Kadampa order of Tibetan Buddhism.

A well-known Tibetan contemporary of Atisha was the translator Marpa. He came from a wealthy family in the Lhodrak region of Southern Tibet and traveled on several occasions to India to gather texts and study with a number of Indian masters. His main teacher was the former abbot of Nalanda Monastery turned tantric yogi, Naropa. Marpa became the teacher of the poet-saint Milarepa, who in turn taught Gampopa, through whom the main lineages of the Kagyu order of Tibetan Buddhism were founded.

At the same time Könchok Gyelpo, a monk from the powerful Khön family in southern Tibet, received the lineages into which the translator Drokmi had been initiated by his Indian masters. In 1073 he founded a monastery in his homeland of Sakya. He and his son Kunga Nyingpo then established the Sakya order of Tibetan Buddhism.

This period of Buddhist revival is often called the Second Dissemination of the Doctrine in Tibet. It was a time when the foundations of much of what we now call Tibetan Buddhism were laid. Translation work was started again, producing a complete reworking of the translations done at the time of the Empire. Monasteries (such as Reting, Tsurpu, Densatil, Drigung, Talung, Tsel Gungtang, and Sakya) were built on a grand scale, and the life of the country became more and more absorbed in religious matters.

Although politically not united, the various chieftains, princes, and head lamas of Tibet lived in relative harmony, and none of them made a serious effort to bring the country under his own control. This period of peaceful, innocent independence came to an end at the beginning of the thirteenth century when the rising power of the Mongols began to make itself felt throughout China and Central Asia. Under the leadership of Genghis Khan, the Mongolians were in the process of forcing the entire area to submit to their rule. Envoys were sent to

Tibet demanding submission, and the Tibetans yielded without any resistance. For the time being this saved them from further interference, but in 1239 Genghis's grandson Godan Khan sent raiding parties into Tibet that penetrated as far south as the monasteries of Reting and Drigung.

The Sakya Dynasty

Five years later, sensing the influence wielded by the great lamas of the land, Godan invited the head abbot of the Sakya order, Sakya Pandita, to his court. In return for a guarantee of no more Mongolian incursions into Tibet, Sakya Pandita offered Tibet into the hands of the Khan, an act that did not endear him to his rivals in Tibet. As a reward he was made regent of Tibet with a post in the Mongolian court. This relationship took on further dimensions under the respective successors of Godan Khan and Sakya Pandita. Godan's heir Kublai was so impressed by the spiritual qualities and teachings of Sakya Pandita's nephew Pakpa that in return for initiation into the secret teachings of Buddhism, he bestowed upon him the title of Imperial Preceptor—in other words, de facto ruler of Tibet.

This arrangement was to have repercussions all the way into the twentieth century. Basically, a deal was struck between a certain religious order and a prevailing political power. The religious order provided spiritual guidance and was rewarded with political control over the internal affairs of Tibet, while the political power became the overlord of the country and guaranteed peace in return for submission. A major consequence of this was the increased politicization of the Tibetan Buddhist orders. They began competing with each other for the favors of the most powerful rulers of the day, thus intensifying the sense of division among them. As it was based upon compromise and sectarian self-interest, this attitude of trading spiritual for political authority weakened the political integrity and independence of Tibet.

Independence

With the support of the Mongolian Yüan dynasty, Sakya hierarchs ruled Tibet for almost exactly a century. But as the power of the Mongolians in China declined, a nationalist movement arose in Tibet under the leadership of Jangchub Gyeltsen of the Pamotrupa family based in the Yarlung Valley. In 1354 he overthrew the Sakya leadership and was acknowledged by the Mongolians as the ruler of Tibet. When the power of the Yüan rulers in China finally collapsed and they were replaced by the indigenous Chinese Ming dynasty, the Tibetans ignored the former "patron-priest" arrangement they had with Mongolian-ruled China and embarked on a three-hundred-year period of independence.

Jangchub Gyeltsen regarded his rule as a return to the golden days of the Yarlung Empire. There was a renewed appreciation of the deeds of Songtsen Gampo and Trisong Detsen that amounted almost to a form of worship. This was also the period of the discovery of texts concealed by Padmasambhava, which further inspired a sense of the greatness of the spiritual traditions of the past. This new dynasty was also governed mainly by lamas, Jangchub Gyeltsen himself becoming a monk of the Kadampa school. Meanwhile, the other Buddhist orders continued to vie for regional political influence and formed alliances with different local chieftains and families in the country. High lamas were also received at the Mongolian and Ming courts, but now as spiritual teachers rather than as potential political allies.

The Pamotrupa dynasty ended around 1435 and was replaced by the secular rule of the princes of Rinpung, an area southwest of Lhasa, which lasted for 130 years, until 1565. They were succeeded by four kings of Tsang, who ruled from Shigatse. Both of these dynasties were governed by lay rulers who were allied with the powerful lama, the Karmapa, head of another Kagyu suborder at Tsurpu monastery near Lhasa.

But this epoch of independence came to a violent end in 1642, when the Mongolians appeared on the scene again and forcibly replaced the last Tsang king with the towering figure of the Fifth Dalai Lama.

THE RULE OF THE DALAI LAMAS (1642–1959)
The Rise of the Gelukpa Order

During the period of Pamotrupa rule in Tibet there lived and taught a monk called Tsongkhapa, named after the region of Eastern Tibet where he was born in 1357. Tsongkhapa was a brilliant and noble figure who studied widely with lamas of the various Buddhist orders of his time. He produced a lucid and synthetic vision of Buddhist thought and practice and lived a monastic life that paid strict attention to the ethical values embodied in the ordained community. He attracted a wide following during his lifetime, including many devoted disciples who sought to preserve his influence after his death.

These disciples established a number of monasteries in Central Tibet that swiftly grew in size, and a distinctive new order of Tibetan Buddhism began to emerge. Initially it was known as the Ganden order, named after Tsongkhapa's monastery near Lhasa, but later acquired the title "Geluk" (Virtuous Order) by which it is known today. The Gelukpa were concerned with the teachings of Tsongkhapa, which emphasized a return to the spirit of the purity of doctrine and ethics introduced in the eleventh century by Atisha. At this stage they must have appeared as a fresh, dynamic, and somewhat idealistic order untarnished by the stains of political ambition that now clung to most of the Sakya and Kagyu schools in Central Tibet.

The leadership of this order passed from the older to the younger disciples of the master, and was finally granted to Tsongkhapa's nephew, Gendun Drup, the founder of Tashilhunpo Monastery in

Shigatse. Following the example of the Karmapas, Gendun Drup announced that he would deliberately take rebirth in Tibet and gave indications to his followers to enable them to find him. His successor was called Gendun Gyatso, a learned and powerful man who, as head abbot of Drepung Monastery near Lhasa, further consolidated the prestige of Tsongkhapa's tradition. During his time Drepung grew into the largest monastery in Tibet, with more than a thousand monks.

The next successor to the leadership of the Gelukpa order was Sonam Gyatso, born in 1543. The prominence of the Gelukpas now began to attract the attention of the Mongolians, who since their eviction from China had returned to their northern homelands. Altan Khan, a descendant of Genghis, invited Sonam Gyatso to meet him. Upon meeting the Khan in northeastern Tibet, Sonam Gyatso was given the title "Ta-le," the Mongolian word for "ocean" (*gyatso* in Tibetan), which is now written as "Dalai." This title was retrospectively bestowed upon Sonam Gyatso's two predecessors, and thus Sonam Gyatso became the Third Dalai Lama. No formal political alliances were entered into by the two men. It seems that Altan Khan was sincerely impressed by the spiritual teachings of the Dalai Lama and encouraged the conversion of the Mongols to Buddhism. But when Sonam Gyatso's reincarnation turned out to be a great-grandson of Altan Khan, the danger of further Mongolian political involvement in Tibet became apparent.

The Fifth Dalai Lama

The rulers of Tibet at that time, the Tsang king and his ally the Karmapa, were understandably alarmed by the prospect of a Mongol-Gelukpa alliance. Tension between the two groups rose, leading to the king's attack of Drepung and Sera Monasteries. The Fourth Dalai Lama, Yönten Gyatso, fled from Central Tibet and later died under suspicious circumstances in 1616 at the age of twenty-five. The following year a successor was found in the figure of Ngawang Losang Gyatso, born to a Nyingmapa family in the Chonggye Valley. The Mongolians continued to support the Gelukpa and make threatening gestures in the direction of Tibet. Finally Gushri Khan, the leader of the newly powerful Qosot Mongols, proposed to the Gelukpas that he invade Tibet and put an end to the conflict with the Tsang king. This he did, emerging victorious in 1642. The king of Tsang was murdered, the Karmapa order stripped of its authority, and Losang Gyatso, the Fifth Dalai Lama, was enthroned as regent over Tibet.

With the support of his Mongolian backers, the newly empowered Fifth Dalai Lama set out to unite the country under Gelukpa rule. He traveled widely, inspecting the state of the monasteries and administration of the different provinces and making changes where he saw fit. By 1656, the year of Gushri Khan's death, most of Tibet from Kailash to Kham was under his control. Since

Gushri's successors showed little interest in Tibet, Mongolian influence waned and the Dalai Lama became virtually an absolute ruler. This was the first time in the history of Tibet that a single, indigenous regime, uniting spiritual with secular authority, truly dominated the land. The Dalai Lama was generally recognized as a wise and tolerant ruler who brought back a sense of national unity and strength to Tibet. The lasting symbol of his rule is still visible in the grandeur of his Potala Palace.

Manchu Overlordship

Despite the Fifth Dalai Lama's achievements, his death in 1682 exposed the weaknesses inherent in the machinery of succession by reincarnation. Because of the inevitable gap of around twenty years before the next Dalai Lama could assume control, an unstable political vacuum was liable to emerge in this interim between one ruler and the next. And since the successor was chosen not on his merits but by the auspiciousness of his birth, it was always uncertain whether he would be a suitable leader. Such were the dangers when the Fifth Dalai Lama died. Initially his regent, Desi Sanggye Gyatso, concealed his death, maintaining that the Dalai Lama had entered a long period of meditation. Later, the choice of successor turned out to be an unfortunate one, for Tsangyang Gyatso, the Sixth Dalai Lama, showed little interest in either religious observances or political responsibility and preferred the life of a poet

and libertine. Tibetans generously explain this behavior as the enlightened, unfettered activity of an advanced tantric yogi, but it nonetheless contributed to events that were to have detrimental and lasting consequences.

Waiting in the background was Lhabzang Khan, a nephew of the Fifth Dalai Lama's patron Gushri. He took the opportunity to murder Desi Sanggye Gyatso and seize power, declaring himself king of Tibet. To dispose of the inconvenient Sixth Dalai Lama, Lhabzang banished him to China, but he died in Eastern Tibet before reaching the border.

Lhabzang Khan's position was soon under threat from another group of Mongols, the Dzungars, who were former allies of Desi Sanggye Gyatso. In 1717 they invaded Tibet, murdered Lhabzang, and set out on a vicious rampage of burning and looting. At this point the founder of the newly established Manchu (Ching) dynasty in China, K'ang Hsi, decided to intervene and stabilize a situation that was spinning out of control on his borders. He invaded with an army of seven thousand men who forced the Dzungars to retreat. To further impress themselves as saviors on the Tibetans, they brought with them the young Seventh Dalai Lama, Kelsang Gyatso, who until then had been in Kumbum Monastery in northeastern Tibet. In 1720 the Seventh Dalai Lama was enthroned and in the following year the emperor decreed Tibet to be a protectorate of China. Two Chinese representatives, called Ambans, were left in Lhasa to oversee relations between the two countries.

The Seventh Dalai Lama was a religious man who played a minor role in the governing of the country. This was left to lay administrator, the most effective of whom was Polha Sonam Topgye, who ruled until 1747. The Eighth Dalai Lama, Jampel Gyatso, was also largely uninvolved in matters of state, but from the time of his rule, the administration was put in the hands of a council of four ministers, one of whom would be a monk. Toward the end of his reign, in 1792, the Chinese army had to be called in to drive out the Nepalese Gurkhas, who invaded from the south and reached as far as Shigatse. This was the final intervention of Chinese forces on behalf of the Tibetans, and for more than a century their role in Tibet became a formality.

None of the next four Dalai Lamas, from the ninth to the twelfth, had any influence over Tibetan affairs, since they all died before reaching the age of majority. Whether they were murdered or died of natural causes is still an open question. A series of regents governed in their stead and the quality of their rule varied considerably with their personalities and abilities. During the nineteenth century Tibet adopted a xenophobic policy and closed its borders to all foreigners. With China occupied by its own internal decline and the suspect British and Russians refused entry, the Tibetans settled into a period of conservative, church-dominated stability.

The Thirteenth Dalai Lama

Tubten Gyatso, the Thirteenth Dalai Lama, 1933

The next great national leader of Tibet to emerge was Tubten Gyatso, the Thirteenth Dalai Lama. He presided over Tibet's entry into the twentieth century and its initial response to the tumultuous events that were to transform the political landscape of Asia. He was a perceptive ruler who recognized the precarious position of Tibet and the need to reach agreement with its neighbors (China and British India) over the exact political status of Tibet. He was forced into exile twice during his reign, first to Mongolia when the

British, suspicious that the Tibetans were dealing with the Russians and eager to establish their own trade agreement with Tibet, sent an expedition under Colonel Younghusband into Tibet in 1904; and second to India when the Manchus invaded in 1910 in a last-ditch attempt to absorb Tibet into China. Although the British won their trade agreement, the revolution in China in 1911 undermined any vestige of authority the Manchus retained in Lhasa, and the Tibetans drove them out. The Dalai Lama returned in triumph to his capital in 1913, declaring an independent Tibet free from even the formality of Chinese overlordship.

Later the same year the British arranged a conference in Simla between themselves, the Tibetans, and representatives of the new Republic of China in order to establish the exact nature of the relationship between them. The Chinese insisted that Tibet was an "integral part of China," the first time such wording had been used. The Tibetans fiercely repudiated this suggestion, and it was up to the British to work out some kind of compromise. The convention carried on for six months, at the end of which a series of points was drafted for official approval by the three parties. The rather complex agreement hinged on the notion that Tibet was an autonomous state under the suzerainty of China. The British and Tibetans were willing to sign the agreement, but the Chinese government refused. A separate Anglo-Tibetan declaration was made instead in which the British recognized Tibetan autonomy but would not recognize Chinese suzerainty over Tibet unless the Chinese signed the Simla accord (which they never did).

For the remainder of his rule the Thirteenth Dalai Lama had to contend with continual tension and fighting on the Chinese border as well as internal resistance to change and modernization from the powerful, conservative elements within the Gelukpa hierarchy. It would not be long before the British, who provided Tibet's tenuous connection to the outside world and only security against Chinese invasion, would leave India, and China would be taken over by a Communist regime with decidedly imperial intentions.

Shortly before his death in 1933, the Dalai Lama issued a stern warning to his people of the dangers they faced in the years ahead. But no sooner had he died than chaos and factionalism beset the government, producing just the instability that Tibet could least afford at that critical time.

The Fourteenth Dalai Lama

The Fourteenth Dalai Lama en route to India, 1959

The Fourteenth Dalai Lama, Tenzin Gyatso, was born to a farming family in northeast Tibet in 1935. At the age of two, he was recognized as the reincarnation of the Thirteenth Dalai Lama, taken to Lhasa and enthroned. He grew up in the seclusion of the Potala and Norbulingka palaces, slowly and painfully becoming aware of the crisis towards which his country was heading. In response to the Chinese army's invasion of Tibet in 1950, when the Fourteenth Dalai Lama was only fifteen, he was officially appointed the political leader of Tibet. In 1959 he fled into exile in India after a popular uprising against the Chinese in Lhasa that resulted in the death of thousands of Tibetans. He was followed into exile by approximately one hundred thousand Tibetan refugees. Settling in the mountain town of Dharamsala, he established a new Tibetan government-in-exile and began the task of organizing the refugee community in India.

In 1974 the Fourteenth Dalai Lama visited the West for the first time, and since then has been a tireless campaigner for the Tibetan cause worldwide. His passionate insistence on a nonviolent struggle against the Chinese occupation and oppression resulted in his being awarded the Nobel Peace Prize in 1989. In addition he has become one of the most respected and well-known spiritual leaders in the world today and his teachings are available through numerous publications. The Chinese government has consistently failed to respond to his many offers of dialogue and is currently engaged in one of its most persistent campaigns to discredit him in Tibet. *Kundun*, a Hollywood film about

his early life, has recently been made by the well known film-maker Martin Scorsese, much to the annoyance of the Chinese government.

THE DALAI LAMAS

1.	Gendun Drup	1391–1474
2.	Gendun Gyatso	1476–1542
3.	Sonam Gyatso	1543–1588
4.	Yonten Gyatso	1589–1616
5.	Ngawang Losang Gyatso	1617–1682
6.	Tsangyang Gyatso	1683–1706
7.	Kelsang Gyatso	1708–1757
8.	Jampel Gyatso	1758–1804
9.	Lungtok Gyatso	1805–1815
10.	Tsultrim Gyatso	1816–1837
11.	Khedrup Gyatso	1838–1855
12.	Trinle Gyatso	1856–1875
13.	Tubten Gyatso	1876–1933
14.	Tenzin Gyatso	1935–

CHINESE OCCUPATION (1950–PRESENT)

India gained independence from Britain in 1947, and two years later Mao Tsetung declared the formation of the People's Republic of China. In the excitement of their new beginnings the two

Chinese trucks arrive in Lhasa, January 1955

countries asserted the renewal of a long, but fictitious, history of mutual friendship (an assertion the Indians were soon to regret). Having successfully liberated the Chinese people, the following year the Communist government decided "to liberate the oppressed and exploited Tibetans and reunite them with the great motherland." The People's Liberation Army invaded Eastern Tibet in October 1950 and swiftly captured Chamdo. A few months later they had convinced the Tibetan governor there, Ngapo Ngawang Jigme, to sign (with no authority from the Lhasa government) a seventeen-point agreement for the "peaceful liberation of Tibet." The Tibetans were ill-prepared to cope with this invasion, and with a minimum of resistance the Chinese army made its way into Lhasa in September 1951.

The Chinese arrived on a wave of optimistic promises and goodwill with which they tried to win the Tibetans over to the idea of a just and equal socialist society. The Dalai Lama's government tentatively agreed to cooperate with a number of measures aimed at improving the Tibetans' lot by introducing certain features of modern life, such as roads and electricity. This uneasy alliance did not last long. Suspicious of the Communists' motives, the Khampas in Eastern Tibet staged a revolt in 1956 that soon became a full-scale insurrection. Tensions mounted in Lhasa, and an armed resistance movement was soon active in Central Tibet. In March 1959 the general of the Chinese forces in Lhasa made an unusual request for the Dalai Lama to attend a theatrical show inside the Chinese military base. This was interpreted by the Tibetans as a ploy to kidnap their leader, and they reacted with a series of popular demonstrations in Lhasa and outside the Norbulingka. This explosive confrontation finally erupted on March 17. The Chinese started shelling the city, and that evening the Dalai Lama and his entourage fled south in the direction of India. The demonstrations turned into an outright rebellion against the unwanted Chinese presence in Tibet that was met with the full fury of the Chinese military. Fierce fighting broke out in Lhasa, but the superior Chinese forces quickly overwhelmed the Tibetans, inflicting heavy casualties and damaging many buildings.

Henceforth, the Chinese dropped any pretense of "peaceful liberation" and set out to incorporate Tibet into the People's Republic. They were assisted in this task by a number of Tibetan collaborators, such as Ngapo Ngawang Jigme. The former institutions of Tibet were dismantled, monasteries were stripped of all authority, and a Chinese-dominated bureaucracy supported by a massive military presence was established to govern the region. The wishes of the Tibetan people were ignored and any hint of resistance was immediately suppressed by force. In September 1965, it was proudly announced that Tibet was now the Tibetan Autonomous Region of the People's Republic of China.

During the following decade China

became embroiled in one of the greatest disasters any country has ever inflicted upon itself: the Cultural Revolution. Although much of Tibet's cultural heritage had already been destroyed as part of the process of peaceful liberation, what remained was now systematically reduced to ruins. Red guards, some of them young Tibetans, tried to uproot every last trace of the former system. Monasteries in the most isolated places were taken down stone by stone. Religious paintings and inscriptions were effaced. "Reactionaries" were jailed by the thousands merely for refusing to denounce their faith in the Dalai Lama. In Tibet the Cultural Revolution served the additional purpose of seeking to obliterate the very idea of a people's separate identity as a nation.

Since the death of Mao in 1976, the policy of the Chinese government has mollified somewhat and become more "realistic." The destruction wrought by the Cultural Revolution is officially mourned, and a program is under way throughout China to repair some of its damage. The Tibetans, too, have benefited from this liberalization and the Chinese have admitted to errors in their handling of the Tibetan situation. Taxes and other restrictions have been lifted and certain economic and religious freedoms have been granted. Tibetans have been allowed to visit relatives and friends exiled in India.

Lhasa was declared an open city in October 1984, enabling foreigners to travel freely in Tibet for the first time.

During the next three years a steady stream of travelers and tourists visited the country. This allowed many people to gain a firsthand impression of the Chinese occupation and contributed to the resurgence of pro-Tibetan activism in the West in the late 1980s. The Tibetans were likewise able to communicate with the outside world directly and more freely.

This climate of liberalization and freedom of movement led to the first of a series of pro-independence demonstrations in Lhasa on September 27, 1987. Four days later police opened fire on a crowd of two thousand demonstrators outside the Jokhang. Foreign journalists and tourists were expelled. This marked a return to a more repressive Chinese policy in Tibet; during the following months hundreds of Tibetans were arrested on charges of subversion, and restrictions were imposed on foreigners traveling to the country. On March 5, 1989, police opened fire and killed a group of demonstrators in Lhasa. The unrest spread and two days later a state of martial law was declared. Up to two hundred people are believed to have been killed and thousands arrested. Three months later the Beijing government suppressed the pro-democracy demonstration in Tiananmin Square.

Martial law was lifted in May 1990, and since then controls on both Tibetans and foreigners have gradually been eased. The Chinese government, however, used the period of martial law to strengthen its hold over Tibet by instituting a more pervasive but less visible apparatus of repression. This allowed ostentatious ceremonies to mark the fortieth anniversary of "peaceful liberation" in May 1991 to pass without disturbance.

Deng Xiaoping's policy of high-speed implementation of economic reform started to take effect in Central Tibet by mid-1992, with a marked increase in shop and office construction and a declaration that Tibet was open to foreign investment. The next pro-independence demonstration in Lhasa in May 1993 was triggered by anger about price increases. It was suppressed by tear gas instead of guns and had no discernible impact on Chinese policy.

Despite a commitment to make China's Most Favored Nation trading status contingent upon improvements in its human rights record (including cessation of the forced migration of Chinese to Tibet), in May 1994 President Clinton renewed MFN for the second year running and formally severed any link between economic agreements and human rights. In July of that same year, Chinese leaders held the Third National Work Conference on Tibet, in which they agreed to implement even faster economic development in the Lhasa area. At the same time they declared the Dalai Lama "an enemy of the people" and forbade government workers to display his image on their altars at home. In April 1996, the ban on Dalai Lama photos was broadened to include the display of portraits of the Dalai Lama by business owners, monasteries, and ordinary lay people. Today it is a crime to display such photos.

Tibetans in Exile

The Dalai Lama left Lhasa on March 17, 1959. Two weeks later, he reached India. In the months that followed he was joined by about a hundred thousand fellow refugees. Prime Minister Nehru readily granted political asylum to the Tibetan leader and his followers but refused to take any further steps against the Chinese. Despite the guarantee by the British that their support for Tibet (as embodied in the Anglo-Tibetan declaration of 1914) would be continued by their Indian successors, Nehru offered no recognition of the Dalai Lama's government. Instead he affirmed his support for the recent Indo-Chinese treaty, which promised that neither country would involve itself in the internal affairs of the other, thereby acknowledging Chinese sovereignty over Tibet.

The Dalai Lama then appealed to the world community for support. The International Commission of Jurists investigated his case and concluded that Tibet was indeed a sovereign state and that the Chinese were guilty of what amounted to genocide. But when the issue was brought up before the United Nations later in 1959, a resolution was passed in Tibet's favor merely demanding "respect for the fundamental human rights of the Tibetan people." Led by the Russians, the Communist bloc countries accepted the Chinese view of the affair and accused the West of fabricating the issue as another weapon in the cold war. The Indians and the British, the only two countries with a good knowledge of the situation, both emphasized the ambiguities of the Tibetan case and refused to take a firm stand for the Tibetans' right to independence.

Although the outside world continued to express sympathy for the plight of the Tibetans, it did nothing to support their cause and simply turned a blind eye to what the Chinese were doing. Discouraged by the ineffective response of the world community, the Dalai Lama recognized that he had no real allies. He turned his attention instead to the immediate problems of sheer physical survival and the preservation of Tibet's unique but threatened culture.

The Tibetans in exile have proven to be a remarkably resilient and resourceful people, establishing in less than twenty years a thriving refugee community in India and abroad. The Dalai Lama has created a government in exile at his home in Dharamsala and critically restructured the political apparatus. Many of the major monasteries have been reestablished in the Tibetan settlements in southern India, and Buddhist teachers have founded centers and monasteries throughout Europe and America, thus making the Tibetan religious heritage accessible to a wider audience than ever before.

In June 1978 the Chinese surprised everyone by allowing Tibetans in exile to return freely to Tibet (the only condition was that on their visa applications they give their nationality as Chinese). Postal communication was also reestablished.

In these ways the refugees suddenly were able to gain firsthand knowledge of their families and friends left behind nearly twenty years before. Even more surprising was the Chinese allowance of a series of fact-finding missions from Dharamsala to travel extensively through the country to evaluate for themselves the present situation. The first of these delegations left in August 1979, composed of senior members of the Dalai Lama's government as well as his immediately elder brother, Lobsang Samten. This was followed in 1980 by two further delegations. Everywhere the missions went they were besieged by crowds of tearful Tibetans imploring the Dalai Lama to return. Feeling rose to such a pitch during the second delegation's visit to Lhasa that a crowd gathered outside the hotel where the delegates were staying and began shouting for Tibetan independence. The delegation was duly dispatched back to Hong Kong the next day, accused of "inciting the Tibetan people to break with the motherland." Although the third delegation completed its tour, a planned fourth team was never sent. The Chinese, aware of the deep national feelings of the Tibetans, realized that they could not possibly contain the presence of the Dalai Lama on Tibetan soil without risking an uprising.

The Dalai Lama's stature as an internationally respected religious and spiritual leader has grown enormously in the past decade. Since winning the Nobel Peace prize in 1989, he has, often under the pretext of being a Nobel laureate, been received officially and privately by foreign governments and leaders throughout the world. In 1987 he proposed a Five-Point Peace Plan for Tibet during a visit to the U.S. Congress, in which he expressed his wish for Tibet to be an internationally recognized zone of peace, committed to neutrality and environmental preservation. The following year he issued a statement to the European Parliament in Strasbourg, in which he suggested the possibility of Tibet's being responsible for its own domestic policy but allowing China responsibility for foreign affairs.

The Chinese have consistently refused, however, to enter into discussions about any of these proposals. The "Strasbourg statement" was subsequently withdrawn because of disagreement within the Tibetan-exile community. While the Dalai Lama continues to be a thorn in the side of Beijing, his efforts, as well as those of the numerous pro-Tibet lobbying groups throughout the world, are yet to produce any significant change in Chinese policy.

CONCLUSIONS

The Tibetans are a race with a language, culture, religion, history, and customs entirely distinct from those of the Chinese. They have functioned as a de facto independent state for thirteen hundred years, for the most part as a peaceful, deeply religious neighbor of India and China. Even during the period of overlordship by Chinese dynasties, it was non-Chinese rulers (Mongolians and Manchurians) who exercised that overlordship. For the Communists to maintain that Tibet has always been an integral part of China has no basis at all in history or fact.

Not only have the Chinese incorporated Tibet into China but they have partitioned it as well. Although the wider area to which Tibetan culture spread was often only nominally controlled by the government in Lhasa, the people of those regions have tended to consider themselves Tibetans rather than Chinese and regard the Dalai Lama as their spiritual and temporal leader. Now Amdo, the northeastern region of Tibet, has become part of Qinghai and Gansu provinces, and much of Kham, the eastern region, has been included into Sichuan and Yunnan. The so-called Tibetan Autonomous Region refers mainly to Central Tibet, Tsang, and Western Tibet.

China's avowed aim of liberating the oppressed masses of Tibet was merely an ideological justification for pursuing the imperialist ambitions of the Han Chinese, first voiced at the outset of Sun Yat-sen's Republic, to incorporate all the bordering territories of Mongolia, Manchuria, Xinjiang (Turkestan), and Tibet into China. Its main purpose was strategic: to secure its western border and to dominate the highland of Central Asia, giving it access to India, the Middle East, and the southern republics of the former Soviet Union. So far it has achieved considerable success with military force, but in so doing has entirely compromised its standing as a socialist society, reverting instead to the role of a colonialist power insensitive to the demands of the people it has conquered. "A people that enslaves others," wrote Karl Marx, "forges its own chains."

The cost of this conquest in terms of human suffering has been enormous. Millions of people (including 1.2 million Tibetans) have lost their lives. Many more have been forced to spend years in prisons and labor camps for such "crimes" as "harboring bourgeois tendencies." Families have been separated, cultures and religions persecuted, and traditional ways of life abandoned. People have been subjected to racist discrimination in education and employment, with the privileged positions almost always being given to the occupying Han Chinese.

In foreign affairs the Tibetans have at times acted naively, preferring a short-term, expedient solution without considering the longer-term implications of their actions. Had they been less willing to acquiesce to the nominal overlordship of the Yüan and Manchu dynasties, been less xenophobic during the nineteenth century, and formed more solid contacts with the outside world during the early decades of the twentieth century, they might have been able to prevent the tragedy that has overcome them. The notion of a "patron-priest" relationship was a conveniently ambiguous one that in traditional Asian political relations could work to the advantage of both parties without making either of them into the underdog. To the politically minded Mongols and Manchus, the patron naturally held a superior position to that of the priest. But to the religiously minded Tibetans, the priest held the real and higher power.

By Western standards Tibet was a backward and feudal society with its fair share of injustices and shortcomings, but by all accounts it was a country where people were content with their lot, adequately fed and clothed, of a cheerful and friendly disposition, and nourished by deeply rewarding spiritual values. It may well turn out that they were preserving something that we in our arrogance have discarded.

TIBETAN BUDDHISM

A common misconception still prevails about Tibetan Buddhism that it is a shamanistic form of Buddhism heavily influenced by the indigenous Bön religion of Tibet. This misconception can be easily reinforced by visiting Tibetan monasteries and seeing all manner of ferocious, seemingly demonic deities peering at you from the murals and tangkas. But in every culture where Buddhism has spread, from Sri Lanka to Japan, the same phenomenon can be observed: instead of denouncing and stamping out the local gods, the Buddhists have simply converted them to their own cause. People are thus able to continue making use of their traditional religious symbols but within the context of a more highly evolved system of value and meaning. Tibet is no exception to this. The traditional religion of the country, in this case Bön, has conditioned the form Buddhism has assumed, but it has had little influence on its meaning. In fact the opposite is true; since the arrival of Buddhism in Tibet both the form and the meaning of Bön have been completely transformed by its presence.

Buddhism entered Tibet from India in two principal phases (about 90 percent of the "demonic" deities one sees are actually Indian in origin). The first phase was during the period of the Yarlung Empire, the Indian figure most associated with this period being Padmasambhava. The second phase was during the eleventh century. Atisha and Milarepa are the best-known figures of this time. Although both Tibetan and Western scholars like to see the introduction of Buddhism as a systematic and almost deliberate effort, it is more likely that it was the gradual product of centuries of cultural and religious influence filtering from India and China into the Tibetan highlands. Only much later was this process simplified and categorized by historians.

Buddhism was the Tibetans' introduction to higher culture as such. Until the Communist takeover in the 1950s it informed their entire view of life: the origin and nature of the world, the role of the individual in society, the relation between mind and matter, the principles of ethics, the arts, medical science, and, of course, religion. Their lives were permeated by Buddhist values. It is impossible to understand Tibetans without knowing the basic tenets of Buddhism and how they interpreted them. And only in this way can we perhaps peel away some of the layers of exotic fantasy that have built up around these people.

One of the most distinctive features of Tibetan Buddhism is the way it has integrated what it sees as the three principal trends of Indian Buddhism into a coherent, systematic whole. These three trends are the Hinayana, Mahayana, and Vajrayana, or the individual, the universal, and the diamond vehicles to enlightenment, respectively. The Hinayana tradition presents the basic teachings of the historical Buddha Shakyamuni; these teachings correspond to the tradition that today is preserved by the Theravada Buddhists of Sri Lanka and Southeast Asia (who, incidentally, object to the term "Hinayana" as being derogatory). The Mahayana tradition introduces a further evolution of ethical and philosophical understanding that started to emerge in India about five hundred years after Shakyamuni. And the Vajrayana, the esoteric or secret form of the Mahayana, is seen as a powerful, direct path that utilizes symbolic imagination, mantric sound, and subtle physical energy to effect a complete psycho-physical transformation from an ordinary person to an enlightened being.

Hinayana

The "small vehicle" of Buddhism starts out by recognizing the frustration and imperfection of normal human existence. It proceeds to explain that the source of this frustration and imperfection lies not in the nature of the world itself nor in the intention of God or the devil, but in the intellectual bewilderment and emotional confusion within ourselves. It maintains that the suffering we experience in life can be brought to an end by ridding ourselves of this confusion. And it offers a way to realize this goal by following a path of personal development that includes the examination and changing of one's attitudes, behavior, livelihood, and psychological habits. According to Tibetan Buddhism, the Hinayana is the path that one takes in order to achieve one's own liberation from suffering and

confusion. It is for this reason that it is called the individual or small vehicle.

The basic teachings of Buddhism emphasize the need for strict moral discipline combined with a rigorous training in meditation and insight as the means to liberate oneself from the negative inner bondage to suffering. These elements are likewise stressed in Tibetan Buddhism and find their classical expression in its monastic institutions. The monk or nun consciously adopts the way of life that has been found to be the most conducive to the cultivation of these qualities. Although many of the minor rules of Indian Buddhist monasticism were put aside in Tibet, usually for practical reasons of climate, local customs, and so on, the main vows, such as not taking life, celibacy, not stealing, and not lying about one's spiritual attainment, were upheld. Ideally a monk would devote the remainder of his life to study and spiritual discipline, aspiring to set an example to society by his own embodiment of the values of Buddhism. In practice, though, many Tibetan monks were also employed in the administration of their monasteries and would spend all but the last years of their lives engaged in official work that often had political implications. Other monks would be specially trained in the performance of the complex rituals found in Tibetan Buddhism, and much of their time would be taken up by long sessions of chanting and praying, either in the homes of the laity or in the monastery itself.

The monks and nuns are also the living symbols of the Buddhist spiritual community, or Sangha. As in most Buddhist societies, Tibetans believe that a continued monastic presence is vital to the preservation of Buddhism. Thus one of the responsibilities of the lay community is to support the monasteries either by donating food or money directly to it or by sponsoring one or more monks or nuns. It was also a custom to donate a son to the monastery both for his education and as a contribution to the order. Although this practice was denounced and forbidden by the Chinese after they assumed power, since 1985 it has been partially resumed, and many of the young monks you see in the monasteries today are there because their parents have sent them to help revive the monastic tradition. The government now sets limits in each monastery as to how many monks can officially reside there. In some monasteries the state provides a small monthly stipend for each registered monk; frequently, however, the actual number of monks in residence far exceeds the official limits, with the result that many monks do not receive a stipend from the government.

Another important feature of basic Buddhism is the commitment of taking refuge in the Three Jewels. The Three Jewels are the Buddha, the Dharma, and the Sangha. It is by committing one's life to these three principles that one is considered a Buddhist. Such commitment is the fundamental spiritual focus of Buddhism. It means directing one's inner life toward the enlightenment and com-

passion personified by the Buddha; practicing the Dharma (the path revealed by the Buddha) as the means of realizing enlightenment; and devoting oneself to the Sangha (community) of men and women who are likewise engaged on this path. In Tibetan Buddhism this triad is often supplemented by a fourth refuge, the lama, or spiritual teacher, and even by a fifth, the *yidam*, or personal tantric deity (about which more will be said below). Quite early in their lives most Tibetans will attend a formal ceremony of "taking refuge" in the presence of a lama. During their daily practice this commitment is repeatedly renewed, and as a preparation for the more advanced tantric practices it has to be recited, together with visualization and contemplation, one hundred thousand times.

Mahayana

The "great vehicle" of the Mahayana is based upon and includes the Hinayana doctrines and practices but emphasizes a different ethical standpoint. The Mahayana grew up in India as a critique of certain tendencies in the early Buddhist community to renounce any further involvement in the plight of the world and strive instead for one's own release in the unconditioned, deathless realm of Nirvana. The Mahayanists believed that by severing every last trace of attachment to the world one failed to acknowledge the essential connectedness one has with life and to discover the meaning of one's fundamental participation in existence. For them true spiritual nobility was found primarily not in detachment and release but in compassion and love. The Mahayana ideal is the bodhisattva, the person who selflessly aspires to realize enlightenment for the sake of all living beings.

From the very beginning of the introduction of Buddhism into Tibet, the Tibetans were exposed to the ideas of the Mahayana. They accepted them readily, and there was never any actual conflict between followers of the Hinayana and Mahayana traditions. The Tibetans understood the Mahayana as a critique of the tendency within oneself to center spiritual practice around one's own personal needs and desires alone. Compassion became a central theme in Tibetan Buddhism and explains the tremendous devotion the Tibetans have for the archetypal bodhisattva of compassion, Avalokiteshvara (in Tibetan, Chenrezi). Avalokiteshvara is the personification of enlightened compassion and is represented in a number of symbolic forms. Songtsen Gampo, the Tibetan king who first accepted Buddhism, and the Dalai Lamas are revered as human emanations of Avalokiteshvara.

When that enlightened compassion is symbolized in sound it becomes the mantra OM MANI PADME HUM. This is the melody of Tibet, murmured constantly by the devout as they count their beads. As a mantra it is used as a means of concentrating the mind upon the meaning of compassion while its associations and

vibratory resonance evoke corresponding feelings in the heart. Its syllables are those most commonly carved on the rocks and stones around holy shrines. In some places you can see them outlined in white rock on distant hillsides. Before the Chinese occupation roads were lined with "mani walls," long piles of stones carved with the mantra slowly built up by pilgrims and local people. Sadly, most of these have been demolished.

The bodhisattva realizes that to overcome the world's frustration and despair, ultimately it is necessary to uproot the spiritual origins of suffering. Since from a Buddhist point of view this is achieved through enlightenment, the bodhisattva sets out to attain this goal in order to be in a position to lead others to a similar state, recognizing that the optimal benefit one can bring to the world is one's inner illumination, compassion, and freedom. The bodhisattva's path is outlined in the Mahayana teachings as consisting of six central qualities: generosity, ethics, tolerance, energy, meditation, and wisdom. Of these six, wisdom is the key to enlightenment which, to be effective, must be supported by the moral and psychological strength of the other five.

The wisdom of enlightenment consists of direct, nonconceptual insight into the ultimate nature of existence. In Mahayana Buddhism, the term used to refer to this truth is *shunyata*, which literally means "emptiness." This notion of emptiness is frequently misinterpreted to mean that Buddhism is life-denying and nihilistic. But nothing could be further from the truth. A well-known Tibetan lama was once asked by a Western student how, if everything were empty, one could still appreciate the beauty of nature. He replied that it is only when you have realized emptiness that you can fully appreciate the beauty of nature.

Emptiness does not deny the presence and beauty of people, animals, trees, mountains, and flowers. It simply negates the fictions we project upon these things that prevent us from experiencing them as they are. Chief among these fictions is the sense that things are static, self-contained, and separate from everything else. This is most evident in the case of our sense of ego-identity. Of course, intellectually we may know that things are neither static nor self-contained, but the doctrine of emptiness does not merely challenge our intellectual views: it also puts into question our pre-intellectual sense of how things are. For it is not false concepts alone that prevent enlightenment, but a much more deeply rooted clinging based upon patterns, tendencies, and habits inherited from past conditioning. Thus the philosophy of emptiness, profound and far-reaching as it may be, has to be driven home by the power of a concentrated, meditative awareness capable of counteracting the very force of conditioning itself.

Tibetan monks may spend many years studying, reflecting, and meditating upon the meaning and implications of emptiness. They read texts, receive explanations, debate among themselves, and go into solitary retreat to deepen their understanding. Volumes of commentaries to the key Indian works on emptiness as well as original writings have been composed over the last thousand years by lamas from all the different orders of Tibetan Buddhism.

The aim of Mahayana practice is to harmonize wisdom and compassion. The wisdom of emptiness in no way diminishes the love the bodhisattva has for the world. By stripping the mind of fictitious notions, the bodhisattva breaks down the barriers that create the sense of separation between self and others. In this way emptiness reveals the rich and dynamic interrelatedness of all things. Wisdom and compassion mutually enhance each other and culminate in the liberated yet engaged enlightenment of the Buddha.

Vajrayana

The "diamond vehicle," the Vajrayana, is considered to be part of the Mahayana. As such, the Vajrayana has the same objective as the Mahayana, the realization of enlightenment for the sake of others, but it employs its own distinctive means to achieve that goal. These methods are based upon the teachings of the Buddhist tantras. As opposed to the sutras (discourses given by the historical Buddha to a general audience), the tantras are esoteric instructions given to selected groups of disciples. Vajrayanists believe that these teachings were also taught by Shakyamuni, albeit through his magically assuming a special form. The tantras reveal a path to enlightenment that is swifter than the ordinary Hinayana or Mahayana paths but no less arduous. They often speak in an evocative symbolic language. States of spiritual attainment are illustrated not by psychological descriptions but by vibrant, personalized gods. By invoking these symbolic figures, the practitioner of the Vajrayana enters into a living relationship and identification with enlightenment as personified by the "deity" with whom he or she has the greatest affinity.

The Vajrayana is a path of transformation. Instead of seeing the spiritual quest as the simple rejection of evil and achievement of good, it recognizes how every psychological condition of humankind—whether beneficial or harmful—is essentially a process of energy. Raw energy is in itself neither good nor bad. Only when it is channeled by people toward constructive or destructive ends does it assume a moral character. The Vajrayana uses yogic techniques to channel energy toward enlightenment instead of allowing it just to perpetuate the cycle of confusion. Contrary to much popular misinformation, the Vajrayana does not abandon ethical constraints; in common with every Buddhist path, it is bound to the ethos of enlightenment. Because of the dangers involved in the utilization rather than the suppression of emotional energies, if anything it demands an even higher degree of ethical integrity.

The often bewildering array of deities you see in Tibetan temples and monasteries personify the multifaceted phenomena of enlightenment that are utilized and developed in the Vajrayana. Some deities depict the peaceful aspects of buddhahood, smiling with encouragement and love. Others show its wrathful side, urging the practitioner to overcome his or her hesitation and engage in the awesome, compassionate dance of liberated consciousness. The numerous waving hands clutch objects that symbolize the spiritual tools needed for the task of transforming an ordinary person into an enlightened one. The stamping feet trample the obstacles that hold you back from the fulfillment of your existential responsibilities.

The circular, symmetrical mandalas you sometimes see are symbolic descriptions of the deity in the context of his or her world. When visualized during Vajrayana practice, mandalas are not flat circles but three-dimensional, luminous spheres. The deity resides in the center of this sphere, often in the company of the minor deities of his or her entourage. The mandala itself symbolizes the complete reorientation of experience wrought by enlightenment. Such transformation affects not only the quality of one's own consciousness but also the way in which the world itself appears.

There are two stages involved in this process of transformation. First it is necessary to rid oneself of delusive ideas and perceptions of who one is and what reality is. On the tantric path this is achieved by imagining oneself as a deity and the world as the mandala of that deity. One's speech likewise becomes the mantra of the deity. The particular deity one chooses for this purpose is called one's *yidam*, or chosen deity. The initial practice of the Vajrayana entails systematically familiarizing oneself with this transformed view until it can be sustained in meditation without any distraction for several hours. In the second stage the practitioner uses his or her powers of imagination and concentration to free and rechannel the subtle energies that are the physical basis of psychic life. This gives him or her access to the founding stratum of existence, which is known by a number of descriptive terms: clear light, primordial Buddha, Great Perfection, Dharmic presence, and others.

In the course of normal human existence, this fundamental clear light only becomes apparent to us shortly after clinical death. But without spiritual preparation during life, we usually pass over it in a haze of inattention. The yogic techniques of the Vajrayana enable one to experience this luminous ground of life and death in meditation and on that basis recreate the quality of one's existence. Through constant practice one learns to arise from this meditation imbued with the dynamics of the deity instead of the habits and conditioning of one's former self.

The Tibetans also possess other methods of meditation that lead to an experience of the clear light but do not necessarily involve the stages of tantric practice described above. These are the practices of the Great Seal (*mahamudra*) and the Great Perfection (*dzog-chen*). Such methods propose a direct breakthrough to the ultimate nature of consciousness and being, in a way similar to the Zen traditions of China and Japan. In most cases, though, they are taught in conjunction with and often as the culmination of the traditional tantric path of deity yoga.

The Wheel of Life

The Wheel of Life thangka painting

These spiritual practices and disciplines are interpreted as a meaningful response to the kind of world the Tibetans believe themselves to inhabit. This world is the one they inherited from India over a thousand years ago, and it is only within the last forty years that it has been seriously challenged by the modern scientific outlook introduced with the arrival of the Chinese. The traditional Buddhist worldview conceives of the universe as temporally and spatially infinite. It has no beginning and only a hypothetical end (should all sentient beings realize Nirvana). It is composed of countless world systems, all of which are inhabited by six basic forms of life: humans, animals, celestials, titans, ghosts, and denizens of hell. These life-forms dwell in the sky, on the earth, in the water, and beneath the ground of a world that is dominated by a majestic mountain called Sumeru, protruding into the heavens from the center of a vast ocean. We humans live on a continent called Jambudvipa, situated in the oceans to the south of Sumeru.

The mind, or stream of consciousness, of each individual being is regarded as beginningless and endless. Until we recognize our dilemma and adopt a spiritual path to liberation, we are condemned to pass through an infinite succession of births within the six forms of life. The driving force of consciousness is the accumulated impetus of our actions, which propels us from one realm to the next according to the ethical quality of our deeds.

This process is vividly depicted by an illustration called the Wheel of Life, a painting of which is sometimes found at the entrance of Tibetan temples. At the hub of this wheel are three animals: a pig, a snake, and a cock, respectively symbolizing the ignorance, hatred, and desire that motivate the actions that keep us bound to a meaningless cycle of birth and death. In the circle around the hub are shown various beings rising to divine heights only to fall again into hellish agony. Around this circle are six (sometimes only five) sections that show the realms of existence into which beings are propelled and then ejected. The outer rim contains a circle of twelve pictures that symbolize the twelvefold sequence of conditioning that leads from ignorance to aging and death. The entire wheel is held by the demonic figure of Yama, the personification of death, who contains it in his mouth, ready to bite at any moment. Outside the wheel stands a Buddha pointing to a moon, symbolizing the completeness of spiritual liberation.

Although the Tibetans often interpret this diagram quite literally, it can also be seen simply as a powerful symbol of the human psyche. It illustrates how our habitual psychological forces propel us into a cycle of frustrating life-situations from which we seem incapable of disentangling ourselves. Yet by recognizing the mechanism of this process we have the potential to counteract the power of conditioning and reach an inner psychological freedom and completeness.

RELIGIOUS PRACTICE

When in Tibet you may be struck by the apparently superstitious aspects of religious practice that conflict with what you have read elsewhere about the profound insights of Buddhist philosophy. From a superficial observation it is easy to conclude that Tibetan Buddhism is just a corrupt form of the original teachings of the Buddha. But as with all religions, the wide spectrum of different spiritual needs and abilities among its followers has led to an equally wide range of spiritual understandings and practices. The way in which a well-trained monk understands Buddhism will be a far cry from the way it is perceived by an old woman or man in the market. But nowadays, since most of the monks were driven into exile or imprisoned or killed by the Chinese, it is rare to meet a learned monk or lama in Tibet itself to counteract the impression of Tibetan Buddhism as a simple folk religion.

In the larger Gelukpa monastic universities around Lhasa the monks who chose to follow the full course of philosophical training would be required to study a number of demanding subjects that would often take fifteen to twenty years to master. They would begin with a three-year course in basic philosophy, epistemology and formal logic before proceeding to the main subjects of Buddhist doctrine, Madhyamaka philosophy, Buddhist phenomenology, and monastic discipline. Upon successful completion of these studies they would be awarded the degree of Geshe, which is more or less equivalent to our Doctor of Divinity. After this they would often go on to do tantric studies and practices. In the Kagyu and Nyingma orders a simi-

lar but usually less extensive course of study was followed; it was more common for monks to enter tantric practice at a younger age to master the meditative and yogic techniques required for completion of the Vajrayana path. In all the orders, a basic tantric retreat was a three-year undertaking, either alone or with a small group of fellow practitioners. Some monks, as well as unordained yogis, would spend several years in the remote mountainous areas as hermits devoted to intensive spiritual practice.

In addition to philosophical and tantric training, most monks also received instruction in the intricacies of monastic ritual life. Large assembly halls are found in almost all the monasteries where the monks would gather daily to recite invocations and prayers. Often these prayers would be accompanied by drums and horns played by monks who specialized in ritual music. Holidays would be marked by increased ritual activity in the monasteries, with chanting monks filling the assembly hall often for days on end. In some cases, the ritual prayers and music would be accompanied by dances performed by monks dressed in bright silk brocade costumes and fantastic masks. Throughout the rituals, the monks are meant to engage in elaborate visualizations, seeing themselves as deities and their environment as a mandala.

Also associated with the monasteries was the tradition of oracles. According to this tradition, local protector deities would speak through a chosen medium, usually a monk, after having first been invited to enter the medium through ritual incantations. Once the medium had gone into a trance, it would deliver predictions and advice to the elders of the monastery. Some oracles, such as the one associated with Nechung Monastery, were highly prized by the Gelukpa rulers of Tibet and were often consulted regarding political as well as religious affairs.

All of these monastic traditions were severely interrupted by the Chinese occupation, and they have been preserved mainly among the exile communities in India. In recent years Westerners have begun to train to become geshes, with so far three or four Western monks being awarded the degree. Many more Westerners and Asians from countries such as India and Taiwan have completed three-year tantric retreats under the guidance of Tibetan lamas in India, Europe, and North America. In Tibet today, cautious moves are being made to restore some of these systems of training, but considerable obstacles, a principal one being the lack of qualified instructors, still stand in the way. While monastic ritual life does continue to a certain extent, it too has been curtailed. Some argue that without the philosophical and meditational training that was meant to accompany it, Tibetan ritual life will lose its meaning, becoming just another tourist attraction.

On the level of popular, devotional practice, Buddhism is still a strong force throughout Tibet. Although public displays of faith were forbidden during the Cultural Revolution, as soon as the restrictions were lifted in the early 1980s, the country witnessed a huge resurgence of religious expression. The recitation of mantras and prayers, prostration, circumambulation, and the making of offerings to the temples constitute the core of popular practice. Whether these acts are accompanied by deeper religious understanding cannot easily be judged from the outside.

Upon visiting temples and monasteries in Tibet, one will meet pilgrims and devotees making offerings to the deities on the altars. They offer white greeting scarves (*katas*) and drape them on statues as a formal gesture of "meeting" the deity symbolized by the image; they pour liquid butter into the lamps to keep them burning and thus symbolically dispel the darkness of ignorance; they offer incense and flowers and ring bells as acts of dedicating the experience of sense pleasure to enlightenment. The simplest offering is that of seven bowls of fresh water lined along the altar, which stands as a gift of one's essential, unpolluted, pure nature to the realization of buddhahood. Prostrations, too, are a form of offering. In performing them one gives up one's pride and arrogance, often combining this with a confession of the things one has done that have caused harm to oneself and others.

The turning of prayer wheels is another ubiquitous practice that for many people has come to typify popular Tibetan Buddhism. The cylindrical wheels—both the hand-held variety and the larger

THE LAND AND ITS PEOPLE

1. Pilgrim outside the Jokhang Cathedral during Losar

2. Harvest festival in Zungkar

3. Harvesting barley in the autumn

4. Milking a goat

5. Nomads with horses

6. Yak amidst mountains and clouds

7. The square in front of the Jokhang Cathedral

8. Pilgrim outside the Jokhang Cathedral during Losar

9. Tibetan elder

10. Yak

11. Elegant Tibetan mother and child in Lhasa

12. Tangkas on the Potala Palace during the Yogurt Festival

13. Protector Chapel at Sakya Monastery

14. Two women and a nun at Drepung Monastery

15. Monks performing at a festival in Nagchu

16. Young monk rehearsing for the cham dance

17. The great tangka at Ganden Monastary

18. Spinning prayer wheel, Sakya Monastery

19. Monk at Sakya Monastery

ones lining the walls of shrines and temples—are filled with rolls of paper printed with mantras and prayers. As one turns the wheel and recites a mantra, usually OM MANI PADME HUM, it is believed that additional merit is gathered because of the spinning of the mantras packed inside. This constant turning of sacred words also represents the continuous turning of the Wheel of Dharma.

Among the stranger aspects of popular practice are the rubbing of hands or other parts of the body on stones, rocks, pillars, walls, or other objects with religious associations. This is done with the hope that merit will be accrued and bodily ailments healed. Pins and needles are stuck into the brocade clothing of statues and around tangkas in the belief that this will sharpen one's intelligence. Clumps of wool are tied to trees and shrubs around monasteries in the hope that the about-to-be slaughtered animal to whom they belonged will benefit. Similarly, sheep and cows may be led clockwise around a monastery as their final act on this earth. The people performing many of these popular practices may not be able to give a reasoned explanation of what they are doing. No more than I was able to explain to a Tibetan lama in Europe what a Christmas tree was.

The Lama

"Lama" is the Tibetan term used to translate the Sanskrit "guru," which simply means "spiritual teacher." Thus a lama is someone who is qualified to guide others along the path to enlightenment. A lama need not be a monk, and most monks are not lamas. Some of the greatest lamas in the Tibetan tradition, Padmasambhava, Marpa, Milarepa, Kunga Nyingpo, and Drom Tönpa, for example, took no monastic vows and lived as laymen and yogis. The term for a monk in Tibetan is *trapa* not lama. Moreover, to call Tibetan Buddhism "Lamaism" is also a misuse of words. The Tibetans call Buddhism *nang-pa'i-chö*, which means "the Dharma of the Insiders" (a term used by Buddhists throughout Asia). "Lamaism" was a term coined by Western scholars and gives the impression that Tibetan Buddhism is something at odds with "orthodox" Buddhism.

In Tibetan Buddhism, the spiritual teacher plays a very important role, especially in the Vajrayana. Before embarking upon a tantric practice it is necessary to find a qualified guide who is willing to initiate you into the mandala of an appropriate deity and instruct you in the subsequent stages of meditation. Such a teacher will henceforth be considered your lama, and you will be expected to devote yourself wholeheartedly to his or her instructions. This special role of the lama in the Vajrayana has been applied throughout the whole of Tibetan Buddhism, giving a strong devotional quality to the religion.

The term "lama" also has some specialized usages. If you go to a monastery and ask how many lamas are there, you will be told, perhaps, that there are two.

This would mean that the monastery honors within its ranks two lines of reincarnating teachers. This system of recognizing the reincarnations of particularly great teachers dates from the end of the twelfth century when a great master called Karmapa declared that he would deliberately take rebirth in Tibet, and a few years later a young boy was subsequently recognized as his successor. Most monasteries of any standing traditionally had at least one such lama, the larger monasteries up to three or four. These men (and, in a few rare cases, women) would serve not as abbot, which is more a post within the monastic administration, but as the spiritual head of the monastery. Such lamas are also referred to by the titles of "tulku" and "rinpoche."

In the West two of the best-known tulkus, or reincarnating lamas, are the Dalai Lama and the Panchen Lama. The First Dalai Lama and the First Panchen Lama were both disciples of the founder of the Geluk school, Tsongkhapa. The present Dalai Lama is the fourteenth in his line and the previous Panchen the tenth in his. Although the Dalai Lama escaped to India in 1959, the Panchen Lama was in China at the time and was unable to leave. Since then he was constantly under the wing of the Chinese authorities. In the early 1960s he disappeared from public life after making some pro-Tibetan statements and did not resurface until the end of the Cultural Revolution. It is fairly certain that he was imprisoned and probably tortured during this time. Until his sudden death while on a rare visit to his monastery in Shigatse in 1989, he lived mainly in Beijing, occupying a high-sounding post. Despite this apparent link to the Chinese, a document written by the Tenth Panchen Lama before his death has recently come to light in which he expressed his doubts about Chinese policies in Tibet.

After the Tenth Panchen Lama died, the traditional search for his successor began. The Chinese appointed Chadrel Rinpoche, a lama from Tashilhunpo Monastery, to conduct the search in Tibet. Unbeknownst to the Chinese authorities, however, Chadrel consulted the Dalai Lama for advice. In 1995 the Dalai Lama's office in Dharamsala announced that a six-year-old boy called Gendun Chökyi Nyima had been recognized by the Dalai Lama as the Eleventh Panchen Lama, effectively preempting any such announcement by the Chinese. This move infuriated the Chinese authorities, and the boy, his parents and Chadrel Rinpoche all disappeared from public view.

Shortly thereafter, the Chinese declared that another boy, Gyanchain Norbu, had been recognized as the Eleventh Panchen. Although Gyanchain Norbu was subsequently enthroned, most Tibetans continue to regard the Dalai Lama's choice as the authentic reincarnation of the Panchen Lama. The whereabouts of Gendun Chökyi Nyima remain unknown. In 1997, Chadrel Rinpoche was sentenced to six years in jail with a further three years stripped of political rights for the crime of "leaking state secrets."

As for the present Dalai Lama, he leads an active life both in the Tibetan community abroad and as an internationally recognized religious leader. As if to prevent any possibility of the Chinese authorities making claims on his reincarnation after he dies, he has recently announced that he will take rebirth in the Tibetan exile community.

The Yellow Hats and the Red Hats

In many books written about Tibetan Buddhism you will come across the orders of the Red Hats and the Yellow Hats. One gets the impression that the history of Buddhism in Tibet is dominated by the conflicts between these two groups, with the Yellow Hats finally emerging victorious. This view is an oversimplification and only adds to the confusion surrounding the four principal Buddhist orders: the Nyingma, Sakya, Kagyu, and Geluk. Although the Yellow Hats can be identified with the Geluk order, it makes no sense to group the other three together as the Red Hats. The historical conflict upon which the Yellow/Red distinction is based is that between the Mongolian backers of the Geluk and the Tsang kings who supported the Karma Kagyu suborder, during the seventeenth century. This becomes all the more confusing when the Karmapa, head lama of the Karma Kagyu, is commonly known as the Black Hat Lama, in distinction from another leader of the

same order, the Shamarpa, the Red Hat Lama. The problem gets even more knotty when you try to include the Sakya and Nyingma orders. To understand the different orders we have to look beyond what they wear on their heads.

The Tibetans sometimes distinguish between the Ancients and the Moderns, the former being the Nyingma order, who base their teachings on the first translations that were done from the seventh century onward, and the latter being the Sakya, Kagyu, and Geluk orders, who base their traditions upon the later translations begun in the eleventh century. Another way of dividing the orders is by historical division: the Nyingma is the earliest order; the Sakya and Kagyu are the middle orders; and the Geluk is the later order. About three hundred years separate the emergence of one group from the next.

Another problem is that around the four main orders there exist several minor orders and suborders. Some of these smaller orders are confined to a handful of monasteries that follow the teachings of a particularly great lama of that area. Examples of these would be the Bu order of Zhalu Monastery and the Bodong order of Samding Monastery. Although no longer a separate tradition, the Kadam order based at Reting Monastery was very influential, and it is often considered the forerunner to the Geluk order.

It is much more difficult to try to distinguish the orders on doctrinal grounds. The differences that do exist between them here have often been emphasized more for sectarian than philosophical reasons. Although representatives of these orders continue to stress the uniqueness of their tradition as opposed to the others, to an outsider the similarities that unite them will appear far greater than the differences that divide them.

Religious Art

A great deal of the religious art of Tibet was destroyed during the Chinese occupation. Many statues and paintings were taken to China, where they were either channeled to the art market in Hong Kong, reduced to their raw materials, or simply stored away. A small amount has been trickling back to Tibet since the mid-1980s, and it remains to be seen how much eventually returns. Tibetans also concealed a considerable number of statues and tangkas and, as the political situation becomes more stable, these too have begun to reappear. The handful of artists and craftspeople who survived the persecutions of the 1960s are now able to work again at their traditional skills and train young apprentices as well. Much of the work on display in renovated temples and monasteries today is theirs.

The most common forms of religious art in Tibet are statues, tangkas, and murals. The vast majority of statues depict lamas, buddhas, bodhisattvas, tantric deities, and protectors. These vary in height from a few centimeters to several meters and are made from substances ranging from clay to gold. The tangkas and murals likewise show lamas and deities, and often surround their subjects with details from the life of the main figure. Mandalas and lineage trees (representations of the entire lineage of teachers belonging to a certain tradition) are also common subjects. Around the walls of many temples are murals depicting scenes from the former lives of the Buddha as well as historical events related to the founding of the monastery.

Apart from a certain number of folk themes, Tibetan art has a purely religious function. The statues that line the altars in the monasteries are a focus of faith and a source of inspiration for the devout. The tangkas serve as aids to meditation, their exact details reminding the practitioner of the deity or mandala he or she is visualizing. Until recent interest from the West, paintings were never evaluated in terms of their antiquity, artistic merit, or monetary value. If a beautiful, old tangka was too faded to be of further use as a meditation aid, it would often be ceremoniously destroyed and replaced with a new one, perhaps of inferior artistic worth. Art for the Tibetans is not an end in itself but merely a means to help realize a higher spiritual meaning.

The motifs found in Tibetan art may strike one as highly formalized, stifling the individual creativity of the artist. Such creativity is also a value not highly regarded in Tibet; more important is a humble submission of the ego to reproduce exactly the sacred forms of the past. But as you study the wide range of sculptures and paintings preserved in the monasteries, you will soon begin to distinguish the works of a master artist from those of an uninspired apprentice. Artistic genius finds its expression nonetheless.

The symbolism of Tibetan religious art is too intricate to discuss here. The symbols operate on a number of levels, possessing different meanings according to the depth of the viewer's spiritual insight. It is worth mentioning the sexual symbolism that is often found in the representation of tantric figures. Certain deities are shown in sexual embrace with a consort. Sexual union is used as a vivid symbol for the integration of the male and female components of the spiritual path. The male aspect is compassion and active engagement, whereas the female aspect is wisdom and depth of understanding. Final enlightenment is present only when these two aspects are fully united with each other. The deities in sexual embrace do not hint at some secret erotic practice, but confront us with the challenge of integrating the male and female dimensions within ourselves, which are often split apart. Similarly, the wrathful and terrifying deities confront us with the challenge of fiercely defying our own negative mental states of anger, greed, and ignorance.

Sacred Literature

Like art, literature in Tibet is almost exclusively used for religious purposes. A script for writing the Tibetan language was devised by Songtsen Gampo's minister Tönmi Sambhota in order that Buddhist scriptures could be translated from Sanskrit. It took the Tibetans about six hundred years to complete that monumental task of translation, the result of which was 108 volumes of discourse attributed to the historical Buddha and a further 227 volumes of Indian commentaries to those discourses. The collection of discourses is called the *Kangyur* in Tibetan, which means "translation of the word," while the set of commentaries is call the *Tengyur*, the "translation of the commentaries." These scriptures, which consist of four hundred to five hundred pages each, are printed on long, unbound leaves of tough, fibrous paper (about thirty inches long), placed between wooden covers, and wrapped in cloth. They are often stacked on shelves in chapels and worshipped as reverently as the statues and other holy objects.

In addition to the Kangyur and Tengyur there is also a vast quantity of indigenous writings by Tibetan lamas that for the most part consist of further commentaries to the Indian texts, although the Tibetans have evolved their own styles of composition and textual structure. Every lama of note has his *Sungbum* (collected works), which frequently runs to ten or twenty volumes. These writings explore in detail the meaning of Buddhist doctrine, philosophy, and logic, as well as more secular subjects such as medicine and astrology. In addition, numerous works deciphering the symbolic meaning of the tantras and a great number of original liturgical texts have also been composed. Only a fraction of this literary heritage has been translated into Western languages and most of it remains unknown to the outside world.

Stupas

When the historical Buddha was cremated, his body was placed in a traditional Indian funeral cask to be cremated. This cask is called a stupa (in Tibetan, a *chöten*) and has subsequently become for Buddhists what the cross is for Christians. It is the preeminent symbol for the Buddha and his enlightenment, and the parts of the stupa represent the different stages on the way to the final goal. There are eight principal forms of the stupa, each of which stands for a particular aspect of the Buddha's career. The Enlightenment Stupa symbolizes his illumination; the Victory Stupa, his conquest of Mara (the Buddhist Satan); the Nirvana Stupa, his passing away; and so forth. There are eight stupas because after Shakyamuni's body had been cremated, the relics were divided into eight parts, placed in eight smaller funeral casks, and taken to the eight major areas of India where the Buddha had been active. In Tibet when a great lama died, his body would likewise be cremated in such a funeral cask and the relics then enshrined in a more ornate stupa. The act of walking around a stupa in a clockwise direction (always keeping the stupa to your right) is considered by Tibetans and by Buddhists throughout Asia to generate great merit, which can then be dedicated toward the attainment of enlightenment.

Sky Burial

Although high lamas and monks are generally cremated, the most common way to dispose of the dead in Tibet is to take the corpse to a specially designated area outside the town or village, often at the top of a mountain, chop it into pieces, and wait for the vultures and other birds of prey to come and eat it. The final religious rites would be performed by monks and relatives before taking the body away. According to Mahayana Buddhist beliefs, consciousness leaves the body about three days after clinical death. From this moment on the corpse is considered truly lifeless, its purpose fulfilled. The manner of disposal is considered a final act of generosity, enabling other animals to be nourished by one's remains.

This practice has greatly aroused the ghoulish curiosity of many foreign visitors. Initially the Tibetans tolerated the presence of foreigners at "sky burial" sites but recently have become offended by the blatant voyeurism of some observers, especially those who try to photograph the occasion. The Chinese are also none too happy about foreigners attending this "barbarian" ritual and in Lhasa now officially forbid it. If you do witness the sky burial, do so with a sense of respect for the dead, their families, and Tibetan custom. Keep a good distance and do not even show a camera. Perhaps follow the example of the Buddhist monks and yogis who deliberately live in such places and use this opportunity to deepen your insight into the transitoriness of life and the certainty of death.

Religious Fesitvals

Monk dressed in tantric costume for religious dance, c. 1940

Prior to 1959 the most jubilant and colorful events in Tibetan life were the various festivals that occurred throughout the year. These were soon banned by the Chinese and denounced as wasteful and indulgent. Since 1985, however, there has been a slow reinstatement of some of them. In the early spring of 1986, the greatest festival of all, the Mönlam, or Prayer, festival, took place again for the first time in nearly thirty years. This festival follows the Tibetan New Year (*Losar*) celebrations and begins on the fourth day of the first lunar month. Traditionally, huge butter sculptures were erected outside the Jokhang Cathedral in Lhasa, monks and pilgrims poured into the city, and there was a long procession around the Barkor carrying a famous statue of the future Buddha, Maitreya. The Mönlam festival was begun by Tsongkhapa in the early years of the fifteenth century and continued uninterrupted until the Chinese occupation. In 1989 the festival was once again banned. The Chinese feared that such a powerful symbol of Tibetan nationalism would be likely to turn into a massive demonstration against their rule. Only very recently have they allowed it to be resumed.

Another important festival is the Sakadawa festival on the fifteenth day (full moon) of the fourth lunar month, which celebrates the birth, enlightenment, and death of Buddha Shakyamuni. On this day Tibetans often devote themselves to religious practices and abstain from eating meat. The monasteries perform elaborate ceremonies and devotees make offerings to the monks. It is said that the merit from whatever virtuous acts one commits on this day is greatly multiplied, thus lessening the time remaining on one's path to enlightenment.

The A-che Lhama Opera at the Norbulingka, c. 1946

Other major religious festivals are the Chökor Duchen, which celebrates the Buddha's first teaching in Sarnath near Varanasi, on the fourth day of the sixth lunar month; the Lhabab Duchen on the twenty-second day of the ninth lunar month, which commemorates the Buddha's return to earth after his ascent to the heavens to teach his mother; and the Festival of Lamps on the twenty-fifth day of the tenth lunar month, which commemorates the death of Tsongkhapa, the founder of the Geluk order.

In addition to these festivals there are numerous other national and regional celebrations. At some of these, monasteries display beautiful embroidered tangkas from high walls often built solely for that purpose. Others are purely secu-lar occasions when people enjoy the performance of open-air opera and sports, along with generous portions of the local barley beer, or *chang*. The Communist government considers such folk festivals to be far less threatening, and many of them are presently in the process of being restored.

The Tibetan lunar month is usually about a month behind the Western calendar, with the new year usually beginning sometime in February. However, each year fluctuates and sometimes a whole month has to be added. Thus in any given year it is impossible to know exactly when these festivals will occur without referring to a Tibetan calendar.

PART ONE
LHASA

1
THE CITY OF LHASA

Lhasa, the capital of Tibet, is situated on the north bank of the Kyichu River in the province of U (Central Tibet). The Chinese consider it to be the regional capital of the Tibetan Autonomous Region (TAR). The Lhasa region may be reached by air from Chengdu (Sichuan, West China) and Kathmandu, or overland from Golmud (Northwest China) and Kathmandu.

EARLY HISTORY

Originally Lhasa was called Rasa. It was a town built by the Otang Lake, and it was so called because when the water in the lake was stirred by wind its waves would make the sound "ralasa." In the seventh century, at the time of Songtsen Gampo, this lake—perhaps it was more of a marsh—was filled in with the help of a mythical goat, and the Jokhang Cathedral was built on the site. It first became the capital of Tibet during his reign. Although the king used Lhasa as his summer capital, the rulers continued to be buried in the Chonggye Valley near Yarlung for the remainder of the dynasty he inaugurated. There are still nine sites in or around Lhasa that are associated with Songtsen Gampo. The most important of these are the chapels of the Potala that he built, and the Jokhang and the Ramoche Cathedrals.

Songtsen Gampo gave the town the name Lhasa, which means "ground of the gods." The Tibetan etymology of the name states that the city is called ground (*sa*) of the gods (*lha*) because it is as though a lofty realm of the gods had fallen to the ground though the richness of the Dharma.

When Songtsen Gampo's Nepalese queen Bhrikuti (known in Tibetan as Trisun) arrived from Nepal, she perceived the land of Tibet as the body of a demoness who had to be subdued in order for a Buddhist civilization to take root. The king then ordered thirteen temples to be built on the most prominent parts of the body. Lhasa lay on the demoness's chest, and the Jokhang was built where the queen thought the heart of the demoness to lie. The other twelve temples are distributed as follows: there are four on the demoness's hips and shoulders; four on her elbows and knees; and four on her hands and feet. The outermost temples were built as far away as Bhutan, where some are still standing. The inner range of "demoness subduing temples" were located in Central Tibet (for examples, see p. 148 and p. 182).

When the Yarlung dynasty collapsed in the ninth century, the unity of the country was destroyed and power reverted to local feudal lords and princes. Throughout this period Lhasa remained an important city but only nominally was it the capital of Tibet. When the country was next united under the Mongols, Sakya became the de facto capital on account of the power given to

The former Great Western Gate of Lhasa

the Sakya lama Pakpa by Kublai Khan. After the end of the Sakya dynasty, the center of political authority shifted to Nedong (near Tsetang) and then to various regions in Tsang. It was only when Gushri Khan, another Mongolian emperor, defeated the local Tibetan king in 1642 and installed the Fifth Dalai Lama as leader of Tibet that Lhasa again became the center of government.

In the meantime, however, the city had been growing as a religious center. In 1409 the founder of the Gelukpa order, Tsongkhapa, initiated the yearly Mönlam, or Great Prayer, festival at the Jokhang Cathedral. In the same year, the first large Gelukpa monastery, Ganden Monastery, was founded at a location 40 kilometers to the east of the city. Within a decade, Drepung and Sera Monasteries were established on the outskirts of Lhasa. These three monasteries continued to grow in both size and influence, especially after the political ascendancy of the Gelukpa order starting at the time of the Fifth Dalai Lama. By the mid-twentieth century, the monastic population of Lhasa was estimated to be in the vicinity of 20,000 monks, most of whom were residents at

one of these major monasteries.

Little remains from the time of the early kings, and most of what one sees in terms of old buildings and monasteries dates back only to the later period of development. The greater part of the Potala Palace was constructed around the time of the Fifth Dalai Lama, while the Norbulingka was begun only during the Seventh Dalai Lama's reign. Many of the older treasures of the city were destroyed after the Chinese occupation. Historic buildings and even entire districts have been razed to the ground. Yet despite these changes, Lhasa still evokes a powerful sense of mystery for its visitors. A view of the Potala Palace from the top of the Chakpori hill can seem as magical and mysterious today as it must have seemed to pilgrims and visitors centuries ago.

THE FORBIDDEN CITY

Lhasa was one of the last places on earth to be visited and described, let alone occupied, by Western imperial powers. As such, it exercised a compelling fascination throughout the eighteenth and nineteenth centuries as the forbidden city. The city was romantically imagined to possess inconceivable treasures, to preserve ancient wisdom, and to be home to great mystics and saints. Yet before the eighteenth century, Lhasa was not a closed city but a vibrant center of trade and learning. One of the very first Westerners to reach Lhasa was the Jesuit missionary Ippolito Desideri, who

Religious ceremony in Lhasa before 1959

received in Europe from two Lazarist priests, Abbés Huc and Gabet, who stayed a few months before being evicted by the Chinese Amban. In Huc's description of their first sight of Lhasa we gain a glimpse of a vanished world:

> The sun was nearly setting when, issuing from the last of the infinite sinuousities of the mountain, we found ourselves in a vast plain and saw on our right Lha-Ssa, the famous metropolis of the Buddhic world. The multitude of aged trees which surround the city with a verdant wall; the tall white houses, with their flat roofs and towers; the numerous temples with their gilt roofs, the Buddha-la (= Potala), above which rises the palace of the Talé Lama—all these features communicate to Lha-Ssa a majestic and imposing aspect.

arrived in 1716 and stayed in Tibet for seven years. He described the city as "densely populated not only by natives, but by a large number of foreigners of divers nations, such as Tartars, Chinese, Muscovites, Armenians, people from Kashmir, Hindustan, and Nepal, all established there as merchants, and who have made large fortunes."

The subsequent policy that excluded foreigners was not unique to Tibet but common to both China and Japan, who likewise feared the threat of growing Western influence and colonization. The last Christian missionaries were forced to leave Lhasa in 1740. The next Westerner to penetrate the city was the eccentric Englishman Thomas Manning, who arrived in the retinue of a Chinese general in 1811. It was not until 1846 that a further reliable account of the city was

After the departure of Huc and Gabet, the city remained closed to Western eyes until the British invasion of 1904 led by Colonel Francis Younghusband. Accompanying the army was a journalist, Edmund Candler, whose account of the expedition, *The Unveiling of Lhasa*, was a best-seller in its time. He described the approach to what he calls "the most hidden city on earth:"

> As we approached, the road became an embankment across a marsh. Butterflies and dragonflies were hovering among the rushes,

The Potala Palace 1904

clematis grew in the stonework by the roadside, cows were grazing in the rich pastureland, redshanks were calling, a flight of teal passed overhead. . . . Some of us climbed the Chagpo Ri and looked down on the city. Lhasa lay a mile in front of us, a mass of huddled roofs and trees, dominated by the golden dome of the Jokhang Cathedral.

Candler acknowledged that by penetrating Lhasa, the British army had "unveiled the last mystery of the East. There are no more forbidden cities which men have not mapped and photographed." He foresaw the dawning of an age where "children will be sceptical and matter-of-fact and disillusioned," but then stops himself and recalls: "But we ourselves are children. Why could we have not left at least one city out of bounds?"

MODERN LHASA

The late twentieth century tourist will barely recognize these charming descriptions of a rural city. The Great Western Gate, a large stupa between Chakpori and the Potala through which travelers entered the city until 1959, has been demolished and replaced by a busy thoroughfare rumbling with trucks and buses. Only a colorful mass of prayer flags stretching across the road reminds one of what once stood here. Present-day Lhasa is dominated by modern Chinese utilitarian architecture. A sprawling "new town" of multistory offices, concrete shops, and garish nightclubs stifles the old Tibetan city and extends far beyond the Potala and most of the way to Sera Monastery. Wide paved avenues divide this new town into neat rectangles and squares. Compared with most towns in China, it is featureless rather than ugly.

And it is still expanding. Plans are under way to extend the urbanized area of Lhasa beyond Drepung Monastery to the village of Tolung, some eight miles farther west of the present city border. The old city is also under threat. Traditional townhouses are being demolished at an alarming rate, to be replaced by rapidly erected stone and concrete structures, which are then sold off to wealthy individuals. Unless something is done to halt this wave of change, in a few years Lhasa might well become nothing but an urban sprawl, with just a handful of historic temples and shrines protruding from its midst.

Official statistics record that in 1949 the population of Lhasa was 30,000. In 1983 it had grown to 110,000. It is estimated that in 1994 there were 150,000, of whom only one third were ethnic Tibetans; the rest were mainly Chinese bureaucrats and military personnel. Government policy is to stabilize the population of the city at 200,000 by the turn of the millennium.

In contrast to the lethargic city I saw in 1985 and 1986, Lhasa in the mid- to late 1990s has the feel of a frontier boomtown. Construction sites are everywhere, traffic is abundant, and the streets are bursting with commerce. Many disadvantaged Chinese and Muslims have poured into the area in search of a quick buck. The garish commercialism of modern China is visible throughout the city in posters, billboards, storefronts, and the blast of pop music from karaoke bars. The government is encouraging foreign investment through generous tax breaks. Joint venture-capital companies are flourishing with funding pumped in from the West. A new five-star hotel complex is being constructed on the Ta-ye-do island to the south of the city with capital from Macao.

THE BARKOR

The old city of Lhasa is the section of town east of the Potala, most of which is contained between the main avenue (Dekyi Shar Lam) and the river. While old townhouses are increasingly being replaced, the layout still remains to some extent what it was in pre-Chinese times. The houses line narrow, winding cobbled streets on which dogs, cattle, sheep, goats, and people are all equally at home. All these alleys are connected in one way or another to the Barkor, the quadrangle of streets surrounding the Jokhang Cathedral. Unfortunately, despite statements made to the contrary, to contrary, the Chinese government's commitment to preserving these historic buildings is uncertain at best.

"Barkor" literally means "intermediate circuit" and refers to the circumambulation route immediately around the complex of buildings surrounding the Jokhang Cathedral. The Barkor is at once the religious and mercantile focus of old Lhasa; pilgrims endlessly walk clockwise around it, pausing in their devotions every now and again to inspect some merchandise and haggle over its price. Both sides of the road are lined with shops and stalls selling all manner of goods from trinkets to tantric ritual objects. The Barkor is unsurpassed for having absorbed whatever traces of ancient Tibet are still present in the souls of the rich diversity of people who religiously pace its well-trodden streets.

In 1985 a large area of old townhouses facing the entrance to the Jokhang was cleared to make way for a spacious plaza giving easy and direct access to the temple. The plaza itself is poorly conceived. The planners seem to have had in mind a European city square dominated by a large cathedral. But the Jokhang impresses not by any lofty Gothic grandeur but by its solemn, weighty presence. Such presence is far more effective when suddenly encountered from a narrow enclosed street. It is only diminished when set off by a large open square. The plaza is further marred by phony, vertical-walled Tibetan-style houses and grotesque street lamps. Unintentionally, the tearing open of the old city to allow entrance from the new serves as a vivid and disturbing symbol of violation.

THE LINGKOR

A longer circumambulation circuit called the Lingkor used to run around the outside of the old city, along the river and around the Potala. While most of this has been erased through incorporation into modern roads, the idea of the Lingkor has nonetheless persisted as a feature of the collective memory of the elder townspeople, many of whom still walk it daily, usually in early morning before the traffic begins. It is a moving experience to get up around 5:00 A.M. and join the figures mumbling mantras and spinning prayer wheels as they trace the course of this largely demateri-alized pathway. At some points they stop beside mounds of stones piled on pavements or asphalt roadsides, remove their hats, and pray in the direction of a site that may no longer physically exist.

The only preserved section of the Lingkor today starts on the riverbank to the southwest of the Jokhang, just east of Thieves' Island, where pilgrims often camp. The footpath follows the river until you see a large cairn on the opposite side of the road. Cross here and enter a walled alleyway that brings you out at the rear of the Chakpori. You climb up the side of the Chakpori past many carved rock images and *tsa-tsa* shrines, then descend to the intricately carved and painted cliff wall and other small shrines. This leads into another walled passageway, which cuts over the back road to the Norbulingka and then continues along another alley. Just before you get to the main road, there is a small alley to the right that takes you to Kunde Ling Monastery (see chapter 4.)

From this point the Lingkor follows the modern asphalt roads of the city. When you reach the Dekyi Nub Lam, turn right and continue to the next main intersection (with the golden yaks), and turn left on the road that takes you around the back of the Potala. Some pilgrims do an additional loop around the Potala before rejoining the Lingkor to proceed to the east end of the old city. The route then swings back around the south of the old city, through the Muslim quarter, and finally reconnects with the surviving old section on the riverbank by Thieves' Island.

2
THE JOKHANG

The old city of Lhasa is literally built around the Jokhang. It is the easiest place in town to find. You can approach it either by following the Barkor (the quadrangle of roads lined with stalls in the center of the old city) until you reach its main entrance, or by going straight to the plaza that faces it. It is open to the public every day except Monday. Note that parts of the Jokhang (such as the second floor) may be closed without warning; in the afternoon especially some of the chapels may be closed.

History

The Jokhang is without a doubt the most sacred temple in Tibet. It was established in the seventh century by King Songtsen Gampo in order to house the image of Akshobhya Buddha (known in Tibetan as the Jowo Mikyö Dorje) offered to him by his Nepalese wife, Bhrikuti (also known as Trisun). At this time it was called the Trulnang temple, or temple of "magical appearance." Later, when the Jowo Shakyamuni statue given to the king by his Chinese wife, Wen Cheng, was moved here from the Ramoche Temple, the temple was given its present name, Jokhang, the "Shrine of the Jowo." (The Akshobhya statue changed places with Jowo and was installed in Ramoche.) The Jowo statue was part of the Chinese princess's dowry. It was originally given to her father, T'ai-tsung, the second emperor of the T'ang dynasty, by a king from Bengal. The Tibetans believe it was crafted by the celestial artist Vishvakarman at the time of the Buddha. When Wen Cheng came to Tibet, she was accompanied by many Chinese artisans, who built the Ramoche Temple to house it. The Jokhang, however, was originally designed by Nepalese craftsmen on behalf of Queen Bhrikuti.

It is unclear exactly why the changeover of the two statues took place. The records state only that when Songtsen Gampo died, Wen Cheng moved the Jowo statue from Ramoche to the Jokhang for protection against an invading Chinese army and concealed it in one of the chapels. There is still a chapel called the Shrine Where the Jowo Was Hidden. On our plan this is Chapel 18, which presently houses Amitabha and the Eight Medicine Buddhas.

Since its founding, the Jokhang has been considerably enlarged and embellished, in particular during the reign of the Fifth Dalai Lama. Some of the worn wooden carvings around the doorways to the chapels, on the capitals of several pillars, and on the ends of some beams may date back to the seventh century, but apart from the Jowo itself, very few statues are that old. Most of the images are modern, remade to replace those destroyed during the Cultural Revolution. There are currently 101 monks living here, 40 of whom have official governmental standing as Jokhang monks.

The Site

Directly in front of the entrance to the cathedral are three stone steles in two separate enclosures. The taller of these carries a bilingual inscription of the Tibetan-Chinese agreement of 821 between the Tibetan king, Tri Ralpachen, and the Chinese emperor, Wen Wu Hsiao-te Wang-ti. This agreement, clearly between equals, makes interesting, although in retrospect ironic, reading. It states, for example: "Tibet and China shall abide by the frontiers of which they are now in occupation. All to the east is the country of Great China; and all to the west is, without question, the country of Great Tibet. Henceforth on neither side shall there be waging of war nor seizing of territory. If any person incurs suspicion he shall be arrested; his business shall be inquired into and he shall be escorted back." The other two steles are inscribed in Chinese and tell of the dangers of smallpox and means to cure it. They have been worn away in many places, presumably by Tibetans who supposed that the stone itself must have curative properties. Immediately behind these two steles there used to grow a large willow tree planted by Queen Wen Cheng, of which now only the dead stump is visible.

The forecourt leading to the main entrance of the Jokhang is invariably filled with devotees prostrating themselves full-length in the direction of the Jowo. To the left are two massive prayer wheels.

As one walks through the main portals, the first images one sees (1), two to the right and two to the left, are large seated statues of the Four Guardian Kings. From here one enters an inner courtyard (2), the center of which opens to the sky. Traditionally, this was the main assembly area for the monks. If you look up to the left you will see an ornate covered balcony adorned with golden figurines and pinnacles. This balcony leads to the private quarters of the Dalai Lama, where he would stay during the Mönlam festival and observe the monks engaged in philosophical debate in the courtyard below.

On your left as you enter the courtyard is a wall painting of the Mongol emperor Gushri Khan in conversation with Desi Sanggye Gyatso, the regent who ruled after the death of the Fifth Dalai Lama. The detailed murals that cover the remaining wall space depict the thousand buddhas who will appear during this current eon. These are all recent paintings commissioned by the Thirteenth Dalai Lama. At the far end of the courtyard is a long altar usually ablaze with butter lamps. Behind the altar is another doorway, which leads to the interior of the Jokhang itself.

To enter the main hall of the Jokhang you proceed down another dark corridor, which runs past two small chapels. On the left (4) is a room containing five figures with wrathful expressions. On the opposite side of the hallway (3) is another chapel with three benign beings. The wrathful figures are rakshas, malefic, cannibalistic spirits, and the benign ones are nagas, an intelligent underwater species. According to tradition, these beings appeared to Songtsen Gampo as he was building the temple and, after having been subdued, vowed to protect it against harmful influence until the end of time.

Facing you as you enter the large inner chamber of the Jokhang are several large statues. To the left sits Padmasambhava (a), to the right Maitreya (c). Between them and slightly behind stands a thousand-armed Avalokiteshvara (b). To the right of the main Maitreya figure are two other images of Maitreya, both facing inwards. The smaller of these two, Barzhi Jampa (d), is named on account

of the Barzhi family who commissioned its construction. The larger is called the Miwang Jampa (e) on account of its being commissioned by the nobleman Miwang Polha. Behind the image of Avalokiteshvara is another small encased statue of Padmasambhava (f).

Normally a queue of Tibetans murmuring mantras and carrying prayer wheels and butter offerings moves clockwise around these central figures. This line of people hugs the walls and weaves slowly in and out of the numerous chapels, which are entered by regularly placed low doorways. The best (and only) way to visit these chapels is to join the queue.

The Chapel of Tsongkhapa and his Eight Pure Disciples (5)

The first chapel, immediately to the left of the entrance, is dedicated to the founder of the Geluk order, Je Tsongkhapa. He is the main figure facing you as you enter, and is accompanied by a group of monks known as the Eight Pure Disciples. The most famous of these are his two chief disciples, Khedrup Je and Gyeltsab Je, who are seated to his right and left. Tsongkhapa once received a vision of Manjushri in the Jokhang and asked him how many disciples he should take with him into retreat. Manjushri told him to take eight. They then departed for Chölung in the Olka Valley (see chapter 23) to meditate.

The Stupa of Examination (6)

The original of this white and gold stupa was made by Sakya Pandita. In the cen-

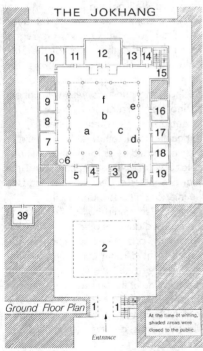

THE JOKHANG

Ground Floor Plan

At the time of writing, shaded areas were closed to the public.

Entrance

ter of the stupa one can see a small gold-
en image of the female deity Vijaya. After
the stupa are newly painted murals of
Maitreya, four-armed Avalokiteshvara,
Amitabha, Vajrapani, Hayagriva, and
Shakyamuni.

The Chapel of the Eight Medicine Buddhas (7)

Eight rather undistinguished images
adorn this small room. Between this and
the next chapel is a statue of Milarepa.

The Chapel of the Fivefold Self-Originated Avalokiteshvara (8)

The main figure in this chapel is a thousand-armed, eleven-headed Avalokiteshvara, the original of which is said
to have miraculously appeared at the
time of Songtsen Gampo. One tradition
maintains that Songtsen Gampo and his
two wives were absorbed into the statue
at death. The original head of the statue
was smuggled out of Tibet during the
Cultural Revolution and is now enshrined
in the main temple in Dharamsala. Two
wrathful protectors stand guard on either
side of the entrance. On the left are
three seated figures: Jigten Wangchuk (a
form of Avalokiteshvara), and Tronyer
Chenma and Ozer Chenma (two forms
of Tara who sprang from the tears of
Avalokiteshvara). The three figures
along the opposite wall are Sarasvati,
Tara, and Avalokiteshvara Karsapani.

The Chapel of the Maitreya of Purification [Jampa Trudzel] (9)

To the right of the main image of

Maitreya, seated along the wall, are
small, fine statues of four principal bodhisattvas: Manjushri, Avalokiteshvara,
Vajrapani, and Tara. To the left of the
main image is a newly installed statue of
Amitabha. On the opposite wall is an
image of Tsongkhapa with a stupa to
either side.

Before reaching the final chapel along
this wall you pass another image of a
thousand-armed Avalokiteshvara enshrined in a golden glass and wood
case.

The Chapel of the Statue That Resembles Tsongkhapa (10)

During Tsongkhapa's own lifetime several
statues of the master were commissioned.
Upon seeing this one, Tsongkhapa is said
to have remarked on how closely it resem-
bled him. Another tradition maintains that
this image was created miraculously by
the protector Dharmaraja. Yet another tradition claims it was commissioned by a
later Mongolian emperor. Behind
Tsongkhapa to his left is a series of his
teachers from the Sakya tradition. This
raised corner section is sometimes called
the Chapel of the Lake on account of a
small doorway there that opens to a stairway that used to take one to a small body
of water. Local people say it is now dry.

The Amitabha Chapel (11)

Guarding the entrance to his chapel are
two wrathful protectors. To the left stands
the blue figure of Vajrapani and to the
right the red form of Tsolme-wa Tsekpa,
an aspect of Hayagriva. Inside, Amitabha

is flanked by two small ferocious guardians. Along each wall are four seated bodhisattvas. This room is sometimes called the "room where obstacles are dispelled." Since this shrine is immediately before that of the Jowo, here the pilgrim prays that his or her karmic hindrances to seeing the Jowo are fully cleared away.

Between the Amitabha chapel and the Jowo are four raised, seated figures. The central image is King Songtsen Gampo. To the left is his Nepalese queen, Bhrikuti, and to the right his Chinese queen, Wen Cheng, before whom is Vajrapani. The fourth, smaller statue in the corner is an old and much revered image of Padmasambhava. This image is markedly realistic and makes an interesting contrast to the traditional stylized representations of the Guru.

The Chapel of the Jowo Shakyamuni (12)

The central and most important shrine in the Jokhang is also the most elaborate and impressive. As you stand at its wide entrance, make sure to look up at the beautifully carved and painted woodwork on the ceiling above. Upon entering the shrine, you first pass two wrathful figures: Vajrapani, on your right, and Achala, on your left. You then pass standing, life-size images of the Four Guardian Kings before climbing a number of steps leading to the interior of the chapel. The Jowo is heavily bedecked with brocade clothing and jewelry. Before him burn massive silver butter lamps. A small doorway on the left and another on the right allow the pilgrims to touch their heads to his leg and make whatever wishes they may have. Immediately behind the Jowo is an old Buddha image of which only the head and shoulders are visible. It is said that this was the main image prior to the arrival of the Jowo. When the Jowo was to be installed in its place, the older statue apparently proclaimed that it would never move but would remain to care for the new image. Around the high walls of this chapel are twelve standing bodhisattvas known as the Six Holy Sons and the Six Holy Daughters. At the back of the room are also found images of the Seventh and Thirteenth Dalai Lamas, Tsongkhapa, and a large seated Buddha.

As you leave the Jowo shrine and proceed to the next chapel, you encounter three seated images. The central figure is that of Atisha. To the left is the translator Ngog Legpa'i Sherab and to the right the layman Drom Tönpa, Atisha's main disciple.

The Chapel of the Protector Maitreya [Tri-Tri Jampa] (13)

The central image is a form of Maitreya mythologically connected with the king Tri-Tri (Krikin), a benefactor of the former Buddha Kashyapa. It is said to have been brought to Tibet by Bhrikuti, the Nepalese queen of Songtsen Gampo. The eight seated bodhisattvas around him are all aspects of Tara. On the walls are newly painted murals of the Thirty-Five Confessional Buddhas. Formerly the stove of Wen Cheng was kept in this chapel in the front left-hand corner.

On your way to the next chapel you will also pass three seated figures. The central figure is that of the Tibetan lama Jonang Taranata. Although strongly criticized by Tsongkhapa and his followers for some of his philosophical statements, he is still highly revered for his erudition and spiritual attainment. To the left is Avalokiteshvara and to the right Amitayus. On the wall behind each statue are paintings of the respective figures.

The Chapel of Avalokiteshvara Who Roars Like a Lion (14)

The main figure worshipped in this shrine is not the large Buddha Amitabha placed at the end of the chapel, but the smaller image of Avalokiteshvara seated on a lion, which is the first statue on the left as you enter. The other five bodhisattvas are also aspects of Avalokiteshvara.

Against the wall between this chapel and the staircase leading to the upper story is a short pillar with a hole at the top. Many pilgrims place an ear to this hole in the hope of hearing the sound of the Anga bird beating its wings. According to legend, the Anga bird lives at the bottom of the lake upon which the Jokhang is built.

At this point one may either follow the majority of pilgrims upstairs or continue to visit the remaining chapels on the ground floor. Here we shall describe these remaining chapels first before covering the upper story.

Shrine to Padmasambhava (15)

Tucked away in a corner beneath the stairs are statues of Padmasambhava flanked by Shantarakshita and King Trisong Detsen.

As you leave this shrine you may notice an image of the Medicine Buddha on the wall to the left protected by a metal grille. This marks the place where nine buddhas are said to have spontaneously manifested from the Clear Light. The murals here depict the Thirty-Five Confessional Buddhas. In addition is Shakyamuni, flanked by Maitreya and Manjushri and surrounded by the eight great Indian *pandits*.

Amitayus Chapel (16)

Above the door as you go in are images of Green and White Tara, together with an Indian mahasiddha. Inside the chapel are nine identical statues of Amitayus with consort, reflected on the walls behind them with identical paintings.

Between this and the next chapel is a mural of King Songtsen Gampo accompanied by his Nepalese and Chinese wives. The third woman, holding the baby, is his lesser-known Tibetan queen. There then follow murals of a thousand-armed Avalokiteshvara, White Tara, Amitabha, and another White Tara.

The Chapel of Maitreya [Jampa Che Zhi] (17)

The small, delicately wrought image of Maitreya that stands as the central figure of this chapel is the one traditionally carried around the Barkor in the procession

during the Mönlam festival. To the left of
Maitreya stands Manjushri and to the
right Avalokiteshvara. An image of Tara
sits to either side of these bodhisattvas.
Four wrathful protectors against the
walls guard the shrine. To the right of
the entrance stands Vaishravana and to
the left Jambhala. Seated by the altar is
a statue of Lama Gyelwa Bum, renowned for having constructed a bar-
rage against the river in Lhasa, thus sav-
ing the city from being flooded. If you
look carefully in the lower left corner of
the chapel as you enter, you will see a
small stone carving of a goat. This is the
sacred goat (Dungtse Rama Gyelmo)
that, according to legend, filled with
earth the lake upon which the Jokhang
was to be constructed.

The Chapel Where the Jowo Was Hidden (18)

On the wall leading to this chapel are
murals of Manjushri and statues of the
five great lamas of the Sakya tradition.

   This is the chapel where the Jowo statue was concealed by Wen Cheng when
she moved it here after the death of her
husband Songtsen Gampo. Now the
central figure is that of Amitabha. Along
both side walls are the Eight Medicine
Buddhas.

The Chapel of the Seven Heroic Buddhas (19)

Above the door are paintings of the
longevity triad, a Victory Stupa, and
Prajnaparamita.

   These seven buddhas, which include

Shakyamuni as the main figure and six
others, are shown here in the *sambhogakaya* or archetypal form. When
depicted in the *nirmanakaya* or
emanated aspect, they are known as
the Seven Heroic Buddhas. Going
clockwise they are called: All
Protecting, Golden Power, All Seeing,
Shakyamuni, World Destroyer, Head
Protrusion, and Kashyapa.

The Chapel of the Dharma Kings (20)

The images in this chapel are some of
the very few that miraculously escaped
destruction during the Cultural Revolution. The central figure is Songtsen
Gampo. To the left is Trisong Detsen
and to the right Ralpachen. These three
rulers reigned at the height of the
Tibetan Empire and were responsible
for the introduction and consolidation
of Buddhism in Tibet. To the left of the
door as you enter is Songtsen Gampo's
minister Gawa. Next to him is his
Nepalese queen and next to her the
first (quasi-mythological) king of Tibet,
Nyatri Tsenpo. To the right of the door
is Tönmi Sambhota, the minister of
Songtsen Gampo who created the
Tibetan alphabet, and next to him the
king's Chinese wife.

   The mural on your left as you leave
this chapel and return to the entrance of
the cathedral describes Songtsen
Gampo's founding of the Jokhang. In the
center of the painting is a lake with a
white stupa in the middle. Songtsen
Gampo had thrown his ring in the air
and proclaimed that he would start

building wherever it fell. When the ring fell into the lake a stupa was miraculously produced. A sacred goat then appeared to fill the lake with earth. On this foundation the Jokhang was constructed. To the left of the lake you can see the image of the Jowo being carried in a palanquin from China. Further to the left is a painting of the Potala in the original form constructed by Songtsen Gampo. To the far left is the medical college founded on the neighboring Chakpori hill.

We continue our visit to the Jokhang by climbing the two flights of stairs leading to the upper story.

The Chapel of the Buddhas of the Three Times (21)

This shrine to the buddhas of the past, present, and future was under construction in 1994. On the wall to the left are murals of the eight manifestations of Padmasambhava, to the right a damaged one of Tsongkhapa.

The Chapel of Shakyamuni and his Disciples (22)

Here the historical Buddha Shakyamuni (or Gautama) is flanked by his two chief disciples, the arhats Shariputra and Maudgalyayana. Standing bodhisattvas surround the room and murals of Shakyamuni and Tara adorn the walls. Note the fine carvings on the old doorway to this chapel.

The theme of the chapel continues along the wall with a mural of Shakyamuni and his two disciples, surrounded by the traditional sixteen great arhats of the Buddha's time.

The Chapel of the Eight Medicine Buddhas (23)

The Medicine Buddhas symbolize the healing quality of the Buddha's enlightenment: the healing of both the mental delusions that lie at the root of suffering as well as physical and mental disease. A protector stands guard at each side of the door: to the right, Gyeltsen Tsenmo and to the left, Chagdor Korchen.

The Chapel of Shakyamuni (24)

Two images of Shakyamuni are found here. The smaller image to the right of the main one is accompanied by the arhat disciples Shariputra and Maudgalyayana.

The Chapel of the Five Protectors (25)

This is one of the several tantric shrines found on this upper level of the Jokhang. The central deity here is the wrathful protector Hayagriva, the "Horse-Headed One." To the left is Pelden Lhamo. Guarding the doorway are (to the left) Dutsen, a spirit being, and (to the right) Lutsen, a naga. The five remaining wrathful deities, who guard the center and the four directions, are the protectors to whom the shrine is dedicated. Around the walls are paintings of Green Tara, Shakyamuni and his two chief disciples in seated posture (which is unusual), and the Thirty-Five Confessional Buddhas.

The Chapel of the Three Great Kings (26)

The three great kings of the Yarlung dynasty are celebrated in this chapel. In the center is Songtsen Gampo, to the left Trisong Detsen, and to the right Ralpachen. To the left of the three kings are Songtsen Gampo's two main wives, and to the right his minister, Tönmi Sambhota. Also on the king's right is one of the seven symbolic jewels of royal power, the precious general. As you enter the chapel, on the left are other images of royal power: the symbolic precious elephant, precious horse, and precious minister.

The Chapel of the Dharma King Songtsen Gampo (27)

This spacious shrine located directly above the main entrance to the Jokhang is dedicated to the founder of the temple, Songtsen Gampo. A large statue of the king dominates the shrine. As usual he is flanked by his Nepalese and Chinese queens. Behind the three main figures are the Seven Heroic Buddhas (see Chapel 19). Against the left wall of the chapel are three smaller images of the king and his two wives. To the right are Tsongkhapa and his two chief disciples. In front of the king is a large, ornate silver pitcher. This was the receptacle in which the king kept his supply of chang (barley beer). The silver casing probably houses an earthenware vessel and is of a later date. Before the Chinese occupation, once a year this pitcher would ceremoniously be carried around the households of the nobility and a serving of chang offered to each family.

The Chapel of Avalokiteshvara (28)

The central image here is a simple representation of Avalokiteshvara. Along the walls are the six buddhas who are the special protectors of each of the six realms of existence: the hells, the hungry ghost realm, the animal realm, the human realm, the titan realm, and the celestial realm. Since the guiding principle of these buddhas' activity is their compassion, Avalokiteshvara—as the personification of compassion—stands as the main image. Numerous small identical images of Amitayus are painted in red on the cream-colored walls.

The remaining chapels in this section of the floor (nos. 29–35) either are empty, are being used as storerooms, or contain a temporary assortment of images. Chapel 34 is regarded as the meditation cell of King Songtsen Gampo and is distinguished by a low, elaborately carved doorway. It is due to be restored as a chapel to the king and his principal meditation deities. Next to chapel 34, immediately above the Jowo image downstairs, is a concealed Chapel called the Zhalre Lhakhang (The Chapel Where One Can Behold the Face) containing murals possibly from the time of Songtsen Gampo. It is described in detail in Roberto Vitali's Early Temples of Central Tibet. It is only accessible with special permission.

You must now retrace your steps in order to find the stairs by which you reach the remaining tantric chapels at the rear of the upper story.

The Padmasambhava Chapel (36)

This chapel houses images of the eight manifestations of Padmasambhava, the Indian tantric master who helped establish Buddhism in Tibet. In the center is an image of the master as Guru Rinpoche, accompanied by his two main consorts.

To the left of the chapel, some steps lead you to an old room that used to be devoted to the Jowo Shakyamuni. It is believed that some of the historical Buddha's robes were stored here. Some very old murals still adorn the walls. On the wall to the right of the chapel is a self-emanated image of the protectress Pelden Lhamo covered by cloth and glass.

The Samvara Chapel (37)

This chapel houses a single statue of the tantric deity Samvara with his consort, Vajravarahi.

The Chapel of Pelden Lhamo (38)

Pelden Lhamo is often regarded as the principal protectress of Tibet, especially among the Gelukpa. There are two statues of her in this shrine: the one to the right is the peaceful form; the one to the left, wielding a sword, with her face covered by a cloth, is the wrathful aspect.

The monk in the Pelden Lhamo shrine may allow you to enter another chamber that is reached by a small flight of stairs at the rear of the chapel. This chamber, the Pelchok Dukhang, has no statues but has been richly decorated with tantric murals.

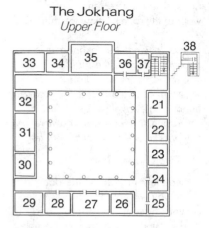

The Jokhang
Upper Floor

The walls are black and the paintings beautifully outlined in white, gold, and red. The figures depicted are the main Geluk protectors: Yamantaka, Mahakala, and Pelden Lhamo. This chamber is the place where the monks who live in the Jokhang gather to perform their rituals, in particular the tantric rite of *gangso*.

This chamber leads directly onto the roof of the Jokhang. Although the monks may be reluctant to let you go up here, it is well worth a visit. [Another entrance to the roof is found by the staircase leading out to the main forecourt, behind (1).]This is where the monks have their rooms; there are no chapels here. The golden rooftops are exquisitely embellished with dragon heads and figurines. Beaten golden plaques placed at regular intervals around the tops of the walls portray all manner of Indian and Tibetan Buddhist symbols. Of particular note are the delightful murals of Tara painted around the entire length of the outer walls of the rooms below the main roof.

Before leaving the Jokhang it is worth circumambulating the main building. As you leave the main entrance, turn right. This will lead you to a long corridor lined with prayer wheels. Just as you approach this corridor, however, you will pass another chapel to your left.

The Tara Chapel (39)

Immediately in front of the door to this shrine you will notice a roundish piece of carved masonry on the ground. This marks a stone that is said to resemble the pointed hat of Tsongkhapa. The chapel itself is devoted to Tara, a large image of whom sits in the center of the room. Behind her in glass cases are the Twenty-One Taras, which are her principal manifestations. On the right of the chapel are six other statues. The first three depict the Indian masters Shantarakshita and Padmasambhava and, to the right, their patron, Trisong Detsen. The remaining three images are of Tsongkhapa and his two chief disciples.

The Circumambulation Path

The circumambulation path takes you around the Jokhang and ends back at the main inner courtyard (2). The walls to both sides are covered with detailed murals depicting 108 stories from the Buddha's previous and final lives. They are based on the *Paksam Trishing (Avadanakalpalata),* a work by the Kashmiri poet Kshemendra, and were commissioned in the early part of the twentieth century by the Thirteenth Dalai Lama.

3
RAMOCHE TEMPLE: GYUTÖ & GYUME

RAMOCHE AND GYUTÖ

Ramoche is in Lhasa, to the north of the Dekyi Shar Lam at the end of a narrow street called the Tun Tril Lam. It is easily reached on foot from anywhere in the old city. It is open daily.

History

The Ramoche Temple is one of the oldest religious buildings in Lhasa. It was erected by Songtsen Gampo's Chinese wife in the seventh century to house the statue of the Jowo Shakyamuni that she brought with her to Tibet. When this statue was moved to the Jokhang after Songtsen Gampo's death, it was replaced by the image of Akshobhyavajra, known in Tibetan as the Jowo Mikyö Dorje, which was brought as part of the dowry of the king's Nepalese wife, Bhrikuti. Originally the temple was built in the Chinese style but after repeated damage by fire it was rebuilt in the Tibetan fashion.

Ramoche was always overshadowed by the Jokhang, and in 1474 it was taken over by Kunga Döndrup, a second-generation disciple of Tsongkhapa, and used as the main assembly hall for the newly founded Upper Tantric College (Gyutö). At its height, up to five hundred monks lived and studied at the Upper Tantric College; their main residential and study area was across the road

from the Ramoche (this has now been converted into a school). As with the Lower Tantric College (Gyume), some of these monks would enter the college at a young age and specialize in the tantric arts of chanting, the construction of mandalas, and the performance of complex rituals; others, however, would enter only after having completed their doctrinal training at one of the principal Gelukpa monasteries around Lhasa.

The temple suffered considerable damage during the Cultural Revolution and was closed until the summer of 1985. The main image of Akshobhyavajra was said to have been broken in two during the revolution and the upper body carried off to China. The two halves were reunited and the image restored to the temple in the mid-1980s, after the Tenth Panchen Lama discovered the statue's torso in Beijing. Technically, 115 monks belong to Ramoche, but only seven live here, as caretakers. The rest live outside the monastery with relatives. They assemble five times each month to perform ceremonies but are unable to follow the traditional courses of intensive tantric study due to the severe shortage of teachers. Their studies at present are limited to major rituals and mandala construction.

The Site

Upon entering Ramoche you pass along a hallway that takes you past a protector chapel on the left and a statue of Dorje Yudruma, the special protectress of the

Upper Tantric College, and Sengdongma, the Lion-Faced Dakini. A large statue of Vajrapani stands on the right as you enter the main **assembly hall**, which is lined with rows of monks' cushions. To the left of the hall is an encased statue of the Thirteen-Deity Yamantaka and to the right a glass-encased statue of Guhyasamaja, next to which is Kunga Döndrup, the founder of the Upper Tantric College. The large throne is reserved for the present Dalai Lama. To its right is a statue of the Thirteenth Dalai Lama and a cabinet with statues of Tsongkhapa and his two main disciples. The remaining cabinets contain images of Tara, Avalokiteshvara, Amitayus, Tsongkhapa, Shakyamuni, and Maitreya.

The main shrine is to the rear of the temple. After passing the Four Guardian Kings you ascend a few steps to face the sumptuously ornamented image of Akshobhyavajra, a representation of Shakyamuni at the age of eight, brought to Tibet by Songtsen Gampo's Nepalese queen. Around him stand the Eight Great Bodhisattvas. Tsongkhapa and Manjushri are in the corners, while two statues of Vajrapani guard the entrance. Behind the main image is a small replica made to replace the original during its absence. An inner circumambulation path takes you beneath this replica.

The upper stories are still to be restored. From the roof one has a good view of Tsomoling Monastery and Zhide Dratsang.

GYUME: THE LOWER TANTRIC COLLEGE

Gyume is on the Dekyi Shar Lam. It is east of the Yak Hotel, on the same side of the road, across from the Tibet-Kansu trade center. From the street it looks like any other Lhasa townhouse, but the doorway can be recognized by the golden Sanskrit lettering painted along the top. A white cloth showing a Dharma Wheel and two deer hangs in front of the main monastery building inside the courtyard. It is open all day.

History

The Lower Tantric College was founded in 1433 by Je Sherab Senge, a disciple of Tsongkhapa who vowed to his teacher that he would take responsibility for preserving his tantric teachings. The college was first known as Se Gyu-pa and was not located in Lhasa but on a mountain called Lhunpo Se in the province of Tsang. It moved to its present site in the city of Lhasa only at the time of the Fifth Dalai Lama. Like the Upper Tantric College, it specialized in training young monks in tantric rituals, and elder geshes in tantric doctrine and practice.

Gyume was completely desecrated during the Cultural Revolution and its buildings turned into houses for the local people. It reopened in May 1985 with the return of thirty-five elderly monks. The reincarnate lama of Gyume is a monk named Dedrul Rinpoche, who currently lives at the nearby Meru Monastery.

The Site

Around the spacious, tidy courtyard are rooms for the monks, a kitchen, and two rooms containing large prayer wheels, the second of which is attended by a nun and has a shrine to Tsongkhapa and his two main disciples.

The altar in the main **assembly hall** bears images of Tsongkhapa and his two main disciples, Je Sherab Senge (the founder of the monastery), the Thirteenth Dalai Lama, and Shakyamuni. In front of the altar is a large throne reserved for the present Dalai Lama. Behind the altar is a room containing huge, three-story-high statues of Tsongkhapa and his two main disciples. These are replicas of the originals, which were destroyed during the Cultural Revolution, made by a recent past abbot of Gyume called Nye Lama. His relics are enshrined in a stupa to the right of the images. To the left is a statue of Vaishravana. A doorway on the right leads to a small protector chapel with a statue of the Thirteen-Deity Yamantaka.

More quarters for monks are found on the second story. There is also a **Tara Chapel**, which contains numerous images, including a statue of Green Tara that is rumored to have spoken. On the roof are guest rooms for the Dalai Lama and a library where the Kangyur is stored. At the back of the roof is a gallery from which you can view the three large statues on the ground floor.

4
ANI SANGKHUNG NUNNERY, THE FOUR LING MONASTERIES, & OTHER SITES IN LHASA

This chapters explores some of the smaller temples that lie hidden among the warren of streets in and around the old city of Lhasa. They were nearly all closed down during the early years of the occupation, but they are now slowly reappearing and resuming their original functions. In contrast to the larger monasteries, such as Sera and Drepung, these smaller places are foci of devotion and practice for the people of the city.

ANI SANGKHUNG NUNNERY

Ani Sangkhung is the largest and most active of the small temples in the city. The nuns here have often been at the forefront of demonstrations against the occupation. I would like to dedicate this chapter to the nun (second from the right in color photograph #33, between pp.118-119) who was arrested and killed by the Chinese authorities. Although the nunnery can be reached by a shortcut through the back streets of Lhasa behind the Jokhang, it is probably easiest to go first to the main mosque. From there take the small road going west. The nunnery is about two hundred yards on your right and is yellow in color. Ask local people for the Ani Gompa. It is open all day.

History

Ani Sangkhung is the only active nunnery in Lhasa today. The foundations for a temple are said to have been laid on this site as early as the seventh century, as the place was associated with Songtsen Gampo. Initially it was a monastery, and only in the fifteenth century was it enlarged and turned into a nunnery by a disciple of Tsongkhapa named Tongten. Prior to 1959 it was under the spiritual direction of the Geluk lama Pabongka Rinpoche. The building was abandoned during the Cultural Revolution and began to collapse through neglect. It has been working as a nunnery again since 1984 and there are now 93 nuns, most of whom are young. In recent years as many as 120 nuns have lived here, but quite a few have been imprisoned for demonstrating against the Chinese, and others have fled to India. The nuns' main duty is to conduct rituals, primarily to Avalokiteshvara and Tara. Some nuns go to Drepung to study basic Buddhist doctrine. In 1993, the present reincarnation of Pabongka Rinpoche, now a young man living in India, visited the nunnery for the first time since the occupation.

The Site

Vajrapani and Hayagriva guard the entrance to the main **assembly hall**, the principal image of which is a thousand-armed Avalokiteshvara. In the cabinets behind are statues (from the left) of: Green

Tara, Pabongka Rinpoche (made in 1941, the year of his death), Trijang Rinpoche, Samvara, Shakyamuni, Tsongkhapa and his two main disciples, Vajrayogini, Mindrugpa, Shakyamuni, and White Tara. At the end is a glass case with a tangka of Pelden Lhamo (the nunnery would like to add a statue). On the upper walls are the only murals surviving from before the Cultural Revolution. They depict Tsong-khapa, Yamantaka, Samvara and Guhya-samaja, Tara, Avalokiteshvara, and Vajrayogini.

If you go down the alley to the right of the nunnery, you come to a long room of unusual shape and design, dedicated to King Songtsen Gampo. He is said to have meditated there and through the force of his concentration diverted the course of the Kyichu River when it threatened to flood the site where the Jokhang was being con-structed. At the far end of the room, cov-ered by a glass canopy, is a sunken pit. At the bottom of this was the king's meditation chamber, and there is now a small statue of him there. Tsongkhapa's student Tong-ten, the founder of the nunnery, is also said to have spent time in retreat here.

THE FOUR "LING" MONASTERIES

There are four "ling" temples of Lhasa: Tenggye Ling, Tsomo Ling, Kunde Ling and Tsechok Ling, all of which were con-structed in the seventeenth century. The Fifth Dalai Lama decreed that the regent of a Dalai Lama should be selected from one of these monasteries (although in practice this was not always done). All *of them were built up into wealthy estab-lishments during the Manchu period.*

Tenggye Ling

Tenggye Ling is situated to the west of the old city, south of the Dekyi Shar Lam, behind the Mentsi Khang and amid a maze of old Lhasa townhouses. A lane opposite the Snowlands Hotel will take you there. In 1912 it was partially damaged for siding with the Chinese in the conflict of the same year and lost its former prestige. Shortly after the Chinese seized power in 1959, most of Tenggye Ling was turned into living quarters for the army and local people. During the Cultural Revolution the last remaining chapels were destroyed.

Over the past ten years it has slowly been restored to its function as a temple. Four monks live here. The chapel, now in reasonable condition, is on two levels. The lower level is rather bare apart from murals that seem to depict a battle scene. The upper level contains a cabinet with butter sculptures and a figure of Padma-sambhava, next to which is a tangka of Mahakala, followed by a scarf-draped image of Dorje Drakden. The main image is that of Tsemar, a Nyingma protector. To the right is the protector Nyingko Nechen. Two Sakya protectors are in glass cabinets on the right-hand wall.

Traditionally, Tenggye Ling was affiliated with Loseling College of Drepung. It was also connected the Samye Monastery, being the Lhasa home for one of Samye's protectors.

Tsomo Ling

Tsomo Ling was connected to Sera Me

College and founded by a former tutor of one of the Dalai Lamas. The large residence of this lama now stands empty opposite the main entrance to Sera Me (see Chapter 10). Tsomo Ling is located to the south of Ramoche and is reached by taking a small alley north from the Dekyi Shar Lam opposite the road that runs to the Jokhang on which is situated the Snowlands Hotel.

During the Cultural Revolution the complex ceased to serve as a monastery, and it is now a home to many lay families. In 1989, however, a small monastery reopened. There are 17 monks living here (as opposed to 175 in the past), all of whom live in the assembly hall. The head lama of the monastery is the fifth incarnation and lives elsewhere in Lhasa. The murals in the hall are reasonably well preserved. Cabinets on the left-hand side contain images of Hvashang Mahayana, Vajrayogini, and Green Tara. A door to the left of the altar leads to a series of dark, empty rooms, which used to be protector chapels. Note the bullet holes peppering their walls. A throne for the Dalai Lama stands in front of the altar, on which are images of the third Tsomo Ling lama, Tsongkhapa and his two main disciples, Shakyamuni, Amitayus, and Padmasambhava.

Kunde Ling

Kunde Ling is located to the west of the city off the Dekyi Nub Lam (the main road leading to the Holiday Inn). You turn onto the Lingkor path and after a few meters turn left, just before the Kunchi Tibetan Restaurant. A winding alley leads you into an unsuspected little pocket of old Tibetan townhouses. The monastery is entered through a low gateway, which takes you into a small courtyard. Formerly the seat of the Kunde Ling regent Chökyi Gyeltsen, who ruled after the death of the Twelfth Dalai Lama in 1875 until his own death in 1886, Kunde Ling was badly damaged during the Cultural Revolution and has only very recently started to function again as a temple. In the small assembly hall is a throne for Daktsar Rinpoche, the sixth incarnate lama of the monastery, who is now a small boy in India. A photo of the previous incarnation hangs from a pillar. The temple, which is dominated by a large statue of White Tara, is taken care of by monks from Palhalupuk. A few tangkas hang around the unpainted walls.

On the hill just behind the monastery is a small retreat hut called Drubtob Lhakhang associated with Tangtong Gyelpo. The main room is still bare, containing only a cabinet with a statue of Tangtong Gyelpo and a couple of wall paintings. Gesar Lhakhang (see p. 76) is further along this same hill.

Tsechok Ling

Founded in the eighteenth century by Yeshe Gyeltsen, the tutor of the Eighth Dalai Lama, Tsechok Ling is located on the south bank of the Kyichu River, seven kilometers (about four miles) from the center of Lhasa. To get there, cross the bridge, turn right, and follow the river.

Just before you reach the army encampment, take a road that bears off sharply to the left. Continue past a long crumbling wall, passing through the village of Tep, until you see the white and red buildings of Tsechok Ling ahead.

The monastery is largely in ruins and has only been functioning again since 1992. Nineteen monks are in residence. On the rear wall of the assembly hall is a painting of the founder, Yeshe Gyeltsen. The murals behind the statue of Shakyamuni are of Jamgön Lama and the Fifth Panchen Lama. The other walls of the hall are painted with the thousand buddhas of this eon.

On the upper story, an enclosure at the rear contains a **Protector Chapel**. Two protectors can be seen: Jangchok Tinley Gyelpo, riding a snow lion, and Pelden Masok Khemo (a form of Pelden Lhamo, an old tangka of whom is in the assembly hall) on a mule. To the right of the statues hangs an old tangka of the Fifth Dalai Lama.

A short flight of steps leads to a long, clean chapel, containing a central image of Yeshe Gyeltsen, in whose heart is a smaller image of one of his predecessors. This room used to be the founder's private quarters. The other rooms on the upper story still lie in ruins.

OTHER TEMPLES AND SHRINES IN LHASA

New Meru Monastery (Meru Sarpa)

This large complex of buildings in poor repair is on the Dekyi Shar Lam next door to Gyume, the Lower Tantric College. It is one of the oldest religious sites in Lhasa, having been founded initially by King Ralpachen in the eighth century, only to be destroyed in the ninth by Langdarma. After its later reconstruction it became one of the largest and most important Geluk monasteries in the city. Many of the buildings now house a printing facility. The Kangyur, which used to be printed below the Potala, is now printed here, and plans are under way to start printing the Tengyur.

Steps from a small courtyard behind the large incense burner lead to a small monastery where twenty or so monks currently live, using an old protector chapel as their assembly hall. In a room at the rear of this hall, behind the throne for the Dalai Lama, is a long altar. Below a tangka of Brahma are four stupas, which were buried during the Cultural Revolution and then retrieved, and the head of Brahma—all that remains of a statue that once stood in Meru. To the right of the Brahma head is a stone bearing the imprint of the feet of the Fifth Dalai Lama.

The original assembly hall is rather decrepit. The murals are faded and damaged. In the center is a solitary statue of Shakyamuni in a glass case. In a large room entered through a doorway in the front wall are some damaged statues. On the left is a well-preserved image of Maitreya with its heart torn out to plunder the relics, gold, and silver that were inside.

Zhide Dratsang

Situated close to Tsomo Ling but further

west, Zhide Dratsang was traditionally connected to Reting Monastery. It was founded by a disciple of the Seventh Dalai Lama and housed around two hundred monks. During the Cultural Revolution the complex was badly damaged, the monks evicted, and the remaining buildings turned into accommodations for lay families. Twenty-five monks now live here, occupying two small temples. The first temple, on the right, is dedicated to Amitayus, a prominent statue of whom is in the chapel, flanked by Shakyamuni and Maitreya.

Mani Lhakhang

This square mani chapel is off the north side of the Barkor, at the beginning of a small street that runs behind the Jokhang. It is connected to Mindroling Monastery. In addition to the large prayer wheel in the center of the building, it contains a thousand small images of Padmasambhava and a notable old statue of Terdak Lingpa, the founder of Mindroling.

Jampa Lhakhang

This chapel is about twenty meters past the Mani Lhakhang, on the right. Completely destroyed in the Cultural Revolution, it began to undergo reconstruction in May 1992 and is now complete. The main image is a two-story-high statue of Maitreya (Jampa), flanked by smaller images of Shakyamuni and Dipamkara, that is, the Buddhas of the Three Times. The chapel is also called the Blessing-Water Chapel, and was originally founded in the fifteenth century by a disciple of Tsongkhapa named Senpa Lodrö Gyeltsen, who spent many years here in retreat. A stupa contains the relics of Drakpa Namgyel, the sixth incarnation of the founder. The present incarnation, the fourteenth, lives as a layman in Lhasa. On the ground floor are two meditation caves (low, sealed entrances in the right hand corner of the front wall), one of the famous fifteenth-century "crazy yogi" Drukpa Kunleg, the other of Drakpa Namgyel.

The Old Meru Temple (Meru Nyingpa)

To reach this temple, continue down the same alley of the Jampa Lhakhang, past a red doorway and a row of prayer wheels. Through the second break in the prayer wheels is a doorway that leads you to the Old Meru Temple. The original building dates back to the time of Songtsen Gampo and is reputed to be where Tönmi Sambhota designed the Tibetan alphabet. It later became the Lhasa seat of the Nechung oracle. The main image in this tiny, ancient shrine is that of Dipamkara, the Buddha of the past. The Eight Great Bodhisattvas are also here. All the images are new. A bare inner circumambulation passage leads around the temple. It is cared for by Geluk monks from the New Meru Monastery.

Gongkar Chöde Branch Temple

On the floor directly above the Old Meru Temple is a Sakya temple affiliated with the Gongkar Chöde Monastery near the Gongkar (Lhasa) airport. At present it is a shrine to the protector Pelgön Dramtse, an aspect of Mahakala, a life-size statue of whom dominates the room. A cabinet also contains images of Padmasambhava, Guru Gönpo, and a four-armed aspect of Pelden Lhamo, called Pelden Dunkham. It is an active city temple, seemingly well supported. Six Sakya monks from Gongkar currently live here.

Nechung Branch Temple

This temple is reached by continuing down the same alley on which is located the Old Meru Temple and then turning left at the end. This brings you out into a small courtyard facing the entrance of the monastery. It is affiliated with Nechung Monastery near Drepung and is mainly involved in the performance of rituals to the various protectors of the Nyingma, Sakya, and Geluk traditions. The main protector is Dorje Drakden, the deity who speaks through the Nechung oracle and is relied on by the Tibetan government. Previously more than a hundred monks lived here. Currently there are twenty-two (the maximum allowed is twenty-five).

The main image in the assembly hall is a thousand-armed Avalokiteshvara in a cabinet. The murals of wrathful protectors around the walls were all restored in 1993–94.

The chapel in the slightly raised room at the back of the assembly hall has Padmasambhava as its main image. Above him is a cabinet with smaller images of Tsongkhapa, Vajradhara, and the Fifth Dalai Lama. Clay statues of the five directional guardians, wrathful

deities mounted on mythical animals, give additional protection. The second to last cabinet on the right is covered by cloth and contains the palace of Dorje Drakden, while the last (uncovered) cabinet houses the palace of Pelden Lhamo.

On the upper story there are no chapels, but the rooftop gives an excellent view of the rear of the Jokhang and its roofs.

Karma Shar Monastery

This old Gelukpa temple with tall and noble stone walls is behind the Jokhang and can be reached only by a narrow cobbled street in the old city. The gold-on-black murals of wrathful protector deities have recently been completely repainted. Only the murals on the upper level of the assembly hall retain the retouched originals. The main image in the shrine is Padmasambhava. The shrine is dedicated, however, to the red wrathful deity with a spear and bow, called Lhakdor (or Chenchik, meaning "one eye"), to the right of Padmasambhava. Further to the right is an old statue of the protector Tsemar, which was rescued by local people and recently returned to the monastery. Hanging from a pillar on the right is a swollen leather bag with a wrathful face. When a parishioner dies, his or her breath is "transferred" into this bag, which is then taken to Samye Monastery, where predictions are made about the person's future rebirth. While traditionally a temple of the Nyingma school, Karma Shar is currently under the supervision of two monks from Sera (the remaining old murals also indicate that the Gelukpas have been active here for a long time).

The Rigsum Gonpo Temples

"Rigsum Gonpo" means the "Protectors of the Three Realms," and refers to Avalokiteshvara, Manjushri, and Vajrapani. Four temples are dedicated to these deities in the cardinal directions of the old city of Lhasa, known as the North, South, East, and West Rigsum Gonpo Temples. Although the East temple is not, the others are now restored and functioning.

The South Rigsum Gonpo Temple

This temple is about three hundred yards west of Ani Sangkhung, on the same road. Reopened in 1990, the tiny chapel is taken care of by three monks from Ganden Monastery, with which it is traditionally connected. In addition to images of Avalokiteshvara, Manjushri, and Vajrapani are statues of Akshobhyavajra and Pelden Lhamo.

The North Rigsum Gonpo Temple

This temple is on the road between the Ramoche Cathedral and the Dekyi Shar Lam, about fifty meters on the right before you reach Ramoche itself. A simple sign indicates a narrow passageway that leads to the temple. It was completely gutted during the Cultural Revolution, and restoration began only in 1993 under the supervision of seven young nuns from Gari Nunnery, located behind Sera. Gold-on-red images of the four-armed Avalokiteshvara are painted on the walls. The room next door, which is still unrestored, was originally the principal shrine of this chapel.

The West Rigsum Gonpo Temple

This temple is about a hundred meters off the southwest corner of the plaza on the way to the local bus station. A sign in English ("The Three Protecting Lords Temple of the West") directs you to the chapel. It was reopened in September 1989 by monks from Drigung Monastery, with which it is associated. In the main shrine room, in addition to the triad of Avalokiteshvara, Manjushri, and Vajrapani, are images of Padmasambhava, Abchi Drölma (the protectress of Drigung), Dorje Drakden (Pehar), and Tsongkhapa. The temple also owns the woodblocks of several important Mahayana Buddhist philosophical texts, copies of which are stored in the shrine and are for sale.

On the upper floor is a small shrine to Padmasambhava and his two consorts, where special celebrations are offered on the tenth day of the lunar month.

Trode Kangsar

Behind and to the west of the Southern Rigsum Gonpo Temple, in a small square beside a newly erected block of apartments, is Trode Kangsar, a shrine founded at the time of the Fifth Dalai Lama. The shrine is dedicated to Dorje Shukden, a controversial deity who became a special protector of the Geluk tradition in the seventeenth century. Trode Kangsar is the traditional home not only of the deity, but also of the medium through which the oracle would speak. The deity's followers recognize him as the reincarnation of a rival of the Fifth Dalai Lama and as an emanation of Manjushri. They see Dorje Shukden as a force for protecting the purity of the Gelukpa lineage—mainly from the influence of other sects, especially the Nyingmapas. Many Gelukpas reject the practice, and the present Dalai Lama has strongly discouraged his followers from propitiating the deity. Although he practiced the deity himself while still in Tibet, he now believes that Dorje Shukden is not an enlightened protector but a worldly being who is a "spirit of the dark forces." The Dalai Lama's strong stand on the issue has led to public demonstrations, primarily by Western converts to the Shukden practice, accusing him of repressing religious freedom. It has also led to divisions within the Gelukpa school that continue to have disturbing repercussions as this book goes to press.

To the right of the portico as you enter Trode Kangsar is a depiction of Dorje Shukden's lineage on a mural. The principal images at the front of the shrine are Tsongkhapa and his two main disciples. On the left are two fine statues of Pabongka Rinpoche and his disciple Trijang Rinpoche. In the cabinet on the far right is an image of Dorje Shukden with the four deities of his entourage in smaller cabinets beside him. A beautiful old silver relief image of Shukden is in a cupboard to the right. The only other objects that have survived from former

times are a ritual hat of the protector hanging from a pillar and some carved vajras and clouds on the stone stairway leading to the shrine. The five monks who care for Trode Kangsar are connected to a monastery in Lhokha called Rawo Chöling, which has recently been rebuilt with funds raised here.

One block south of the Trode Kangsar is the **Trijang Lhabrang**, the residence of Trijang Rinpoche, the former incarnation of whom was junior tutor to the present Dalai Lama. He died in India in 1981. The Trijang Rinpoches were traditionally spiritual directors of Trode Kangsar. The building has been converted to flats and offices and performs no religious functions.

Kar-nga Dong Shrine

This small, untidy-looking shrine is built at the base of the Potala, against the easternmost flank of the hill, and can be easily recognized by the rows of prayer wheels outside. Carved on the rock wall inside are Avalokiteshvara Who Roars Like a Lion and a thousand-armed Avalokiteshvara. The chapel also contains a number of relief carvings on large slabs of stone, some of which are supposed to date back to the founding of the Jokhang. In 1986 the caretaker-monk said that the carvings, which are not engraved on the rock wall of the hill, were taken from the Jokhang and placed here in 1980. Currently five nuns take care of the shrine.

Just past the Kar-nga Dong Shrine is the **Tukje Lhakhang**, another small shrine containing a large mani wheel. The shrine gets its name (Tukje means "compassion") from the image of the thousand-armed Avalokiteshvara in the main, glass-fronted altar. The shrine has been open since 1987 and is tended by three monks from Chökhorgyel Monastery, near Lhamo'i Latso.

Gesar Lhakhang

Gesar Lhakhang is situated on the Bompo hill to the west of Chakpori, south of the Dekyi Nub Lam before you reach the turnoff to the Lhasa Hotel. The temple is the large building at the east end of the hill. The hill is associated with the taming of the demoness of Tibet at the time of Songtsen Gampo, and it is believed that Trisong Detsen built a structure here in which Padmasambhava meditated. The present temple dates back to the end of the eighteenth century. It has traditionally been dedicated to the mythic hero of Eastern Tibet, Gesar of Ling.

You enter through a gateway in the west of the building that leads into a split-level courtyard. The main temple is dedicated to Gesar, and an image of him as Ngawo Töndrup is the central figure on the altar. On the right are a large Guru Tradok and Ekajati, on the left Sengdongma and Damchen Dawa Norbu. A large Padmasambhava with his consorts Yeshe Tsogyel and Mandarava is on the left of the room, and various lamas, mahasiddhas, and buddhas are in glass-covered niches around the walls.

Instead of turning back into the courtyard, go left to circumambulate the building. This will lead you to a small temple on your left. The main figure is a large orange Manjushri, to whose sides sit Vajrapani and Avalokiteshvara (the Rigsum Gonpo). On the shelves to either side are a thousand small images of White Tara. An Avalokiteshvara mandala is in the back right-hand corner.

The temple has been open since 1989. Although it is under the jurisdiction of the Geluk order, there are currently three Nyingma monks in addition to three Geluk monks living here.

The Lhasa Mosques

There has been a Muslim quarter in Lhasa for at least four hundred years. The original Muslim community came from Kashmir and settled in the city as butchers. The Tibetans, it seemed, preferred others to accumulate the karma of killing the animals whose flesh they proceeded to eat. A Uighur community also established itself in this quarter, and it is to them that the main mosque in the southeast of the old city belongs. This mosque was destroyed by fire in 1959 and has subsequently been rebuilt. It is of interest to note the same Tibetan-style decorative motifs and pillar design found in Buddhist monasteries adorning the mosque. Non-Muslims are not permitted inside.

The mosque of the Kashmiri Muslims is a couple of hundred yards west of the main mosque, past the Ani Sangkhung. Until 1991 it was indistinguishable from the other Lhasa townhouses around the Barkor. Two pillars, a dome, and a crescent now adorn the front of the building, making it readily identifiable.

5
THE TIBETAN MEDICAL CENTER (MENTSI KHANG)

The Medical Center is easy to find. It is the long white concrete building by the plaza that faces the Jokhang. If you wish to make an appointment with a Tibetan doctor, go to the administration office on the ground floor as soon as you arrive. There is a small consultation charge in addition to the cost of medicine. The poorest Tibetans are treated free of charge. It is not possible to have an astrological consultation. There is also a pharmaceutical factory, where the traditional medicines are manufactured, and a specialist institute for the study of Tibetan medicine and astrology, but these are closed to visitors.

History

Tibetan medicine is an ancient tradition of healing that is rooted in the Buddhist tradition. It is based on four medicinal tantras translated from the Sanskrit by Vairochana in the eighth century. These texts were edited (some say compiled) by the father of Tibetan medicine, Yutok Yönten Gonpo (729–854). Yutok, who came from a long line of doctors, traveled extensively in India, Nepal, and China to study medicine and incorporated the medical knowledge of all these traditions into the four tantras, which are still the basis for Tibetan medical studies

today. He became the personal physician to the Tibetan king Trisong Detsen and founded the Gongbu Menlong medical school, 400 kilometers (250 miles) east of Lhasa, where he trained more than a thousand students.

The next great revision of the four tantras was done by another Yutok descendant, Sarma Yönten Gonpo (1126–1201), who also wrote a commentary on them called *The Eighteen Branches*. Another influential figure in Tibetan medical history was Desi Sanggye Gyatso (1653–1706), the regent of the Fifth Dalai Lama. In addition to being a politician, he further revised the four tantras and composed the *Baidurya Ngönpo*, a word-by-word commentary on the four tantras, and the *Baidurya Karpo*, a treatise on astrology. In 1696 he founded the medical monastic institute on Chakpori and commissioned the famous eighty medical tangkas, which were completed in 1703.

The most renowned physician of this century was Khyenrab Norbu (1883–1962). Born in Tsetang, he went to Ngangcho Monastery before studying at Chakpori. He was assigned as a personal physician to the Thirteenth Dalai Lama, who in 1916 appointed him as the director of the Mentsi Khang (literally, the Institute of Medicine and Astrology).

Tibetan Medicine

One of the principles of Tibetan medicine is that the basis of good health is the maintenance of harmony between the three vital humors of the body: energy (or wind), bile, and phlegm. Psychologically, these three humors are related to the three mental poisons described in Buddhism: ignorance, desire, and anger, respectively. Illness occurs through imbalance of the humors and can be treated by applying remedies that reestablish their harmony. Diagnosis is made mainly through a careful analysis of the pulse, whose beat and subtle movements can be used by the doctor to recognize the nature and location of the particular imbalance. Treatments vary, but the most common is a course of herbal remedies in the form of pills, which are usually chewed and swallowed along with hot water.

Astrology plays a significant role in Tibetan medicine, for when a pulse diagnosis is being made, the doctor must be conscious of the external influences upon its beat. These influences include the season, the budding of certain plants, and the movement of heavenly bodies. If these factors are not detected and accounted for, an exact diagnosis of the patient's ailment is not possible. The study of astrology enables the doctor to understand these influences and recognize them in the pulse beat. Astrology is also used to determine the course of action to be taken by relatives (that is, the prayers and rituals to be performed) when a close one dies. By studying a person's chart, a doctor is also able to prescribe preventive treatments to counteract negative astrological influences that are liable to occur at certain times.

The Site

The present building that houses the Mentsi Khang was opened in 1977. Its doctors currently see four hundred to five hundred patients daily. Each of the rooms on the first two stories specializes in either certain maladies or forms of treatment. There are facilities for treating external wounds, internal ailments, ear and eye disorders, heart problems, and gynecological complaints. Rooms are set aside for minor surgery, "golden needle" treatment, astrological calculations, and diagnostics. A large herbal dispensary is right across from the main entrance. A limited amount of Western medication is also available. There are around two hundred qualified Tibetan doctors working here and in the other medical institutes in the city.

As you come up the stairs to the second floor, the second door on the left leads into a museum. In glass cases around the room are old medical texts, medical diagrams, natural ingredients, and prepared medicines. At the far end of the room is a large statue of Yutok Sarma Yönten Gonpo. In the cabinet to the left of the statue are examples of the four tantras written and illuminated in gold. On the walls are four astrological tangkas and photographs showing details of Tibetan medical history and practices.

On the top floor, at roof level, it is possible to visit two rooms. The one on the left is a kind of shrine to the Tibetan medical tradition. Behind glass at the

end of the room are statues of Yutok
Yönten Gonpo (center), Desi Sanggye
Gyatso (left), and Khyenrab Norbu
(right). The texts in cabinets around the
room are the Kangyur, the Tengyur, and
the major medical treatises. In two smaller cabinets to the right of the window
are images of the Medicine Buddha,
Shakyamuni, and White Tara. On the
right is Yutok Sarma Yönten Gonpo.

On the opposite side of the corridor is
a room with medical tangkas, which are
copies of the seventeenth-century originals. They depict the anatomy of the
body, both its skeletal and organic
makeup and the subtle energy channels
as described in the four tantras. They
also show the various plants used in the
preparation of medicines. The large
appliqué tangka on the end wall is of
Yutok Yönten Gonpo with the Medicine
Buddha, Padmasambhava, Vairochana
the translator, Chakpori, and the old
Mentsi Khang. The wrathful figure at the
bottom left is the medical protector Dorje
Dundul.

6
THE POTALA

The Potala is a landmark impossible to miss. It is located at the west of the city and is reached simply by following the Dekyi Shar Lam westward from the old city. It is open from 9 A.M. to 4 P.M. every day except Sunday. Many rooms are closed from around noon to 2:30 P.M. Foreigners are expected to enter the palace from the rear, at a gate where tour vehicles will deliver them. On certain days (in recent years it has been on Wednesdays and Saturdays) it is possible to enter in the traditional way via the front steps. Here we will follow the pilgrim route starting from the front steps, ascending to the roof of the Potala, and descending clockwise down through the building to exit at the rear. If you come with a tour group, read the description of chapels in the reverse order. Be warned that chapels are opened and closed somewhat indiscriminately.

Also included in this chapter is the Lukhang, or Naga Chapel, situated in the small lake behind the Potala.

History

Songtsen Gampo was the first Tibetan ruler to establish a palace on this outcrop, the Red Hill, which dominates the city of Lhasa. Although his palace, which was called the Kukhar Potrang, was burned down by an invading Chinese army during the reign of his successor,

Mangsong Mangtsen, there are still two rooms inside the Potala that supposedly date from his time. But it is impossible to tell how extensive this first palace was and what it was like.

Old pictures of the Potala often show a tall stone stele rising up from the ground in front of the palace. It now stands on the opposite side of the main road by the Potala. This is the ancient Zhöl pillar, erected about 764 by the loyal minister and general of Trisong Detsen, Ngenlam Tagdra Lugong. It modestly records how the Tibetan armies successfully overran most of Central Asia and finally occupied the Chinese capital of Chang-an (Xian). The rewards bestowed upon Tagdra Lugong by the king are also recorded on the pillar.

Construction of the present palace began in earnest in 1645 during the reign of the great Fifth Dalai Lama. By 1648 the White Palace was completed. To finish the rest of the building, known as the Red Palace, his chief advisor, Desi Sanggye Gyatso, had to conceal the Dalai Lama's death and pretend that he was in a prolonged retreat. The Red Palace was completed in 1694, twelve years after the Dalai Lama's death.

The building is named after Mount Potala in South India, one of the holy mountains of the Hindu god Shiva. Buddhists, however, dedicated this same mountain to Avalokiteshvara, the bodhisattva of compassion, and gave the name "Potala" to the Pure Land where Avalokiteshvara resides. Since both Songtsen Gampo and the Dalai Lamas were considered to be incarnations of Avalokiteshvara, Potala was the obvious name for their dwelling.

The Potala has served as the home of successive Dalai Lamas and their monastic staff from the time of the Fifth until that of the present Dalai Lama, the Fourteenth. From the latter half of the eighteenth century it has been used as the Winter Palace, and the Norbulingka as the place where the rulers would retreat during the summer months. With the exception of a section added on to house the tomb of the Thirteenth Dalai Lama, the palace is much the same as when it was first built.

The Potala was slightly damaged during the popular Tibetan uprising against the Chinese in 1959 and was fortunately spared from further destruction during the Cultural Revolution, apparently through the personal intervention of Chou En-lai, the Red Guards being kept at bay by the Chinese military.

Before 1959, the Red Palace was home to the 175 monks of the Namgyel Tratsang as well as monks from all the major Geluk monasteries who were responsible for staffing the individual chapels. At present there are thirty-two monks from Sera, only five of whom are fully ordained. Although for Tibetan pilgrims the Potala is still a place of worship, the government prefers to treat it as a museum.

Another controversy rages around the fate of the Zhöl, the cluster of traditional houses at the foot of the Potala, which were recently demolished by the local government. The area has since been converted into a plaza. Alternative modern housing has been built for the previous inhabitants at a site a mile or so behind the Potala.

The Site

The first impression you may have of the Potala is that it is not located at the great height that most photographs suggest. Compared to the surrounding mountains, the rocky outcrop on which it stands is tiny. Nonetheless, as you slowly acquaint yourself with the dimensions and proportions of this incredible building, the awesome grandeur of its architecture becomes so much more tangible and real that even the most rapturous description seems inadequate.

"The Potala is superbly detached," wrote Edmund Candler, a journalist who accompanied the Younghusband expedition in 1904. "It is not a palace on a hill, but a hill that is also a palace." This is as true today as it was then. It is well worth circumambulating the Potala with Tibetan pilgrims, riding around it by bicycle, and observing it under different light conditions, in order to appreciate fully its architectural complexity. The circumambulation path starts opposite the lane that leads to Palhalupuk. It passes between two high walls and opens out into a park with three large stupas at the rear of the building. Boats can be rented to row on the small, fish-filled lake in the park. On a small island in the lake is the **Lukhang** (see pages 89-91 for details). The circumambulation path leads you out of the park through a set of large gates and via a corrugated-iron-roofed bazaar back into the built-up area of Lhasa.

The Dalai Lamas lived and worked in the Red Palace, the central, squarish structure that rises out of the mass of the surrounding White Palace. If you enter from the front steps, you will reach an enclosed inner courtyard. You enter the Red Palace by a steep wooden stairway to find yourself in the main foyer. On the left of this opening are two handprints of the Thirteenth Dalai Lama placed beneath an edict written in the cursive Tibetan script. Around the other walls are murals depicting the construction of the Jokhang, the Potala, and the medical college on Chakpori. The Four Guardian Kings are also portrayed.

Several more flights of stairs bring you out onto the roof of the palace, and it is from here that you actually enter the building itself, slowly working your way down. This is where the Dalai Lama's personal monastic staff, the Namgyel Tratsang, also lived. They were responsible for performing all the complex rituals required by the Tibetan head of state, and for the upkeep of the numerous chapels and shrines situated in the maze of rooms that make up the four stories of this multistoried labyrinth. The roof affords a superb view over Lhasa and the Kyichu Valley basin.

The Dalai Lama's Quarters

The only room on the roof level that is permanently open at present is the **offi-cial reception hall,** which is just around the corner as you come up the stairs. This opulent room is dominated by a large throne, to the right of which hangs a realistic portrait of the Thirteenth Dalai Lama and to the left of which the Fourteenth. Small antechambers to each side of the raised platform lead to their respective private quarters.

Some tour groups are also allowed to visit the Dalai Lama's private quarters behind the official reception hall. The first room you enter is a smaller audience chamber where individuals and private groups would be received. Set in the right-hand wall are three large cabinets containing a number of exquisite bronzes. The three animal-headed deities and the statue of Vijaya are of particular note. From here you will enter a small, square protector chapel. The principal deities are a six-armed Mahakala, Pelden Lhamo, and Dorje Drakden. The final room in the third section is the small but very ornate bedroom of the Dalai Lama. The large altar houses statues of the longevity triad of Amitayus, White Tara, and Vijaya. A beautifully painted mural of Tsongkhapa is visible above the bed.

The Upper Floor

The visit to the main section of the Potala begins as you enter a doorway on the far side of the roof from the reception hall.

The Maitreya Chapel (1)

The main statue here is a large, beautifully made, seated Maitreya. Inside the

THE POTALA

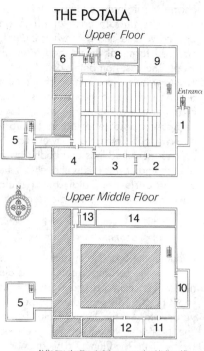

Upper Floor

Upper Middle Floor

At the time of writing, shaded areas were closed to the public.
These floor-plans are for orientation only and are not to scale.

Eighth until the Fourteenth. To the left of the throne is an altar. The image on the far left is of the Fifth Dalai Lama, commissioned shortly before his death by Desi Sanggye Gyatso. In it are some hair clippings from the Great Fifth's head. To the right of the throne is a large cabinet with an image of a deity called Lhamo Öser Chen riding a boar. Many other deities surround the room: Kalachakra; Padmasambhava; the triad of Manjushri, Avalokiteshvara, and Vajrapani; Kshitigarbha; and Achala. Of particular interest is the wrathful form of Tara to the right of Maitreya. In the far corner is a small wooden mandala of Kalachakra erected at the time of the Eighth Dalai Lama. The scriptures in the upper wall are a complete edition of the Kangyur and Tengyur. The collected works of the Fifth Dalai Lama are in the wall to the left as you go out.

In 1984 this chapel was badly damaged by fire—presumably caused by an electrical fault—and many fine tangkas were destroyed.

The Chapel of the Three-Dimensional Mandalas (2)

This chapel was constructed by Kelsang Gyatso, the Seventh Dalai Lama. An image of him sits at the far end of the room next to his throne. The very fine murals also date from his time. Before the three magnificent mandalas were erected, this room used to be Kelsang Gyatso's personal residence. The mandalas are those of the three principal tantric deities practiced in the Geluk

head of the image is said to be the brain of Atisha and a piece of skull from the last human incarnation of Maitreya, inscribed with his own writing. The statue was commissioned by the Eighth Dalai Lama in honor of the recently deceased mother of the Sixth Panchen Lama, Pelden Yeshe, a relative of his. It was also the Eighth Dalai Lama who turned this room into a chapel; from the time of the Sixth Dalai Lama it had served only as a living area. The throne facing Maitreya was used by all the Dalai Lamas from the order: Guhyasamaja, Samvara, and Yamantaka. When looking at them from the monk's seat by the window, the mandala of Guhyasamaja is in the middle. To the right is that of Samvara—of the Luipa tradition—and to the left that of the thirteen-deity form of Yamantaka. To the left of the dark passageway along which you come in are collected about five hundred small statues. In addition to the usual images of the Thirty-Five Confessional Buddhas, the Twenty-One Taras, and so on are found many of the principal lamas and deities of all four orders of Tibetan Buddhism.

The Chapel Celebrating Victory over the Three Worlds (3)

This room is located in the very middle of the upper story of the Red Palace. It, too, was constructed by the Seventh Dalai Lama and the throne in the room was at one time used by him. The most outstanding figure is that of a thousand-armed Avalokiteshvara, commissioned by the Thirteenth Dalai Lama and made from Chinese gold. The glass-covered altar by the entrance contains images of Tsongkhapa and the Thirteenth Dalai Lama. A painting of the Chinese emperor Ch'ien-lung (1735–97), the last of the great rulers of the Manchu dynasty and the one responsible for driving the Gurkhas out of Tibet, hangs at the back with an inscription in Chinese beneath. On the wall to the left of the altar is a 120-volume edition of the Manchu version of the Kangyur. There are three standing cases in a fenced-off part of the

chapel containing examples of these texts. The middle case displays an opened volume clearly showing the precise red forms of the jagged Manchu script. The cases on both sides show the ornate wooden covers in which the texts are bound and demonstrate superb craftsmanship: each cover displays embossed gold lettering in Tibetan, Manchu, and Chinese and jewel-encrusted images of buddhas and bodhisattvas at each end. It was in this chapel that the young Fourteenth Dalai Lama would have performed his religious observances.

The Chapel of Immortal Happiness (4)

Although the Sixth Dalai Lama used this room as his personal residence, he did not convert it into a chapel during his short reign. This was done some fifty years later by the Eighth Dalai Lama. The throne, however, was the one used by the Sixth. The Eighth Dalai Lama dedicated the chapel to Amitayus, and a thousand small statues of the deity can be found in niches around the walls. There is also a standing Avalokiteshvara and a beautiful red statue of the wrathful principal guardian of Dzogchen practice, Ekajati.

The Tomb of the Thirteenth Dalai Lama (5)

You enter the chapel through a long corridor that connects it to the Red Palace. This brings you to an anteroom from which you can either descend to enter the chapel from the ground floor or enter a special viewing pavilion at a higher level. A well-executed modern mural adorns the wall to either side of the entrance. It depicts the Thirteenth Dalai Lama surrounded by his teachers, ministers, and other contemporary figures, and shows scenes from his life, including his 1910 pilgrimage to India. The stupa is two stories high and well illuminated by sunlight from the many windows (in contrast to the tombs of the other Dalai Lamas). It is a mass of softly glowing gold, adorned with an image of eleven-faced Avalokiteshvara. On the altar is the much-depicted three-dimensional pearl mandala, said to be constructed out of two hundred thousand pearls.

The Tomb of the Eighth Dalai Lama (6)

The stupa in which the Eighth Dalai Lama is entombed was constructed in 1805. It is adorned with a gold statue of eleven-faced Avalokiteshvara. Other images in this room include a statue of the Eighth Dalai Lama, a statue of Shakyamuni Buddha that was commissioned by the Ninth Dalai Lama, and a tangka that depicts Nyatri Tsenpo, the first king of Tibet according to Tibetan lore.

The Lokeshvara Chapel (7)

This shrine together with the room beneath (10) are the two oldest chapels in the Potala, dating back to the time of Songtsen Gampo in the seventh century. The Tibetans consider this shrine to be the holiest in the Potala. You enter it by climbing a steep wooden staircase beneath a large inscription hanging over the door that reads, "The Amazing Fruits of the Field of Merit" in the Chinese, Tibetan, and Manchu languages. Immediately on the left as you enter is a large wheel, which symbolizes the union of spiritual and temporal authority in Tibet achieved by the Fifth Dalai Lama. In the case on the left-hand wall there are three pieces of gilded stone with footprints embedded in them; from the left, these belong to Padmasambhava, Tsongkhapa, and Nagarjuna. The small central statue is a heavily jeweled and gilded standing figure of Avalokiteshvara, which is said to be made of sandalwood and to be of Indian origin, as are the two accompanying images to either side. They are said to be "self-arisen" images, which were found inside a sandalwood tree when its trunk split open. To the left of the main images are the Seventh Dalai Lama and Tsongkhapa; to the right are the Fifth, Eighth, and Ninth Dalai Lamas. Numerous other statues fill the cases to either side, including the Sakya lama Pakpa as well as the Kagyu teachers Marpa and Milarepa. A large ferocious figure of Vajrapani stands guard by the opposite wall. To the left of the door as you leave is an old encased image of Atisha.

The Tomb of the Seventh Dalai Lama (8)

To the right of the Lokeshvara Chapel, you come to the multicolored door to the shrine room that contains the Seventh Dalai Lama's reliquary stupa. This stupa is heavily encrusted with gold, and is said to contain nearly one hundred thousand jewels and semiprecious stones. In front of the stupa there is a three-dimensional Maitreya mandala. This room is often closed to the public. A closed room next to the Ninth Dalai Lama's tomb is called the Lama Lhakhang, which contains murals depicting stories from the lives of the Third, Fifth, Eighth, and Thirteenth Dalai Lamas, as well as images of Tara.

The Tomb of the Ninth Dalai Lama (9)

Next door to the tomb of the Seventh Dalai Lama is the tomb of the Ninth. In addition to the golden stupa, it contains a silver statue of the Ninth Dalai Lama. There is also a silver image of Tsongkhapa and an edition of the Kangyur written in gold.

The Upper Middle Floor
The Kalachakra Chapel (10)

The superb three-dimensional mandala of Kalachakra was brought from Jonang Puntsok Ling by Desi Sanggye Gyatso in 1680, as part of the suppression of the "heretical" Jonang school by the Gelukpas (see chapter 31). This well-preserved gold and copper divine mansion, the residence of the deity Kalachakra, is twelve meters (forty feet) in circumference. On the mandala itself are statues of 734 deities. When you stand by the window where the caretaker-monk sits, you can see to the right a life-size statue of Kalachakra and consort. To the left of the statue, in shelves along the wall, are small

images of the 176 lamas who have passed the Kalachakra lineage down to the present day. In similar shelves to the right are the seven religious kings of Shambhala and the twenty-five *kalki*, or spiritual presidents, who have been ruling Shambhala since the time of the religious kings. We are now in the reign of the twenty-second kalki, Aniruddha. At the far end of the chapel opposite the door is a statue of Manjushri riding a lion, also surrounded by the lamas of his lineage. A small shrine to Pelden Lhamo is in the right-hand corner by the window. To your left as you leave is an image of Padmasambhava seated on a throne.

The Shakyamuni Chapel (11)

Work began on this chapel at the time of Desi Sanggye Gyatso, but it did not reach its present form until the reign of the Eighth Dalai Lama. The main figures are those of Buddha Shakyamuni flanked by the Eight Great Bodhisattvas. The throne is one used by Kelsang Gyatso, the Seventh Dalai Lama. In the wall opposite the throne is a handwritten edition of the Kangyur, above which hang tangkas of the Eight Medicine Buddhas.

The Amitayus Chapel (12)

Nine statues of Amitayus dominate this small chapel built by the Eighth Dalai Lama. A White Tara and a Green Tara are also present. The throne was one used by the Eighth Dalai Lama and the fine murals probably date back to his time. The murals include a depiction of the fifteenth-century architect and builder Tangtong Gyelpo, together with one of his famous iron bridges.

The Practice Chamber of the Dharma King (13)

As with the Lokeshvara Chapel (7), this cell is one of the very oldest rooms in the Potala. Songtsen Gampo is said to have used this dark, small cavelike room as his meditation chamber. It is now filled with statues; the main one of Songtsen Gampo is behind the central pillar. There are other images of the king as well as similar-looking figures that represent his ministers Tönmi Sambhota and Gawa. On a shelf in the right-hand wall is a small statue of the king's mother. Maitreya is to the immediate left as you enter, and behind a pillar at the far end of the room is a somewhat atypical image of the Fifth Dalai Lama. A stove that was supposedly used by King Songtsen Gampo stands at the base of the central pillar.

A door to the right of the practice chamber leads to a room containing a white stupa. The room leads to another room, also with a white stupa, immediately behind the practice chamber. A further empty room can also be reached from here down a flight of stairs. The history and purpose of these rooms is unclear.

The Lima Chapel (14)

This chapel, constructed with an outer and an inner chamber, holds tiers of shelves with approximately 1,600 small bronzes of figures (*li-ma*) from all four schools of Tibetan Buddhism. Most of the gilded statues were made during the time of Tsongkhapa and offered by Chinese Buddhists. Larger statues within this room include Tsongkhapa, Mahakala, Amitayus, and Pelden Lhamo.

The Lower Middle Floor

All the chapels and rooms on this floor are closed. It is nonetheless worthwhile to study the many detailed murals on the walls of the quadrangular walkway which depict the construction of the Potala and other major Tibetan monasteries. Also portrayed is the funeral procession of the Great Fifth Dalai Lama, as well as the festivities associated with the annual Mönlam festival in Lhasa.

The Lower Floor

The Great Western Assembly Hall (15)

After climbing down a number of steep, dark stairwells you arrive in a spacious assembly hall, the largest room in the Potala. Eight tall and thirty-six small solid pillars, all draped in thickly woven white material with black markings, rise from the floor to support the roof. On the western wall are two huge tapestries that were a gift from Emperor K'ang Hsi. These depict the early religious kings, the Dalai Lamas, and other important religious personages. A large throne used exclusively by the Sixth Dalai Lama dominates the area. The subsequent Dalai Lamas from the Seventh to the

THE POTALA

Lower Floor

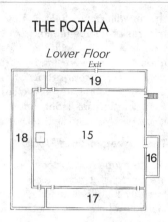

These floor-plans are for orientation only and are not to scale.

Fourteenth used a newer assembly hall in the White Palace close by, which is not open to the public. The walls of the assembly hall are painted with scenes from the Pure Land of Potala and Tibetan religious history.

The Chapel of the Stages on the Path to Enlightenment (16)

The Stages on the Path to Enlightenment *(lam-rim)* is a tradition of instruction detailing all the various steps the meditator needs to take to reach the final goal of enlightenment. For the Gelukpa, this tradition found its definitive statement in Tsongkhapa's major work, *The Great Exposition on the Stages on the Path to Enlightenment.* Thus this shrine, founded by Desi Sanggye Gyatso, has as its main figure Tsongkhapa, surrounded by the teachers of the *lam-rim* lineages. To the left are the masters of the "extensive" lineage, starting with Maitreya and

Asanga. Their teachings deal with the aspects of the path such as compassion, ethics, tolerance, and perseverance. To the right are the masters of the "profound" lineage, including Manjushri, Nagarjuna, and their disciples. Their teachings are concerned with the contemplative understanding of the ultimate truth of emptiness. To the far right are two Enlightenment Stupas.

The Knowledge Holders' Chapel (17)

The Eight Knowledge Holders *(rig-dzin)* to whom this chapel is dedicated are Padmasambhava and seven more or less contemporary Indian masters. These eight masters are each said to have received a particular tantric practice *(sadhana)* from a cremation ground near Bodh Gaya, the site of the Buddha's enlightenment. Padmasambhava brought these teachings, which belong to the Mahayoga tantric tradition, to Tibet and taught them to the twenty-five adepts of Chimpuk near Samye. The Eight Knowledge Holders are located in the left of this long, high room. To the right are the eight manifestations of Padmasambhava himself, which show the richness and diversity of his creative power to appear in whatever form is suitable for a particular occasion. In the center of the room sits a fine ornate image of him as the Lotus-Born Guru in the traditional posture. He is flanked by his two principal consorts, Yeshe Tsogyel and Mandarava. The shrine also contains an edition of the Kangyur written in gold and black ink.

The Chapel of the Dalai Lamas' Tombs (18)

This is one of the most awesome rooms in the Potala, mainly because of the massive golden stupa of the Fifth Dalai Lama, called the "Sole Ornament of the World," which reaches all the way to the upper story. Its spire is lost in darkness while its bulbous base glows softly in the light of silver butter lamps. To the right is a smaller stupa containing the relics of the Tenth Dalai Lama and, on the left, one with the relics of the Twelfth. To either side of the three principal tombs are eight Tathagata Stupas, which commemorate eight major events from the life of the historical Buddha (for example, birth, victory over Mara, enlightenment, turning the wheel of the Dharma, entering Parinirvana). The shrine was erected by Desi Sanggye Gyatso in commemoration of his master, the recently deceased Fifth Dalai Lama.

The Chapel of the Holy Born (19)

The esteem in which the Fifth Dalai Lama was held by his contemporaries is vividly demonstrated here by a silver image of him being placed on a joint throne with an identically sized gold image of Shakyamuni. To the right and left of these two central statues are numerous other figures seemingly placed in this chapel at random, since no obvious theme unites them. At the far left, by the entrance, stands a forlorn stupa with the relics of the seventeen-year-old Eleventh Dalai Lama, who died in 1855. Between this stupa and the main statues are the Eight Medicine Buddhas and the Buddhas of the Three Times (past, present, and future). To the right of the Fifth Dalai Lama are Avalokiteshvara, Songtsen Gampo (in an unusual form), Drom Tönpa, and the first four Dalai Lamas. Lined up along the bases of these figures are several small statues of Padmasambhava. At the far right of the hall, facing inward, is a statue of the Sakya lama, Tsarchen Losel Gyatso, the founder of the Tsar suborder of the Sakyapa.

You leave the Potala from this chapel along a corridor that leads around the back of the statues and finally deposits you in glaring daylight at the back of the building.

THE LUKHANG: THE NAGA CHAPEL

This chapel is immediately behind the Potala on an island in the middle of a small lake, connected to the shore by a footbridge. It is open daily.

History

When the construction of the Potala Palace was finally completed at the end of the seventeenth century, removal of the earth used for the mortar had left a large depression behind the building. This was filled with water and named the Lake of the Naga King, due to the reputed presence of the king of the snakelike naga spirits in the artificial lake. Desi Sanggye Gyatso is said to have made a pact with the naga king, promising to have a shrine to him built on the site. Shortly afterward, the Sixth Dalai Lama built a small chapel on an artificial mound created in the middle of the lake both as a shrine to the naga king and as a personal retreat. This "Naga Chapel" is a three-story building constructed in the form of a mandala.

The Site

After crossing the footbridge to the island, and before entering the chapel, you can circumambulate the temple along an attractive verandah and view the murals on the outer walls. On the right are paintings of Shakyamuni's "celestial mansion," with orange and white forms of Manjushri to the Buddha's sides. On the left is the wrathful protector Dorje Trolo (a form of Padmasambhava) and the "celestial mansion" of Samantabhadra.

From the verandah you enter a bare anteroom that leads down into an almost empty chapel. Here you will find a raised platform with an image of the King of the Nagas riding on an elephant. Also present is a statue of White Tara.

The image in the chapel on the second floor is a form of the Buddha Shakyamuni, known as Luwanggi Gyelpo, or the King of the Naga Lords. This is the form of the Buddha that is dedicated to teaching the nagas and is recognizable by the cluster of snakelike beings (nagas) rising behind his head as a kind of hood or halo. To the left of this figure

stands Avalokiteshvara, and on the right are images of the Twenty-One Taras. In front of the statue is a self-arisen image of Padmasambhava.

The chapel also contains some excellent murals in very good condition. The mural on the west and south walls is an illustration of the story of the mythical youth Pema Obar. Starting from the left and proceeding clockwise, the paintings recount how Pema Obar's father is drowned while searching for jewels in the ocean; how the boy is cared for by his mother and protected by taking refuge in the Triple Gem of Buddhism; how he too goes off in search of jewels and returns home with his riches; how the evil king of the country confiscates the jewels and banishes Pema Obar to the land of the cannibal spirits (rakshas); how Pema Obar converts the cannibal king to Buddhism and is freed to return home; how he is then killed upon his arrival by the evil king; how his ashes are returned to life by the dakinis; how the evil king sees the boy and the dakinis flying through the sky and is tricked into going with them; how they take him to the cannibal king where he is eaten alive by the cannibal spirits; and how Pema Obar returns triumphantly to his home country, becomes king and turns the kingdom into a Buddhist state.

The murals on the east and north walls show deeds from the lives of two legendary Indian kings, the "northern king" and the "southern king."

On the third story, the chapel contains an image of Avalokiteshvara. At the front of the room, facing the Potala, is a section separated off by a screen that the Dalai Lamas would use as a retreat chamber. The Thirteenth Dalai Lama, for example, spent much time meditating here.

Of greatest interest in this chapel, however, are the murals that cover three of the walls, depicting subjects that are rarely seen elsewhere in Tibet today. Unfortunately, but perhaps for the good of the paintwork, they are protected by a chicken-wire grille that hinders the viewing of the finer details. Namkhai Norbu's book *The Crystal and the Way of Light* contains photographs and further explanations of these images.

If you have just walked clockwise around the main altar, the first wall to your left (west) is illustrated with images of yogis demonstrating the physical postures required for the practice of the six yogas of Naropa and other tantric methods. On the next wall (north) are paintings of the stages of human life, beginning with sexual intercourse and conception and culminating in sickness, aging and death. Detailed anatomical pictures of the human body with its various inner organs and energy channels as conceived in the Tibetan medical tradition are also shown to explain how the body is subject to imbalances that result in sickness and decay.

Mahayana Buddhism teaches that after death one enters an intermediate state (*bardo*) before the next rebirth. The mural now continues with detailed images of the peaceful and wrathful deities that appear as visions to the person passing through this postdeath state. These paintings are based on the descriptions found in *The Tibetan Book of the Dead*. At the end of this wall is a picture of Padmasambhava holding a vajra to the head of a horse-riding demon. He is thus shown converting a Bön deity to Buddhism. To the upper left the same demon is shown transformed into the lion-riding protector called Mana, a special guardian relied upon by the Dalai Lamas.

The third wall (east) depicts the eighty-four mahasiddhas of India in their eccentric and often provocative poses, their faces expressing the bliss and inner power conferred upon them by tantric realization. One can also see the twenty-five adepts who worked with Padmasambhava in the conversion of the Tibetans to Buddhism, as well as the Six Ornaments and Two Supreme Indian philosophers. The old and damaged mural past the window shows the construction of Samye Monastery.

7
PALHALUPUK TEMPLE

A convenient time to visit this small temple, as well as the Tangtong Gyelpo Temple next door, is after you have finished seeing the Potala and return to the main road beneath Chakpori. Just cross the road and turn right down a small street, which leads you around the base of the hill. Palhalupuk is about three hundred yards on your right.

History

This curious and delightfully alive temple is formed from a cave at the base of the Chakpori hill. Its name means the "Naga's Grotto of the Stone Gods." The slightly dank, subterranean cavern suggesting an abode of the underwater nagas is filled with the wonderful treasures these beings are supposed to possess. The cave is believed to have been used as a retreat by King Songtsen Gampo in the seventh century and is also associated with his Nepalese queen. Whether this is true or not, the cave is of undoubted antiquity and fortunately has survived the destruction wreaked upon the rest of Chakpori above.

The Site

As you approach the temple you will reach two staircases. The stairs on the right lead to the Palhalupuk. Nearly all the images in the Palhalupuk are brightly painted relief stone carvings emerging from the walls and the central column of rock that seems to support the cave. The main image facing you as you come in is that of Shakyamuni. By his shoulders stand Shariputra and Maudgalyayana, his two chief arhat disciples. Maitreya and Avalokiteshvara stand to either side of them. Rows of bodhisattvas greet you from the walls as you circumambulate the central column. On this column you pass larger carvings of three buddhas: Akshobhya, the Medicine Buddha, and Shakyamuni. Along the left-hand wall you may notice a hole with a loose stone inside. Tradition maintains that Songtsen Gampo would beat this stone on the wall whenever it was time for his attendants living above to bring him his meals. At the back of the cave is an uncarved section of the wall behind which are said to be concealed the jewels of the king's Nepalese wife. A small altar stands to the right with an archaic representation of Pelden Lhamo as well as a small Padmasambhava and Yamantaka carved in stone. The final images you see are those of Songtsen Gampo, his two wives, and his two foremost ministers.

Below the Palhalupuk Temple is another temple with murals of the Thirty-Five Confessional Buddhas and a variety of smaller images. Between the two caves is also a small room where the monks perform their daily services.

Returning again to the foot of the double stairway, you can now take the stairs on the left to the small monastery of fifteen monks who take care of the temple.

At the top of these stairs is a rock pasted with coin offerings to an image of Vajrapani in a small niche. Nearby is the entrance to a small cave with an image of Avalokiteshvara. It is believed that the attendants of Songtsen Gampo would wait here for signals from the meditating king via a channel in the rock from Palhalupuk below. This channel is to the right of the shrine.

The main entrance to the monastery leads into a small chamber in which are located statues of Tsongkhapa and his two main disciples. From here you can enter the main shrine room of the monastery, the principal statues of which depict Shakyamuni. The Sixteen Arhats are displayed in cabinets around the room. An image of the Chinese Ch'an (Zen) master Hvashang Mahayana (see chapter 20) is also found here.

Close by the Palhalupuk is small temple built on the side of the same hill. This is the **Tangtong Gyelpo Temple.** Tangtong Gyelpo was one of those remarkable people whose genius and skill make a lasting impression in numerous fields. Born in 1385, he was a contemporary of Tsongkhapa and a lay adept of the Zhangpa Kagyu order of Tibetan Buddhism. He traveled extensively throughout Tibet as well as in India and China. Wherever he went he would construct temples and, where needed, his famous iron bridges, the remains of which were still observed by travelers visiting Tibet in the early decades of this century. He scored a number of operas relating the lives of the early Tibetan kings, which until recently were performed during the A-che festival. He was also a doctor and is credited with the discovery of two particular medicinal compounds. He died in 1509 at the ripe old age of 124.

Tangtong Gyelpo himself founded a temple on Chakpori. It was renovated in the 1930s by a well-known physician named Khyenrab Norbu but was completely destroyed in the Cultural Revolution. Only in the last few years has it been reconstructed at its present site on the lower slopes of the hill.

The old sagacious and smiling figure of Tangtong Gyelpo with long white hair, beard, and robes is the main statue in the small temple. To either side are a thousand smaller identical images, lined up on shelves along the back wall. On the left is Yutok Yönten Gonpo, the discoverer of the four medical tantras. Below this is a stupa containing the relics of Khyenrab Norbu. The temple is cared for by six nuns from the Shugtseb Nunnery in Lhokar.

8
THE NORBULINGKA

The Norbulingka, "Jewel Park," is a large open area about four kilometers (2.5 miles) to the west of Lhasa. Sometimes referred to as the Summer Palace of the Dalai Lama, its official name now is the People's Park. The most attractive way there is to follow the small road that bears off left from Dekyi Nub Lam, just after the Chakpori. This is the old, direct route that the Dalai Lama would take each summer when he left the Potala for the bucolic charm of the Norbulingka. It is open daily.

History

Kelsang Gyatso, the Seventh Dalai Lama, was the first Dalai Lama to make use of this rural park. He came here not only to rest but to bathe in a curative spring to treat his legs. Since the time of the Eighth Dalai Lama, the park has been used as a summer residence, retreat, and recreation area for the successive Dalai Lamas. Most of the main buildings were constructed during this century by the Thirteenth and Fourteenth Dalai Lamas. It was from here that the present Dalai Lama escaped from Tibet in March 1959. The palaces suffered considerable damage from Chinese artillery fire during the popular uprising that followed his departure. They have now been somewhat repaired, but much of their wealth has disappeared, probably forever, into China and beyond.

The Site

The Norbulingka compound is divided

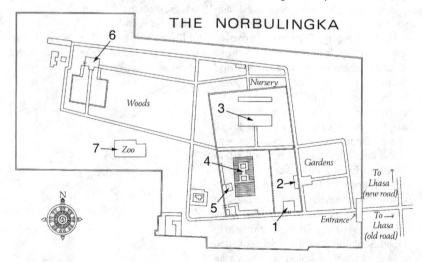

THE NORBULINGKA

into two main sections: the eastern section, which includes the opera grounds, several palaces, and a complex of governmental offices; and the western section, which contains several palaces, a forest, fields, and a zoo. We will start with the sites in the eastern section, since this is the area where one arrives after entering the main gate.

The Kelsang Palace (1)

The first building one encounters in the eastern section of the Norbulingka is the Kelsang Palace. This residence derives its name from Kelsang Gyatso, the Seventh Dalai Lama, under whom construction began in 1755. The palace was then completed during the second half of the eighteenth century by Jampel Gyatso, the Eighth Dalai Lama, and was subsequently used as a summer palace by all the Dalai Lamas up until the Thirteenth. One of its uses was as the audience hall where the monks from Drepung and Sera would receive a blessing from the Dalai Lama on completion of the traditional "summer rains" retreat. This main **audience hall** can be entered from the courtyard. With the morning sun, the hall is magnificently illuminated. Rich brocades hang from the pillars and two giant butter lamps stand in the middle of the room. Sixty-five identical tangkas of White Tara from the time of the Thirteenth Dalai Lama hang from the walls and rafters. A large throne is raised on a platform at the rear of the chapel, behind which are encased statues of the Eight Medicine Buddhas.

Images of Tsongkhapa and his two chief disciples, Amitabha, and the Thirteenth Dalai Lama (which is said to resemble him closely) are ranged nearby.

Upstairs are two chapels, a study, a reception room, and a library. The first chapel you reach contains images of the Buddha and the Sixteen Elders. The second room is a protector chapel, with images of Guhyasamaja, Chakrasamvara, and Vajrabhairava painted on the walls. In the south of the building is the Dalai Lama's study. This contains murals showing the five visions of Tsongkhapa and Manjushri riding a lion. In the reception hall there are life-size images of Kalachakra and Shakyamuni, as well as murals depicting the main events in the life of the Thirteenth Dalai Lama. Finally, off the reception room there is a library.

Just behind the Kelsang Palace is the **Uyub Chapel**. This is the oldest building in the Norbulingka compound, and many of the Dalai Lamas since the time of the Seventh have meditated here. The main chamber contains a golden throne set before an image of Shakyamuni. There are also murals showing the Potala Palace, the Jokhang Temple, Reting Monastery, and the Norbulingka itself. The meditation chamber is behind the main room.

Khamsum Zilnön Viewing Pavilion (2)

Built into the wall surrounding the palace grounds, this pavilion served as a viewing spot for the Dalai Lamas during the opera performances at the time of the annual Yogurt Festival, held in the sixth Tibetan month (July or August). This delightful structure was rebuilt in the early twentieth century to include a second floor, which houses the Dalai Lama's personal chambers as well as rooms for the Dalai Lama's tutors and other officials.

The New Summer Palace [Tagtu Migyur Potrang] (3)

North of the Kelsang Palace and the Khamsum Zilnön Viewing Pavilion stands the New Summer Palace, or the Eternally Indestructible Palace, built as the official summer residence of the Fourteenth Dalai Lama between 1954 and 1956. An ornate and opulent building, it contains examples of exquisite Tibetan craftsmanship, several very old images, and a number of incongruous twentieth-century objects imported from the West. A Tibetan guide will lead you around the rooms that are open, all of which are on the second floor.

The first room is the **south assembly hall**. Three beautiful silver images of Vajradhara, Maitreya, and Manjushri are enshrined here. From the ceiling above and to the front of them hangs a fine piece of embroidered brocade depicting the most important thinkers from Buddhist India: these include Nagarjuna, Asanga, Vasubandhu, Dignaga, and Dharmakirti. To the right is the Dalai Lama's throne, above which hangs a tangka of Yamantaka.

Around the walls is painted a detailed account of Tibetan history from its earli-est mythical beginnings until the finding of the Fourteenth Dalai Lama and his return to Lhasa in 1939. It begins at the upper left-hand corner with Shakyamuni Buddha declaring that since there were no human beings in Tibet, his teachings would, for the time being, be restricted to India. He passes the responsibility of teaching the Tibetans to Avalokiteshvara. Avalokiteshvara then assumes the form of a monkey and descends into Tibet on a mountain in Tsetang. He mates with a demoness and they produce six children—half human and half monkey. These eventually grow into the first Tibetans. The Tibetans are next depicted cultivating the first field in Tibet, again in the region of Tsetang. The first Tibetan king is called Nyatri Tsenpo. According to legend, he was descended from the Shakya clan in India, and thus is distantly related to the historical Buddha Shakyamuni.

The history continues with King Songtsen Gampo and the founding of the Jokhang in Lhasa. His minister Tönmi Sambhota is depicted studying Sanskrit in India and returning to Tibet to create the Tibetan alphabet and grammar. This written language enabled Buddhism to be introduced on a wider scale.

The murals on the back wall recount the reign of King Trisong Detsen, the founding of Samye Monastery, and the ordination of the first monks. They conclude with events from the time of the last great Tibetan king, Tri Ralpachen, and the demise of that dynasty with the anti-Buddhist policies of King Langdarma.

On the right of the enshrined deities are images of Lhasa and several of the most important monasteries founded from the eleventh century onward. There are fine traditional-style representations of Reting, Ganden, Sera, Drepung, and Tashilhunpo. It is worthwhile to take note of these paintings and compare them with what remains of the monasteries today.

The wall above the Dalai Lama's throne shows the history of the Dalai Lamas from the First until the Fourteenth. The visits of the Fifth and Thirteenth Dalai Lamas to China are depicted as well as the Thirteenth's brief exile in India. It concludes with the present Dalai Lama being escorted from Amdo to Lhasa as a young boy.

The **study chambers** of His Holiness are the next rooms to be visited. The study room contains a silk-appliqué tangka of Atisha, Drom Tönpa, and Ngog Legpa'i Sherab. In the second chamber are images of a thousand-armed Avalokiteshvara and the Gelukpa "assembly tree." An old tangka of Avalokiteshvara, Manjushri, and Vajrapani hangs above the Dalai Lama's seat. The square seat to the right is where His Holiness's tutors would sit while instructing their pupil. An old-fashioned radiogram and armchair are also here.

One now enters the **bedroom** of the Dalai Lama. At right angles to an art-deco bed is a small silver shrine containing some very beautiful old images of Vajradhara, Yamantaka, Samvara, Vajrayogini, and Manjushri. A small door leads from one side into a very functional, Western-style bathroom.

North of the bedroom is the **library**, which contains a throne and a central image of Manjushri. The murals in this room depict scenes of some of the most important Buddhist pilgrimage places in India. Adjacent to the library is a **meditation chamber**, which contains tangkas of Guhyasamaja, Chakrasamvara, and Vajrabhairava. There is another image of Padmasambhava surrounded by King Trisong Detsen and Shantarakshita. On a small, low table there is a cabinet that contains a three-dimensional representation of the Potala Pure Land of Avalokiteshvara.

The next room is the reception hall called **Ganden Chöling**. In the very center is a magnificent, intricately carved golden throne. This throne would be carried outside on special occasions for His Holiness to address the people and give teachings and initiations. Well-executed murals adorn the walls. Famous deeds from the lives of Shakyamuni and Tsongkhapa are shown. Beyond them is a rather bizarre realistic representation of the Dalai Lama and his court circa 1956. Above him sit his tutors, while below are a strange assortment of Tibetan officials, members of the Dalai Lama's family, and other dignitaries including the former British representative Hugh Richardson (in a trilby); Indian, Kuomintang, and Mongolian ambassadors; and, in yellow robes, a shaven-headed Japanese monk who managed to stay illegally in Sera

Monastery for three years. The painting was done by Amdo Jampa, an artist who has now returned from exile in India and lives in Tibet. The main statues behind the throne are those of Maitreya, Atisha, and Tsongkhapa. On the opposite wall is a group painting of the fourteen Dalai Lamas. Note that the upper four figures have no wheel in their hands, whereas the rest do. This shows that only from the time of the Fifth were the Dalai Lamas endowed with political power. Beneath the Fifth Dalai Lama, Desi Sanggye Gyatso is depicted in conversation with the Mongolian king Gushri Khan. In this way the three figures are symbolically aligned as manifestations of Avalokiteshvara, Manjushri, and Vajrapani (the "Protectors of the Three Worlds"), respectively.

The guide might now take you to the Dalai Lama's **dining room** (it is not always open to the public). The murals are mainly concerned with the life of Tsongkhapa. The master is depicted with the eight disciples with whom he went into retreat in Olka. Another disciple, Tsakpo Ngawang Drakpa, who built many monasteries in Kham and received the key teaching of the "three principal aspects of the path," is painted over the bed. The four great deeds of Tsongkhapa are portrayed to the right of an image of the Fifth Dalai Lama surrounded by all other Dalai Lamas. By the door are a symbolic diagram of the stages of concentration leading to complete mental quiescence, some illustrations of certain monastic customs and rules, and

a Wheel of Life. An altar on the left has images of Atisha, Drom Tönpa, and Ngog Legpa'i Sherab, all made from medicinal pills.

The **quarters of the Dalai Lama's mother** are in the adjoining room. The most remarkable object here is a delightful sandalwood shrine carved at the time of the Thirteenth Dalai Lama. The casing as well as the figures inside are made of sandalwood. On the right is an exquisite statue of Milarepa. Smaller images of Shakyamuni and the Six Ornaments and the Two Supreme Ones of Indian Buddhist thought sit to the left of Mila. A door leads to another sitting room for visiting Indian and other dignitaries. It contains a painting of an Indian bodhisattva donated by Nehru and a miniature painting of the twelve deeds of the Buddha. Because she was a woman and the Norbulingka a monastery, the Dalai Lama's mother would use these quarters only for daytime visits. In the evening she would return to Lhasa.

On the **landing** above the staircase are four fairly interesting paintings. On the left is a peculiarly Tibetan square diagram divided into many smaller colored squares; this is called a *kunsang korlo*, or "circle diagram of utter goodness." Each square has a letter or syllable in the middle. Reading it either horizontally or vertically gives one the names of all the Tibetan kings from Nyatri Tsenpo to Ralpachen. To its right is a picture of the origins and structure of the world according to the *Abhidharmakosha* of Vasubandhu.

There then follows another kunsang korlo, this one containing the names of all fourteen Dalai Lamas. On the adjacent wall is a symbolic painting of Padmasambhava and the two translators Vairochana and Shantarakshita. At the time of King Langdarma Buddhism was suppressed and it was forbidden to paint images of any Buddhist figure; thus, Buddhist artists had to resort to symbols. This painting is an example of that style. Padmasambhava is indicated by the sword, and the two translators by the two-headed duck and parrot. The birds have two heads to symbolize translators, that is, people capable of speaking two languages.

The Lake and Its Shrines (4)

This artificial lake with two shrines was dug at the time of the Eighth Dalai Lama, Jampel Gyatso, during the latter half of the eighteenth century. The whole area was designed primarily for recreation purposes. The central shrine, decorated with playful, lightly colored images set in panels, has no overtly religious qualities and must have been used as a sheltered summerhouse to entertain friends and drink tea. The second shrine, with the pagoda-style roof, has murals depicting familiar religious figures that still show signs of desecration. Inside are some excellent paintings of some of the main monasteries. This shrine is dedicated to the nagas, snakelike beings believed to inhabit the lake. Various rituals would be performed here as offerings to appease and gratify them.

As you leave this park you will notice a row of long, nondescript buildings to the right of the lake. These locked rooms contain many of the Dalai Lama's possessions not confiscated by the Chinese. The buildings you pass on the left as you leave the entrance courtyard are the stables.

Drunzig Palace (5)

The square building facing the usually dry artificial lake to the left of the Eighth Dalai Lama's palace was constructed by the Thirteenth Dalai Lama as a library and personal retreat. "Drunzig" is a synonym for Chenrezi, or Avalokiteshvara. To the right of the small palace is a pile of pebbles, placed there by the Thirteenth Dalai Lama as he walked around the palace and gardens. Behind this grows an apple tree that he planted with the prayer that it would help him complete a three-year retreat of Yamantaka. By studying the growth of the tree, the Dalai Lama tried to see how his meditation was progressing.

On the right as you enter the **assembly hall** on the ground floor is a stuffed tiger. The story goes that during the time of the Thirteenth Dalai Lama a tiger was reported roaming the grounds of the Norbulingka. One of the forbidding palace guards caught the beast by its tail and killed it by picking it up and hurling it to the ground. In addition to the nearly four thousand volumes of scripture that are packed into its walls, this dimly lit room houses a newly made wooden statue of Avalokiteshvara and a larger image of Amitayus. A thousand smaller images of Amitayus are newly painted on the walls. A tall glass cabinet that used to contain a silver image of Tara stands empty. The Eight Great Bodhisattvas stand beneath the scriptures at the base of the back wall. When the Thirteenth Dalai Lama returned from India in 1913, he brought with him a number of Indian images that are enshrined in this room. The ornately carved shrine containing a smaller shrine decorated with serpents contains a sandalwood statue of Shakyamuni that belonged to the eleventh-century translator Rinchen Zangpo. The larger shrine used to contain a gold and silver image of Tara that was destroyed during the Cultural Revolution.

Upstairs are the Thirteenth Dalai Lama's **retreat quarters.** The main chamber is a small audience room where His Holiness would occasionally interrupt his retreats to deal with matters of state brought to him by his ministers. No other people were ever allowed in here. The room itself contains a throne immediately above which is a restored painting of the five Dhyani Buddhas. In the glass cabinet to the right of the throne are some very old statues, including Tsongkhapa and his two chief disciples, Padmasambhava, Samvara, Manjushri, Avalokiteshvara, Amitayus, Shakyamuni, and a very rare "Eye-Opening" Avalokiteshvara—the only other known depiction of this figure is a mural in the Jokhang.

The meditation cell itself is reached by passing through a bare anteroom with a single bed where the Dalai Lama would rest and eat. A mural of the five manifestations of Tsongkhapa as he appeared in a vision to his disciple Khedrup Je is on one wall. There are also five boundary markers, which look like carved pedestals. During a retreat they would mark, often with an umbrella inserted in them, the physical limits beyond which the retreatant would not be allowed to go. The cell itself is very small with richly painted walls. A large painting of Yamantaka, the Thirteenth Dalai Lama's personal deity, is on the wall behind the seat. It is said that he spent many years meditating on this deity, receiving visions and words of advice from him. On the left is a white offering scarf given to His Holiness by the Ninth Panchen Lama.

Upstairs is another small room that would have been used by the Dalai Lama's attendants for making tormas and other ritual offerings. The broken remains of a three-dimensional mandala of Yamantaka can still be seen here.

Behind this palace are a row of rather insignificant buildings that previously served as servants' quarters and kitchens.

The Thirteenth Dalai Lama's Palace [Chensek Palace] (6)

This palace, located in the northwestern section of the compound, was built in 1922 for Tubten Gyatso, the Thirteenth Dalai Lama, by a wealthy lay Buddhist supporter named Chensek Kumbu. It is still known by the Tibetans as the Chensek Palace. Frequently only the

main assembly hall on the ground floor of this three-story building is open to the public. This large and spacious room used to house a superb collection of old tangkas, which unfortunately have been removed. Thirty-six gilded copper images of Amitayus, Vijaya, and Tara, the triad of deities most strongly connected with longevity, are encased along the rear wall to both sides of the raised platform on which the Dalai Lama's throne is placed. In 1948, when he was thirteen years old, the present Dalai Lama commissioned a silver statue of his predecessor, the Thirteenth, and had it enshrined behind the throne. The carvings along the tops of the pillars above the throne are worth studying. The detailed murals around the skylight depict the deeds of Tsongkhapa.

Upstairs on the second floor are the private quarters of the Thirteenth Dalai Lama. They consist of a private **living room** and adjoining **bedroom**. The living room is a narrow rectangular chamber with a grandfather clock and a small shrine. The bedroom is even smaller, containing a bed that indicates the diminutive stature of its occupant. A beautiful old statue of Tara on the bedside table is the only religious object in the room. It is reputed to have spoken directly to His Holiness. An unusual mural of a Thousand Armed Avalokiteshvara in lotus posture is on one wall.

On the third floor are a number of rooms, which have been maintained much as they were left in 1933 when Tubten Gyatso died. The main room is the Dalai Lama's private **teaching hall.** This was where the Thirteenth would perform monastic ordination ceremonies and tantric initiations and deliver discourses on Buddhist philosophy and doctrine. The two most outstanding images in this room are standing forms of a thousand-armed Avalokiteshvara and a thousand-armed Sitatapatra (Dugkarma). They are placed side by side, and both radiate a sense of warmth and insight. To their right is a small encased figure of Dorje Drakden, the special protector propitiated by the Tibetan government through the Nechung oracle. Portraits of earlier Dalai Lamas—the First, Second, Third, Fifth, and Seventh—adorn the walls along with some paintings of the principal Geluk monasteries. On the wall high above the throne at the back are depicted the seven religious kings and the twenty-five kalki of the Shambhala legend. The murals depict several important monasteries: Kumbum in Amdo, Reting, Chökhorgyel (with Lhamo'i Latso, the oracle lake), Tashilhunpo, and Sera.

A door leads into an adjoining room notable mainly for its murals of the Dalai Lamas, including a large one of the Thirteenth himself. To the left is a painting of the Norbulingka and the Dalai Lama surrounded by his entourage. On the right is the Potala.

By going through a door at the back of this room one enters first a bare anteroom and then the small **prayer chamber** where the Dalai Lama would perform his daily recitations and other practices. The walls of this tiny cell are richly painted with tantric deities.

Across the courtyard from this palace is a smaller building, the **Kelsang Dekyi Palace,** where the Thirteenth Dalai Lama would retire each night. Most of the main images have been removed to the Chensek Palace, but restoration work is now underway to redecorate the rooms. It may be closed to the public. The first main room you enter contains a detailed mural of Tushita (Ganden), the Pure Land where the future Buddha Maitreya now resides. A portrait of Tsongkhapa is beside it. There is a small altar with a fine statue of the Jowo Shakyamuni with two buddhas seated beside him. The adjoining room, partitioned off by screen doors, has a mural of the Dhanyakataka stupa of Kalachakra. On the opposite wall is a case with some old statues, including Avalokiteshvara and two images of Tsongkhapa's disciple Khedrup Je. You can see where the golden ornaments have been removed from some of these statues. The one other room worth visiting on this floor (the others are bare) possesses a mural of the pure land of Avalokiteshvara (Potala) with a fine thousand-armed representation of the deity in the center. The wooden carvings on the screen door beautifully depict the Kadampa masters Atisha, Drom Tönpa, and Ngog Legpa'i Sherab.

Close by to the Kelsang Dekyi Palace is the Chime Chokkyil, the small building in which the Thirteenth Dalai Lama died.

This is closed to the public.

The Zoo (7)

Between the Thirteenth Dalai Lama's Palace and the Kelsang Palace is a zoo with a small collection of deer, mountain goats, large cats, bears, monkeys, and other Tibetans animals, none of whom seem particularly pleased to be there.

9
DREPUNG MONASTERY

Drepung is about eight kilometers (five miles) west of Lhasa. It is reached by leaving the city along the Dekyi Nub Lam, going west (toward the airport). The turnoff for the monastery is on your right. It is one kilometer up the hillside; you must walk up this last stretch unless you come by jeep or private tour bus. The bus, which departs from designated stops along the Dekyi Shar Lam, leaves you on the main road beneath the monastery. A return service takes you back to Lhasa in the afternoon. The colleges and chapels are open daily.

History

Drepung is one of the three great Gelukpa monasteries near Lhasa, the other two being Sera and Ganden. Until the Chinese occupation it served, like its two sister monasteries, as a center of learning and monastic training to which monks from all corners of Tibet would come to spend as long as fifteen or twenty years methodically studying and debating the meaning of the Buddhist scriptures. Thus for centuries it existed as a small monastic township housing thousands of fully ordained monks, novices, workers, and other functionaries. Founded in 1416 by Jamyang Chöje Tashi Pelden, a disciple of Tsongkhapa, Drepung soon grew into the largest of all Gelukpa monasteries, housing more than seven thousand monks. It could well claim to have been the largest monastery the world has known.

Drepung also quickly became a major center of Gelukpa religious power. The Second, Third, and Fourth Dalai Lamas all lived and were entombed here. During the time of the Fifth Dalai Lama, Drepung became a center for political power as well, as the Dalai Lama's personal residence was transformed into the first administrative center of the Tibetan government under Gelukpa rule.

The monastery was also renowned for its scholastic training. It produced many great lamas, including Jamyang Zhepa, the founder of Labrang Monastery in Amdo. Most of the monks who came from Mongolia to be trained would join

The abbots and disciplinarians of Drepung Monastery before 1959

the Gomang College of Drepung. It was
here that Agvan Dorjiev, the Buryat
lama who became a tutor to the
Thirteenth Dalai Lama and tried to bring
Tibet under the protection of the Russian
tsar, studied.

Like all other Tibetan monasteries of
similar size, Drepung is organized in a
system of colleges (dratsangs) and houses (khangtsens). The colleges are the
main units of the monastery, distinguished from each other by the kind of
studies the monks follow there. Each college has an abbot (khenpo), who is
responsible for administrative matters,
and a disciplinarian (ge-kö), who is in
charge of the monks' conduct. Affiliated
with each college are a number of houses, where the monk-students live for the
duration of their training. The houses are
divided according to the regions of the
country that the monks come from.
Although each college has its own
assembly hall and chapels, the monastery usually has another main assembly
hall (tsog-chen) where, on important
occasions, the monks from all the colleges can gather.

Of all the Gelukpa monasteries
around Lhasa, Drepung suffered least
during the Cultural Revolution. Although
several buildings at the rear of the complex were destroyed, the main colleges
and assembly hall were left fairly intact.
Since 1982 over four hundred monks
have joined the monastery, most of them
young men, and an attempt is now
being made to begin the courses of
study again.

The Site

The Ganden Palace [Ganden Potrang](1)

Built by the Second Dalai Lama, Gendun
Gyatso, this palace was the home of all
the subsequent Dalai Lamas through the
great Fifth Dalai Lama. When the Fifth
Dalai Lama attained political control of
Tibet in the mid-seventeenth century, the
palace also became the main governmental headquarters for Tibet. Even after
the Potala Palace was completed after
the Fifth Dalai Lama's death, the
Ganden Palace remained a powerful
symbol of the Geluk order's political
power and prestige in Tibet. This was
where the subsequent Dalai Lamas and
their entourage of monks would stay
when they visited Drepung. Apart from a
small retaining staff, the palace would
stand empty when the Dalai Lama was
not there.

To enter the palace you must climb a
flight of stairs that leads you into a spacious courtyard with a large tree. The
main edifice of the palace looms up at
the back of the courtyard and at the
upper right-hand corner a balcony
bedecked with cloth hangings indicates
the Dalai Lama's personal quarters
(which are not open to the public). Steps
to the left of the courtyard lead into a
large, spacious assembly hall, called the
Sangapa Tratsang, where in former
days the Namgyel Tratsang, the Dalai
Lama's personal monastic staff, would
gather for their services. Statues of several deities are enshrined behind glass

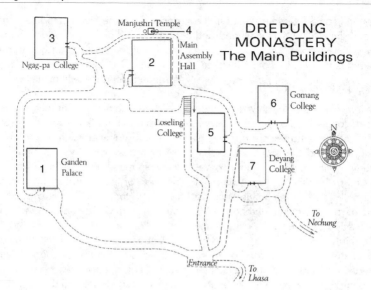

DREPUNG MONASTERY
The Main Buildings

3 — Ngag-pa College

Manjushri Temple — 4

2 — Main Assembly Hall

6 — Gomang College

Loseling College

5

1 — Ganden Palace

7 — Deyang College

N

To Nechung

Entrance
To Lhasa

and metal grilles in dark recesses along the front wall. In the rear left-hand corner is a trapdoor that leads down into a room where the Fifth Dalai Lama held audiences.

At the back of the hall is a protector chapel with a formidable thirteen-deity Yamantaka statue with a frowning statue of the Fifth Dalai Lama in front, beside which is a smaller image of the Seventh Dalai Lama. On the right of the chapel are large statues of Kalarupa and Pelden Lhamo, and a small, wrathful Gyelpo Kunga.

Upon returning to the outer courtyard, proceed up the two-tiered set of steps to the main courtyard, which is surrounded by residential quarters and storerooms. This is where the Cham dances of the Yogurt Festival would be performed

each summer before moving on to the Norbulingka. A flight of stairs at the back of this courtyard leads you up to the palace's main assembly hall, which is presently quite bare. The hall contains a statue of Atisha's tutelary deity, the so-called Speaking Tara (Tara Sungjönma) and one of Chenrezi, the bodhisattva of compassion. At the back of the hall is a protector chapel, which contains statues of Bhairava, Pelden Lhamo, Mahakala, and the Fifth Dalai Lama.

Above the main assembly hall are the private quarters of the Dalai Lamas, as well as offices where they would conduct governmental affairs. Usually it is only possible to visit one of these rooms, a chapel that contains the Fifth Dalai Lama's elaborate throne. Cabinets around the room feature a range of deities and texts. The main statues in the center of the altar are Tsongkhapa and his two chief disciples.

The rest of the Ganden Palace is closed.

The Main Assembly Hall (2)

The Main Hall. This lavishly decorated hall is no longer used as the main assembly hall at Drepung except on special occasions. Instead, the 450 monks gather regularly in the smaller but more convenient hall of Loseling College. The main image at the front of the hall is Maitreya seated on a huge golden throne. To the left is a stupa containing the relics of the Ninety-Fifth Ganden Tripa, the titular head of the Gelukpa order (for more information on this position see chapter 12). To the right is a statue of Sitatapatra, in front of whom are Shakyamuni Buddha and Ling Rinpoche, who was the Ninety-Seventh Ganden Tripa. After Sitatapatra come Tsongkhapa, the Thirteenth Dalai Lama, Jamyang Chöje (the founder of Drepung), a youthful Seventh Dalai Lama, then the Third, Fourth, Fifth, Ninth, and Eighth Dalai Lamas. The Sixteen Arhats are placed in two groups of eight at each end of the altar.

The steps to the left of the central Maitreya statue lead into the main chapel. This is a high-ceilinged, spacious room that is one of the oldest structures in Drepung; the assembly hall was added on at a later date. The chapel is dedicated to the Buddhas of the Three Times. The Eight Great Bodhisattvas line the walls, and the wrathful forms of Vajrapani and Hayagriva guard the

doorway. Nine stupas modeled on the stupa in India where Buddha Shakyamuni first taught the Kalachakra tantra, the Shri Dhanyakataka stupa, are arranged along the wall at the back. The name "Drepung" is the Tibetan translation of Dhanyakataka, which literally means "rice mound." This name well describes the first visual impression one receives of the monastery when approaching it from the main road below, although when construction of the monastery first began it probably consisted of only a handful of buildings and was yet to resemble a mound of rice.

A doorway at the front left of the main hall leads to a protector chapel dedicated to Pelden Lhamo, whose statue (usually covered with offering scarves) is to the left of an ornate "palace" of the deity made of thread in a tall cabinet at the end of the room.

The Upper Story. None of the chapels on the second floor is open. On the third floor the main chapel reveals the exquisite head and shoulders of a giant statue of Maitreya at the age of eight, the base of which is in one of the closed chapels on the floor below. This image is called "The Maitreya Who Fulfills Your Wishes on Beholding Him."

Stairs to the left of this chapel lead to a chapel dedicated to Shakyamuni. Thirteen stupas are found arranged to either side of the Buddha. At the far end of the room is a high wooden throne with the Fifth Dalai Lama.

Leaving this chapel by the far door

brings you to a chapel with an image of Maitreya (Miwang Jampa) at the age of twelve. To the left is Tsongkhapa and to the right Jamyang Chöje, between whom are White Tara, Togme Zangpo, Seu Rinzen (founder of the Tara chapel in the Jokhang), and Namgyelma. Behind these statues are four stupas. From the left they contain the remains of Panchen Sonam Drakpa, Jamyang Chöje, and Gendun Gyatso, the Second Dalai Lama. The fourth is a Medicine Buddha stupa. The remains of the Third and Fourth Dalai Lamas are also enshrined in stupas in this building, but traditionally these have never been open to the public.

The next room is the **Tara Chapel**, which dates back to the time of the Fifth Dalai Lama. There are three images of Tara side by side encased behind glass. The image on the left is Nartang Chime Drölma, the Tara responsible for preserving Drepung's drinking water; the middle image is Yamdrok Yumtso Drölma, the Tara responsible for Drepung's wealth and prosperity; and the image to the right is Gyeltse Tsechen Drölma, the Tara who empowers Drepung with authority. A superb 114-volume edition of the Kangyur, commissioned by the Fifth Dalai Lama, bound in sandalwood with ivory ends and written in gold ink, is enshrined along the wall. This edition was stolen by the Chinese in 1959 and returned to Tibet only in 1985. A statue of Prajnaparamita, the "Mother of the Buddhas," sits midway between these volumes, holding in her lap an amulet containing a tooth of Tsongkhapa. Three standing cases down the middle of the room contain examples of the casings and text of this edition of the Kangyur as well as a volume from another edition painted in red ink on a continuous sheet of paper.

It is possible to ascend yet one more story to the level of the roof, where you will find three more chapels. To the left is a large room containing statues of all the rulers of Tibet, from the earliest kings to the later Dalai Lamas. The Fifth Dalai Lama sits on a raised throne at the center of the back wall, and there seems to be no particular order in the arrangement of the other images. The statues are nonetheless well made and expressive. There is also a small Maitreya Chapel, which possesses the conch shell reputedly donated to the monastery by Tsongkhapa, as well as a Shakyamuni Chapel that contains an image of the Buddha surrounded by about fifteen stupas.

Ngag-pa College (3)

The Chapel. This one chapel open at the rear of the main hall is one of the oldest buildings in Drepung. It was erected by Tsongkhapa himself, before the existence of Drepung, as a shrine to Yamantaka. The main image is still that of a single Yamantaka, reputedly made by Tsongkhapa. According to tradition, Tsongkhapa molded the body around the relics of the great translator Ra Lotsawa, one of the most important figures in the Yamantaka tradition. When he had finished the neck and was about to make the heads, it is said that they appeared spontaneously. In addition to statues of Tsongkhapa and the Fifth Dalai Lama, the room contains many of the major Gelukpa protectors: Mahakala, Kalarupa, Vaishravana, Dorje Drakden, and Pelden Lhamo. The prayer wheel in the right-hand corner is consecrated by the mantras of Yamantaka and is regarded as a shrine to the deity's speech.

The Main Hall. The hall and the rest of the Ngag-pa (Tantric) College was built onto Tsongkhapa's Yamantaka Chapel at a later date. Along the front of the main hall are a number of texts, some statues of Tsongkhapa and various Dalai Lamas, and, in the center, a throne for the Dalai Lama, in front of which is a thousand-armed Avalokiteshvara in a case. More interesting are the smaller images of the Indian and Tibetan teachers who make up the lineage of the "Stages on the Path to Enlightenment." They are enshrined on the left-hand side of the hall. Some of the figures, such as Nagarjuna and Asanga, can easily be recognized but most of the lamas are hard to identify.

There are no chapels open on the upper story of the Ngag-pa College.

The Manjushri Temple (4)

This small temple is situated immediately behind the Main Assembly Hall. The main figure inside is a stone image of Manjushri, carved on a large boulder around which the temple is built. To the left and right of the temple stand white stupas. The one on the left contains one hundred thousand verses of scripture; the one to the right, the relics of Lama Umapa, the teacher through whom Tsongkhapa was able to communicate directly with Manjushri.

Loseling College (5)

Tsar Khangtsen. This is situated on the left of the entrance to Loseling. Steps lead you to a courtyard, whence you can enter the dimly lit assembly hall of Tsar Khangtsen (Tsar House of Loseling College). On the left of the hall are the Buddhas of the Three Times. The main statues on the altar at the front are (from the left): a standing Avalokiteshvara, the Seventh Dalai Lama, Tsongkhapa flanked by his two chief disciples, then Shakyamuni, the Fourth Dalai Lama, followed by several Taras and Tsongkhapas. The texts at the ends of the altar are the Kangyur and Tengyur.

Main Assembly Hall. In niches along both sides of this vast hall are images of Amitayus and an aspect of Tsongkhapa. These statues were made around seventy years ago. Formerly there were a thousand of each deity, but about six hundred were removed or destroyed during the Cultural Revolution. The main statues on the altar at the front are (from the left): two aspects of Tsongkhapa, a large stupa with the relics of Legden Rinpoche, the first abbot of Loseling; the first

Kangyur Rinpoche, another famous Loseling lama; the Fifth, Eighth, and Seventh Dalai Lamas; Jamyang Chöje; Panchen Sonam Drakpa, Loseling's textbook writer; Tsongkhapa on a silver throne; the Thirteenth Dalai Lama; and a final image of Sonam Drakpa in debating posture. Mandalas of the three main Geluk tantric deities (Yamantaka, Samvara, and Guhyasamaja) can also be seen here. In the center is a large throne reserved for the Dalai Lama. Beyond the throne, after a series of smaller images including one of Tsongkhapa that is said to have once spoken, is a huge stupa with the relics of the first Dedrup Rinpoche, another renowned Loseling lama. Finally (beyond the door) are Manjushri, Tsongkhapa and his two main disciples, and Sitatapatra.

The Chapels. One enters the three chapels at the rear of the assembly hall by a door in the wall at the left. The first chapel is dominated by a large Enlightenment Stupa, behind which, on raised platforms, are Atisha, Green Tara, Tsongkhapa, and Jamyang Chöje. The Sixteen Arhats are also displayed in tiers around the room.

The second chapel is dedicated to Maitreya, represented in a large statue in the center and two smaller images elsewhere. Shelves filled with texts reach from floor to ceiling. Shakyamuni, Tsongkhapa, and the Thirteenth Dalai Lama can be seen as well as images of Atisha, Drom Tönpa, and Ngog Legpa'i Sherab.

The third chapel houses a small statue of Shakyamuni. Four stupas contain the relics of former Ganden Tripas. The walls are filled with texts.

The Upper Story. The only chapel open on the upper story is a protector chapel. You first enter an antechamber with a range of wrathful protector deities in cabinets. From here pass beneath a stuffed goat draped with offering scarves into the main chapel. On the left in a small cabinet are Dharmaraja, Dorje Drakden, and Vaishravana, and on the right, in a large gold cabinet, is Damchen. The longer cabinet on the left includes Mahakala, Yamantaka, Samvara, and Guhyasamaja; that on the right, Tsongkhapa and his two main disciples, Sengdongma (the lion-faced dakini), Vaishravana, and Dorje Drakden.

Gomang College (6)

The Chapels. The first chapel contains the longevity triad of Amitayus, Tara, and Vijaya. Scriptures are stored in the walls.

The second chapel is the largest and most important of the three on the ground floor of Gomang. A wide assortment of lamas and deities, raised on several tiers, fills the room. The central figure on the uppermost level at the back is Buddha Akshobhya. To the left is Shakyamuni and to the right a smaller Akshobhya. Immediately beneath are three more statues; the central image is Shakyamuni, with Maitreya to the left and Avalokiteshvara to the right. Beneath sits a youthful Tsongkhapa, the principal figure of the thousand other images of the master found in the main hall. Below and in front of Tsongkhapa is a row of five smaller statues depicting the first five incarnations of the famous Gomang lama Jamyang Zhepa (the founder of Labrang Monastery in Amdo). Many other smaller images surround these central figures, and there are two stupas containing the remains of the second and third abbots of Gomang.

The third chapel is rather messy. The Twenty-One Taras are arranged in three tiers along the back wall. Along the left wall, in four tiers, are the Sixteen Arhats.

The Main Hall. In the far left-hand corner of this hall are two images of six-armed Mahakala. Above and around the statue are many small images of Tsongkhapa, of which there used to be a thousand but half have been stolen. The first statue past the doorway to the first chapel is of the rarely depicted Tsangyang Gyatso, the Sixth Dalai Lama. Continuing to the right are Tsongkhapa; Dipamkara, the Buddha of the past; two more images of Tsongkhapa; and the Seventh Dalai Lama. Instead of a central image, there is a large opening that leads to the main chapel in the rear. This opening is presently barred. Further to the right are images of Maitreya, Amitayus, Jamyang Chöje, Tsongkhapa, and an eleven-headed, eight-armed Avalokiteshvara. The walls are painted with new murals.

The Upper Story. As with Loseling College, there is just a single protector chapel on the upper story in Gomang. The main image is a gold-framed Mahakala, behind which is concealed a self-originated Mahakala in rock. The protector is associated with Chankya Rölpa'i Dorje, the second incarnation of Jamyang Zhepa, a statue of whom is in the gold case. To either side are other aspects of Mahakala and to the far left a statue of Yamantaka. Some minor local deities, converted to protect Buddhism, are also present. Women are not usually permitted to enter this chapel.

Deyang College (7)

The Chapel. The main image in the single chapel of Deyang College is Maitreya. To the left are Manjushri, Tara, the Fifth Dalai Lama, Tsongkhapa, and Shakyamuni. On the right sit the Seventh Dalai Lama; the first Nechung oracle, who was also the first abbot of Deyang; Jangchub Pandenpa, a renowned lama of the college; the First and Second Reting Rinpoches; Yönten Gyatso, who was a debating partner of the Fifth Dalai Lama, the first abbot of Ratö Monastery, and the second abbot of Deyang; and the Third Dalai Lama. A small cabinet to the far right contains an image of Tangtong Gyelpo.

The Main Hall. Old statues of Tsongkhapa and his two chief disciples are the main images in this hall. The female deities Sitatapatra, White Tara, and Tara Cintamani are also on the altar. The Fifth Dalai Lama is the only other lama present; he is especially important in Deyang College as traditionally the monks have based their philosophical studies on a text composed by him. In the far left-hand corner of the hall is the protector Dorje Drakden, and in the opposite corner Pelden Lhamo.

On the upper story is a small protector chapel dedicated to Dorje Drakden. To the left is a cabinet with Hayagriva and consort, Pelden Lhamo, and Dorje Drakden. On the wall on the left is a self-originated Dorje Drakden that has been painted. Above the door as you come in is an old collection of weapons and armor.

NECHUNG MONASTERY

Nechung is only a few minutes' walk from Drepung Monastery.

History

Nechung Monastery has an important place in the history of Tibet. Until 1959 the medium for the state oracle of Tibet lived here. The medium was a monk through whom the special protector of the Tibetan government, Dorje Drakden, would give advice to the Dalai Lamas and leaders of the country. No major decisions of the Tibetan government would be made without first consulting the Nechung oracle.

The Nechung community of monks have always had a special relationship with the deity Dorje Drakden. It is believed that this deity was first recognized and propitiated in India, where it was known as Pehar, and the Nechung community was initially established somewhere near the Indo-Tibetan border. Because of war it then moved to Samye Monastery, and at the time of the Fifth Dalai Lama came to its present site near Drepung Monastery, where it was given the name Nechung (literally, "small place").

In 1959 the medium for the oracle escaped to India with the Dalai Lama, settled in Dharamsala, and continued to serve the Tibetan government in exile. Although the medium died in 1985, a successor was found and through him the Dalai Lama still continues to consult the deity Dorje Drakden. (John Avedon's *In Exile from the Land of Snows* has an excellent chapter on the Nechung oracle.) Nechung Monastery was severely damaged during the Cultural Revolution, and restoration began in the 1980s. Eighteen monks now live here, compared with the sixty or seventy who ran the monastery before the Chinese occupation. The monks are not strictly affiliated to any of the four orders of Tibetan Buddhism.

The Site

You enter the monastery through a set of doors painted with human skins and walk into a newly restored **assembly hall**, its walls beautifully painted with images of relatively obscure wrathful deities. At the far left-hand corner a door leads into the protector chapel dedicated to Dorje Drakden. Two images of the protector are found here; one in a large cabinet with his face covered, the other in a smaller cabinet facing the door. Between these two images are the remains of a large tree trunk. It is believed that when the monastery was founded on its present site, Dorje Drakden took up residence in this tree. Consequently, the chapel is called the Wrathful Tree-Trunk Chapel. Several other large statues fill the room: Ling Rinpoche, the Seventh Dalai Lama, Tsongkhapa, Padmasambhava, and the Eight Medicine Buddhas.

The adjacent chapel on the ground floor contains a central image of Jowo Shakyamuni and a small cabinet with a statue of Dorje Drakden. None of the other statues that surrounded the central figure has yet been replaced. Above where the caretaker-monk sits are three very fine tangkas of Ekajati, Yamantaka and consort, and Tsedrekma. More tangkas of various lamas and deities hang from the other walls.

The final chapel at the back of the assembly hall is a somewhat bare **Protector Chapel**. On the right are statues of Ekajati, Pelden Lhamo, and Lhamo Nyima Shonu. The curtained wood and glass cabinet in one corner contains the symbolic celestial mansion of Dorje Drakden.

To reach the upper stories of the monastery you must go out the way you came in and enter a small door to the right. This takes you to the second floor, where two adjacent chapels have been restored. The first is a large room that

was used as an **audience room** of the Dalai Lama whenever he visited Nechung. The large throne at the back of the room was used by the Fifth to the Fourteenth Dalai Lamas. There are a number of old and beautiful statues along the altar that were recently offered to Nechung by the monks of Drepung. On the far left is a wonderfully expressive image of the Fifth Dalai Lama. Next to him are Tsongkhapa and two Buddhas. Jowo Shakyamuni is enshrined in a glass case. Next to him is Maitreya. To the right of the throne are Tsongkhapa and his two chief disciples and Avalokiteshvara. In front is a new statue of Manjushri. A fine old tangka of Samvara hangs to the far left by the door.

Adjoining this chapel is a smaller room dedicated to Tsongkhapa. A large, newly made image of the master sits behind glass flanked, as usual, by Gyeltsab Je and Khedrup Je, his two chief disciples. There are also smaller images of the Buddha, Avalokiteshvara, Tara, and Tsongkhapa.

Climbing to the roof you find a single chapel containing a magnificent statue of Padmasambhava, made in 1981 by a Tibetan sculptor living in Lhasa. It is six meters (eighteen feet) high, and sits with an angry expression. The Guru is bedecked in robes of very fine, old Chinese brocade. The chapel used to serve as the quarters of the Dalai Lama.

Next door to Nechung is another complex of buildings that has recently been turned into a monastic school. Young monks from different parts of

Tibet and from all four main orders of Tibetan Buddhism come here to study Buddhist philosophy and doctrine, using mainly Gelukpa texts. There are at present around fifty monks training here. One can visit the school, but the main chapel-cum-assembly-hall is newly and functionally decorated with little that would interest a visitor.

Behind Nechung is a white-walled compound, built by the Thirteenth Dalai Lama in order to perform a retreat focused on the deity Yamantaka. It is said that he did this in order to secure the independence of Tibet against Chinese intervention. The Fourteenth Dalai Lama also stayed here as a young man. A large empty anteroom leads into a three-roomed apartment. Only the murals indicate what purpose this building once served. One wall depicts an eleven-headed Avalokiteshvara, the Pure Land of Amitabha, and the Pure Land of Tara. The front room is the meditation cell. A large photo of the Dalai Lama is above the bed-throne, and paintings of Tsongkhapa, Drom Tönpa, and Ngog Legpa'i Sherab (without Atisha), Pelden Lhamo, and Dorje Drakden adorn the walls. To the left of the altar are murals of Padmasambhava, Hayagriva, and Yamantaka. A thousand-armed Avalokiteshvara and other images stand on the altar.

High on the peak of the crest of rock behind Nechung you can make out a small hermitage where the Second, Third, and Fourth Dalai Lamas did retreats.

10
SERA MONASTERY

Sera lies about five kilometers (three miles) to the north of Lhasa along the base of the mountains at the edge of the valley. It can be reached by bus from the bus station near the Mentsi Khang. You can also bicycle or walk. The colleges and chapels are open daily, with the usual long lunch break.

History

Sera Monastery was built below a small hermitage where Tsongkhapa spent several years in retreat both meditating on and writing commentaries to the Buddhist scriptures. A leading disciple of Tsongkhapa, Shakya Yeshe (1352–1435), started constructing Sera in 1419, the year of his teacher's death. Ten years earlier Tsongkhapa had been invited by Emperor Yung-lo of Ming China to visit his court in Beijing. Unable to go himself, Tsongkhapa sent Shakya Yeshe in his stead. A subsequent emperor showed his appreciation of Shakya Yeshe's teachings by giving him in 1434 the title Jamchen Chöje (Great Gentle Dharma Lord), the name by which he is best known today.

Although many of the outlying residential buildings in Sera were destroyed during the Cultural Revolution, the principal buildings were left relatively intact. Four hundred monks now live here, many of them recently ordained, and an attempt is being made to recommence the traditional course of study for which the monastery is renowned.

Sera Monastery before 1959

Sera Monastery is divided into two main colleges (*dratsang*), Sera Me and Sera Je.

In the last few years, as Sera Monastery has revived as an active monastery, a number of houses (*khangtsen*) have been restored to lodge the monks from different parts of Tibet who come here to study. It was these buildings that suffered the greatest damage during the early years of Chinese occupation. Some were pillaged and left to crumble, others were even used to billet soldiers. Since most of these *khangtsen* are still being rebuilt and contain nothing of particular interest to the Western visitor, I will only mention them in passing.

One of the most sacred objects in Sera is the vajra (Tib. *dorje*) that is considered

to be the prototype of all other vajras in Tibet. It was found by the tantric adept Dacharpa in Padmasambhava's cave in Drak Yerpa and is now shown to the public only one day a year.

The Site

I shall describe the interiors of the colleges and halls in Sera according to the route followed by Tibetan pilgrims. Upon entering the main hall of each building, you turn left and follow the left-hand wall until you reach the first of the chapels that are connected along the back of the building. Only after studying these chapels do we look at the images in the main hall. Finally we visit the shrines on the upper story.

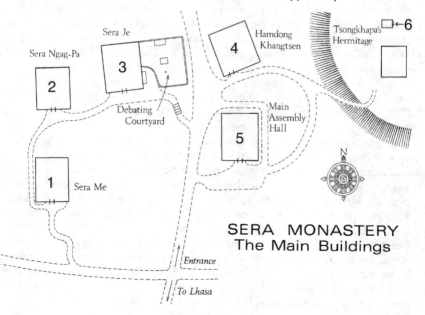

SERA MONASTERY
The Main Buildings

Sera Me College (1)

The Chapels. The first chapel is dedicated to Ta-og Chögyel, the worldly Dharma protector of the East. He is the wrathful deity to the left of the chapel with consorts to either side. The dominant statue is that of Yamantaka and consort, a large, beautiful, and fearful image. Numerous old vajras can be seen hanging from one of the beams on the roof. Three iron scorpions are attached to one of the pillars, apparently as a means of warding off the negative influence of the nagas.

Three large Buddhas dominate the following chapel: Shakyamuni, the Buddha of the present; Maitreya, the Buddha of the future; and Dipamkara, the Buddha of the past. Many volumes of the *Perfection of Wisdom Discourses* line the upper walls. Images of the Sixteen Arhats, in Chinese-style pseudo-grottoes, are also enshrined in the room.

The next chapel houses the most sacred image in Sera Me, a statue of Shakyamuni called the Miwang Jowo, the Jowo commissioned in the fifteenth century by the influential Miwang family, one of the principal benefactors of Tsongkhapa. Although heavily ornamented, this is a fine piece of work and probably the original. A large figure of Amitayus sits at the rear of the chapel, and the Eight Great Bodhisattvas stand along the walls. The wrathful forms of Hayagriva and Achala guard the shrine.

The last of the rear chapels is dedicated to Tsongkhapa, who sits in the company of many important lamas from the Geluk tradition. The First, Second, Third and Fifth Dalai Lamas are represented, as are Jamchen Chöje, the founder of Sera, and Gyeltsen Zangpo, the monastery's first abbot. Atisha and Drom represent the Kadampa tradition. The founder of Sera Me College, Kunkhyen Jangchub Bum, is seated to the right of Drom. On the wall near the exit are two more recent masters: Gyelwa Ensapa and a very expressive Purchok Ngawang Jampa.

The Main Hall. The central figure in the main hall is an image of Shakyamuni with delicate and sensitive features. The workmanship of the halo is worth noting. In front of the Buddha are small statues of Jamchen Chöje and Jangchub Bum, the founders of Sera and Sera Me, respectively. Maitreya and Manjushri are to either side of the main image. In the left-hand corner of the hall is a large three-dimensional Medicine Buddha mandala. The rest of the long altar running along the front of the hall is occupied by statues of lamas, some more easily recognizable than others. Tsongkhapa and his two chief disciples are there along with lesser-known lamas of Sera Me. A modern image of a portly, smiling Pabongka Rinpoche beneath an umbrella is in front of Manjushri. At the back to the right is a stupa containing some of Pabongka's remains. In the right-hand corner of the hall is a statue of Jamchen Chöje surrounded by other lamas.

The Upper Stories. Upstairs are two small shrines. On the left as you come up is a chapel devoted to Tuwang Tsultrim, a form of Shakyamuni represented here by a small, standing statue with notably aquiline features, suggesting its possible Indian origin. A small stone figure of Tara is to the right of the main image. This used to be the most revered image in Tsang Khangtsen of Sera and has only recently been moved to this shrine. The other figures are modern and for the most part easily recognizable.

On the opposite side of the roof, connected by a small walkway, is a Tara chapel. This used to be where an edition of the Kangyur was kept, but all 108 volumes were destroyed during the Cultural Revolution. In its place a thousand small images of Tara made in China during the last century have been moved up from a smaller khangtsen. The larger Tara amongst these is said to have once spoken. To the right of the shrine are three larger images of Tara, Amitayus and Vijaya, the longevity triad.

Between Sera Me and Sera Ngag-pa are three khangtsens: the Tsang and Lar Khangtsens of Sera Je, and the Bompora and Tsar Khangtsens of Sera Me. The debating courtyard (*chöra*) of Sera Me is between the Bompora and Tsar Khangtsens.

Sera Ngag-pa College (2)

This is the oldest structure in Sera. The first building Jamchen Chöje erected, it served as the main assembly hall for the monks until, over the years, Sera expanded to its pre-1959 size. When it was replaced by the larger assembly hall (5), it became the tantric (*ngag-pa*) college of Sera. The pillar capitals in the entrance hall are some of the finest I have seen in Tibet.

The Chapels. There are only two chapels to the rear of Sera Ngag-pa. The more interesting is that of the Sixteen Arhats to the left. Seated in niches halfway up the wall are Tibetan images of the sixteen saints. Below them, standing on a ledge, are another sixteen images that are small, lacquered Chinese statues. These were offered by Emperor Yung-lo to Jamchen Chöje when he visited China. A large figure of Shakyamuni is in the center with a finely carved wooden halo behind him.

The chapel to the right is the Protector Shrine. The main figure is a single Yamantaka, the only one remaining in Tibet to have been built at the time of Tsongkhapa and seen by the master. Dharmaraja, two aspects of Pelden Masung Gyelpo, a four-armed and a two-armed Mahakala, Gompo Guru, Dharmaraja with consort, Vaishravana on a lion, a large image of Jamsing, and a White Brahma are also present. Also of note are the beautiful wrathful masks hanging from the walls and the armor from the pillars.

The Main Hall. The outstanding image here is that of Jamchen Chöje himself.

The smiling, radiant face of the statue is crowned with a distinctive black hat around which are Sanskrit letters. (Such a hat was probably given to him by Emperor Yung-lo, who gave a very similar one to the Fifth Karmapa just two years before Jamchen Chöje arrived at the court in Nanking.) It is said that when the new main assembly hall (5) was built, it was planned to move this statue there, but at the moment of departure, the statue announced that it would prefer to stay put. A copy was placed in the main assembly hall instead.

Many other Sera lamas sit to either side of Jamchen Chöje. An expressive image of the first abbot of Sera, Gyeltsen Zangpo, sits to the left between Maitreya and Pabongka Rinpoche. He is recognizable by his stern expression and goatee. Second from the end on the right is a large figure of Jetsun Chökyi Gyeltsen, the Sera lama who wrote the standard textbooks for the college. Next to him is a smaller statue of Lodrö Rinchen, the founder of Sera Je college. Sanggye Tenzin, the first abbot of Sera Ngag-pa, is one of the figures in the front row.

The Upper Story. The long front room on the upper story is the Rabse Lhakhang, a meeting room for the monks with a number of tangkas on the walls. The only chapel on the upper floor is dedicated to Buddha Amitabha, a rather unattractive but perhaps ancient statue of whom sits as the central image. To the left is a stupa containing the relics of Gyeltsen

Zangpo, and to the right a stupa with the relics of the great debater Chökyi Gyeltsen. The Eight Medicine Buddhas surround the shrine. The fifteen buddhas painted on the walls outside the chapel are connected to the fifteen days of the Mönlam festival.

Sera Je College (3)

The Chapels. The first chapel is not entered from the rear of the main hall but through a doorway in the left-hand wall. This leads you into a shrine with tall figures of the Buddhas of the Three Times, accompanied by the Eight Great Bodhisattvas. However, this chapel serves more as an anteroom that leads into the most holy shrine in Sera Je, the Hayagriva chapel.

You may have to join a long queue of people waiting to enter the Hayagriva chapel, circumambulate the deity, and press their heads respectfully to his feet. Hayagriva (the Horse-Headed One) is the main protector of Sera Je. This dark and mysterious shrine was erected by the college's founder, Lodrö Rinchen, and since then has become an important place of pilgrimage. Hanging from the blackened upper walls and ceiling are numerous suits of armor, chain mail, helmets, swords, and other weapons. These were offered long ago by Tibetan soldiers as gifts of peace after the sufferings of a long campaign. The beaten bronze front of the deity's shrine is noteworthy for the craftsmanship.

The first chapel behind the back wall is a shrine to Maitreya: a large image of

PART ONE: LHASA

20. Pilgrims in Lhasa

21. Typical Tibetan window with flowers

22. Pilgrims' market in Lhasa

23. Roof ornaments on the Jokhang Cathedral

24. Kashmiri Mosque in Lhasa

25. Performing prostrations in front of the Jokhang Cathedral

26. Main shrine at the Jokhang

27. Jowo Rinpoche image in the Jokhang

28. Padmasambhava statue in the Jokhang

29. Making statues of Padmasambhava in the Jokhang

30. Statue of Songtsen Gampo's wife, Wen Cheng, in the Jokhang

31. Nun offering a mandala in the Jokhang

32. Nomadic sang merchant in front of the Jokhang

33. Nuns at Ani Sangkung

THE POTALA

34. Potala Palace

35. Statue of Songtsen Gampo in the Potala Palace

36. Mural depicting yogic techniques at the Lukhang

37. Three dimensional Kalachakra mandala with deity at the Potala

38. Sang burner outside Palhalupuk

39. Palden Lhamo in Palhalupuk with images of Guru Rinpoche and Yamantaka

40. Door ornament, Norbulingka Palace

41. The Norbulingka Palace

42. Monks at Drepung sewing the great Shakyamuni tangka

43. Courtyard of the Ganden Palace at Drepung

44. Yogurt festival at Drepung Monastery

45. Destroyed buildings at Drepung Monastery

46. Senior monks and students at Sera Monastery

the future Buddha with Tsongkhapa and his two chief disciples before him adorns the chapel. Other famous Geluk and Sera lamas, the Eight Medicine Buddhas, and several stupas are also here. In the wall facing the shrine are the Sixteen Arhats in grottoes. Scriptures of the Kangyur are housed in the surrounding walls.

The following chapel is in honor of Tsongkhapa, a large statue of whom overshadows the two Buddha images seated to either side. A number of other images of the master with his two main disciples are present, as are several other important lamas from the Geluk order. Nagarjuna and other Indian masters are also represented. The chapel is guarded by the ever-watchful Hayagriva and Achala.

The final chapel has as its main figure a delightful image of Manjushri in the posture of turning the wheel of Dharma. You will notice that the smiling head and torso are slightly inclined toward the window on the right (which has recently been bricked up for security against thieves). The debating courtyard is immediately outside, and it is said that Manjushri is listening eagerly to the discussion taking place beyond the wall. Maitreya and a simple form of Manjushri sit to his sides.

The Main Hall. Since the Hayagriva chapel houses the holiest image in Sera Je, there is no obviously central image in the main hall. The empty seat reserved for the Dalai Lama has pride of place; beneath it is a smaller throne reserved for the Panchen Lama. The altar is crowded with images. To the left of the throne are a statue of the Thirteenth Dalai Lama; three stupas containing the relics of lamas from Sera who had reached eminent positions in the Geluk hierarchy, such as Ganden Tripa (Throne Holder of Ganden) or tutor to a Dalai Lama; and a stupa containing the relics of Miwang Paluwa, a scion of the powerful Miwang family who sponsored the construction of Sera Je. A row of lamas including Tsongkhapa sit to the right. The founder of Sera Je, Lodrö Rinchen, is fourth to the right. More smaller stupas with the relics of Sera lamas are at the end.

The Upper Story. The first chapel to the left is again consecrated to Hayagriva, but this time to a small, nine-headed, multi-armed aspect of the deity. Two statues of Padmasambhava also adorn the shrine as does one of the Fifth Dalai Lama. In a row of glass cases in the wall above the Fifth Dalai Lama are many small, well-executed images of various wrathful deities and protectors, as well as a lama-artist called Kunkhyenpa (Omniscient One) who constructed the main image of Hayagriva downstairs. A new chapel is being erected on the upper floor of this one.

Opposite is a newly opened Tukje (compassion) Chapel with a thousand-armed Avalokiteshvara as the main statue. Among the various images on display are three large old tangkas of

Amitabha, Shakyamuni and the Sixteen Arhats, and the Eight Medicine Buddhas by the exit door.

The Debating Courtyard. This large, walled courtyard is to the right of Sera Je. Here hundreds of red-robed monks would sit, often in the shade of its many magnificent trees, engaged in philosophical debate. In the center of the courtyard is a small stone shrine covering a large bare rock. According to tradition, while Tsongkhapa was composing his commentary to Nagarjuna's *Root Verses on the Middle Way* in his tiny hermitage above what would later be Sera, thirteen letter A's hovered in the space above him. When the work was completed, the letters descended to the ground below and embedded themselves in this rock. Because of the offerings thrown onto the rock by devout Tibetans, they are barely discernible today. At the far end of the courtyard is the raised platform where formal examinations are held. The monks may still be seen engaging in this old Indian form of debate.

On the way to Hamdong Khangtsen, on the far side of the debating courtyard, is a rock with some painted carvings of Avalokiteshvara, Manjushri, and Vajrapani, as well as Green Tara and some mantras.

Hamdong Khangtsen (4)

This khangtsen is one of the largest and best preserved in Sera. It was built by later generations of the Miwang family, who had supported Tsongkhapa and built Sera Je College. Many of the monks studying at Sera Je would live here.

The Chapels. There are two chapels at the back. The first is a long room containing a central image of Maitreya. To his left is a statue of a recent lama, Tubten Kunga, who died only in 1962 and was responsible for a great deal of restoration work shortly before the Cultural Revolution undid his labors. Attached to a pillar on the left is an encased statue of Tara. This revered image is said to have spoken on several occasions. She safeguards the spring that supplies Sera with its water. A long train of offered bangles and other items hangs beneath her. Gold-on-red images of Amitayus are painted over the back wall.

The other chapel is a protector shrine to Gyelchen Karma Tinley, a minor manifestation of Hayagriva who is regarded as the special protector of Hamdong Khangtsen. An assistant deity stands to either side of him and Vaishravana looks on.

The Main Hall. The central place is occupied by a throne for the Dalai Lama. To the left are Amitabha, Drubkhang Gelek Gyatso, Purchok Ngawang Jampa, and Chökyi Gyeltsen; to the right are Shakyamuni, Jamchen Chöje, a Medicine Buddha, and the longevity triad of Tara, Amitayus, and Vijaya.

Below Hamdong Khangtsen, directly

opposite the debating courtyard, is Denma Khangtsen, a smaller house that is part of Hamdong.

The Assembly Hall [Tsog-chen] (5)

This is the largest building in Sera. Traditionally, it was the place where, on special occasions, all monks from the three colleges would congregate. Since nowadays there are fewer monks, this hall is used for all the gatherings of the monastery. If you approach the assembly hall from the Sera Je debating courtyard, enter the building from the rear, which brings you in at the upper story.

The Upper Story. On the left at the back you will find an old and rather appealing chapel dedicated to Avalokiteshvara. The central figure, with a thousand arms and eleven heads, is a small standing image with delicate features. To the left are two encased images made of stone that must be either Indian or Nepalese in origin. They represent a four-armed Mahakala and Vaishravana.

Crossing over an empty room, which leads out to the ground level behind the hall, you enter the chapel into which the head of the Maitreya statue below protrudes. It is revealing to observe the features from above as well as from below. A small image of Tsongkhapa can be seen enshrined in Maitreya's heart. Several other images are present, including, in the far right-hand corner, a Buddha whose bronze or copper halo seems Indian in design.

The final chapel contains a simple fig-ure of Shakyamuni surrounded by several deities and lamas.

The Chapels. The first chapel is dedicated to the Buddha and the Sixteen Arhats. The second houses a tall, seated Maitreya flanked by the Eight Great Bodhisattvas, with Hayagriva and Achala as protectors. The third chapel contains Tsongkhapa and his two chief disciples, behind whom hangs a very fine silk-appliqué tangka of the Fifth Dalai Lama. The protector chapel to the far right is dominated by Yamantaka and his consort.

The Main Hall. Of particular note in this huge room are the two magnificent appliqué tangkas that hang from ceiling to floor depicting Green Tara on the left and Mahakala on the right. The murals are older than usual and worth studying; they include Yamantaka, Guhyasamaja, Samvara, Kalachakra, and scenes from the life of Shakyamuni. This hall also has a more lived-in feel to it: the rows of padded seats are clearly in daily use. Several times each month one can participate in the services held here with all four hundred monks of Sera.

The main images behind the large throne for the Dalai Lama are Jamchen Chöje, the founder of Sera, flanked by the Fifth and Thirteenth Dalai Lamas. Just to the right of center is a giant and very beautiful seated statue of Maitreya, whose head reaches to the upper story. To the left is the Seventh Dalai Lama in front of whom sit Chökyi Gyeltsen,

Tsongkhapa, and a small unusual image of Desi Sanggye Gyatso.

The Printing Press. Across the road from the Main Assembly Hall is a recently opened printing press. Stored in here are many of the woodblocks rescued from the famous Sherig (Cultural) Printing Press, which was located in the Zhöl village below the Potala and destroyed during the Cultural Revolution. The monks have recarved many of the missing or worn blocks. The complete works of Tsongkhapa and his two chief disciples, Gyaltsab and Khedrup, are now available here.

Tsongkhapa's Hermitage [Chö Ding Khang] (6)

To reach the hermitage you must find the narrow path that leads up the mountainside opposite the assembly hall. (The easiest way is to follow the telegraph wires.) On your way you will pass several interesting painted reliefs on large boulders. The most striking ones are those of Dharmaraja and consort, Tsongkhapa, and Jamchen Chöje. A fine relief of several Taras can also be found a little farther up.

The hermitage is a simple, ocher-colored, square building. The original was destroyed during the Cultural Revolution, but a replica has been built on the same site. The room inside is quiet and austere, with a simple altar with a mandala on it. The image of Tsongkhapa adorned the altar until 1992, when it was stolen along with two rare texts. The walls are

painted with murals of Tsongkhapa and his disciples, Indian pandits, deities, and protectors. It was here, at the beginning of the fifteenth century, that Tsongkhapa composed two of his last works: his commentary to Nagarjuna's *Root Verses on the Middle Way* and his study of the two principal schools of Mahayana Buddhist philosophy, *The Essence of True Eloquence.*

The larger building in front of the hermitage used to be a retreat house for the monks of the tantric colleges in Lhasa. You enter by stairs leading to the upper story. The temple itself is bare, with images of Tsongkhapa and his two disciples, to the left of whom sits Sherab Senge, the founder of the Lower Tantric College (Gyume).

To the east of this temple is a level, fenced-off area, which used to be a debating courtyard. The newly built structure up the hill farther to the east contains the old teaching throne of Tsongkhapa. Beyond that are the ruins of the hermitage of his disciples Gyeltsab Je and Khedrup Je. Below these ruins is a shady grove with a spring that was supposedly created by Tsongkhapa's protectress deity while he was in retreat here.

The elevated vantage point of the hermitage offers a good panoramic view of Sera. The easternmost complex of buildings is Tsamlo Khangtsen, which is still to be renovated. In front of the yellow roof below is Gomde Khangtsen of Sera Je, which is being restored. Tehor Khangtsen of Sera Je is also visible.

High in the barren hillside above Sera are the remains of the small hermitage built by Drubkhang (Meditation Cell) Gelek Gyatso during the time of the Seventh Dalai Lama. After his death the place grew into a retreat complex able to accommodate twenty to thirty monks. It was destroyed during the Cultural Revolution but partially restored by the Panchen Lama in 1986. A single chapel has been built around the meditation cell of Gelek Gyatso, and a handful of monks reside there.

11
PABONGKA PALACE & CHUB SANG NUNNERY

The historically important site of Pabongka is seven km (about four miles) northwest of Lhasa. Take the road to Sera and turn left at the hospital. After five km the road forks. Take the left fork for Pabongka. The right fork leads to Chub Sang Nunnery, which is also described in this chapter.

History

Before Songtsen Gampo built the Jokhang and his palace on the Red Hill, he established a retreat house on a large flat rock at Pabongka. At the end of the eighth century, during the reign of Trisong Detsen, the first seven monks ordained in Tibet by Shantarakshita also stayed here. A number of buildings have stood at this site over the centuries. At the beginning of this century, Pabongka was the seat of the powerful Geluk lama of the same name who lived 1871–1941. Pabongka Rinpoche composed many Geluk liturgical works that are still used in the monasteries today. A lama at Sera Monastery, he was a powerful religious and political figure and the main teacher of Trijang Rinpoche, the junior tutor of the present Dalai Lama. Many Geluk lamas active in the West today trace their lineages back through him.

The Site

The buildings, which dated back to the seventeenth century, were razed during the Cultural Revolution. Reconstruction started in 1986, and today the complex of buildings at Pabongka functions as a small Geluk monastery with twenty-six monks.

The first building you reach is the large, square **Nyung-ne** (Fasting) **Temple**. At present the assembly hall is largely unpainted and contains only a throne for the Dalai Lama and a few statues. The most important place here is the chapel at the rear built over the self-originated images in the rock of the Protectors of the Three Realms (Avalokiteshvara, Manjushri, and Vajrapani). This shrine possibly dates back to the time of the early kings.

The path winds up the hill to the somewhat forbidding structure of the Heruka Palace, built on the large rock where Songtsen Gampo had his original retreat. You enter the building by circumambulating to the left. Just before some steps is a door to the right that takes you into the small **Lhamo Temple**, a cave in the rock dedicated to Pelden Lhamo, a self-originated image of whom is the first figure on the wall on the left. Images of Songtsen Gampo and his wives, Shantarakshita, Trisong Detsen, and Padmasambhava are on the altar. Follow the steps up and go round to the back of the building, where you will find stairs that take you into the **Heruka Palace** itself.

The palace is essentially a shrine to the early Yarlung kings who established Tibet as a nation and introduced Buddhism. You follow a long corridor until reaching a door on the left, which leads into a chapel containing images of the early kings on the left and more recent Geluk lamas on the right. The next doorway on the right leads to the main assembly room called the Potrang Khang (palace room). The main figure on the altar is Shakyamuni. Images of the early kings and the Fifth Dalai Lama are to the left as you come in. Other statues include the Thirteenth Dalai Lama and Tsongkhapa and his two chief disciples. A doorway leads from here to a protector chapel at the back with the main Geluk tantric deities and protectors.

There is a small shrine room on the roof, which contains a miscellaneous collection of statues of well-known lamas and deities. The room is reserved as quarters for the Dalai Lama. A bed awaits him in the far right-hand corner.

Farther up the hill past the ruins of stupas that contained the relics of former Pabongka Rinpoches is a yellow building containing two chapels: on the right one dedicated to Tsongkhapa, with five large statues representing, perhaps, the five aspects of the master as he appeared to his disciple Khedrup Je; and on the left one dedicated to the Eight Medicine Buddhas. On the roof is a small room called the Gyeltsab Potrang (regent's palace) with a selection of small statues.

On leaving this building take the right-hand path toward the two restored stupas.

There used to be four stupas at Pabongka, enshrining beads from Tsongkhapa's rosary. The beads were lost or destroyed with the stupas. On the left of the two stupas is a square **Mani Temple**, containing a large prayer wheel, an altar, and some statues. In the house above the temple are living ten or so nuns.

CHUB SANG NUNNERY

The nunnery is two kilometers up the right-hand fork before Pabongka.

Chub Sang Nunnery was founded in the seventeenth century at the time of the Fifth Dalai Lama. Its name literally means "good water." Prior to 1959 it was home to three hundred nuns. Badly damaged during the Cultural Revolution, it has now been partially restored and houses more than a hundred nuns.

The nunnery itself is on the hill behind the complex of buildings. Follow a tortuous path up to the left through the residential area until you reach a small shaded courtyard. The shrine on the rock to the right is to the female deity Vijaya. Other carved images are also painted on the rocks nearby. The path edges around a ravine to the west, bringing you to a rock shrine to White Tara. Finally you reach a tree-lined yard. A gate at the left leads into the courtyard of the nunnery's small temple. The main image is of Tsongkhapa and his two disciples, to the right of whom is a stone image of the Buddha that was presented to the nuns by the Fifth Dalai Lama when the nunnery was opened. The statues on the long altar are, from the left, Ling Rinpoche, Pabongka Rinpoche, and Trijang Rinpoche, followed by an unusual image of the Indian pandit Chandrakirti.

The newly restored, main **assembly hall** is above the temple in a large, open area planted with many young trees. The first room is a mani temple with two large prayer wheels and the Thirty-Five Confessional Buddhas around the walls. A door at the back brings you into the main hall itself, where a throne for the Dalai Lama has pride of place. Images of the Kadampa triad of Atisha, Drom Tönpa, and Ngog Legpa'i Sherab are to the left of the main Buddha image on the altar. The Fifth Dalai Lama and Tsongkhapa and his two main disciples are to the right. In front of them are old statues of a rare triad of lamas: Chongsawa, Tsongkhapa, and Pamotrupa.

A large red building containing the quarters of the Panchen Lama is further down the hill, but this is still in poor repair.

On a hill high above the nunnery one can see Tashi Chöling, a monastery with twenty monks affiliated to Sera.

PART TWO
U—CENTRAL TIBET

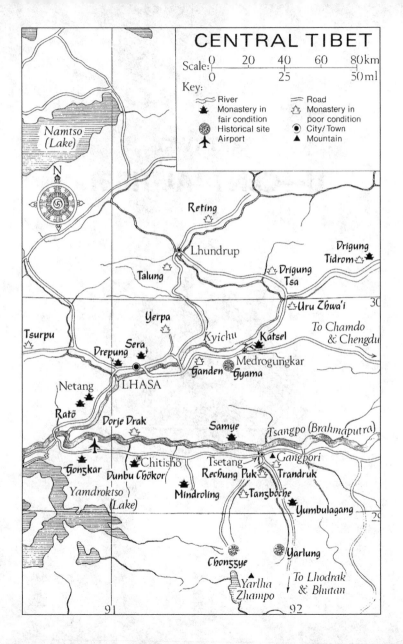

CENTRAL TIBET

Scale:

| 0 | 20 | 40 | 60 | 80 km |

| 0 | 25 | 50 ml |

Key:
- ~~~ River
- 🏛 Monastery in fair condition
- ⊚ Historical site
- ✈ Airport
- ═══ Road
- ☆ Monastery in poor condition
- ◉ City/Town
- ▲ Mountain

Namtso (Lake)

N

Reting

Lhundrup

Drigung Tidrom

Talung

Drigung Tsa

Uru Zhwa'i

Yerpa

Kyichu

Katsel

To Chamdo & Chengdu

Tsurpu

Sera

Drepung

Medrogungkar

Ganden

Gyama

Netang

LHASA

Ratö

Dorje Drak

Samye

Tsangpo (Brahmaputra)

Gongkar

Chitishö

Tsetang

Gangpori

Dunbu Chökor

Rechung Puk

Trandruk

Yamdroktso (Lake)

Mindroling

Tangboche

Yumbulagang

Chongzye

Yarlung

To Lhodrak & Bhutan

Yarlha Zhampo

91

92

12
GANDEN MONASTERY

Ganden, the fifteenth-century monastery of Tsongkhapa and main center of the Geluk order, is located about 40 km (25 mi) east of Lhasa. To reach it you must cross the Lhasa bridge and head out along the main road in the direction of Medrogungkar. The monastery is on the hillside, hidden from the road itself. About halfway to Medrogungkar you turn sharply right, and after a couple of kilometers sharply right again. For the next half hour you climb up a tortuous series of hairpin bends that lead to the monastery itself. The monastery is open daily.

FROM LHASA TO GANDEN

About 10 km (6 mi) out of Lhasa you pass nearby Tselgungtang Monastery. This is off the road, on the hillside to the right. Tselgungtang was a major Kagyu monastery, founded in 1175 by Tsöntru Trakpa (or Lama Zhang), a disciple of Gampopa's nephew. It became the center of the Tsel suborder of the Kagyupa and in the twelfth and thirteenth centuries wielded considerable political influence. In the sixteenth century, the monastery was taken over by the Gelukpa and suffered the ironic fate of being burnt down in 1546 by followers of the Kagyu order who were struggling for power against the Gelukpa in

Central Tibet. Although it was rebuilt, it thereafter ceased to be an important center. It was completely destroyed during the Cultural Revolution.

Farther along the road to Ganden you pass through Taktse Dzong (formerly Dechen Dzong), a small town recognizable by the steep hillock around which it is built. A small temple can be found amid the ruins of the castle on the hilltop. Shortly after this town is the newly built Taktse Zamchen (Great Taktse Bridge) where the road crosses the river on its way to Penyul (see chapter 14).

Ganden and Taktse Dzong are the starting points for the four- to five-day hike across the mountains to Samye Monastery. Taking you through wild and spectacular scenery, these are tough walks and should not be undertaken without adequate preparation. One has to cross remote passes above 5,000 m (16,000 ft) and there are no provisions along the route.

History

Tsongkhapa was born in 1357 in Amdo, the northeastern province of Tibet. During the time of the Third Dalai Lama his birthplace was marked by the erection of the Kumbum Jampa Ling Monastery near Xining. While still very young he was recognized as possessing unusual spiritual qualities and as a young man was sent to Central Tibet to further his understanding of Buddhism in the more cultured region of the country. The first monastery he visited was that of Drigung, where he studied medicine and

Ganden Monastery, 1949

the doctrines of the Kagyu lineage. From here he proceeded to Netang, Samye, Zhalu, and Sakya Monasteries. He met his main teacher, Rendawa, at Tsechen Monastery just outside Gyantse. For many years he studied the full range of Buddhist philosophy, including the more esoteric tantric systems. He then retreated to Olka, north of the Brahmaputra downstream from Tsetang, and spent the next four years in intensive retreat. Upon returning to society he found himself much in demand as a teacher. One place where he taught was the hill in Lhasa on which the Potala was eventually built. Together with Rendawa he stayed for some time at Reting, where he composed his most famous work, *The Great Exposition of the Stages on the Path to Enlightenment*. After another meditation and writing retreat at Chö Ding Hermitage (above where Sera Monastery now is), he founded, in 1409, the famous annual Mönlam

(prayer) festival in Lhasa, which, after a twenty-five year hiatus, was reinaugurated in 1986. (In the political unrest that followed the demonstrations of 1987 and 1988, it was canceled in 1989 and by 1994 had not been resumed.)

After the prayer festival Tsongkhapa decided to found his own monastery. He selected Mount Drokri, a mountain upstream from Lhasa, and called the monastery Ganden, Tibetan for "Tushita," the Pure Land where the future Buddha Maitreya resides. Within a year seventy buildings had been completed, but it was not until 1417 that the main hall of the monastery was consecrated.

Tsongkhapa died at Ganden two years later, in 1419, and shortly before his death passed the mantle of succession to Gyeltsab Je, one of his two chief disciples. Gyeltsab Je held the position of Ganden Tripa (Throne Holder of Ganden) until his own death twelve years later, when it passed to Tsongkhapa's other chief disciple, Khedrup Je. The post of Ganden Tripa was later given to the senior Dharma Master of one of the two main Ganden Colleges, Jangtse and Shartse. It was a five-year post for which to qualify one must first have obtained a geshe degree with highest honors (*lharampa*), proceeded to the abbotship of one of the two Lhasa tantric colleges, and from there been appointed Dharma Master of either Jangtse or Shartse College. The tradition has been continued in India; it is the Ganden Tripa, *not* the Dalai Lama, who heads the Gelukpa order.

During his lifetime Tsongkhapa was regarded as a remarkable spiritual figure whose genius and saintliness held him above the sectarian differences of his times. Although greatly inspired by the example of Atisha, to the point of attributing authorship of his own major written work to him, and by the spirit of the Kadampa tradition, Tsongkhapa nonetheless studied widely with representatives of all the major orders in Tibet and assimilated their lineages. It is uncertain whether he intended to form his own order, though he must have realized it was liable to happen. He could not have foreseen, though, the dimensions this order (the Gelukpa) would eventually assume and the political power it would wield.

Over the following centuries Ganden Monastery grew to the size of a small township, delicately perched along the high sheltered slopes of the mountain. By 1959 this calm, secluded center of learning and contemplation housed more than five thousand monks, but with the Chinese occupation the monks were forced to scatter, and by the mid-1960s the monastery was nearly deserted. The final blow came with the Cultural Revolution. Coerced by the Chinese and caught up in the frenzy and terror of the times, the local Tibetans demolished the buildings. For many years only jagged ruins remained. The greater religious freedom permitted after the death of Mao allowed the laborious and gradual reconstruction of the monastery to begin. One by one the buildings emerged from out of the rubble and monks trickled back to their former home. Yet, perhaps because of its symbolic power as the stronghold of the previous spiritual rule as well as its distance from the capital, Ganden has been rebuilt largely through private funds and has received scant support from the government. Four hundred monks are officially allowed to live here now, although there are around six hundred actually in residence.

The Site

Ganden is one of the most spectacular as well as the most tragic of the sacred sites in Tibet. With very few exceptions, everything in the monastery today is new. Nonetheless, great effort has been made to recreate exactly what was there before. The route we will follow through the monastery is somewhat arbitrary, but it does allow one to visit all the places of importance in a roughly clockwise direction without having to retrace one's steps.

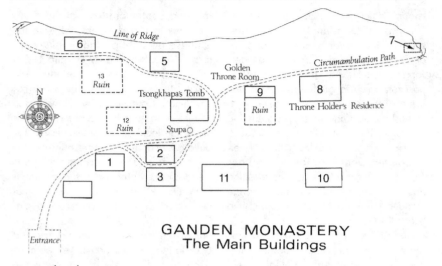

GANDEN MONASTERY
The Main Buildings

Ngam Chö Khang (1)

As you enter the monastery along the main pathway this is the second building on your right. It is a small temple built on the site where, in the earliest days of Ganden's history, Tsongkhapa and his monks would assemble for their daily services. As with nearly every temple in Ganden, the main images in the shrine room are those of Tsongkhapa and his two chief disciples, Khedrup and Gyeltsab. To the left of this triad is a statue of Shakyamuni and to the right another form of Tsongkhapa, in which he is depicted holding a golden vase. To the left of the shrine room is a small chapel dedicated to four protectors: Pelden Lhamo, Mahakala, Dharmaraja, and, on the far right, a large statue of Yamantaka. As with most protector chapels in Ganden, women are not allowed to enter this darkened chamber.

Gomde Khang (2) and Tepu Debating Courtyard (3)

The next building you encounter on your way along the main path is the Gomde Khang (house of meditation). It is now merely used as accommodation for the monks. Immediately below is the Tepu Debating Courtyard. This is a good example of a formal debating courtyard (*chöra*) where the monks would meet after their daily lessons to analyze the meaning of what they had learned. The raised dais at the back is where examinations would be held.

Tsongkhapa's Golden Tomb [Ser Dung] (4)

This impressive structure is the most prominent building in Ganden. It is easily recognized by its high, inward-sloping, red walls with four small windows at the top. Immediately below it is a recently completed white stupa containing a variety of sacred scriptures and other artifacts, presumably some of the scattered, broken remains recovered after the destruction.

As you enter the Ser Dung from the upper right side you find yourself in the monks' **assembly hall**. A large throne for the Dalai Lama is at the front. On tiered shelves around the room are clay images of Tsongkhapa. Also in this room are images of Tsongkhapa and his two disciples, as well as a three-dimensional mandala of Dharmaraja.

To the left as you enter is a door leading into a large bare room containing a single copper and gold statue of Shakyamuni. Neatly arranged on shelves around the room are a thousand painted clay images representing the thousand buddhas of this eon.

A doorway at the back right leads into a **Protector Chapel**. The main image is of a single Yamantaka. To his sides are a four-armed Pelden Lhamo, a six-armed Mahakala, and three smaller Mahakala images. To the far right is a large statue of Dharmaraja. On the black walls are paintings of various aspects of Dharmaraja.

The stairs to the right of the doorway lead into a large empty assembly room with a throne for the Dalai Lama. From here a doorway on the right leads to the slightly raised chapel called the **Yangchen Khang**, where Tsong-

khapa's remains are entombed in a giant silver and gold stupa. It is said that when Tsongkhapa died his body assumed the form of a sixteen-year-old youth. This was then embalmed and enshrined in a massive stupa. When the stupa was broken open during the Cultural Revolution, the Red Guards were horrified to discover the body in perfect condition, its hair and fingernails still growing. It was destroyed nonetheless. Only some fragments of the skull were saved, and these are now housed in the present stupa. Seated before the stupa are images of Tsongkhapa and his two chief disciples.

The chamber is called the Yangchen Khang because of a large stone that is believed to have flown miraculously to this spot from the Buddhist city of Yangpachen (Vaishali) in India. The stone is visible, embedded at the base of the wall in the rear left-hand corner of the room. It is of interest to study the contents of a small glass case in front of the stupa to the left, which are said to be the begging bowl and wooden teacup used by Tsongkhapa; a thirteen-deity Yamantaka owned by Khedrup Je; a large vajra once held by Tsongkhapa; a small silver stupa in which one of the master's teeth is kept; and a horn from Tsongkhapa's *dzo* (a cow-yak hybrid) with twenty-one self-originated images of Tara inside.

A doorway on the far side of the room from where you entered leads to the **Dezhek Lhakhang**. The two largest images are those of Shakyamuni and Maitreya surrounded by bodhisattvas and stupas, one of which (in a separate case) contains the relics of Paso Rinpoche from Ganden. To the right are statues of Atisha, Drom Tönpa, and Ngog Legpa'i Sherab.

On the roof of the Ser Dung is a newly opened printing house. It contains recently carved woodblocks made in Nyemo (west of Lhasa) of the Sera and Drepung college textbooks. The collected works of Tsongkhapa and his two disciples are now being carved. The chapel next door houses many small, old bronzes from Ganden recently returned to the monastery.

Immediately behind the Ser Dung is a newly constructed **Maitreya Chapel** containing a large image of the future Buddha and statues of Tsongkhapa and his two disciples.

Also newly constructed behind the Ser Dung is the **Zungjug Khangtsen**. The main chapel on the upper story is fairly bare; the largest statue on the altar is of Pabongka Rinpoche, an influential Gelukpa lama of the early part of this century. Other images in cabinets in the room are: Vaishravana, Tsongkhapa and his two main disciples, the Twenty-One Taras, and Shakyamuni. The downstairs room is empty.

The building beside Zungjug Khangtsen is the **Tsar Khangtsen.** Further up the hill is a chapel. These were reconstructed only in 1991.

Amdo Khangtsen (5)

The Amdo Khangtsen is where monks from the northeastern province of Amdo (now Qinghai) were housed when they came to train in Ganden. Since Tsongkhapa came from Amdo, even today monks from this region consider themselves to have a special affinity with Ganden.

The main chapel in Amdo Khangtsen is richly decorated with brocade hangings and murals. On the wall to the left are found paintings of the Thirty-Five Confessional Buddhas. The main statues along the back wall are (from the left) Amnye Machen, the protector deity of the famous mountain of the same name in Amdo, devotion to which was introduced by Tsongkhapa into Central Tibet; what is believed to be an eye of the protector Dharmaraja in a small glass case; and a small painted stone image of Tara that is said to have spoken.

Dreu Khangtsen (6)

There is little of note in this khangtsen. The main images are again those of Tsongkhapa and his two chief disciples. To their left one can see a small painted stone image of Manjushri, regarded by the monks as being miraculously formed.

If one walks further along the ridge of the mountain past Dreu Khangtsen, one will find the beginning of a path that leads around the back of the hill, allowing pilgrims to circumambulate the monastery. From the path you can look across the wide Kyichu basin at the distant valleys and mountains that recede to the far horizon. The clear, thin air at this altitude allows an extraordinary feeling of spaciousness. All along the path you will notice small, crudely made shrines covered with prayer flags and other devotional objects. Allow about one hour for completion of the circumambulation route.

Tsongkhapa's Hermitage (7)

This small building suddenly protrudes from the mountainside as the path curves around the hill on its way back to the monastery. This is one of the places where Tsongkhapa stayed in retreat when he first came to Central Tibet. Inside the cave an image of Tsongkhapa is carved in relief on the stone wall, and to show his particular connection with the Kadampa tradition, carved images of Atisha and Drom Tönpa are placed above his shoulders. A handprint of Tsongkhapa is visible in one corner.

Shortly after this hermitage, one can see another shrine built higher up on the mountain slope. This was where Tsongkhapa would worship his protector deity Dharmaraja, a painted relief carving of whom is visible from the path.

The Residence of the Throne Holder of Ganden [Tri Dok Khang] (8)

The Tri Dok Khang is the official residence of the Ganden Tripa, the Throne Holder of Ganden, the monk elected to be the titular head of the Gelukpa order. The difficulties in describing this labyrinthine building are compounded by the fact that one can enter either from the top or the bottom.

If you enter from the front (bottom), climb up two flights of stairs. After pass-

ing through a doorway on your left, turn right. The first room on your right is where Tsongkhapa died. This bare and dimly lit room contains only a vacant throne. The walls, however, are richly painted with deities, predominant among which are various aspects of Manjushri, with whom Tsongkhapa had a special relationship. The other images are of Guhyasamaja, Vijaya, and Amitayus. Dharmaraja and Mahakala guard the doorway.

The next room on the right is where the Dalai Lama would traditionally stay on his visits to Ganden. In addition to the cabinets with various deities and Tsongkhapa are two beds. The room across the corridor is similarly reserved for visits of the Panchen Lama.

A well-illuminated chapel on the upper story houses a complete set of the Kangyur. These long, cloth-wrapped texts are set in the rear wall to either side of statues of Tsongkhapa and his two chief disciples. To the far side of the room is one of the thrones used by the Ganden Tripa (the main one being in the Golden Throne Room next door).

At the end of this upper courtyard, on the left, is the **Samvara Chapel**. This typically darkened tantric shrine with black walls covered with ferocious images contains, in addition to the main figure of Samvara, statues of Tsongkhapa's disciple Khedrup Je and Mahakala. To the right of the altar is a cabinet with a small figure of Vajrayogini and an ancient image of Mahakala. On a beam in front of the altar is a face of Yamantaka that survived the Cultural Revolution.

Straight ahead as you come up the stairs is the Dzom Chen Khang. The main images in this well-lit and spacious room are Tsongkhapa and his two main disciples. To the left is a large image of Shakyamuni and to the right one of Trijang Rinpoche, the late junior tutor to the present Dalai Lama. In addition to cabinets containing various images is a throne for the Dalai Lama.

To the left of the Tri Dok Khang is the small debating courtyard of the Throne Holder of Ganden.

The Golden Throne Room [Ser Tri Khang] (9)

This narrow, red building between the residence of the Throne Holder of Ganden and the Golden Tomb of Tsongkhapa was one of the first to be reconstructed in the early 1980s. In 1994 it was demolished as part of the reconstruction of the massive Ganden assembly hall immediately in front of it. It will be rebuilt once the assembly hall is completed. Until then, the throne and other relics are housed in the Maitreya chapel behind the Ser Dung. The description that follows was made in 1986.

The Ser Tri Khang contains a single high-ceilinged chapel in which the golden throne of Tsongkhapa and the Ganden tradition stands beneath three giant images of the master and his two disciples. Lying on the throne in a grimy cloth bag are the shoes of the present Dalai Lama, left behind after his flight to India, and the hat of the Ninety-sixth

Throne Holder of Ganden. Only three lamas have been allowed to sit on this throne: Tsongkhapa, the Ganden Tripa, and the Dalai Lama. It faces a large doorway that looks out onto the main assembly area of Ganden.

On the middle story is a room containing an edition of the Tengyur, and on the upper story two rooms with an edition of the Kangyur, which the monks will unlock upon request. These texts were removed by the Chinese and returned only recently through the efforts of the late Panchen Lama. In one of the Kangyur rooms is a long, carved, ornate altar with many small images of deities, lamas, and stupas.

Nyare Khangtsen (10)

The chapel of Nyare Khangtsen consists of a small room, warmly lit with butter lamps. In the cabinets are images of Mahakala, Shakyamuni, Maitreya, Green Tara, Atisha, Drom Tönpa and Ngog Legpa'i Sherab, Vaishravana with a spear, and Sertrakpa.

Ngari Khangtsen (11)

The well-maintained chapel in Ngari Khangtsen contains a set of images that distinguishes it from the other khangtsens. The main figure is a large image of Tsongkhapa seated alone without the company of his chief disciples. The facial features of this statue are very pronounced, perhaps in an attempt to capture the expression preserved on the images dating from the time of the master himself. To his left are Atisha, Drom

Tönpa, and Ngog Legpa'i Sherab, and to his right Panchen Sonam Drakpa, the Second Panchen Lama, with Chökyi Gyeltsen and Dondze Drakpa Gyeltsen, a renowned lama from Ganden.

Jangtse and Shartse Colleges (12–13)

Jangtse and Shartse were both founded by disciples of Tsongkhapa, the former by Namkha Pelzangpo, and the latter by Neten Ronggyelwa. These two principal colleges of Ganden are largely still in ruins, although in 1994 reconstruction of the Shartse assembly hall was under way. Their approximate locations are shown on the plan by dotted lines. Traditionally, monks from the different khangtsens would belong to one of these two colleges, where they would gather for services and engage in their studies. Both these colleges have been reestablished in South India, where they continue to train monks.

13
DRAK YERPA

Drak Yerpa is 45 km (28 mi) northeast of Lhasa, a journey that takes between one and a half and two hours by jeep. From Lhasa you follow the road toward Ganden until you reach the large Tagtse Bridge 26 km (16 mi). Cross the bridge and continue for 2 km (1.2 mi) until the T-junction. Here turn left and continue west along the foot of the mountains for 11 km (6.8 mi) until you reach the old Lhasa road. Turn right up the valley, heading north. Continue for 7 km (4 mi) until you reach a village. From here it is a half-hour walk to the site of Drak Yerpa.

History

Giuseppe Tucci, the Italian scholar and traveler, recorded his first impression of Yerpa in 1949 thus: "Yerpa appeared suddenly before my eyes at a bend of the road, a cascade of small white buildings along steep, green overgrown cliffs. One could have thought one was not in Tibet. Giant junipers and tufts of rhododendron topped a thick tangle of undergrowth, brushwood and grass victoriously fighting the hard barrenness of rocks. The cliffs were riddled with burrows and caves, some of which were so high up on the face of the abrupt hill that it would have been risky to climb them."

Yerpa is said to be the "life tree," or spiritual axis, of Lhasa itself. With more than eighty meditation caves, it was a village of several hundred hermits, monks, and nuns who lived on a site sanctified by Songtsen Gampo, Padmasambhava, Yeshe Tsogyel, Padampa Sanggye, and Atisha. Since the seventh century it has been considered one of the most sacred sites in Central Tibet. Although it suffered terribly during the Cultural Revolution—its monasteries destroyed and its caves

Drak Yerpa with caves in background, 1937

defaced, its trees and shrubs uprooted for firewood—Yerpa still retains the extraordinary natural beauty and dignity of its setting. Drawn by the force of the memory of those who inhabited it before, hermits are slowly returning to its caves, and the shrines are being restored.

The Site

The view from the foot of the towering escarpment at Drak Yerpa is spectacular. Immediately before one is the sacred Lhari, a small domed hill with the words OM MANI PADME HUM inscribed with white rocks on its lower surface. Beyond, the valley descends to the Kyichu River, and in the far distance snow-capped mountains line the horizon.

As you reach Drak Yerpa from the village, the first buildings you reach are the ruins of the summer residence of the Upper Tantric College in Lhasa (see Chapter 3). The five hundred monks of this college would come up here every summer for about two months and continue their study of the tantric doctrines. Not a single chapel remains standing. From this lowest point on the hill one can see another row of ruins slightly higher up to the right. They are all that is left of Yerpa Drubde, a Kadam monastery founded by followers of Atisha, and subsequently a Geluk monastery with up to three hundred monks until 1959. By 1993 a couple of monks had returned to live here.

If you look out toward the distant mountains from here, you can see two isolated ruins down to the left just below the saddle of the ridge that gently rises to the Lhari hill. The farther of these two was the place where Atisha had a small monastery and used to teach; the nearer is where the community of disciples would live. An old Vajrapani stupa and a newly rebuilt white Victory stupa are visible to the left and right of these temples. Behind the ruins can be found the remains of Atisha's teaching throne.

Some of the most important caves are also clearly visible from this vantage point. They lie along the base of the cliff about 150 m (500 ft) from the ruins of the monastery. To the far left is a fissure in the rock face. To the left of this is the tiny cave where Atisha once meditated. This is the **Tendrel Lhakhang** (Chapel of Auspicious Coincidence), so called because when Atisha entered it a rain of flowers fell. Inside the cave is an altar with statues of Atisha, Drom Tönpa, and Ngog Legpa'i Sherab. The cave has been occupied by retreatant Geluk lamas for several years.

Continuing to the right (east), one passes the **Chagna Dorje Puk** (Vajrapani cave), on the ceiling of which is a self-originated head of that bodhisattva, and the **Tse Chu Puk** (tenth-day cave), so called because offering ceremonies are performed here to Padmasambhava, with whom the cave is associated, on the tenth of every lunar month. One then arrives at the largest cave in this complex, the **Jampa Drup Khang** (Maitreya practice chamber). Originally it was believed that the eighty tantric adepts of Yerpa, all of whom were disciples of Padmasambhava, meditated together here (or in the **Druptob Puk**, a smaller cave complex nearby). In the thirteenth century a temple was founded in the cave by Martön Tsultrim Jungne, who commissioned a renowned seated statue of Maitreya. The temple was completely destroyed by the Red Guards but restored in 1987. A two-and-a-half-story replica of the Maitreya statue is now in place. Chapels and an edition of the Kangyur occupy the upper stories of this tidy and well-illuminated temple.

Below the Jampa Drup Khang is the recently restored, small, square **Rigsum Gonpo Chapel** built around rock carvings of Manjushri, Avalokiteshvara, and Vajrapani, believed to have been carved by Songtsen Gampo. A statue of the king is to the left, beneath which is a footprint of Yeshe Tsogyel.

Further along from the Jampa Drup Khang is the **Chögyel Puk** (Dharma King cave), where Songtsen Gampo meditated. You enter through a narrow corridor. On the left is a self-emanated image of the Lion-Faced Dakini. Since the king is credited with introducing the worship of Avalokiteshvara into Tibet, the main statue on the altar is that of his personal deity, the thousand-armed, thousand-eyed Avalokiteshvara—notable for all its faces being wrathful except those at the front and the top. The other image is of Vairochana and is said to come from the Jokhang. The murals are being restored. A prominent figure of Vajrakila,

the Nyingma protector, has been completed. A narrow doorway leads to a tiny cave with a small recess with a statue of Songtsen Gampo on an altar.

Below and slightly to the right of Chögyel Puk is the **Lhakhang**, a well-restored temple that leads inside to two caves. The one on the right is the **Lhalungpa Puk**, associated with the monk Lhalungpa Pelgyi Dorje, who escaped here after assassinating the Bönpo king Langdarma in 842. His hat was enshrined here until 1959. A large image of Padmasambhava is seated before a central pillar. To his sides are his consorts Yeshe Tsogyel and Mandarava and in front of him is a stone with Lhalungpa's name carved on it—brought here from Talung. In the recesses around the walls used to stand images of the Dhyani Buddhas.

Directly above the Lhakhang is the famous **Dawa'i Puk** (moon cave) of Padmasambhava. For the Nyingma tradition Drak Yerpa is the sacred place associated with Padmasambhava's speech. Stairs lead to a large cave with three entrances to a room on the right. Imprints of Padmasambhava's feet (above which is an image of the female deity Ekajati) are found on the far left-hand wall. The chapel also contains images of the eight Taras who protect from fear and the eight manifestations of Padmasambhava. A low doorway on the left takes you into a small, low-ceilinged shrine with Padmasambhava's meditation throne and one of his footprints on the right-hand wall. Still higher up the mountain face are the **Nyima'i Puk** (sun cave), where Padmasam-bhava also meditated, and the **Sang Puk** (secret cave) of Yeshe Tsogyel.

Below and to the east of Dawa'i Puk can be seen the ruins of **Neten Lha-khang** (arhat temple), one of the earliest structures at Yerpa housing images of the Sixteen Arhats brought from China in the eleventh century.

14
TALUNG & RETING MONASTERIES

Both Talung and Reting played roles of great historical importance in Central Tibet. Today they lie largely in ruins, and a visit to the somewhat remote area north of Lhasa to see them may be of limited interest to many visitors.

Talung Monastery is about 120 km (75 mi) from Lhasa depending on the various routes that can be taken through the fertile Penpo Valley (or Penyul) north of the Kyichu. From Lhasa you follow the road toward Ganden until you reach the large Taktse Bridge (26 km; 16 mi). Cross the bridge and continue for 2 km (1.2 mi) until the T-junction. Here turn right and follow the river upstream for 10 km (6 mi) until the road veers left into the Penpo Valley. After 30 km (19 mi) you will reach a crossroads. To follow the main route to Talung, turn right here, and proceed another 35 km (21 mi) via Lhundrup Dzong to the Chak-la pass (5,330 m; 17,300 ft). 11 km (7 mi) below the pass you can see Talung 3 km (2 mi) up a side valley called the Pakchu.

PENYUL

A number of sites in this fertile and culturally important region are worth mentioning. In the eleventh century Penyul was a major center for the teachings of the Kadam school. Atisha taught extensively here, and his disciples subsequently founded Kadampa monasteries. In the following centuries of sectarian and political strife, however, nearly all of these establishments either disappeared or were taken over by monks of the Sakya, Kagyu, or Geluk schools. During the Cultural Revolution, all the monasteries in the area were seriously damaged.

Langtang Monastery can be visited by turning left instead of right at the crossroads mentioned at the beginning of the chapter. This takes you across the Penpo River (often dry) to the remains of the complex, now partly a farming commune with a few buildings restored to their original use. Founded in 1093 by the Kadampa geshe Langri Tangpa (author of the well-known *Eight Verses of Mind Training*), it eventually became a Sakya monastery. The most revered image in the main chapel is one of Tara that has been heard to talk. A few kilometers southwest of Langtang is the famous **Nalendra Monastery**, founded in 1435 by Rongtön Mawa'i Sengge, an exceptionally learned contemporary and rival of Tsongkhapa who trained in the Kadam tradition but was quickly appropriated by the Sakyapa. Since the end of the fifteenth century Nalendra (named after the famous Nalanda Monastery in India) was one of the most extensive and important Sakya monasteries in Tibet. It was totally demolished during the Cultural Revolution, and only a handful of chapels, dwellings, and stupas have so far been restored from the ruins.

If you go straight ahead at the aforementioned crossroads, the road will allow you a view of both Langtang and Nalendra to the left, across the river. It then turns right up a valley. A right turn after about 3 km (2 mi) will take you via the **Shara Bumpa Stupa** to Lhundrup Dzong. This stupa dates back to the twelfth century, when it was erected by a Kadampa master named Sharapa Yönten Drak. Other Kadampa stupas, in various states of repair, surround it. A nearby nunnery is being restored.

Down the valley from Talung, on the road to Pongo Chu and Reting, you pass the rebuilt **Tashi Gomang Stupa**, originally constructed by the former Tibetan government because it was believed that this was the spot from where waters started flowing into Lhasa. Perched on the hillside high above the stupa is the **Sili Götsang Hermitage**, the cave retreat of the third abbot of Talung in the thirteenth-century. It is also associated with the thirteenth century Drukpa Kagyu lama Götsangpa. It used to provide for up to thirty retreatants from Talung but was badly damaged during the Cultural Revolution. It has since been restored and is again in use.

TALUNG MONASTERY
History

Talung Monastery was founded in 1180 by the sage Talung Tangpa Tashi Pel on the site where the Kadampa masters Drom Tönpa and Potowa lived. Talung Tangpa was a disciple of Pamotrupa Dorje Gyelpo in the Kagyu line descended from Gampopa and Milarepa. He was renowned not only for his contemplative insights and powers but also for his austere and simple life. Under the inspiration of its founder, Talung Monastery became well known for its strict adherence to the monastic rules. It grew into a huge monastic establishment, at one time housing up to seven thousand monks. It also became involved in the political upheavals that raged during the thirteenth century and suffered from occasional conflicts with its sister monastery, Drigung. It managed to steer clear of politics until the seventeenth century, when it fell under the control of the Lhasa government. By the time of the Cultural Revolution the number of monks had dwindled to about six hundred, among whom were three lines of incarnate lamas.

The Site

Although reduced to ruins during the Cultural Revolution, four temples in the upper part of the complex have now been restored and 160 monks are in residence. The lower parts are still occupied by local villagers. The site is dominated by the impressive ruins of the Great Jokhang of Talung built in the thirteenth century and one of the most celebrated religious edifices in Tibet.

In 1991 a new assembly hall was opened behind the ruins of the Jokhang. Vajrapani, Hayagriva, and the Four Guardian Kings greet you in the hallway. The main chapel is largely undecorated and devoid of images. In the front of the hall are three thrones: one for the

Dalai Lama (center), one for Mar Rinpoche of Talung (left), and one for Shadrung Rinpoche of Talung (right). The former lives in Dharamsala, India; the latter in Sikkim.

To the left of the assembly hall a gateway leads into a courtyard. On the left-hand side of the courtyard is a protector chapel, while straight ahead steps guarded by wrathful protectors take you to an enclosed verandah. The entrance hallway has murals of Dutse (right), a special guardian of Talung, and Yama on a horse (left). Among the figures on the left-hand wall of the main chapel is a painting of the founder of the monastery, Talung Tangpa. A door on the left leads into a shrine with editions of the Kangyur, Tengyur, and other writings.

A doorway on the right of the veranda leads into a smaller courtyard. The newly built temple on the left is a shrine to the Talung Tangpa, and the main statue on the altar is of him. It is here that the lama went into retreat to perform prostrations. A newly commissioned tangka shows how the monastery used to be.

The building at the left-hand corner of the courtyard is the Sherig Khang, a room mainly used for special ceremonies connected with the lines of lamas of the monastery. The images in the room are predominantly of the present and former incarnations of Talung.

RETING MONASTERY

Reting Monastery is about 150 km (95 mi) north of Lhasa. Instead of turning left to Talung after the Chak-la pass, continue on the same road for another 20 km (12 mi), passing the Tashi Gomang Stupa on your left, to the small town of Pongdo Chu (or Pongdo Dzong), where the road rejoins the Kyichu River. Reting is 24 km (15 mi) from Pongdo on the north bank of the Rongchu Valley.

History

Reting Monastery in its former splendor, 1950

Reting Monastery was the first Kadampa monastery to be founded. Drom Tönpa, Atisha's chief disciple, began building it when he settled here in 1057, three years after his teacher's death. He brought with him some of Atisha's relics and remained until his own death in 1064, both teaching and meditating. Many others who had been similarly inspired by Atisha's approach joined him and around them crystallized what came to be know the Kadam (Spiritual Advice) order of Tibetan Buddhism.

These founders of the order were known as the Kadampa geshes. Only later did the Gelukpa, a later outgrowth of the Kadampa ideal, use the term "geshe" to designate an official degree of learning. After Drom the abbotship passed to his disciple Neljorpa Chenpo, who considerably enlarged the monastery. The well-known Kadampa geshe Potowa also served as abbot for three years in the late eleventh century. In 1240, however, the armies of the expanding Mongol empire penetrated Tibet as far as Reting and laid waste the monastery.

Tsongkhapa joined the monastery in 1397, when he was forty years old. While here he received a vision of Atisha, which inspired him to compose his magnum opus, *The Great Exposition on the Stages on the Path to Enlightenment*. In the wake of Tsongkhapa's reforms, the monastery ceased to be Kadampa and was taken over by the Gelukpa (initially called the New Kadampa Order).

In 1738 the Seventh Dalai Lama appointed his tutor Ngawang Chokden as the abbot of Reting, whose successive incarnations became known as the Reting Rinpoche. Two of these Rinpoches served as regents during the minorities of Dalai Lamas. This regency was effectively the most powerful political office in Tibet. From 1845 to 1855 Tibet was ruled by a Reting Rinpoche, as it was from 1933 to 1947, while the present Dalai Lama was a child. This Fifth Reting Rinpoche was responsible for discovering the Dalai Lama through a vision he saw in the Lhamo'i Latso Lake. But he became caught up in

sexual scandal and political intrigue and was probably murdered in 1947 for his role in an attempted pro-Chinese coup.

The Site

The hill on which Reting stands is scattered with gnarled juniper trees, believed to have sprung from the hair of the monastery's founder, Drom Tönpa. The extensive monastery of Reting was virtually razed during the Cultural Revolution. Over the past ten years monks have returned to the monastery, and reconstruction is slowly proceeding. Today 115 monks are officially registered at Reting, but no more than 60 are in residence at any one time. Tenzin Jigme, the Sixth Reting Rinpoche, lives in Lhasa.

The main assembly hall at Reting was formerly four stories high and supported by one hundred and forty pillars. Since 1984 a more modest building has been erected on its foundations to serve as the main hall. Its walls are decorated with murals of Kadampa and Gelukpa lamas and tantric deities, and the main chapel is surrounded by an internal circumambulation path. The main images in the chapel are preserved from the days of Reting's former glory. The small central gold statue of Manjuvajra (Jampel Dorje) is believed to have been brought from India. Nearby hangs an old tangka of a standing Tara, who is said to have once spoken. In a small cabinet is a black rock with a gray self-originated image of Avalokiteshvara. Also on the walls are three surviving tangkas of a set depicting Atisha and his teacher

Serlingpa and Atisha with Drom Tönpa.

Further up the hill is one other quad-rangle of newly restored buildings. This was formerly one of the most sacred sites of Reting, as both Drom Tönpa and Tsongkhapa taught here. Inside the main chapel are four large statues of Ngog Legpa'i Sherab, Atisha, Maitreya, and Drom Tönpa. To the right of Drom is a throne from which Tsongkhapa first gave his teaching, *The Foundation of All Excellence*, a versified synopsis of the path to enlightenment. To the right of this throne is another that marks the place were the Kadampa geshe Gonpopa had his meditation cell.

To the left of these buildings are the ruins of stupas that contained the remains of many great Kadampa mas-ters, including Atisha and Drom. Behind and to the right of this quadrangle is a small protector chapel dedicated to Damchen Garwa Nagpa, a local deity converted to Buddhism at the time of Padmasambhava. In front of the chapel is the tree in which the protector is sup-posed to live.

The remains of **Yangön Hermitage**, where Tsongkhapa composed *The Great Exposition on the Stages on the Path to Enlightenment,* is located higher on the hill behind the monastery. Drom Tönpa and Talung Tangpa also lived and medi-tated in this hermitage. Even farther up the hill is a red-painted rock that marks the place where the traditional protector deities of Reting dwell.

A further 4 km (2.5 mi) beyond Reting is a small nunnery called **Samdrup Ling** which has expanded considerably over the last few years. At present 150 nuns are connected to the nunnery.

15
DRIGUNG TIL

The head monastery of the Drigung Kagyu order, Drigung Til is located 130 km (81 mi) northeast of Lhasa. It rises spectacularly from a high mountainside at the end of the long valley that begins at Drigung Chu, where the Kyichu makes its last sharp bend before flowing down to Lhasa. It can be reached either downstream from Pongdo Chu or upstream from Lhasa. Both routes offer a number of side trips to other sites which will be described in this chapter.

PONGDO CHU TO DRIGUNG TIL

The road from Pongdo Chu follows the course of the Kyichu along a wide and beautiful valley. From Pongdo you continue for 33 km (20 mi) until you arrive at a village. On the hill behind it is a small monastery called Pemba Gompa, visible from the road. Affiliated with Reting, about twenty monks currently live there.

The small and dilapidated monastery of Drigung Tsa is 56 km (35 mi) from Pongdo, shortly after a large roadside stupa. Drigung Tsa, named "Tsa" (root) because of the belief that it stands over an important water source, was founded by a Drigung Kagyu lama named Tinley Zangpo. It is situated in the middle of a village and hemmed in by houses. You climb up a steep staircase to a small chapel with a variety of tangkas and statues. To the right is a protector shrine

dedicated to the Drigung protectress Abchi Drölma. Drigung Chu and the turnoff to Drigung Til are a further 11 km (7 mi) along the road.

LHASA TO DRIGUNG TIL

From Lhasa you follow the main road toward Medrogungkar, the medium-size town and administrative center for the area, 70 km (44 mi) from the capital. About 8 km (5 mi) before reaching the town is the wide opening to the Gyama Valley, the birthplace of King Songtsen Gampo. The actual birthplace is marked by a small square shrine called Gyelpo Khang (king's house) on the hillside on the left, 2 km (1.2 mi) from the turnoff. It is only open when the caretaker-monk happens to be present. As you continue further up the valley you pass the small Gyama Shar stupa, then, on the right of the valley, Dumbu Ri, the site of a former Kadampa monastery, now marked only by three stupas. A further 4 km (2.5 mi)

Katsel Temple near Medrogungkar, 1949

beyond Gyelpo Khang brings you to Gyama Trikhang, also a former Kadampa monastery, now a village with a small, disused temple and the remains of a large stupa. A third Kadampa (and subsequently Sakya) monastery, Rinchen Gang, is reported to be further still up the valley.

Two km (1.2 mi) west of Medrogungkar is the **Katsel Temple**, one of the "demoness-subduing temples" of Songtsen Gampo (see p. 48). Although damaged during the Cultural Revolution, the temple has been restored in its original design and offers a good example of early Tibetan temple architecture. The wide range of images in the temple reflects the historical significance of the site, while the predominance of Drigung Kagyu lamas and deities indicates the tradition currently in charge of Katsel. The main statues in the assembly hall are the Buddhas of the Three Times. Attached to a pillar on the left is part of a prayer wheel that purportedly belonged to Songtsen Gampo, as well as part of a skull of a deer that appeared while the king was planning the temple. At present thirty-two monks are based at Katsel, and reconstruction is still in progress.

Another place worth visiting in Katsel is the Swedish School, officially opened in September 1994. The school has a hundred students from the age of six to fourteen, fifty of whom are from impoverished villages in the outlying districts. It is a good example of how a Western country can offer concrete help to the Tibetan people.

From Katsel to the bend in the river at Drigung Chu is a further 33 km (20 mi). A kilometer behind Drigung Chu, up a small side valley, is the **Uru Zhwa'i Temple**. Founded at the end of the eighth century by Nyang Tingedzin Zangpo, a minister of Trisong Detsen and later the first Tibetan abbot of Samye, Uru Zhwa'i marks the place where the Kashmiri teacher Vimalamitra composed and concealed the Inner Essence (Nying Tik), a seminal Dzogchen text of the Nyingma school. The monastery was completely destroyed during the Cultural Revolution but is now being rebuilt. The one artifact to have survived is the stele (doring) to the left of the courtyard in front of the temple. It records government grants of land and entitlements to Nyang Tingedzin and his heirs. The remains of a similar stele can be seen on the right. The only shrine so far restored is a protector chapel with images of Padmasambhava, Damchen (on a lion), a ten-headed Tsamdrup, Ekajati, and the great Nyingma lama Longchen Rabjampa. Seven monks have returned to the monastery.

At Drigung Chu you turn right up the deep valley towards Drigung Til. On the north bank of the river, 10 km (6 mi) from Drigung Chu, is **Yangri Gon Monastery**. Founded by Tinley Zangpo, the eighth Drigung Kyapgon, the monastery was destroyed by the Chinese and its grounds turned into a military camp. On the left-hand side of the newly restored building is a painting of how the monastery used to be. At the front of the main hall are three thrones, for the Dalai Lama and the two principal lamas of the Drigung lineage. To the left of the thrones is a statue of the founder of the monastery, and to the right, in a white cabinet, a peaceful aspect of Abchi Drölma, the special protectress of the Drigungpa. Forty-two monks are now settled here, with another forty living at an old hermitage close by.

Drigung Til is a further 30 km (19 mi) up the valley.

History

Although a hermitage was first built on this site by the Kagyu yogi Minyak Gomrim in 1167, in 1179 it became the base of the Drigung suborder of the Kagyu tradition. The monastery was founded by a monk from Kham (1143–1217), a disciple of the great Kagyu lama Pamotrupa, subsequently known as Jigten Sumgon, Lord Protector of Drigung. Due to his influence, the monastery quickly grew in size and reputation and by the thirteenth century was vying with the powerful Sakya order for political power over Tibet. Although Drigung managed to survive an attack in 1240 by the Mongol patrons of the Sakyapa (the same force that destroyed Reting), in 1290 it was burned to the ground by a Sakya army. While Drigung never again aspired to national political power, it continued to be a monastery renowned for training monks in the contemplative tradition. In 1959 there were around 300 monks living here.

The first twenty-three successors of Jigten Sumgon were appointed by a hereditary lineage. Since then Drigung has been headed by two lines of reincarnate lamas, the Chetsang Rinpoche and the Chungtsang Rinpoche. The present Chetsang Rinpoche is the seventh in the line and lives in Piyang Monastery in Ladakh, having escaped from Tibet in 1975. He speaks English and has started teaching in the West. The present Chungtsang Rinpoche resides in Lhasa.

The Site

Although the monastery was badly damaged during the Cultural Revolution, it has recovered remarkably well. Several buildings have been restored and now 116 monks live here, many of whom are in long-term retreat in hermitages on the top of the mountain. Pachung Rinpoche, the meditation master of Drigung who remained here uninterruptedly from 1959, died in 1987. It is possible to stay overnight (usually in a school below the monastery), but you must bring your own food.

You enter the large newly restored Tashi Gomang assembly hall directly from the courtyard (which also serves as a parking lot). The room has thrones for the two lamas of the monastery and houses a variety of statues and texts. The main chapel located on the story above the assembly hall is the Serkhang, whose central image is Jigten Sumgon, the founder of Drigung. Below him is a slab of rock bearing his footprint and to the right a small stupa containing his relics.

Elsewhere in the room are several statues of the protectress Abchi Drölma. The other chapel on the top story, reached by a somewhat circuitous route, is the Denchö Dzamling chapel from which you can view two giant restored stupas.

To the east of this main building is the **Abchi Lhakhang**, dedicated to the protectress Abchi Drölma. It is believed that Abchi Drölma was originally a dakini who married an ancestor of Jigten Sumgon. She subsequently became the guardian deity of Drigung. A white peaceful and a golden wrathful image of the protectress sit side by side in the chapel. A number of small bronzes that were saved from destruction are placed in no particular order around the room. A pair of *dri* (female yak) horns hangs from one of the pillars, which are believed to have acted as the basis for a vision that inspired Jigten Sumgon to build his monastery here and possibly name it Drigung (the exact etymology of which is unclear).

Further up the hill and to the east of the Abchi Lhakhang is the former residence of Pachung Rinpoche, built on the site of Jigten Sumgon's own retreat hut. Another footprint on rock of the founder of the monastery is enshrined here.

An easy forty-five-minute circumambulation from the monastery takes you to the famous sky burial site at Drigung, situated on the far western end of the ridge. This is still in use, and visitors are allowed to observe the proceedings but are generally asked *not* to take photographs. A number of stupas, shrines, and prayer flags surround the boulders of the burial site itself, which is symbolically associated with the mandala of the tantric deity Samvara.

TERDROM

In 772 King Trisong Detsen offered his wife of two years, Yeshe Tsogyel, to the Indian tantric guru Padmasambhava. This caused such an uproar among the king's Bön ministers that the couple were forced to flee the royal court. They took refuge at Terdrom, where they lived alone practicing tantric yogas in a cave, subsequently called the Tsogyel Sangpuk (Tsogyel's Secret Cave). After the Guru departed, Yeshe Tsogyel returned to Terdrom with another consort from Nepal. She later spent three years in solitary retreat on the snow line practicing Dzogchen.

The side valley that leads to Terdrom is 2 km (1.2 mi) west of Drigung Til. A half-hour drive of 8 km (5 mi) leads you up to a point where the small river divides into two and you see a profusion of small houses and prayer flags where most of the 115 nuns currently settled here live. The nunnery clearly stands out from the other smaller dwellings. The altar of the simple, earth-floor chapel displays the eight manifestations of Padmasambhava and the peaceful and wrathful aspects of Abchi Drolma.

From the springs it is possible to walk to the higher reaches of Terdrom, where a number of hermitages and caves are located. A pleasant four-hour loop will take you to the magnificent **Nyizer Puk**, the cave where Yeshe Tsogyel gained insight into the nature of mind. A much longer (eight-hour) hike will take you along the Nangkor (inner circuit) of Terdrom to the **Khandro Tsogkhang Chenmo** (great dakini assembly hall), a 50-meter-high (160 ft) cave inside which are two hermitages, now in use again by the nuns. Concealed in the roof of the cave is the **Tsogyel Sangpuk** where Yeshe Tsogyel received the Khandro Nying Tik instructions from Padma-sambhava. Be warned that this walk is fairly arduous and ascends to more than 5000 m (16,300 ft).

16
TSURPU

Tsurpu is 70 km (44 mi) northwest of Lhasa. Leave the city by the Dekyi Nub Lam, pass Drepung, and turn right when the road forks left to Netang and the airport. After 24 km (15 mi) at km marker 1897, turn left over a small bridge that takes you up a picturesque side valley to Tsurpu itself. By jeep or land cruiser, it takes about an hour and three-quarters. Because of the political sensitivity around the young Seventeenth Karmapa, Tsurpu is occasionally restricted to foreigners. Some Westerners, however, have received permission to conduct meditation retreats here. When the Karmapa is in residence, a brief blessing ceremony is held daily. There is a bus that leaves from in front of the Jokhang in the morning.

History

Tsurpu Monastery was founded in 1189 by the First Karmapa, Dusum Khyenpa, who was born in the eastern province of Kham. He came to Central Tibet to study and at the age of thirty became a disciple of Gampopa. He returned to Kham and founded Karmapa'i Densa, the monastery from which the Karma Kagyu order derived its name. Only toward the end of his life did he return to Central Tibet to found Tsurpu. Shortly before he died he said that he would be reborn in Tibet and gave indications as to how he could be

Tsurpu Monastery, 1946

found. He thus became the first lama to introduce the unique Tibetan custom of lines of recognized *tulkus* (incarnate lamas), a practice that eventually became popular with all the main orders.

Dusum Khyenpa returned in 1204 as Karma Pakshi, the Second Karmapa, nine years after his death. Again he was born in Kham and came to Tsurpu only when he was forty-three years old. He stayed there for six years. In 1256 he was invited by Kublai Khan to the imperial court. By the time he arrived, the Sakya lama Pakpa had established himself as Kublai's teacher, and the Karmapa chose to leave. On his way home he received another invitation from Möngke Khan, then head khan of the Mongol Empire. Möngke became a disciple of the Karmapa and gave him the title Pakshi, which means "master" (*acharya*) in Mongolian. However, in 1260, as a result of the struggle for succession after the death of Möngke, he found himself banished from Tibet by Kublai, who supported the Sakya hierarch Pakpa. Upon his release four years later he went to Kham. After eight years of teaching he returned to Tsurpu and spent the rest of his life renovating and enlarging the monastery.

Tsurpu was further enlarged during the time of the Fifth Karmapa, Deshin Shekpa, in the fifteenth century. During the sixteenth and seventeenth centuries the Karmapas were the spiritual advisors to the kings of Tsang and thus became powerful political figures. They vied with the early Dalai Lamas, but when the Mongolian army of Gushri Khan defeated the king of Tsang and enthroned the Fifth Dalai Lama as ruler of Tibet in 1642, they lost their political influence. Although many smaller monasteries belonging to the Karmapa subsect of the Kagyu school were then forcibly turned into Gelukpa centers, thus diminishing the power of the Kagyupa in Central Tibet, Tsurpu survived as a stronghold of the Kagyu order until the Chinese occupation in 1959, at which time there were over a thousand monks living there.

As the seat of the Karmapa, Tsurpu was the headquarters of the Karma Kagyu order in Tibet and had numerous other submonasteries and temples scattered throughout the country, many of which were in Kham. Monks from the order would travel here for their doctrinal and contemplative training and, once qualified, return to their home province to take charge of their local monastery.

Rangjung Rigpa'i Dorje, the Sixteenth Karmapa, went into exile in Rumtek, Sikkim, and directed the Karma Kagyu order from there. A powerful and charismatic figure, he played an important role in preserving the doctrines of the Kagyu tradition and introducing them to the outside world. He died in Zion, Illinois in 1981.

Four senior tulkus—Tai Situpa, Shamarpa, Goshir Gyeltsab, and Jamgön Kongtrul—were then appointed as a collective regency to oversee the transition and find the next incarnation. It was commonly believed that the Sixteenth Karmapa had left the traditional letter containing details of his future rebirth. But no such letter was found until 1989, when Tai Situpa announced that he had discovered one, with precise instructions, concealed inside a talisman given to him by the Karmapa. This was not shown to the other regents until March 1992. Shamar Rinpoche, however, expressed doubt concerning its authenticity.

From this point on, events moved rapidly. On April 26 Jamgön Kongtrul, who had been delegated to find the new incarnation in Tibet, was killed in a car crash near Siliguri, India. At some point, a boy, as described in the letter, was discovered in Eastern Tibet and dispatched to Tsurpu. On June 12 Shamarpa arrived in Rumtek Monastery with an Indian army bodyguard to meet with Tai Situpa and Gyeltsab to discuss his reservations, but the presence of troops caused a violent clash between different monastic factions and the discussion was abandoned. Three days later the boy arrived at Tsurpu. On June 29, Beijing acknowledged the boy as a "Living Buddha"—the first time a tulku has been recognized by the Chinese government since 1959. On July 3, the Tibetan government-in-exile announced the Dalai Lama's recognition of the boy. On September 27, in Tsurpu itself, the official enthronement of eight-year-old Ugyen Tinley, the Seventeenth Karmapa, took place. Shamar Rinpoche, however, did not attend, and in 1994 declared another young boy, Tenzin Chentse, to be the Seventeenth Karmapa. The whole affair has been divisive and acrimonious, exposing to the world at large the degree of political infighting sometimes involved in the struggle to establish a successor to a powerful lama.

The Site

Although it is still largely in ruins, a great deal of reconstruction has taken place at Tsurpu since 1986 and continues apace. In 1993, 370 monks were resident in the monastery, and the retreat centers in the hills nearby were fully operational. Since the monastery is now the residence of a young tulku, it is likely to become a major spiritual center in Tibet. The senior lama in Tsurpu in 1994 was Drubpon Dechen Rinpoche.

About a kilometer before you arrive at the monastic complex, you pass on your left the ruins of the Karmapa's former summer palace and gardens. Reconstruction is under way.

You enter the main complex of Tsurpu from a large courtyard with an old stone stele, on which is described the history of the monastery. A veranda to the left of the assembly hall is where monks perform annual dances to Padmasambhava (on the tenth day of the fourth lunar month) and Mahakala Bernakchen (on the twenty-ninth day of the twelfth lunar month).

The main steps lead into the courtyard of the **Protector Hall**, around which are chapels to the various protector deities of the monastery. On the far left is a shrine to the chief protector of Tsurpu, a form of Mahakala called Bernakchen. There is a large statue of the dark blue deity, holding a curved flaying knife and a skull cup. To the right in a cabinet is an old smaller image of the deity, considered to be the most sacred object in Tsurpu. The next chapel to the right is dedicated to Yönten Gonpo, a protector riding a horse, in union with a consort. The next room is a shrine to the tiger-mounted Dorje Trolo, a manifestation of Padmasambhava and an important protector in the Nyingma and Kagyu traditions. The figure next to him, on a horse, is Gönpo Tashi. The small black statue of Mahakala in front of the cabinet was made by a Westerner in France. The following shrine is to the Nyingma and Kagyu protector Vajrakilaya (Dorje Purba), an image of whom in consort is on the right. The final chapel is dedicated to the protectress Tseringma.

From here one enters the **assembly hall**. You climb up some steps on the front left to a raised platform with the altar. You first see a large stupa with relics of the Sixteenth Karmapa. The main figures on the altar are Amitabha, Shakyamuni, and the Sixteenth Karmapa. The murals around the walls depict the Sixteen Arhats, while those around the skylight show Padmasambhava with Gampopa to the left and Marpa to the right. Other Kagyu lamas, including incarnations of the Karmapa and the Tai Situpa, are painted around them. It was in this room that Ugyen Tinley was enthroned as the Seventeenth Karmapa in September 1992.

On the upper story are three rooms, the central one being the audience chamber of the Karmapa, where he gives his daily blessings. Outside this room are large murals of Tsurpu (right), and the two main Karma Kagyu monasteries in Kham (left): Karma Gon and Karma Kangri. The other rooms on this level are a library and the living quarters of the Karmapa, Tai Situpa, and Goshir Gyeltsab when they are in residence.

Behind and to the left of this complex is the newly reconstructed **Serdung Chenpo**, which serves primarily as the Karmapa's residence. To the right of this site is where the old **Lhakhang Chenmo** stood, a vast structure with one of the largest statues in Tibet: a 20-meter-high (65 ft) Jowo Shakyamuni, made from a single mold by the Second Karmapa, Karma Pakshi. Reconstruction has not yet begun.

The first building to rise from the rubble is now dwarfed by the assembly hall complex. This is the **Zhiwa'i Dra-tsang**, to the left of the Serdung Chenpo, a modest building, completed in 1984 and containing a small assembly hall and, on the upper floor, some residential rooms and a protector chapel dedicated to Mahakala, Pelden Lhamo, and Dharmaraja. Next door to this building is the monastic kitchen.

Behind the Serdung Chenpo is another building under reconstruction: the **Chökang Gong Monastery** of Goshir Gyeltsab. To the right of the assembly hall is the **Zhangkhange Serpo**, a building currently used for storage and guest accommodations. Above that is a small rebuilt temple called **Ösel Ling**. Further to the east is the **Kunga Delek** guesthouse, where foreigners can stay and do retreat. There is a good library with many books in English. The ruins closest to the electricity plant by the river are the **Zuri Lhakhang**, the residence of Zuri Rinpoche.

High on the hillside, behind the buildings, is a center for the traditional Karma Kagyu three-year intensive meditation retreats. It was built by Goshir Gyeltsab and completed at the end of 1992. Further up the steep mountainside is **Drubtra Samten Ling**, a facility with eight retreat cells. The first retreat since it was rebuilt ended in July 1993; a second began in November of that year. Perched on the hillside beside this hermitage is another small building, built by Karma Pakshi, the Second Karmapa, as his personal retreat. At one time the hillsides around Tsurpu were dotted with retreat huts, most of which were destroyed.

Many Tibetan pilgrims will do the *rikor* (mountain circumambulation), a two- to four-hour hike up the mountain depending on how long you stop at each shrine. You proceed west, straight up the valley until you reach a large open park (*lingka*) area. For a week each summer the Karmapa camps here with his monks and followers, who relax, play games, and watch traditional operas performed. (Nowadays they also watch Buddhist videos.) Beyond the *lingka* you climb to the burial ground for the monastery and the villages of the valley. The next stage of the ascent brings you to various sacred places: a narrow stone passage through which you crawl to be purified of your sins; a rock bridge over a sheer drop that will psychologically prepare you for the fears of the intermediate state between death and rebirth. Then you come to the meditation caves of the Ninth Karmapa and others. On the summit are some huts where nuns are in retreat. The path does not continue over the back of the mountain.

Across the river from the monastery is a large structure built for the display of huge tangkas on special occasions. Although the ancient tangkas of the monastery were destroyed, new ones have been made and are now on display on festival days.

THE KARMAPAS

1.	Dusum Khyenpa	1110–1193
2.	Karma Pakshi	1204–1283
3.	Rangjung Dorje	1284–1339
4.	Rolpa'i Dorje	1340–1383
5.	Deshin Shekpa	1384–1415
6.	Tongwa Dönden	1416–1453
7.	Chödrak Gyatso	1454–1506
8.	Mikyö Dorje	1507–1554
9.	Wangchuk Dorje	1556–1603
10.	Chöying Dorje	1604–1674
11.	Yeshe Dorje	1677–1702
12.	Jangchub Dorje	1703–1732
13.	Dudul Dorje	1733–1797
14.	Tekchok Dorje	1798–1868
15.	Khakhyab Dorje	1871–1921
16.	Rigpa'i Dorje	1922–1981
17.	Ugyen Tinley	1985–
17a.	Tenzin Chentse	1984–

17
NETANG:
TASHIGANG,
DRÖLMA LHAKHANG,
& RATÖ

Netang is the region 25 km (15 mi) south-west of Lhasa where the western bank of the Kyichu River broadens out into a small plain, just after (when driving from Lhasa) the prominent seated Buddha carved in the cliff to your right. Of the three surviving religious sites, the most important and best preserved is the Drölma Lhakhang. You can also visit the nearby monasteries of Tashigang and Ratö.

TASHIGANG MONASTERY

Approximately 4 km (2.5 mi) past the Buddha in the cliffside is a turning on the left, marked with a sign in Tibetan and English, to the newly restored Tashigang Monastery. Its white stupa can be seen from the main road amid the village houses. The monastery arranges traditional Tibetan-style picnics by the riverside, which can be booked through travel agencies in Lhasa.

Founded in the thirteenth century by the Sakya hierarch Pakpa, the small monastery of Tashigang was the first overnight stopover for the Dalai Lamas when traveling southward from Lhasa. It is being restored by a charitable foundation established by Beru Khyentse Rinpoche, a senior Karma Kamtsang

(Kagyu) lama currently in exile in India, who was born in the village in 1947. Badly damaged during the Cultural Revolution, Tashigang is now being rebuilt. The work was started by the abbot Ngawang Dorje, who returned from his mountain hideaway as soon as the political situation allowed him. Restoration is now under the direction of a Belgian-born disciple of Beru Khyentse, Norbu Repa. At present twenty-seven monks are resident here. Plans are under way to turn Tashigang into a larger monastic educational center and to provide a health care facility for the local population. Thus far the restoration of the chapels has been limited to some murals and a few new statues.

Over the mountain to the north of the monastery lies **Modchok Ritro**, a Shangpa Kagyu hermitage, now being restored with the help of Tashigang. Two monks and six nuns live there.

DRÖLMA LHAKHANG

6 km (3.7 mi) past the Buddha on the cliffside, Drölma Lhakhang is clearly visible on the right-hand side of the road.

History

Atisha is the honorific Sanskrit name given to Dipamkara Shri Jnana, the Indian Buddhist master from Bengal who was instrumental in the so-called second dissemination of Buddhism in Tibet. Atisha, or Jowoje (Precious Lord) as he is called by the Tibetans, was born to a noble family in Bengal in 982. He renounced his home and wealth at an early age and dedicated himself to the extensive study of Buddhism. He even traveled as far as Java (probably to the region of the Borobodur Temple) to receive instructions on the development of the compassionate resolve to attain enlightenment (*bodhichitta*). Upon his return to India he taught widely and became one of the most revered Buddhist teachers of his time, probably settling at the Vikramashila monastery.

In the early decades of the eleventh century Buddhism started to undergo a revival in Tibet. The communities of monks who had been living in the east of the country since the time of Langdarma began to return to Central Tibet. In the west the Tibetan Rinchen Zangpo had returned from eighteen years' study in India and was actively teaching and translating Buddhist scriptures. It was also from the western kingdom of Guge that the local king, Lha Lama Yeshe Ö, sent out repeated invitations to the greatest Indian teacher of the time, Atisha, to visit Tibet. After much supplication and personal sacrifice from the Tibetans, Atisha finally accepted and arrived in Western Tibet in 1042, aged sixty.

His teaching aimed at resolving the conflicts that were present within the Buddhist community of Tibet at that time. Above all he emphasized the need for a sound ethical basis before engaging in the more advanced tantric practices. He composed a short text, *The Lamp of the Path to Enlightenment;* it became the basic writing of the Kadampa school,

which formed after his death under his chief disciple, the layman Drom Tönpa. He spent a total of twelve years in Tibet. He spent his last years in Netang and died here in 1054. Since his death, the Drölma Lhakhang, dedicated to the female deity Tara, with whom he had a particularly strong connection, has been preserved as a shrine in his memory.

The Drölma Lhakhang was one of the few religious sites to escape much damage during the Cultural Revolution. The temple (or at least the statuary) was spared because of a request from the Bengali government that no harm be caused to the most sacred site of Atisha, even today a revered national figure in Bengal. Consequently, the images preserved in the temple are fine examples of the Tibetan religious art and craftsmanship of the eleventh century, often reflecting a distinct Indian influence that is no longer so evident in more recent works.

The Site

Protecting the small temple are life-size statues of the Four Guardian Kings, quite different from the customary Tibetan representations of them. Less ornate and stylized, they possess a simplicity and power that other versions often lack. Two recently repainted murals adorn the front of the building, the one on the left showing Atisha flanked by Drom Tönpa and Ngog Legpa'i Sherab.

The first of the three chapels you visit is dominated by a large Victory stupa. To the left are other metal stupas containing relics of Kadampa teachers and to the right a larger bronze stupa that is supposed to contain some relics of the Indian master Naropa, a teacher of both Atisha and Marpa and the father of the Kagyu order. A statue of a reflective Atisha is the main image, and to either side of him are the Eight Medicine Buddhas.

The middle chapel used to house Atisha's own statue of Tara, which he brought from India. This has been lost over the course of time. On the main altar one can still see two of Atisha's other possessions: on the left, a small Indian stupa, and on the right, an Indian statue of Shakyamuni. Above the altar is another Buddha Shakyamuni. To the left of the Buddha sits a fine statue of Tara, the main image among the twenty-one statues of her that fill both sides of the room. To the right of the Buddha is a statue of Guru Suvarnadvipa, the teacher Atisha visited in Indonesia in order to receive special instructions on the development of compassion. To the left of the altar is an urn that used to contain the remains of Atisha. (These were returned to Bengal during the sixties.) The five Dhyani Buddhas sit by the right wall above the Taras. Until February 1993, concealed among the lower row of Taras, there used to be a small standing statue of Maitreya called the A-tsa Jampa, so called because he is said to have once exclaimed "A-tsa!" (ouch!) upon being pricked by a needle. Sadly, this was stolen. It was recovered in 1994 but has not been returned to the monastery.

The third room is where Atisha used to teach. In the middle of the room is the solid back of what used to be his throne, immediately in front of which is a small statue of Atisha that is said to be one of only two such images made during his lifetime. Around the walls of this room one meets the gaze of three huge seated images. At the back is Amitayus. Tradition maintains that Atisha blessed thousands of small lumps of clay with the mantra of Amitayus and the statue was then constructed out of them. To the right is Buddha Kashyapa and to the left Buddha Dipamkara, both Buddhas of the distant past. The Eight Great Bodhisattvas stand noble and erect between them. All these statues give the room a sense of exceptional lightness and purity.

As you leave the final chapel you will see two white stupas to either side of the doorway. The one to the left contains the monastic robes of Atisha and the one to the right the leather jerkin of Drom Tönpa (a layman). It is also possible to circumambulate the shrine along a tall, inner corridor containing several old prayer wheels.

On the upper story three chapels are currently being restored: a central chapel to the longevity triad (Tara, Amitayus, and Vijaya), with a Kangyur and Tengyur chapel to the right and quarters for the Dalai Lama on the left.

Across the road from the Drölma Lhakhang is a dirt track that in 2 km (1.2 mi) arrives at Kumbum, a restored temple that marks the place where Atisha died.

RATÖ MONASTERY

A further 7 km (4 mi) past Drölma Lhakhang, a road on the right leads to the village and monastery of Ratö.

Ratö Monastery was founded by a lama called Taktsang, who was born in 1045. It was an important early Kadampa monastery and was eventually taken over by the Geluk order. Ngog Loden Sherab, the great translator, as well as Tsongkhapa, spent time here. Latter it was renowned as a center for the specialized study of logic and debate. Two of the monastery's incarnate lamas live and teach in the West: Ratö Kyongla Rinpoche in New York, and Dagyab Rinpoche in Bonn. The third, Ratö Rinpoche, died in exile in Dharamsala in 1992. Photographs of all three are displayed on the altar. Eighty-four monks now live here (compared to 500 before the Chinese occupation).

The most revered image in the temple is a small Indian figure of Tara, a replica of which is now enshrined in a glass case to the left of the throne. It is said that Atisha paid homage to this image and it spoke to him. The other images on the altar along the rear wall depict celebrated lamas associated with the monastery. To the left and right are three intriguing statues of Tsedrekpa, the converted Bön deity who is the special protector of Ratö.

Without doubt the most impressive images in Ratö are the beautiful murals that cover all four walls of the temple. Unlike those in so many other temples today, these have survived the Cultural Revolution and are not restorations. Since they include images of the Fifth Dalai Lama, however, it is unlikely they would be much more than two hundred years old.

Approximately 6 km (4 mi) after the Drölma Lhakhang a suspension bridge on the left takes you up a valley to the **Zhong Tseb Nunnery**, formerly home to two hundred nuns and recently reopened. I was unable to visit.

18
GONGKAR: SAKYA MONASTERIES ON THE TSANGPO

*While its historical significance origi-
nates in the period of Sakya rule of Tibet
in the thirteenth century, Gongkar today
is best known to the visitor as the site of
Lhasa's airport. Formerly the agricultur-
ally prosperous domain of a dzongpön
(commissioner), Gongkar is now an
administrative district stretching from
Chuwo Ri, the small mountain below
which the road from Lhasa crosses the
Tsangpo, to Rawame, on the southern
shore of the river.*

CHUWO RI TO GONGKAR CHÖDE

65 km (40 mi) from Lhasa the Kyichu
flows into the Tsangpo (Brahmaputra) at
the village of Chaksam. The name
"Chaksam" (iron bridge) refers to the
suspension bridge constructed by the
Tibetan sage Tangtong Gyelpo six hundred years ago at this site. It was
destroyed when the present bridge was
constructed by the Chinese. Tangtong
Gyelpo's monastery and the stupa containing his relics were located at the foot
of Chuwo Ri on the south bank of the
river but were destroyed without a trace.

Chuwo Ri itself is one of the four sacred
mountains of Central Tibet. On its summit
is a cave where Padmasambhava meditated, which has been restored and can

be visited. A hermitage of King Trisong
Detsen was also on the mountain. Many
great lamas and hermits have been
associated with Chuwo Ri since the earliest days of Tibet's history.

As the road continues eastward you
pass the ruins of Gongkar Dzong, the
former castle of the *dzongpön* of
Gongkar. Shortly thereafter you reach
the monastery of Gongkar Chöde about
100 m off the road.

GONGKAR CHÖDE
History

Gongkar Chöde (or Gongkar Dorje Den)
was founded by Dorje Denpa Kunga
Namgyel in 1464 and belongs to the
Zung tradition of the Sakya order.
Kunga Namgyel was renowned as a
scholar and master of tantric ritual. The
monastery is also noted as the home of
the sixteenth-century Kyenri style of
Tibetan iconography, many fine examples of which are still preserved here.
The main temple building remains more
or less intact. During the Cultural
Revolution all the statues were removed
and the gilded roofs dismantled. The surrounding monastic buildings were either
destroyed or converted to other uses.
Before 1959 the monastery housed 160
monks. It now has 49.

The Site

The murals that survive throughout the
monastery are well worth seeing. During
the 1960s all the walls of the ground floor
were whitewashed in order to conceal the

murals. Since the early 1980s the monks have been carefully removing this wash. Covering the two side walls of the spacious assembly hall are some excellent scenes from the Buddha's previous lives, as told in the *Paksam Trishing*. Each scene is shown in minute detail, painted with careful and delicate brushstrokes, and bears a short numbered text in Tibetan beneath it. Before entering the chapel at the rear, you will see two other older-looking murals to either side of the doorway. The one on the left is a beautiful representation of the Sakya lama Kunga Nyingpo, with smaller images of Drakpa Gyeltsen to the left and Sonam Tsemo to the right. This Sakyapa triad is traditionally called the Three White Ones. To the right of the doorway is a mural in a similar style of the Two Red Ones. Sakya Pandita is the main figure and is accompanied by his nephew Pakpa. The newly made statues in the assembly hall depict the founder of the monastery, Kunga Namgyel (center), Sakya Pandita and Padmasambhava (left) and two Buddhas (right).

There are two dimly lit protector chapels through a door to the left of the assembly hall. The walls are black, and fearsome animal-headed deities can be discerned traced in gold, red, and white. The first of these chapels is dedicated to Padmasambhava and contains images of the eight manifestations of the Guru. The second is dedicated to the Sakya protector Gönpo Guru, an aspect of Mahakala, a giant statue of whom dominates the room. Women are not allowed in this chapel.

The large, high-ceilinged chapel to the rear of the assembly hall has recently been restored and now houses a large statue of the historical Buddha Shakyamuni, accompanied by his four main arhat disciples: Shariputra, Maudgalyayana, Subhuti, and Ananda. The walls have been decorated with newly painted murals. Along the inner wall of the circumambulation corridor around this chapel are painted scenes of the twelve major deeds of the Buddha and on the outer wall the thousand buddhas of this eon.

The upper story of the monastery is largely empty and unused but contains the most remarkable **Yidam Chapel**, which you may have to ask a monk to unlock. The walls of this small room are covered with finely painted images of the main tantric deities (*yidams*) of the Sakya tradition. The main image, which faces you as you enter, is that of Hevajra, in front of which used to be a life-size statue of the deity. The colors of these murals have been well preserved, and the attention to detail is exceptional. Not only the main figures but also all the smaller attendant deities and dakinis associated with their mandalas are shown; the artwork indicates a craftsman of considerable spiritual sensitivity. The deities depicted include Yamantaka, Manjushri (in several forms), Kalachakra, and Samvara.

At the front of the upper story is a series of rooms, in fairly good condition, reserved for both visiting dignitaries and the principal lamas of the monastery. The rooms give a good impression of the kind of surroundings in which a high lama would live. One of the four, well-preserved painted oval panels depicts how Gongkar Chöde looked in former days.

About 4 km (2.5 mi) behind Gongkar Chöde lies the site of a Drukpa Kagyu monastery called Dechen Chokor, which is slowly being restored.

RAME TO CHITISHÖ

About 20 km (12 mi) east of Gongkar Chöde the road reaches the village of Rame, a pleasant, tidy village lined with trees. In the center of the village is the monastery of Rawame, founded by two Sakya lamas Kunga Lhundrup and Sherab Pelden in the fourteenth century. It was badly desecrated during the Cultural Revolution, and serious restoration began only in 1989. The murals and images, most of which depict lamas and deities of the Sakya tradition, are new. The lama of the monastery is Peljor Yeshe Rinpoche, who returned here after working for twenty years as a farmer. His quarters are on the upper story. Another lama of this monastery, Ngawang Khyentse Tubten Nyingpo, currently resides in France. Around forty monks live here at present.

Just before entering Rame from Gongkar Chöde is a road on the right that leads up a wide valley to the village of Namrab, in which is situated Dakpo Dratsang Monastery, founded in the fifteenth century by the Sakya lama Tashi Namgyel. The structure of the monastery has been well preserved, and some of the original murals are in reasonable condition.

20 km (12 mi) from Rame is the small town of Chitishö, formerly an important trading center on the old caravan route from India. Its castle is now in ruins. The main monastery at Chitishö is Dunbu Chökor, situated through the town, about 300 m south of the road.

DUNBU CHÖKOR
History

Dunbu Chökor was originally founded in the eleventh century by a *tertön* called Drapa Ngonshe (1012–1090), who came from the nearby village of Dranang (the monastery built at his birthplace still survives in Dranang, 20 km [12 mi] east of Chitishö). He was a Nyingma lama who was a disciple of the Indian sage Padampa Sanggye, served as the abbot of Samye, and was the first teacher of the Tibetan woman mystic Machik Labdrön. As a tertön he was responsible for revealing the *Four Medical Tantras*. He died, however, during a medical operation while having lymph drawn out of his heart with a golden straw. During his lifetime he is reputed to have established 128 temples and shrines. Dunbu Chökor was subsequently taken over by the Sakya order, and was expanded to its present size in the fifteenth century by the lama Shedrong Panchen, a disciple of Gorampa Sonam Sengge. The present Dalai Lama stayed here briefly during his flight into exile in 1959 (his room, with bed and altar, are still preserved on the top story). There are now 72 monks living here.

The Site

The main temple building is in fairly good condition despite the fact that all its images were removed. The murals, too, are in good repair. In the entrance porch are two interesting paintings, one of the Wheel of Life and another of the world according to traditional Buddhist cosmology. On the wall on the left immediately as you enter are painted four protectors. The first is Pekor She, a Bön deity converted to Buddhism. Next follow Guru Gönpo, Mahakala, and Pelden Lhamo. Down the left-hand wall are shown the twelve major deeds of the Buddha. Just before you enter the chapel at the rear of the assembly hall you can see a beautiful old wall-painting of the famous Sakya lama Kunga Nyingpo.

The assembly hall itself is still being restored, and no statues of note are installed there yet. In former times the monastery is reputed to have housed an Indian image of Tara that was worshipped by the pandit Chandragomin. In the rear of the main chapel is a weird, poorly constructed artificial grotto in which are perched the Sixteen Arhats. The main image is a large statue of Maitreya.

As you leave the rear chapel, the mural to the left shows the five major Sakya lamas with Sakya Pandita in the center. An opening further down this wall leads to a chapel that used to house an image of Vairochana Buddha made by Drapa Ngonshe. This has now been restored and is accompanied by the other four Dhyani Buddhas and their consorts. The walls are richly decorated with murals of the thirty-two deities of Vairochana's retinue and the Twenty-One Taras.

On the upper floor is a chapel dedicated to Green Tara, surrounded by the other Twenty-One Taras. On the left is a large statue of Sachen Losel Gyatso, a former abbot. Also on this story is a protector chapel to Mahakala with some damaged murals of tantric deities. The room where the Dalai Lama stayed in 1959 is on the story above.

19
MINDROLING: NYINGMA MONASTERIES ON THE TSANGPO

Two important centers of the Nyingma tradition in Central Tibet are found on the north and south banks of the Tsangpo between Chitishö and Dranang. These are the monasteries of Dorje Drak and Mindroling and the related hermitages, caves, and historically significant sites around them.

DORJE DRAK MONASTERY

Dorje Drak, on the northern bank of the Tsangpo, is clearly visible from the road as you approach Chitishö from Lhasa. It can only be reached by ferry from a landing 6 km (3.7 mi) west of Chitishö near a small Tibetan restaurant, whose staff will summon the boat.

Dorje Drak was founded in the sixteenth century by the Nyingma lama Tashi Tobgyel, the third incarnation of Godemchen, the tertön who discovered the Northern Treasure (*jang-ter*) of the Nyingma tradition. Subsequent incarnations of Tashi Tobgyel developed the teachings of the Northern Treasure, making Dorje Drak the home of this important lineage of Nyingma practice. The monastery was razed by the Dzungar Mongols in 1718, who launched a violent anti-Nyingma cam-paign when they arrived in Central Tibet to challenge the Qosot Mongol king Lhazang Khan, whom they murdered. Although subsequently rebuilt, it was again reduced to ruins during the Cultural Revolution and only since 1984 has reconstruction again been started.

The assembly hall and main temple have been rebuilt since 1986, and the monastery now functions again, although on a much smaller scale than before 1959, when four hundred monks lived here. An image of Padmasambhava dominates the main temple.

MINDROLING MONASTERY

The area around Mindroling is famous as the birthplace of many renowned Nyingma teachers: Drapa Ngonshe, Orgyen Lingpa, Terdak Lingpa, and Longchen Rabjampa, all of whom spent much of their lives meditating, studying, and founding monasteries in the region.

The town of Dranang is about 20 km (12 mi) east of Chitishö. The eleventh-century temple Dratang Gompa, a for-mer residence of Drapa Ngonshe, still stands in the center of town. Although it was badly damaged and converted to a storehouse during the Cultural Revolu-tion, some of the original murals have survived. These rare and fine examples of art, executed as Buddhism was revived in Tibet in the early eleventh cen-tury, are well worth seeing. It is not always possible, however, to get permis-sion to see them. They are described in Roberto Vitali's *Early Temples of Central*

Tibet (Serindia, 1990).

To reach Mindroling you leave Dranang and shortly afterward turn right up the Drachi valley. The monastery is 8 km (5 mi) from the main road.

History

In recent times Mindroling has served as the most important Nyingma monastery in Central Tibet. In fact it was the first large monastic establishment of the school, which until the seventeenth century was based in small temples and hermitages throughout Tibet. It was founded by the tertön Terdak Lingpa (1646–1714) in 1676. Terdak Lingpa is renowned as the discoverer of the texts that form the basis of the Southern Treasure (*lho-ter*) of the Nyingma school (in contrast to the Northern Treasure of Dorje Drak). He was ordained at a young age by the Great Fifth Dalai Lama, who came to power four years before Terdak Lingpa was born. He nonetheless renounced his monastic vows later in life and raised a family, whose male descendants continued to serve as throne holders of Mindroling until 1959. The main disciple of Terdak Lingpa was a monk named Lochen Dharmashri, a master of a wide range of subjects including medicine, poetry, and painting. In 1718 Mindroling suffered the same fate as Dorje Drak and was razed by the Dzungars. It was reconstructed by Terdak Lingpa's daughter, Jetsun Mingyur Peldrön, and subsequently became both a training monastery for Nyingma monks from as far afield as

Kham and Amdo as well as a study center for officials from the Lhasa government. Hermitages and a nunnery were built in the hills behind it, and just below it there used to be a massive thirteen-story stupa (*kumbum*). Mindroling was badly damaged during the Cultural Revolution. Previously home to around three hundred monks, the monastery currently houses eighty.

The Site

As you enter the courtyard, on your left is a distinguished temple made out of the characteristic brown stone of the local area. A hundred years ago the Indian scholar Chandra Das remarked that "the neatness of the stonework and the finish of all the masonry about the temple were very remarkable." This is still true today and can be observed on the ruined walls around the monastery.

To the left of the steps that lead into the temple are paintings of major figures from the Nyingma school: Longchen Rabjampa, Vairochana, Shantarakshita, Padmasambhava, and Trisong Detsen. To the right are depicted Terdak Lingpa, members of his family (grandfather, father, son, and daughter) and his student Lochen Chopel Gyatso. Murals depicting numerous images of Amitayus cover the inside walls. These were restored by the monks who painstakingly removed a layer of white paper pasted over them during the Cultural Revolution.

Off the far left-hand corner of the main hall is the **Celestial Palace Chapel**, with eight Kadam stupas of various sizes dominating the altar. Two excellent statues of Shakyamuni and Padmasambhava stand among them, along with two newer images of Padmasambhava and one of Terdak Lingpa. Finely painted old murals of Manjushri cover the walls. Off the far right-hand corner of the hall a protector chapel is currently being restored.

At the back of the hall is a **Shakyamuni Chapel**. Only the head of the main Buddha is of the original statue, as the body was destroyed during the Cultural Revolution. Shariputra and Maudgalyayana stand to either side of the Buddha, and restored statues of the Eight Great Bodhisattvas stand along the walls.

There are three chapels open on the upper story. First is the **Deser Chapel**, which used to enshrine mandalas of the monastery's protectors. In the center of the altar is a small, finely made stupa containing the relics of Ngawang Chodrak, a lama from Mindroling who was jailed in 1959 and released twenty-five years later. He spent the last years of his life in Lhasa and after his death he sat meditating on the Clear Light for ten days. A tangka of Terdak Lingpa commissioned by the Fifth Dalai Lama also hangs here. The handprints and footprints of the master are clearly visible on the painting.

Next door is the **Dewachen Chapel**, dedicated to the memory of Lochen Dharmashri. The small room houses a newly made statue of the master. On the rear wall are restored paintings of the early Tibetan kings Songtsen Gampo, Trisong Detsen, and Nyatri Tsenpo.

Up some steps in the adjacent room is the **Lama Chapel**, a bare room with exceptional and highly original murals of the lamas of the Nyingma tradition. The central image is a newly made statue of Samantabhadra, considered in the Nyingma school as the primordial buddha. In front of Samantabhadra is the wrathful protector Shang-ling. The small altar houses a number of bronzes recently returned to the monastery by the local people. To the right of the altar is a rock bearing what is supposed to be the hoofprint of Terdak Lingpa's horse.

To the far left of the main courtyard is a smaller building that serves as the monastery's **assembly hall**. The striking portrait of Padmasambhava painted by the entrance is reputed to have once spoken. The central statue in the hall is that of Terdak Lingpa, a large figure with a white beard, seated in a glass case. To the right is a throne for the Dalai Lama and to the right of that one for the present throne holder of Mindroling, Kunsang Wangyel, now in exile in India. The walls are covered with images of the thousand buddhas of this eon as well as scenes from Shakyamuni's life. In the chapel in the rear are large statues of Padmasambhava, Shantarakshita, and Trisong Detsen.

THE DRANANG VALLEY

The Dranang Valley is reached by a dirt road from behind the town of Dranang.

Just south of the town are the ruins of

a once extensive Geluk monastery called Jampa Ling, which formerly boasted an enormous multistory stupa dedicated to Maitreya. Work has started on its restoration. Across the valley, on the steep slopes of the facing hill, are the scant remains of the Geluk monastery of Chökhorling. A further 7 km (4 mi) up the valley is Gyeling Tsokpa, a Sakya monastery still serving as a storehouse. Not far behind it, however, is a small hermitage called Gasa Puk, which has been restored and is again in use.

After a further 6 km (4 mi) you reach the ruins of the Drukpa Kagyu Dingboche Monastery high above the village of the same name in the valley. Still further up the cliff wall is a cave where Padmasambhava is said to have meditated and Orgyen Lingpa to have found treasure texts. Törong, the birthplace of the Nyingma sage Longchen Rabjampa, is in the nearby valley that opens to the southeast of Dingboche. The nunnery that marks the site is being restored. Finally, 4 km (2.5 mi) up the Dranang valley, you arrive at the Yarje Lhakhang, a small temple that marks the place where the tertön Orgyen Lingpa was born in 1323.

20
SAMYE MONASTERY

Samye, Tibet's first Buddhist monastery, is of unique significance in both the political and religious history of the land. Formerly on the old caravan route from the Yarlung Valley to Lhasa, its location on the north bank of the Tsangpo, surrounded by sand dunes and with no paved road, makes access difficult today.

Since 1990 there have been two ferries, one for tourists and one for locals, that leave from the south bank of the river early each morning. The tourist ferry is 12 km (7.5 mi) west of Tsetang, the local ferry 22 km (13 mi). Since the tourist boat runs infrequently (and sometimes not at all) it is often necessary, despite government regulations forbidding it, to take the local boat. From the landing-stage on the north bank a truck or dilapidated bus will drive you to the monastery. It takes about an hour.

It is also possible to trek to Samye either from Dechen Dzong or Ganden Monastery in the Kyichu Valley. The most direct route from Dechen Dzong takes two and a half to three and a half days, while from Ganden the average time is between four and five days. Taking you through wild and spectacular scenery, these are tough walks and should not be undertaken without adequate preparation. One has to cross remote passes above 5,000 m (16,300 ft), and there are no provisions along the route.

History

Samye was the first monastery to be built in Tibet. It was probably founded during the 770s under the patronage of King Trisong Detsen, with the work being directed by Padmasambhava and Shantarakshita, the two Indian masters the king had invited to Tibet to

Samye Monastery, 1949

help consolidate the Buddhist faith. The monastery was designed on the plan of the Odantapuri temple in present-day Bihar, India, and mirrored the basic structure of the universe as described in Buddhist cosmology. The central temple represents Mount Sumeru, the mythical mountain at the center of the cosmos. Around it are four temples called "ling," which represent the four continents *(ling)* situated in the vast ocean to the north, south, east, and west of Sumeru. To the right and left of each of these temples are two smaller temples called "ling-tren," representing the subcontinents (*ling-tren*) of the Buddhist universe. There are even two chapels representing the sun and the moon. The entire monastery is surrounded by a circular wall topped with numerous small stupas, and four great stupas in four colors (white, red, blue, and green) stand facing the southeast, southwest, northwest, and northeast corners of the main temple, respectively.

Samye is located at the foot of one of Central Tibet's four holy mountains, Hepori, on which Trisong Detsen is supposed to have had his palace in ancient times. The king was born in the nearby village of Drakmar further up the valley, where a small shrine still marks the spot. The surrounding landscape consists of barren mountains and sand dunes, with the monastery and village occupying a small fertile patch of land in a valley leading to the mountains in the north.

Samye is an especially important monastery because it was here, toward the end of the eighth century, that the first Tibetans were ordained as monks by the Indian abbot Shantarakshita. Seven men from noble families were tested by Shantarakshita to see if they were suitable for the monastic life and then ordained, presumably in the company of other Indian monks accompanying the abbot. They are known even today as the Seven Examined Men.

When the monastery was first built, both Indian and Chinese monks were invited there to work on the translation of Buddhist scriptures from their respective languages into Tibetan. (The Indians lived in the Aryapalo (Hayagriva) Ling temple to the south, while the Chinese lived in the Jampa Ling to the west.) Conflicts arose between the two factions concerning doctrinal interpretation, and the king had to call for a public debate to settle the matter. This took place around 792 between a representative of Indian Buddhism, the scholar Kamalashila (a disciple of Shantarakshita) and a Chinese Ch'an (Zen) teacher named Hvashang Mahayana. The debate was presided over by King Trisong Detsen and was intended to establish which form of Buddhism should prevail in Tibet: the Indian tradition of systematic study, firm adherence to ethical rules, and a practice that entails the gradual ascendance of stages leading to enlightenment; or the Chinese tradition of Ch'an, which emphasizes the possibility of "sudden," instantaneous bursts of enlightenment and the following of a spiritual life that lays itself open to these possibilities. The records of the outcome of the arguments pursued in the debate are ambiguous: both sides claimed to have won. The actual outcome, though, is beyond doubt: the Indian view was favored, and from then on the Chinese influence waned. Hvashang Mahayana had to leave Tibet, and the Ch'an tradition was effectively proscribed. The place where the debate took place was the Jampa Ling, the residence of the Chinese monks.

At the time of the founding of Samye there were no separate schools of Tibetan Buddhism, but because Padmasambhava is so closely connected with the creation of the monastery it has always been strongly associated with the Nyingma tradition. The monks who returned in the eleventh century from Kham and Amdo, where their predecessors had gone into exile during the suppression of Buddhism by Langdarma, established Samye as an important Nyingma monastery. It was later taken over by the Sakya tradition and more recently came under the influence of the Gelukpa. But this holy, ancient shrine has always been rather eclectic. Even today the monks insist that the monastery does not belong to any particular school, although it is inhabited primarily by adherents of both the Nyingma and Sakya traditions.

In the course of its history the monastery has been repeatedly damaged by fire and then restored. The original buildings erected in the eighth century were burned down in 986 and rebuilt by the famous translator Ra Lotsawa. Other restoration work was carried out by the Sakya lama Kunga Rigdzin, Demo Ngawang Jampel Delek Gyatso (a regent who ruled during the minority of the Eighth Dalai Lama), and the Tenth Dalai Lama, Tsultrim Gyatso.

The monastery was damaged during the Cultural Revolution but not totally destroyed as is sometimes suggested. The greatest harm it suffered was the removal of the magnificent upper stories of the main temple. The four ling temples and most of the eight ling-tren temples were emptied and turned into storerooms. The four giant stupas were destroyed without a trace, and much of the encircling wall was allowed to collapse. The village encroached on the monastery grounds to the extent that the whole place seemed like a farmyard, with cattle, yaks, pigs, and chickens roaming everywhere. In the last eight years, however, the upper stories have been replaced, the surrounding wall has been rebuilt, and restoration of the smaller temples and four stupas is rapidly nearing completion. Over one hundred monks are currently resident at or registered with the monastery.

The Site

About 5 km (3 mi) beyond the landing-stage on the way to Samye you will notice a couple of white stupas emerging dramatically from the brown rock hillside on your left. This is Zurkar Do, the place where the Tibetan king Trisong Detsen first met Padmasambhava. According to a traditional account of the meeting, the proud ruler of Tibet was reluctant to pay obeisance to the Indian Buddhist teacher, so Padmasambhava "turned his hands and, springing up from his finger a miraculous flame seared the king's garments. King, ministers, courtiers could not withstand him. Bowing in unison, they gave greeting as though swept by a scythe." To commemorate this event, the king ordered five stupas to be erected at the site. Although damaged during the Cultural Revolution, the stupas are now in good repair.

As you stand in front of the entrance to the main temple (Samye Utse), you will notice an ancient stele on the left. This is the record of an edict made in 779 by King Trisong Detsen, proclaiming, for the first time, Buddhism to be the religion of Tibet. An old bell hanging from the roof directly above the entrance might also date back to the times of the early kings. A cobblestone hallway lined by prayer wheels takes you to the actual entrance, beside which are two attractive stone elephants.

The main temple is renowned for each story's being designed in a different architectural style. The ground floor is Chinese, the second floor Indo-Tibetan, and the third Khotanese.

The large, cavernous ground floor is divided into two main sections: an assembly hall and, connected to it, the main chapel, dedicated to Shakyamuni.

The statues throughout the **assembly hall** are a nonsectarian celebration of many of the greatest teachers in the history of Tibetan Buddhism. On the left-hand side of the hall are Tangtong

Gyelpo, Butön, Kamalashila, and Vimalamitra. At the front of the room, to either side of the entrance of the chapel, are (from the left) the translator Vairochana, Shantarakshita, Padmasambhava, Trisong Detsen, and Songtsen Gampo. To the right are Drom Tönpa, Atisha, and Ngog Legpa'i Sherab—the familiar Kadampa triad. (Atisha is recorded as having visited Samye, where he discovered in the library, even in the eleventh century, Sanskrit texts no longer extant in India.) Longchenpa, Sakya Pandita, and Tsongkhapa—a less common triad known as the Three Incarnations of Manjushri—sit next to the Kadampa masters. The murals around the walls of the assembly hall date back to the time of the Thirteenth Dalai Lama. A fine portrait of Hevajra surrounded by attendant dakinis on one wall suggest a strong Sakyapa influence.

The entrance to the **main chapel** consists of three tall doorways, a feature of Chinese temple design rarely found in other Tibetan temples, symbolizing the Three Doors of Liberation (emptiness, signlessness, and wishlessness). This beautiful and impressive chamber has as its centerpiece a large statue of Shakyamuni, carved in the eighth century from a stone on Hepori. During the Cultural Revolution the head was destroyed, but it has been replaced with one of clay. Lining the walls are ten tall bodhisattva figures. These images, which are replacements of the originals, depict the buddhas of the ten directions in the aspect of bodhisattvas. They consist of the Eight Great Bodhisattvas plus two others: Drimamepa and Kawa'i Pe. Behind each is a painted mural of the corresponding buddha. Two giant wrathful deities, known as King and Kang (Rahu and Achala) guard the shrine. The high, paneled ceiling depicts, in each panel, a tantric mandala. A throne reserved for the Dalai Lama is just outside the chapel on the right.

It is possible to follow an inner circumambulation path around the chapel. Murals of the deeds of the historical Buddha and some *jataka* tales adorn the walls.

A doorway in the right-hand wall of the assembly hall leads you into the **Protector Chapel**. This dark and eerie room powerfully evokes the shamanic dimension of Tibetan culture. The nine figures represent Indian Buddhist protectors as well as indigenous Tibetan deities converted into guardians of the Dharma by Padmasambhava. From the left the figures are: Ngag Chang Kunkar Rinchen, Vaishravana, Ekajati, Hayagriva, Dorje Kurkyi Lönpo, Pelkor, Pelden Masung Gyelpo, Ekajati, and the Kursha Sum—three figures collectively identified as one. Tied to one of the pillars are a gigantic stuffed snake, an old musket, and a sword.

To the left of the assembly hall is an **Avalokiteshvara Chapel**, which is entered from the front of the building. This small shrine was built by the Sakya lama Sonam Gyeltsen on the death of his mother. It contains in relief on the back wall a wonderful thousand-armed Avalokiteshvara made of clay. An old statue of Padmasambhava is in the right-hand corner and next to him an unusual image of Songtsen Gampo. The remains of Kunga Zangpo, a disciple of Tsongkhapa, are enshrined in a glass case to the right. On the wall by their side is what is reputed to be the staff of the translator Vairochana. Seven relief carvings (of Milarepa, Atisha, Tara, and Padmasambhava), which were salvaged from the large white stupa to the southeast of the monastery, are also in the shrine.

There are a number of rooms open on the second floor of the temple. Directly above the Shakyamuni chapel below is a **Padmasambhava Chapel**. A large, imposing, and slightly wrathful statue of the Guru is the central figure in this spacious and rather bare, square room. In front of him is Longchen Rabjampa, and to his right in a small cabinet, Jigme Lingpa. An ancient and miraculously undamaged statue of Amitayus is to the far left and an old Buddha figure to the far right. As with the chapel downstairs, paintings of the buddhas of the ten directions are found on the walls, in front of which stand the same ten bodhisattvas. An internal circumambulation path surrounds the room, and its walls are decorated with images from the Buddha's previous lives.

The fine murals by the entrance to this chapel are worth studying. On the left are numerous scenes from the life of Padmasambhava as described in the

Padma Ka Tang, a biography of the Guru discovered by Orgyen Lingpa in the thirteenth century. Also to the left of the door is the Fifth Dalai Lama, while to the right, surrounded by former kings and Dalai Lamas, is the Eleventh Dalai Lama—suggesting perhaps that these murals date back to the time of his brief life from 1838–1855.

To the right of the Padmasambhava chapel is a small protector chapel dedicated to Hayagriva and, next door, an Amitayus chapel with nine large and a thousand small statues of the bodhisattva.

To the left of the Padmasambhava chapel are the **quarters of the Dalai Lama**. The first of the three rooms is a bare antechamber that leads into a throne room, which presumably served as a small audience chamber. Of greatest note here is a very fine old mural of Samye protected by a cloth drape. It is worth comparing the details of this painting with what remains of the monastery today. The bedroom has some beautiful old murals of the Buddha, Tara, and Maitreya. The glass cabinet on the left contains a number of statues, texts, and artifacts recently returned to Samye by a man from Kham who had concealed them in his home. The objects include: a footprint of Padmasambhava, the skull of Shantarakshita, an amulet box with seven strands of Padmasambhava's hair, the statue of Shakyamuni present at the ordination of Nagarjuna, and Ra Lotsawa's personal statue of Yamantaka.

Access to the newly rebuilt third floor is by a stairway to the left of the doorway to the Padmasambhava chapel. A "pillarless" (i.e., Khotanese) **Mandala Chapel** occupies the entirety of this floor. The outside walls are brightly painted with lamas and deities of the Nyingma tradition. The interior of the room, which can be entered by any one of its four doors, is dominated by a large square structure, possibly the base for a three-dimensional mandala. The newly made statues around the room are deities from the Sarvavid (an aspect of Vairochana) mandala. On the ceiling above is painted a mandala of Vairochana. The four statues facing the front of the chapel are Vairochana, Samantabhadra, Padmasambhava (in his aspect of the Lotus-Born One), and Yudra Nyingpo.

From here you can climb to the unfinished **Samvara Chapel**, located immediately beneath the golden roof. Pillars are arranged around the chapel to represent the Twenty-One Taras and the Sixteen Arhats. The five pillars inside are for the five deities of the Samvara mandala. In the very center is a six-pointed star, symbolizing the inner structure of the mandala itself.

The main temple can be circumambulated by way of a covered cloister that runs around the inside of the courtyard. It is lined with prayer wheels on one side and extensive, though partially defaced, murals on the other. Large images of the Thirty-Five Buddhas of Confession are depicted at regular intervals, surrounded by scenes from a *jataka* text that describes the five hundred pure and five hundred impure previous incarnations of Shakyamuni. The pure incarnations refer to the times he was born as a human or a god, the impure to the times when he was born as an animal. On the front wall (to the left and right of the entrance) paintings of the mythic land of Shambhala, the world as conceived in traditional cosmology, and Samye itself can be seen.

The Ling Temples

A period of rapid reconstruction from 1993 to 1994 has resulted in the restoration of the perimeter wall and the four great stupas. This haste, along with the poor-quality materials (concrete and synthetic gloss paint), suggests a large injection of government money as an investment in the tourist industry. Samye is on the way to becoming Tibet's first Buddhist theme park.

The massive and rather unattractive white, red, black, and green stupas are placed equidistantly around the complex. They were rebuilt by a lama from Kham named Karma Tobgyel, reportedly in consultation with the Dalai Lama. It is possible to enter the green stupa and visit shrines inside.

Circumambulation in a clockwise direction from the front of the main temple takes you first to the Southern Ling temple, **Aryapalo Ling**. Some very fine murals survive in the upper landing of the courtyard. The chapels have been restored, but I was unable to get in. Next door is the **Indian Translation Temple**, which was completely restored in 1988. It has a single chapel dedicated to Akshobhya Vajra with gold-on-red images of Amitayus around the walls and inner circumambulation passage. Statues of Padampa Sanggye and Indrabodhi stand beside the central figure. On the upper floor is a charming chapel to Shakyamuni with Indian and Tibetan translators. A small Dzogchen Mani Temple is next door.

The Western Ling temple is **Jampa Ling**, home of the Chinese monks at the time of the great debate, recognizable by its reddish color and apselike protrusion at the rear. On the right-hand side of the entrance hall is a fine mural of Samye as it was originally. The prominent figure in the main chapel is Padmasambhava with nine thousand small clay images on shelves around the walls. The few images in orange cloth are those that survived the Cultural Revolution. The rear chapel in the apse is dedicated to the Buddha of the future, Maitreya (Tib: Jampa, hence "Jampa Ling"), beside whom are Shakyamuni and Dipamkara, Buddhas of the present and past, respectively. The murals of Maitreya in the unusual circular circumambulation passage are original and of high quality. As you leave the temple you pass the throne where Kamalashila and Hvashang Mahayana debated. A damaged old mural is all that remains.

You pass a tiny shrine called the **Rinchen Natsok Ling** on your way to the Northern Ling Temple, the **Jangchub Semkye Ling**, which is dedicated to the cultivation of *bodhichitta*, the altruistic resolve to attain enlightenment. The main image is that of Padmasambhava on a high lotus throne. A three-dimensional scale model of Samye is also found in this temple. As you continue around past the green stupa, you reach a large, red protector palace called the Samye Chok. The main figure in the chapel on the upper story is Tsemar, his face covered with a red cloth.

The Eastern Ling Temple, **Jampel Ling**, dedicated to Manjushri, was in 1994 still in complete disrepair. The small temple next door to it, the **Namdak Trimang Ling** was where Shantarakshita stayed during his sojourn at Samye.

*About a quarter of a mile to the south of Samye is a large compound with high walls called **Khamsum Sanggak Ling**. This impressive, multistory structure was converted into living quarters and storerooms. Its current state is not known.*

It is well worth climbing Hepori, the small mountain behind Samye. It affords an excellent view of the monastery and the valley and vast Brahmaputra basin. There are also several carvings on the rocks and the remains of some fortifications and stupas.

YAMALUNG AND SAMYE CHIMPU

These two sites are both important retreat centers associated with Padmasambhava. To reach Yamalung one walks from Samye north up the sandy Drakmar Valley. After an hour and a half one reaches Drakmar Drinzang, the birthplace of King Trisong Detsen. Only a tiny shrine bedecked with prayer flags marks the site of the small house where the king was born, possibly during a journey of his parents from Yarlung to Lhasa. A further hour and a half's walk takes you to the village of Ngamgo, where the river divides into two, the left branch leading via the Gokar pass to Dechen Dzong, the right to Ganden Monastery. Yamalung is two hours up the right (eastern) valley. Both Padmasambhava and his consort Yeshe Tsogyel stayed in this cave retreat in the cliff face, over which a small chapel has been erected and where a monk caretaker now lives. Higher up is the smaller meditation cave of the translator Vairochana. The founder of Mindroling Monastery, Terdak Lingpa, subsequently found *terma* at Yamalung in the seventeenth century.

Samye Chimpu is a warren of caves located in a scenic natural amphitheater four to five hours by foot (each way) north of Samye Monastery up a side valley running parallel and to the east of the Drakmar Valley that leads to Yamalung. In 776 it was here that Padmasambhava initiated the Twenty-Four Adepts of Chimpu (among whom was King Trisong Detsen) into the secrets of the Mahayoga tantras. Both he and Yeshe Tsogyel lived here for extended periods. Although all the caves were desecrated during the Cultural Revolution, they have now returned to their original use as places for retreat, and as many as a hundred monks, nuns, and lay practitioners (even the occasional Western Buddhist) might be at Chimpu at any one time. The main cave is the Drakmar Ketsang, where Padmasambhava is said to have given teachings to his eight main disciples. A prominent white temple has been built around the cave. Above this cave is a small residential building, not far from which is the Vairochana Cave, where the great early translator of the same name meditated. Towering above Chimpu is the Sangdok Pelri peak, buried in which are many other retreat caves where several notable figures within the Nyingma tradition such as Longchen Rabjampa and Jigme Lingpa stayed. Two circumambulation paths will take you around the peak.

21
TSETANG

Tsetang, the third largest town in Central Tibet, is 196 km (122 mi) from Lhasa on the south bank of the Tsangpo River. The town is in the heartland of historical Tibet, at the head of the Yarlung Valley and adjacent to the ancient capital of Nedong. Like Lhasa, the old Tibetan town is now hemmed in by a large urban Chinese administrative district. Tsetang is a good base for making day trips to Samye, Yarlung, and Chonggye as well as sites further east along the Tsangpo.

History

The old town is built on the eastern bank of the Yarlung River, at the point where it flows into the Tsangpo. It nestles at the base of the Gangpo Ri, one of the four sacred mountains of Central Tibet, where Avalokiteshvara descended into the country in the form of a red monkey and mated with a mountain demoness (herself an emanation of Tara) to produce the first six members of the Tibetan race. "Tsetang" literally means "playground," the place where the children of the monkey and the demoness came down to play. Avalokiteshvara gave these Tibetans grains and instructed them how to cultivate them in the fertile valley. (Tibet's "first field" is located behind Tsetang's modern hospital.) Symbolically, this legend tells of how under the compassionate influence of Avalokitesh-

vara the Tibetans became agriculturists and thus began the process of civilization. Avalokiteshvara to this day guides the Tibetan people through his continuing appearance in this world as the Dalai Lama.

The town itself was founded in 1351 by Jangchub Gyeltsen, the powerful leader of the Pamotrupa dynasty who rose up against the Sakya rulers of the land. In 1358 he conquered Sakya itself and thus became ruler of Central Tibet and Tsang. Jangchub Gyeltsen was born in 1302 to the influential Lang family, who since the twelfth century had provided the spiritual leaders for the nearby Densatil Monastery, founded in 1158 by the Kagyu lama Dorje Gyelpo (known as Pamotrupa, "the One from Sow's Ferry"), as well as the rulers of the local area. At this time the main town of the region was Nedong, which has now been incorporated into Tsetang, the ruins of its extensive castle are visible today on the hillside at the southern end of the modern town. In addition to being the civil ruler, Jangchub Gyeltsen was also a monk; it is said that during his reign neither wine nor women were allowed into the castle. Under his rule the "dzong" system of districts ruled by an administrator (*dzongpön*) was established. He also reformed the Sakya legal system and inaugurated the building of roads, ferries, and rest houses for travelers. Jangchub Gyeltsen and his successors, who ruled for a century before the center of power shifted to Shigatse and Tsurpu, paid no formal tribute to the Chinese emperors, thus initiating a period of independence for Tibet that would last until the seventeenth century.

Today Tsetang is the capital of the Lhoka region of southern Tibet, which extends to the Indian and Bhutanese border.

GANDEN CHÖKOR LING

If you walk up the main street of the old town of Tsetang, you will arrive at a sort of square with the monastery of Ganden Chökor Ling to the left. Founded by a monk called Sonam Tobgyal, it was previously home to 130 monks. During the reign of the Seventh Dalai Lama (1708–1757) it was converted from a Nyingma to a Geluk monastery under the abbotship of a geshe from Gyu-me called Tenzin Peljor Drakpa. In 1986 it was crumbling, deserted, and used only for storage. Now ten monks are allowed to live here again; it has been brightly painted and the chapels are being restored. The main assembly hall is sparse, with even some of the murals removed. At the back left-hand corner is the entrance to a Tara chapel with images of the Seventh Dalai Lama and the first abbot. A low doorway leads from here into the main chapel, which enshrines three huge statues of Tsongkhapa and his two chief disciples. Stairs on the right of the entrance lead to a protector chapel on the far left-hand corner of the upper story. The main images, with faces covered, are Pehar and Tsemar.

From the roof you have a good view over Tsetang. Below you to the left, near two green storage tanks, are the remains of a Sakya monastery, possibly either Drebu Ling or Samten Ling, the latter having been founded in the fourteenth century by Sonam Gyeltsen, who taught Tsongkhapa as a boy at Atisha's monastery in Netang.

NGAMCHÖ MONASTERY

Although Jangchub Gyeltsen's family was historically connected with the Kagyu tradition at Densatil Monastery, Jangchub Gyeltsen himself was a monk in the Kadam tradition. It was around the Kadam monastery he founded, known simply as Tsetang Gompa, that the village of Tsetang evolved. Jangchub Gyeltsen's successors, however, aligned themselves with the newly emerging Geluk school of Tsongkhapa. From oral information given by the Geluk monks at Ngamchö Monastery, it would appear that this was the original monastery of Jangchub Gyeltsen.

From Ganden Chökor Ling, you continue a short distance uphill eastward toward Gangpo Ri. Ngamchö Monastery is on your left. There are now twenty-two monks at Ngamchö (compared to two hundred in its heyday), and restoration has begun. At the time of the Thirteenth Dalai Lama the monastery was under the leadership of Serkong Dorje Chang, one of the few Geluk lamas of this century who disrobed in order to pursue advanced tantric practices. His son, Serkong Tsenshap Rinpoche, became an assistant tutor to the present Dalai Lama and a teacher to many Western Buddhists. Images of both lamas are found throughout the monastery. The ruins of a retreat complex connected to the monastery can be seen high on the ridge of Gangpo Ri.

SANG-NGAK ZIMCHE NUNNERY

By turning right from Ngamchö Monastery and continuing to the upper edge of the old town, you reach a small rebuilt temple on the lower slopes of Gangpo Ri. This small Geluk nunnery is reputedly one of the first nunneries of the order. It was founded on the site of a cave where a lama named Kyerong Ngawang Drakpa meditated. Above it, according to the nuns, are the ruins of another Kadam monastery called Chözom Ling. (Keith Dowman's *The Power Places of Central Tibet* maintains that these are the ruins of the Sakya monastery Samten Ling.) Eighteen nuns live here at present.

The main chapel and assembly hall of the nunnery has as its central image an old statue of a thousand-armed, thousand-eyed Avalokiteshvara. A small protector chapel dedicated to Pelden Lhamo is reached by returning to the courtyard and climbing the steps to the left.

GANGPO RI

An arduous hike will take you up this mountain that dominates the town to the "Monkey Bodhisattva Cave," where Avalokiteshvara descended to mate with the demoness. The main pilgrim route starts 8 km (5 mi) along the main road out of Tsetang eastward toward Nyingchi and ascends the steep hill, passing the ruins of the Tongdu Nunnery, before reaching the cave, which is marked by a small shrine, just below the ridge. Traditionally, Tibetans walk up here on Sakadawa, the day that celebrates the birth, enlightenment, and death of the Buddha. To complete the circumambulation route, which returns you to the Tsetang side of the ridge (just north of Trandruk Temple), takes ten to twelve hours. A more direct path takes you straight up from Tsetang in about four hours.

SHELDRAK

Looking across the town and valley to the west you can see a high, pointed mountain standing out from the surrounding hills. Just below the summit is the famous Sheldrak (Crystal Rock) Cave of Padmasambhava, which has recently been restored as a shrine. A small temple nearby houses a handful of monks who tend the site. It was here in the fourteenth century that Orgyen Lingpa discovered the Guru's biography, the *Padma Ka Tang*, hidden by Yeshe Tsogyel. Three hundred years later Terdak Lingpa of Mindroling also discovered *terma* here. As with the Gangpo Ri route, it can take between ten and twelve hours to walk to Sheldrak and back. The path starts 8 km (5 mi) south-west of the town along a dirt road that runs up the western bank of the Yarlung Valley. The pilgrimage trail starts from behind the Tsechu Bumpa, recently rebuilt on the site of the original eighth-century stupa, and winds up to the rocky summit.

An easier walk that also starts behind the Tsechu Bumpa takes you to the Lhabab Ri (Mountain of the God's Descent), where the first king Nyatri Tsenpo is believed to have magically descended to earth to rule over the Tibetans. Since Songtsen Gampo (b. 617 C.E.) is regarded as the thirty-third king in the Yarlung line, this would mean Nyatri Tsenpo would have lived several centuries B.C.E. This quasi-legendary and shamanic figure was regarded as having an Indian Buddhist ancestry. Before his arrival the Tibetans lived in caves, and it was he who erected the first hous-es, in particular Yumbulagang (see p. 143-184). Lhabab Ri is the summit that protrudes from a ridge to the south of the Tsechu Bumpa. It can be reached by a number of paths in an hour or so from the stupa. At present there is no shrine to mark the spot.

22
THE YARLUNG & CHONGGYE VALLEYS

Most of the sites in these historically important valleys can be visited in a day from Tsetang. Here we discover what remains from the great period of the Tibetan Empire, two centuries during which Tibet dominated Central Asia, threatened the borders of India and China, achieved its identity as a nation, developed a written script, and imported Buddhism. The Empire collapsed in 842, and Tibet was never again to experience such unity and political eminence.

TRANDRUK TEMPLE

Trandruk is situated in the middle of the village of the same name 5 km (3 mi) south of Tsetang up the Yarlung Valley. It houses sixty-six monks (formerly there were four hundred).

History

Trandruk is one of the first Buddhist temples built in Tibet. As with the Jokhang and Ramoche temples in Lhasa, its founding is attributed to King Songtsen Gampo in the seventh century. He is said to have erected it to house a spontaneously formed image of Tara. It is also said to have served as a winter palace for the king. Like the Katsel Temple near Medrogungkar, it is a "demoness-subduing" temple (see p. 48). It was repaired and enlarged by King Trisong Detsen,

further expanded in the fourteenth and seventeenth centuries, damaged by the Dzungars in the eighteenth century, and subsequently repaired by the Dalai Lamas. The buildings suffered both damage and neglect during the Cultural Revolution; only a few of them remain intact, and a mere handful of artifacts survive. Restoration continues.

The Site

Through the main gate is a spacious outer courtyard with a prayer wheel chapel to the right of the entrance. Around the walls are some carved relief images. A doorway leads to a middle courtyard with old and attractive murals, which in turn takes you into the inner courtyard and the temple itself. Newly installed prayer wheels surround the temple, taking you past a single Padmasambhava chapel at the rear.

The new **assembly hall** (rebuilt since 1986) contains little of note apart from Vijaya and Enlightenment Stupas in the far left-hand and right-hand corners. Most of the rooms off this hall are still empty. An exception is the first room on the right, which is a **Padmasambhava Chapel**, where the Guru sits with his two consorts. Just before the start of the inner circumambulation passage is a new **Amitabha Chapel** with three seated figures: Amitabha Buddha with Avalo-kiteshvara to the left and Vajrapani to the right. By the exit of the passage is a small **Amitayus Chapel**, featuring the traditional longevity triad of Tara, Amitayus, and Vijaya. Next door is a chapel

47. Ganden Monastery

48. Protector Chapel at Ganden Monastery

49. Preceptor and novice monks at Tashilhunpo

50. Hermit's cave at Drak Yerpa

51. Pilgrims line up to meet a high lama at Drigung Monastery

52. Drigung Monastery

53. Sky burial site near Drigung

54. Terdrom Nunnery

55. Cave of the dakinis above Terdrom Nunnery

56. Nuns roasting barley at Terdrom Nunnery

57. Tsurpu Monastery in winter

58. One of the Twenty-One Taras at the Drölma Lhakhang 59. Monk distributing "nectar" to pilgrims at Samye

60. Stone stupa marking the spot where King Trisong Detsen first met Padmasambhava near Samye Monastery

61. Statue of Guru Rinpoche at Samye built by Namkhai Nyingpo

62. Annual cham dances at Samye Monastery

63. Partially defaced mural of Manjushri, Samye Monastery

64. Samye Monastery

65. Morning sang offering at Hepori (above Samye)

66. The tomb of King Ralpachen

dedicated to the Eight Medicine Buddhas.

There are three doorways at the rear of the assembly hall. The one on the left leads to a **Songtsen Gampo Chapel**, in which the founder of the monastery is seated between his Chinese and Nepalese wives. Beside them are his ministers Tönmi Sambhota and Gawa, Manjushri, and Tara.

The large central doorway leads to the main **Tara Chapel**. The five main statues in the front are the five Dhyani Buddhas; the middle three are the restored stone originals, while the smaller two are modern replicas. The Eight Great Bodhisattvas plus an additional Manjushri and Tara (with a vase) stand to each side.

The right-hand doorway takes you into the oldest chamber in Trandruk, a **Compassion Chapel**, where the main figure is a thousand-armed image of Avalokiteshvara, embedded in which (just below his folded hands) is a self-manifested image of the bodhisattva in white stone on black. A replica of Songtsen Gampo's stove is also in here, with what is reputed to be his bowl on top.

The upper story houses the most precious relics of Trandruk to have survived. In the center of an ornate gold altar in the first chapel at the rear of this story is the famous tangka of Avalokiteshvara made from 19,928 pearls. Small niches in this carved shrine contain other paintings and statues of well-known deities. An inner shrine room within this chapel contains a similarly ornate altar with an ancient and startling gilt statue of Padmasambhava, which is said to date back to the Guru's time and to have originally been the main object of worship at Sheldrak. During the Cultural Revolution it was preserved in the Jokhang. At the rear of the chapel hang two fine old appliqué tangkas. On the right is one of Shakyamuni, purportedly one of three made by Wen Cheng (one of which is in the tomb of the Fifth Dalai Lama in the Potala, the other in the Maitreya chapel in Tashilhunpo). On the left is another, Chinese in style, of Lokeshvara, which originally came from Rechung Puk.

As you leave this chapel you will come to a small protector chapel on your left dedicated primarily to the Indian god White Brahma.

YUMBULAGANG

A further 6 km (4 mi) up the Yarlung Valley a small road winds up to the left and takes you to what is regarded as the site of the oldest building in Tibet.

History

Yumbulagang is believed by Tibetans to have been originally built by the first king of the Yarlung dynasty, Nyatri Tsenpo. This tall, dignified building rises erect on the spur of a hill, commanding an impressive view of the entire valley. Scholars aver that the building that stood on this site until the mid-sixties probably dated back to the seventh or eighth century and may well have been built by either Songtsen Gampo or Trisong Detsen. Tibetan murals suggest that it found its final form during the time of the Fifth Dalai Lama. It was destroyed during the Cultural Revolution; the present structure is a replica, built in 1982. It is cared for by seven Geluk monks.

The Site

Yumbulagang has long ceased to be used as a fortress or a dwelling and has been turned into a shrine to the Tibetan Empire. The central figure on the ground floor is a Buddha called Jowo Norbu Sampel, who presides over the assembled kings and ministers. To the left of it is Nyatri Tsenpo and to the right Songtsen Gampo. Along the left-hand wall are lined the minister Tönmi Sambhota and the kings Trisong Detsen and Tori Nyentsen. Facing them along the opposite wall are kings Tri Ralpachen and Ö Sung, followed by the minister Gawa.

The upper story houses a delightful chapel built around a balcony from which you can look down into the shrine below. The main images are of Avalokiteshvara and Shakyamuni. The statue of Avalokiteshvara is a replica of the one originally here, which was in the same style as the one enshrined in the Lokeshvara chapel in the Potala. An old tangka, recovered from the ruins of the original building, is framed behind glass to the left of the altar. To the left of Shakyamuni is a small encased image of the Medicine Buddha, retrieved by the Panchen Lama in 1987. Murals depicting key events in the early history of Tibet are newly painted in a folkloric style. Starting from the

left, Nyatri Tsenpo is shown descending from the heavens and settling near Lhabab Ri. A Sanskrit Buddhist scripture (symbolizing the very first intimation of the Dharma in Tibet) is seen descending from the sky at the time of King Lhatotori (b. 173 C.E.) and settling on the tower of Yumbulagang. Padmasambhava is seen meditating in a cave, probably Sheldrak.

RECHUNG PUK

From Yumbulagang head back in the direction of Tsetang until you come to a road on the left that crosses the valley into a long tree-lined lane. Rechung Puk is high on the spur that divides the Yarlung and Chonggye Valleys, clearly visible from afar. Vehicles are parked at the base of the mountain. An easy climb on foot takes you to the monastery.

History

One of Milarepa's foremost disciples was a yogi named Rechungpa (1083–1161). He was eleven years old when he met Milarepa and spent many years practicing under his guidance. He traveled twice to India, where he also studied extensively with Indian teachers. In contrast to Milarepa's other main disciple, the scholar-monk Gampopa, Rechungpa was a lay yogi. Rechung Puk (Rechung's cave) is one of the places where Rechungpa spent time meditating. Three hundred years later the site was associated with another famous lay yogi, Tsangnyön Heruka (1455–1529), who claimed to follow

Rechung Puk, 1949

Rechungpa's oral tradition rather than the clerical approach of Gampopa. Tsangnyön (The Crazy One from Tsang) is best known for his outrageous behavior and as the author of the biography and collected songs of Milarepa. Tsangnyön Heruka spent the last years of his life at Rechung Puk. Ironically, perhaps, the site subsequently became the base for a large monastic institution. By 1959 the population had dwindled to sixty monks. Today there are eight.

The Site

All that remains at Rechung Puk is a small cluster of white buildings, which have been rebuilt around the site of the cave, below the ruins of the main monastery. The monastery belongs to a tradition called the Rechung Nyinggyu, which combines the Kagyu and Nying-ma lineages.

The main chapel is reached by a stairway that leads to a balcony. The principal figures on the altar represent the major teachers in the lineage of the monastery: (from the left) Vairochana, Manjushri, Rinchen Drakpa (a disciple of Rechung-pa), Padmasambhava, Milarepa, Marpa, and Rechungpa. Rechungpa's cave—a small recess in the rock wall—is in the far left-hand corner of the chapel. The main statue is of Tsangnyön Heruka, surrounded by buddhas, stupas, and other Kagyu lamas. To the right is an old desecrated statue of Tsangpa Gyare Yeshe Dorje, a disciple of Pamotrupa and founder of the Drukpa Kagyu order.

TANGBOCHE MONASTERY

17 km (10 mi) down the Chonggye Valley from Tsetang, you will notice to your left a square temple building at the base of the hillside in a village. This is Tangboche.

History

Tangboche means "great plain." This area in the lower Chonggye Valley derives its name from the time when the vast forest on the hillside burned down and showered the valley below with ash and charcoal, causing people to call it *solnak tangboche*, the "great plain of coals." It is believed that a monastery was founded here as early as the seventh or eighth century by a disciple of the Indian master Chandragomin. It was revived in 1017 by a monk named Tsultrim Jungne, a disciple of Lumpa Lumepa, one of the main figures responsible for the reestablishment of the monastic order in Central Tibet and Tsang after the suppression of Buddhism by Langdarma. During the eleventh century the abbot of Tangboche, Tsöndru Yungdrung, invited Atisha to live in the monastery. The Indian master accepted and for some time resided in the small hermitage on the hillside facing the main temple. Two relics from the time of Atisha were cherished by the monastery: a statue of the master and a set of twelve texts brought by him from India. These were lost during the Cultural Revolution, and efforts are still being made by the monks to retrieve them. The lama of the monastery, Jampa Kelsang, currently lives as a layman in Germany.

The Site

From the outside, the monastery still gives the impression of disrepair, despite the fact that thirty-three monks have now returned. The altar in the main assembly hall of Tangboche contains few images, most of them small bronzes offered to the monastery by the government to replace what had been lost. There are several Buddhas, a fine red dakini, and Atisha. To the left of the assembly hall a door leads to a protector chapel with images of the five wrathful guardians, painted in gold on black walls. Small cabinets line the wall leading from the door of this chapel to that of the main chapel at the rear, which houses images of Shakyamuni, Tsongkhapa, and Vajrayogini. Facing them on the front wall are fine old murals of the Eight Great Bodhisattvas in standing pose.

The striking feature of Tangboche is not its statuary but the excellent murals that have been preserved on all four walls of the assembly hall. These were commissioned in 1915 by the Thirteenth Dalai Lama and are still in good condition. Starting from the left as you enter through the main doorway, the deities depicted are as follows: Pelden Lhamo, accompanied by two lion-headed beings and painted with extraordinary attention to detail; Vaishravana; Manjushri; Vajrasattva; Vajrapani; Sarvavid; Vairochana; Samvara and consort surrounded by the principal dakinis of the mandala; Shakyamuni; Yamantaka and consort; and Atisha. Going past the altar to the opposite wall you find the triad of Padmasambhava, Trisong Detsen, and Shantarakshita; the Eight Medicine Buddhas; and an exquisite Avalokiteshvara mounted on a lion (Chenrezi Sengge Dra); the Eight Taras who Dispel Fear; Mahakala; and Dharmaraja.

From the upper story one can study the fine murals of the Buddha and the Sixteen Arhats, and the Fifth and the Thirteenth Dalai Lamas painted along the back of the raised, skylight section of the main hall.

If you climb the hill immediately in front of the monastery, you will reach the **Atisha Chapel**, where the great Bengali teacher lived during his stay at Tangboche. A creaking gate leads into a pleasant courtyard. The small shrine room has been recently decorated with murals. On the right are Atisha, Drom Tönpa, and the Kadampa lama Tsöndru Yungdrung, a disciple of Atisha and abbot of Tangboche during the master's stay. The same three figures also dominate the altar in the raised shrine at the back of the hall. The

Fifth and Seventh Dalai Lamas are depicted on the left-hand and right-hand walls, respectively. A single torn fragment survives of a painting depicting the travels of Atisha through Tibet.

CHONGGYE: THE TOMBS OF THE TIBETAN KINGS

At the end of the Chonggye Valley, 13 km (8 mi) from Tangboche or 30 km (19 mi) direct from Tsetang, are the tumuli erected as tombs for the kings of the Tibetan Empire during the seventh and eighth centuries. To reach them you pass through the recently expanded modern town of Chonggye.

The Site

Chonggye was the site chosen by the early Tibetan kings as their burial ground. The large, eroded tumuli that

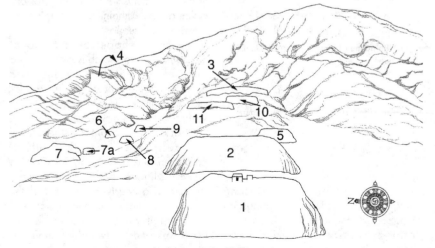

The Chonggye Tombs of the Tibetan Kings

mark the tombs are found at the end of the valley. The biggest and most easily recognizable tomb—with the small temple on top—belongs to King Songtsen Gampo. It is probable that his two queens were also buried with him here. There are conflicting accounts as to the identity, and even the number, of the other tombs. I will follow here the description given to me by one of the monks responsible for the temple atop Songtsen Gampo's tomb; the numbers correspond to those on the accompanying plan.

1. Songtsen Gampo (617–649), reigned from 629.

2. Mangsong Mangtsen (646–676), the grandson of Songtsen Gampo, enthroned 650.

3. Dride Tsugten [Me Agdzom] (704–754), enthroned in the year of his birth.

4. Trisong Detsen (742–797), reigned from 754.

5. Mune Tsenpo (d. 800), a son of Trisong Detsen, reigned from 797.

6. Tride Songtsen [Se-na-lek], a son of Trisong Detsen, (776–815), reigned from 800.

7. Tri Ralpachen [Tritsug Detsen] (805–836), reigned from 815.
   7a. Stele erected by Tri Ralpachen.

8. Langdarma (803–842), reigned from 836.

9. Ö Sung (843–905), the son of Langdarma.

10. Lhe Bön (d.739), the son of Dride Tsugten.

11. Luna Trukyi Gyelpo (n.d.), the son of Lhe Bön (?).

With the exception of Dusong Mangpoje, the successor of Mangsong Mangtsen, all the kings of the powerful Yarlung dynasty are buried here.

Songtsen Gampo (1), Trisong Detsen (4), and Tri Ralpachen (7) occupy the prominent positions in early Tibetan history. It was through their efforts that Tibet was transformed from an insignificant border area into a major Central Asian power and Buddhism introduced and established as the religion of the land. The stele (7a) erected by Tri Ralpachen at the side of his tomb is sunk into the ground and enshrined in a small, bare chapel. The runelike inscriptions on it are hard to decipher. Apparently the notorious Langdarma (8), who brought the dynasty to an end through his factionalism and anti-Buddhist policies, is also entombed here, albeit in a rather insignificant tumulus. His son Ö Sung (9), who established the kingdom of Gu-ge in the west of Tibet, lies beside him. Some distance away, about 1 km (.6 mi) further down the valley, is another barely visible tumulus in which, the Tibetans claim, are the remains of the first king of Tibet, Nyatri Tsenpo.

The small chapel on the top of Songtsen Gampo's tomb is reached by a flight of stone stairs from the road below. From the tumulus one has a clear view of all the other tombs except that of Trisong Detsen, which is out of sight on the back of the mountain. The chapel was destroyed during the Cultural Revolution and rebuilt only in 1983. In 1994 additional buildings were constructed in a courtyard in front of the shrine. The main figure is a statue of King Songtsen Gampo flanked by his two wives and his two chief ministers,

Tönmi Sambhota and Gawa. The newly painted murals depict the Eight Taras Who Dispel Fear, the Thirty-Five Buddhas of Confession, Padmasambhava and his eight main manifestations, and the protectors Mahakala, Ekajati, Pelden Lhamo and Vaishravana. Anoth-er chapel behind the main room is dedicated to the Buddhas of the Three Times: Maitreya is the central figure, to the left is Dipamkara, and to the right Shakyamuni. Amitayus sits to the far left and Padmasambhava to the far right. Vajrapani and Hayagriva stand on guard. Five Nyingma monks now live in the temple.

Close by but out of sight of the shrine is Tsering Jong, a hermitage of the eighteenth-century Nyingma sage Jigme Lingpa, where twenty-five nuns currently live.

RIWO DECHEN MONASTERY

Just before arriving at the tombs of the ancient kings in Chonggye you pass through the village of the same name, above which are the clearly visible ruins of the Chingwa Taktse Castle, a series of ramparts climbing the ridge of the hill. A castle was originally built here by King Shatri, the tenth ruler in the Yarlung line, and was the principal residence of the Yarlung kings until the time of Songtsen Gampo. In a later construction below the royal palace was the home of the locally powerful Nyingma family into which the Fifth Dalai Lama was born in 1617. All these buildings were already in a state of disrepair before the Chinese occupation.

Beneath the ramparts are the remains of the once magnificent Riwo Dechen Monastery. The mighty, crumbling walls of the main assembly hall are all that still stand of the original monastery, whose seventy buildings once covered the upper part of the hillside. This main assembly hall was founded by the fifteenth-century lama Lowo Pelzang according to a design of Gartön Chöje, a disciple of Khedrup Je. At the time of the Fifth Dalai Lama it was associated with Drepung. The monastery grew in size and by 1959 housed about six hundred monks.

In 1985 the first few monks returned to start reconstruction. There are now ninety monks living in or affiliated with the monastery (out of a maximum of ninety-nine allowed by the state). A completely new and smaller assembly hall with three chapels has been built to the left of the old one. The main chapel houses large images of Tsongkhapa and his two disciples, accompanied by Tara, Maitreya, and the Fifth and Thirteenth Dalai Lamas. Steps to the right lead to a small protector shrine dedicated to Yamantaka. Extensive restoration is currently under way.

23
LHAMO'I LATSO: THE ORACLE LAKE

Tsetang is the gateway from Central Tibet both to the Southern province of Lhodrak and the Eastern provinces of Kongpo and Kham. Lhodrak was where both Marpa and Milarepa lived. A day's drive will bring you to Serkargutok, the nine-story tower that Milarepa built for his teacher to prove his sincerity and atone for former evils. The basic structure still stands and is a pilgrimage site. Non-Tibetans, however, are still officially prevented from visiting the area.

The main highway continues eastward from Tsetang along the south bank of the Tsangpo to Nyingchi, where it joins the northern road from Lhasa and Medrogungkar, and heads for Kham. This chapter will concentrate on the area between Tsetang and Nyingchi, taking as its focus the famous "oracle lake" of Lhamo'i Latso, whose waters would be contemplated for visions by monks in search of the next incarnation of the Dalai Lama.

DENSATIL MONASTERY

About 25 km (15 mi) east of Tsetang at the village of Rong, the Tsangpo narrows and the road veers south away from the turbulent course of the river. A ferry will take you from Rong to Sangri on the northern bank. The ruins of the once magnificent Kagyu monastery of Densatil, situated in a valley high above the Tsangpo, lie several kilometers to the west of Sangri.

Densatil was founded in 1158 by Dorje Gyelpo (1110–1170), a monk from Eastern Tibet, who was a leading disciple of Gampopa. Initially, Dorje Gyelpo built himself a simple meditation hut in the valley, but as his fame and teachings spread, a large monastic community was formed around him, thus establishing the first major Kagyu monastery in Tibet. He became the teacher of three founders of Kagyu sub-orders: Talung Tangpa Tashi Pel, who established Talung Monastery and the Talung order (chapter 14), Jigten Sumgon, who established Drigung Monastery and the Drigung order (chapter 15), and Ling Repa, who established the Drukpa Kagyu order. Dorje Gyelpo was also known as Pamotrupa ("the One from Sow's Ferry"), and this name was adopted by the powerful Lang family from Nedong who became patrons of the monastery and, in the fourteenth century under Jangchub Gyeltsen, founders of the Pamotrupa dynasty. Unlike his fellow student of Gampopa, the First Karmapa, as well as his three main disciples, whose orders survived into the twentieth century, Dorje Gyelpo's monastery did not become a base for a distinct Kagyu order. This was due largely to the Pamotrupa family's support for Tsongkhapa and the Geluk order in the early fifteenth century. The monastery's fortunes inevitably became tied to the political power of its patrons.

After the Pamotrupa dynasty collapsed, Densatil declined as a monastic center. It was destroyed during the Cultural Revolution, and only a few small shrines (the principal one being on the site of Dorje Gyelpo's meditation hut) have been rebuilt on the ruins.

THE OLKA VALLEY

The Olka Valley is the traditional route from Lhasa to Lhamo'i Latso, which was followed by the Dalai Lamas and their regents. Remnants of the stone-paved pathway can still be seen as you ascend the higher reaches of the valley toward the Gyelong pass.

Several kilometers east of Sangri, before meeting the Olka River, you come to the ruins of **Sangri Karmar**, the site of the hermitage of one of Tibet's greatest yogis, Machik Labdrön (1049–1129). Machik Labdrön's first teacher was Drapa Ngonshe of Dranang. Her main guru, however, was the Indian yogi Padampa Sanggye. As his consort and main disciple, Machik received and developed the zhije (pacifying) and chöd (cutting) traditions of tantric practice, becoming the only woman to found a major teaching lineage in Tibet as well as reputedly the only Tibetan whose teachings were transmitted back to India. Toward the end of her life she settled in Sangri and became a nun. A monastery subsequently grew up around her hermitage. It was later taken over by the Geluk order and razed during the Cultural Revolution.

As you head upstream, the river divides into northern and eastern tributaries at the village of **Olka Taktse**. The northern tributary ultimately leads over the mountains to Medrogungkar. Eight km (5 mi) upstream you come to **Dzinchi**, famous as the site of a chapel that housed an ancient statue of the future Buddha Maitreya. In 1393 the statue was restored by Tsongkhapa, an act regarded as the first of the master's four great deeds. The connection with the Gelukpas continued at Dzinchi through its becoming the residence of the incarnation line of Gyeltsab Dharma Rinchen, one of the two chief disciples of Tsongkhapa, and his immediate successor as Throne Holder of Ganden. Ironically, the relics of Taranata, founder of the Jonang school, whose philosophical writings were severely criticized and proscribed by the Gelukpa, were enshrined here. Dzinchi was also the birthplace of Khedrup Gyatso, the short-lived Eleventh Dalai Lama. Little of this historic site has been restored.

The eastern tributary of the Olka River is the one you follow to reach Lhamo'i Latso. Shortly after Olka Taktse, on the southern slopes of this tributary is **Chölung**, where Tsongkhapa spent five years in retreat and in 1397 experienced his deepest insight into emptiness. Several indentations in rocks where Tsongkhapa performed prostrations and offerings will be shown to you by the monks. Since 1986 this historically important monastery has been restored and now houses a number of Geluk monks. Another important meditation retreat, originally used by Padmasambhava and subsequently by both Gampopa and Tsongkhapa is the cave of **Olka Garpuk**. It can be reached by a path to the north of the tributary, three to four hours from Olka Taktse, via the ruins of **Samten Ling Monastery**. From Chölung it takes two days to cross the Gyelong pass and descend to **Chökorgyel Monastery**, the last staging post on the old route to Lhamo'i Latso.

BY ROAD TO CHÖKORGYEL MONASTERY

From the ferry crossing at Rong, the main Tsetang-Nyingchi road leaves the river and heads southeast to rejoin the Tsangpo at the town of Gyatsa.

South of the road, a couple of kilometers after leaving the river, is the Geluk monastery of **Chökor Chöde**. Although in poor condition, the original building was not destroyed, and the murals in the main assembly hall have been fairly well preserved. They depict the Sixteen Arhats and a number of protectors. The main images on the altar are of Tsongkhapa and the Buddha. A somewhat dilapidated protector chapel on the upper story is dedicated to Pelden Lhamo and contains a very old statue of Yamantaka. Ten monks are resident here, but the incarnate lama of the monastery, Ngawang Norbu, lives in exile in India. From the roof one can view the ruins of the former *dzong* (fort).

In a further 32 km (20 mi), after the road has turned south up a deep valley, one reaches **Lhagyari** (or Chusum), the site of a palace built by King Songtsen Gampo and the Geluk monastery of Rikung Chöten. Coming from Tsetang you will notice the ruins of the palace looming ahead of you just before the road bears to the right. What remains of the palace is exposed to the elements, and all the surviving rooms appear to be empty. There is little to see but some old defaced murals, the best preserved of which is one of Songtsen Gampo and his two queens. **Rikung Chöten** is reached by a steep path to the right just before you get to the palace road. It was founded by Rikung Ngawang Drakpa during the time of the Second Dalai Lama (1476–1542) and in its heyday housed 170 monks. It was destroyed during the Cultural Revolution and rebuilt by local people in 1985. At present 17 young monks and 30 elder former monks live here. Two buildings have been restored: the assembly hall and a Jowo Chapel.

After crossing the Potang La Pass (5030 m; 16,404 ft) the road winds down through a fertile valley into the harsh and barren region of Gyatsa. The town of Gyatsa Xian is 141 km (88 mi) from Tsetang, about a five-hour drive. A single monastery, **Dakpo Shedrup Ling**, emerges from the tin-roofed development of the modern town. It has around sixty monks and belongs to the Kagyu school, with a room set aside for the Karmapa. Shortly after the town, turn left up a road that takes you to a suspension bridge across the Tsangpo to the village of Gyatsa Chu, where Songtsen Gampo's Chinese queen, Wen Cheng, is reputed to have stayed. Although it is only 43 km (27 mi) from here to Chökorgyel Monastery, the road that climbs up the valley is in such poor repair that it takes more than four hours to complete the journey.

Chökorgyel Monastery was founded in 1509 by Gendun Gyatso, the Second Dalai Lama. During his lifetime he was regarded as the incarnation of Tsongkhapa's disciple Gendun Drup, the founder of Tashilhunpo Monastery near Shigatse, but not as the Dalai Lama, since that title and office were first given to his successor Sonam Gyatso, the Third Dalai Lama, and then retrospectively applied to the former incarnations. Gendun Gyatso entered Tashilhunpo at the age of nine and subsequently became abbot not only of his home monastery but also of Drepung and Sera. It was he who consecrated Lhamo'i Latso as enshrining the spirit of Pelden Lhamo, the protectress of Tibet, hence the name the Goddess's (*Lhamo'i*) Spirit (*La*) Lake (*tso*). Chökorgyel, the only major monastery Gendun Gyatso founded, was built as close as possible to his sacred lake near the cave that served him as a retreat. It became a sizable and important Gelukpa monastic college, with rooms for the Dalai Lamas and their regents. Both the Thirteenth Dalai Lama and the Regent Reting Rinpoche, who discovered the whereabouts of the present Dalai Lama

through a vision in the lake in 1935, stayed at Chökorgyel on their way to Lhamo'i Latso. The monastery was reduced to rubble during the Cultural Revolution.

Only one solitary building, a rather cramped assembly hall, arises from the midst of these ruins. In the mid-1990s building materials still competed for space with tangkas, texts, thrones, and statues. One of the higher thrones to the right bears a statue of Gendun Gyatso. Fifteen monks are currently registered at the monastery, but not all of them live here. A square utilitarian building to the south of the ruins functions as a primitive guesthouse.

LHAMO'I LATSO

It is possible to hire both a guide and a horse at Chökorgyel, thus making the walk to the lake relatively straightforward. Nonetheless, it is an arduous ten- to twelve-hour hike to reach Lhamo'i Latso and return to Chökorgyel by nightfall.

Just below the ruins of the monastery you cross a bridge and turn left. The path soon brings you into a large valley with a fast-flowing river. Follow the valley until you reach a primitive bridge (stepping-stones supporting planks) over the river. This is about one and a half hours from the monastery, near a huge sweep of loose red shale. Cross the river and proceed up the hillside for twenty minutes until you enter a smaller valley (the first tributary on the left). This takes you across a series of level pastures until you reach the small Yoni Lake. From here you continue ascending to an open yak pasture with a stream, which brings you to the base of the final ridge. A very steep climb of half an hour takes you to the narrow pass at the top, from where you overlook the U-shaped valley, with Lhamo'i Latso at the far end. It was here that the Dalai Lamas and their regents would sit to contemplate the lake for visions. A narrow path zigzags down from the pass into the valley and circumambulates the lake, at the far end of which is a recently built square shrine covered with prayer flags and filled with numerous small statues.

DAKLHA GAMPO MONASTERY

The site of Gampopa's monastery above the banks of the Tsangpo can be reached either by a jeep road from Gyatsa Chu or by a two-day walk from Lhamo'i Latso.

By following the course of the stream that runs from the northeast corner of the lake, you will join (in about four hours) a large, wider valley. The descent along the narrow trail down the banks of the river takes you through delightful forests of oak, mixed conifer, and rhododendron, interspersed with alpine meadows, occasional villages, and the remains of watchtowers. It is the first forested area east of Lhasa. Eventually you emerge onto the barren, windswept banks of the Tsangpo. By turning west along the jeep road back to Gyatsa, you will soon

come to a village high above which are visible the ruins of Daklha Gampo. It takes about two hours to climb up there.

As a young man Gampopa, or Dakpo Lhaje, (1079–1153) was trained as a doctor. His young wife died when he was twenty, causing him to reflect deeply on the purpose of human life. Six years later he was ordained as a monk in the Kadampa tradition of Atisha and devoted himself to the study of Buddhism. At the age of thirty-two, having heard of the great yogi Milarepa, he sought him out and received instruction from him in tantric meditation. Ten years later, in 1121, he founded Daklha Gampo. He combined his understanding of Kadampa doctrine and the Mahamudra teachings of Milarepa in his famous study of the Buddhist path, *The Jewel Ornament of Liberation* (translated by H.V. Guenther, 1959). His disciples included the First Karmapa and Dorje Gyelpo (Pamotrupa).

Daklha Gampo never reached the eminence of the great Kagyu monasteries of Tsurpu, Talung, and Drigung. In the early eighteenth century it suffered from the ravages of the Dzungars. It was completely destroyed during the Cultural Revolution.

PART THREE

TSANG

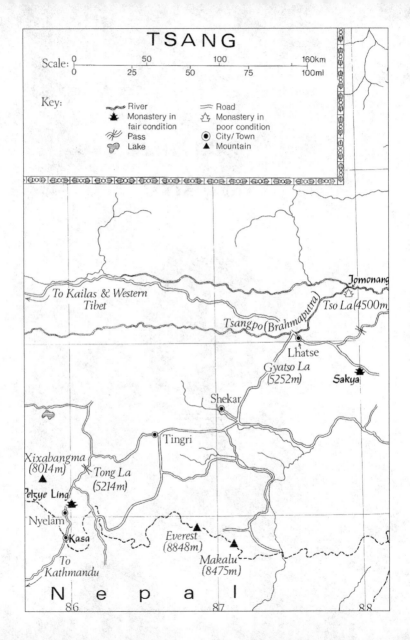

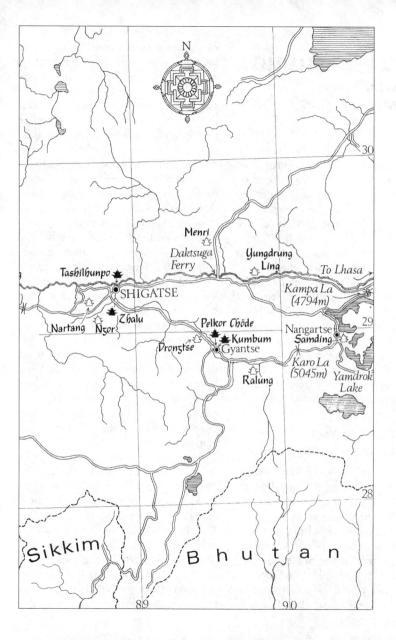

24
SAMDING, TALUNG, & RALUNG MONASTERIES

There are two ways to reach the province of Tsang from Central Tibet. Since the recent improvement of the main road from Lhasa to Shigatse that follows the course of the Tsangpo, most traffic takes that route. Traditionally, the caravan route climbed over the Kamba-la Pass to Nangartse, then over the Karo-la Pass and on to the town of Gyantse. From there the main trading route continued south via Pari and Yadong to Sikkim and India. (Although this border is open again to Indian traders, it still remains closed to tourists.) This chapter will follow the latter route, visiting Samding, Talung, and Ralung Monasteries. The former route to Shigatse is covered in chapter 28.

YAMDROK YUMTSO: THE TURQUOISE LAKE

Having crossed the Tsangpo at Chaksam, one turns right (as opposed to left for the airport and Tsetang) onto a smaller unmetalled road that soon begins the long, winding ascent of the Kamba-la Pass. On the opposite hillside you can see an access road leading to a mine, which the Tibetans say is used by the Chinese to extract "white gold." The first view you have of the breathtakingly beautiful, deep blue-green water of Yamdrok is when you look down from the top of the pass at 4,794 meters (15,724 feet). In fact you see only one arm of this irregularly shaped lake with a circumference of 240 km (150 mi). (A fine view can be had of the whole lake from the airplane window as you fly from or to Kathmandu.) The Italian scholar Giuseppe Tucci described it as being "as still and as deep blue as the sea can be at Naples on one of these days when heaven and earth seem to clasp each other in an embrace of love." Since 1986 the Chinese have built a hydroelectric plant in the valley below, supplied by a tunnel that drains the lake's water. Although it provides electricity for the region, many Tibetans object to what they consider this desecration of one of Tibet's most sacred lakes.

The road descends to the shore of the lake and follows its winding course to the dismal little town of Nangartse (154 km or 96 mi from Lhasa). In earlier times, Nangartse had been a provincial capital of some importance, its main claim to fame being that a daughter of a Nangartse prince gave birth to the Fifth Dalai Lama. The town was already run-down when Tucci passed through in 1949.

On the ridge of the hill that descends at the back of the down is **Ngön Kar Chöde**, a monastery that was totally ruined during the Cultural Revolution and has just started to be restored. It belongs to the Bodong tradition of Samding Monastery (see below). It used to be a large monastery containing sixteen chapels, with fifty monks. At present there are only twelve monks, since that is all the local community can support. It receives no government funding, and all the cost for rebuilding is raised by the monks in Lhasa. The main chapel on the ground floor has a statue of the Buddha and Bodong Chokle Namgyel, the founder of Samding, as well as some small bronzes. A tiny protector chapel contains an image of Pelden Lhamo and a local protector who appears as an old man holding a skull cup. On the upper story is a chapel to Padmasambhava, the statue of whom is surrounded by copies of the Kangyur.

Dorje Pagmo (seated), abbess of Samding, in July 1935

SAMDING MONASTERY

Samding is 10 km (6 mi) east of Nangartse, visible from the town on the ridge of a hill. About halfway to the monastery is a small village with a rare copse of trees, which the local people believe to have sprung from locks of Padmasambhava's hair. The monastery overlooks a smaller lake of the Yamdrok complex.

History

Samding Monastery was probably founded by Khetsun Zhonu Drup during the latter part of the thirteenth century, but it is best known for its association with the eminent lama Bodong Chokle Namgyel (1306–1386). Bodong was an immensely learned scholar, a poet, and a prolific writer. He composed a total of a hundred volumes of writings. He stud-

ied with Sherab Gyeltsen of the Jomonang Monastery and at one time gave instruction to Tsongkhapa, but the order he founded, the Bodong tradition, was soon overshadowed by the Geluk and never gained any widespread prominence. The Bodong order was a syncretic school based on the Nyingma and Sakya teachings. It survived until 1959 as a small sect based at Samding, with thirty subtemples in the nearby regions affiliated with it.

Samding was most noted for being headed by one of the only female incarnate lamas in Tibet, Dorje Pagmo, named after the female tantric deity Vajravarahi (Adamantine Sow), the yidam of Bodong Chokle Namgyel. The community under her was unusual in that it consisted of both monks and nuns. Sarat Chandra Das, in his *Journey to Lhasa and Central Tibet,* recounts that

In 1716, when the Dzungar [Mongol] invaders of Tibet came to Nangartse, their chief sent word to Samding for Dorje Pagmo to appear before him, that he might see if she really had, as reported, a pig's head. A mild answer was returned him; but incensed at her refusing to obey his summons, he tore down the walls of the monastery of Samding, and broke into the sanctuary. He found it deserted, not a human being in it, only eighty pigs and as many sows grunting in the congregation hall under the lead of a big sow, and he dared not sack a place belonging to pigs. But when the Dzungars had given up all idea of sacking Samding, suddenly the pigs disappeared to become venerable-looking monks and nuns, with the saintly Dorje Pagmo at their head. Filled with astonishment and veneration for the sacred character of the lady abbess, the chief made immense presents to the monastery.

The peculiar arrangement of having a community of monks under the direction of an abbess has spawned a number of fictitious tales in the West, best-known of which is Lionel Davidson's entertaining but scurrilous novel *The Rose of Tibet*. There the monastery is called Yamdring, a compound of Yamdrok and Samding. The present incarnation of Dorje Pagmo, the twelfth in the line, is a woman in her late forties who initially renounced the religious life and apparently supported the Communist regime. In 1989 she started to assume some of the responsibilities of the late Panchen Lama. In 1994, however she had resumed her role as head of the monastery and was once again teaching and giving initiations. She lives in Lhasa.

The Site

Samding was destroyed during the Cultural Revolution but has been considerably rebuilt since 1986 and currently houses thirty-four monks.

A steep road leads you to the rear of the monastery, where you enter an untidy courtyard with the monks' residences on the left. A stairway on the right takes you into the monastery proper. At the front of the **assembly hall** are cabinets with newly made statues of Padmasambhava, Bodong Chokle Namgyel (the monastery's founder), and Dorje Pagmo (the abbess). To the right are a throne for the Dalai Lama, which he used in 1956 while on his way to India to attend the celebrations for the 2,500th anniversary of the Buddha's

Samding Monastery before 1959

enlightenment, and a smaller one for the abbess. A chapel at the rear of the assembly hall contains statues of Shakyamuni accompanied by the Eight Great Bodhisattvas. A door at the back right-hand corner of the chapel leads into a protector chapel dedicated to Pelden Lhamo. There is also an image of a local deity, Tashi Obar. To the right of the assembly hall a passage leads to a Kangyur chapel. A carpet on the left of this corridor portrays how Samding used to look before its destruction. Shelves on the back wall of the **Kangyur Chapel** contain an edition of the Buddhist canon, in the midst of which is a cabinet with statues of Shakyamuni and Vajradhara and a Kadampa stupa. The room also contains a large mani wheel.

The only other temple in the monastery (off to the left of the assembly hall) is a **Tsechu Chapel**, where presumably monks gather on the tenth of each lunar month (*tsechu* means "tenth of the month"), containing an image of Padmasambhava, who is traditionally celebrated on this day. A small cabinet on the right contains a small statue of Vajrayogini.

TALUNG MONASTERY

Eight km (5 mi) west of Nangartse a small, unmarked road turns south, crosses a river, and enters a valley. This road will eventually take you to the southern province of Lhoka. After 12 km (7 mi) you see a hill ahead of you. The road swings into a village called Yamdrok Talung clustered around the far side of the hill. Talung Monastery is at the foot of the hill. "Talung" is a common name in Tibet. To distinguish this Talung Monastery from the one of the same name north of Lhasa described in chapter 14, it is sometimes called Lho Talung (Southern Talung).

While there was probably a monastery on this site at the time of the early Tibetan empire, it rose to prominence during the fourteenth century through its association with the famous Sakya lama Tatsang Lotsawa, after whom it is named ("Talung" means "place of Tatsang"). Until 1959, there were two monastic complexes: Sangngak Chökor Ling, a Nyingma monastery higher up on the hill, which was affiliated with Dorje Drak and is now in ruins, and Tarling Chöde, the Sakya monastery founded by Tatsang at the foot of the hill, which is being restored. Eleven monks, some Nyingma and some Sakya, lived here in 1994 and performed their major ceremonies together. Carved images of the Buddha, Avalokiteshvara, and Padmasambhava have been repainted on the cliff wall and covered with makeshift shrines. To their left are further carvings of Virupa, Sakya Pandita, and Avalokiteshvara. Nearby on the hillside are also the remains of Tatsang Lotsawa's residence.

The hall on the right of the courtyard as you enter is dedicated to Padmasambhava. A two-story image of the Guru, completed in 1991, occupies nearly all the space on both floors. In grottoes behind him are images of his eight manifestations. On the ground floor, you stand below his lotus throne and his two consorts Mandarava and Yeshe Tsogyel. On the upper story, you can see his large, startling face. A statue of the protectress Ekajati is in a cabinet in the small room before him.

The building on the left of the courtyard is the main **assembly hall**, built in the fifteenth century. The structure was not destroyed during the Cultural Revolution; the statuary, however, is new. The main image is Tara, to whose side is the wrathful deity Dorje Drakpoze. Old murals of the five great Sakya lamas and the Thirty-Five Confessional Buddhas are depicted on the upper wall above the throne. The chapel dedicated to Shakyamuni at the rear of the hall is believed to date back to the time of the Empire. The ornate halo around the Buddha, the murals, and the pillars seem to be ancient, but in 1994 one could only view them through a skylight from the roof. There are also said to be old wooden images of the teachers in the Sakya lam-dre lineage here.

From the roof of the monastery you can see at the foot of the hills in the west a vase-shaped stupa, which is believed to have been erected by the "crazy yogi" Drukpa Kunleg, who once had a hermitage higher in the hills.

RALUNG MONASTERY

From Nangartse the road to Gyantse heads for the Karo-la Pass (5045 m, 16,400 ft). The Karo-la was the site of a crucial military engagement on May 6, 1904, between the invading army of Colonel Francis Younghusband and the Tibetan forces, who had erected a line of defense across the pass in order to prevent the British from reaching Lhasa. The Tibetans were routed by superior troops and firepower and from that point on offered little further resistance to the British, who reached Lhasa—by the very route we have been following—at the beginning of August.

After descending the Karo-la, the turnoff to Ralung is 221 km (138 mi) from Lhasa (67 km/42 mi from Nangartse) and is indicated by a signpost on the left of the road in Tibetan and English. The ruins and buildings of the monastery are 4.5 km/3 mi along the riverbed from the road.

History

Ralung was founded in 1180 by Tsangpa Gyare Yeshe Dorje (1126–1211), the first Gyalwang Drukchen. Yeshe Dorje was a disciple of Ling Repa, who in turn studied with the famous Kagyu lama Pamotrupa at Densatil. Ling Repa is considered to be the spiritual founder of the Drukpa Kagyu suborder and Yeshe Dorje the one who established the order's main monastery. Ralung grew into one of the largest and most influential Kagyu centers in Tibet. The fourth Drukchen was the renowned Tibetan polymath Padma Karpo (1527–1592), who composed twenty volumes of philosophy and literature. A dispute over the recognition of Padma Karpo's reincarnation, however, caused the Drukpa line to split into two. One of the tulkus, Shabdrung Ngawang Namgyel, settled in Bhutan, and it was under his spiritual leadership that the Bhutanese resisted incorporation into Tibet under the Fifth Dalai Lama and subsequently established a system of government with the reincarnations of the Shabdrung as head—a system which lasted until the beginning of this century. (The Tibetan name for Bhutan, "Druk Yul," literally means "land of the Drukpas.") The other reincarnation, meanwhile, was born into the Fifth Dalai Lama's family, and his successor was discovered by the Great Fifth in 1641.

It is this line that continues today through the current head of the order, the Twelfth Gyalwang Drukchen Rinpoche, who was born in exile in India in 1963 and now teaches worldwide. Another well-known Tibetan lama who lives in Italy and teaches throughout the West, the Dzogchen master Namkhai Norbu Rinpoche (b.1938), is also connected with the Drukpa lineage, having been recognized both as the Thirteenth "Mind incarnation" of the Shabdrung Ngawang Namgyel and as Adzom Drukpa, a tulku of the Ninth Gyalwang Drukchen. The order is also strong in Ladakh, its principal monastery being Hemis, founded by Tatsang Repa, a disciple of the Fifth Gyalwang Drukchen in 1602.

Ralung developed a reputation in recent centuries for being a mixed community of monks and nuns, whose offspring would grow up to take the place of their parents. It seems that rather than

being nonmonastic tantric practitioners with shaven heads and robes, the inhabitants were simply lapsed monastics who cohabited.

The Site

On the orders of the Chinese, Ralung was completely destroyed in 1965 (two years before the official beginning of the Cultural Revolution) by the local villagers. The golden images were taken to China, while the wooden pillars were torn out and burned. The ruins of the monastery overlook a beautiful long, wide valley. The upper jagged, desolate ruins mark the site of the Ralung Tsuklhakhang (cathedral), while those below mark the Khamsum Zilnön Monastery, where the twenty-one chapels and residential quarters would have been. It is these lower ruins that have been undergoing restoration since 1985 and now house around twenty young monks, under the direction of four elderly lamas who survived twenty years of imprisonment to return here in 1985. Outside these walls are a newly built mani chapel, a wall with prayer wheels, and a small stupa.

A gate into the lower ruins leads to a dilapidated courtyard, where the present **assembly hall** is located. At the center of the long altar is a large stupa whose base was unearthed from hiding only after the end of the Cultural Revolution. Many of the images in the cabinets to the left were likewise retrieved. The bronzes on the right were donated by the local government in

Lhasa. On the far left of the altar is what is claimed to be the walking stick of the Indian siddha Maitripa. A large photograph of the Twelfth Gyalwang Drukchen is displayed farther along, together with statues of Shakyamuni, Padmasambhava, Vajradhara, and Green Tara. To the right of the stupa are statues of Vajradhara, Dipamkara, Shakyamuni, and, wearing a red hat, a previous abbot. The pages of text piled on the right were retrieved from the ruins of the Kumbum.

A door to the far right of the room leads to a **Lama Chapel** with a throne for the current Gyalwang Drukchen, next to which is a smaller throne for Namkhai Norbu. The main image is of Padmasambhava. The texts are the Nyingma Gyubum, the tantric canon of the old translation period. This used to be a Samvara chapel with a mandala of the deity made of pearls.

As you are facing the assembly hall, you will see to the left a newly constructed **Kangyur Chapel**, housing an edition of the Buddhist canon donated by Namkhai Norbu Rinpoche. In addition to the texts is a shrine devoted to the Buddhas of the Three Times, to the left of which is the walking stick of Naropa. In a small glass case to the left of the room is a statue of Shabdrung Ngawang Namgyel, the former incarnation of Namkhai Norbu.

About five hundred meters from these main ruins are the ruins of the **Kumbum**, which was smaller than that at Gyantse but similar in design, and was reconstructed and redesigned by the regent Polhane in the early eighteenth century. Only a crumbling ruin now remains. Between the Kumbum and the monastery is a small newly rebuilt house that used to be the residence of Tsangpa Gyare Yeshe Dorje, the founder of the monastery. In the hillside below the lower monastery is a small retreat cave that shows signs of being in use again.

25
GYANTSE: PELKOR CHÖDE & THE KUMBUM

Gyantse is a small, friendly town on the eastern side of the province of Tsang, 287 km (179 mi) southwest of Lhasa. It is situated on the northern bank of the Nyang River, which flows into the Brahmaputra at Shigatse. Only recently having suffered from extensive modern expansion, much of this sizable town still retains its traditional appearance. Although many of the monastic buildings were destroyed, the Kumbum and the adjacent Pelkor Chöde Monastery have been preserved and are two of the most historically and artistically impressive monuments remaining in Tibet. You may see photos of the Chinese-chosen Panchen Lama in some of the temples in Gyantse; these have been placed here recently at the insistence of the Chinese authorities.

History

Gyantse first came to prominence during the fourteenth century, when it served as the capital of a principality established by the enterprising Pelden Zangpo. This prince lived at a time of great political turmoil. He nonetheless skillfully survived the change of power in Tibet from Sakya overlordship to that of Jangchub Gyeltsen of the Pamotrupa dynasty in 1358, as well as the subsequent change of dynasty in China from the Yüan to the Ming in 1368. He established Gyantse as an autonomous fiefdom, while acting as a mediator between Sakya and Nedong as well as paying homage to the Chinese emperor. The Kumbum, the Pelkor Chöde Monastery, and the daunting castle still bear witness to the dynasty founded by Pelden Zangpo and brought to its apogee by his most important successor, Rabten Kunzang (1389–1442),

The monastic complex of Pelkor Chöde and the Kumbum, c. 1935

under whose rule the power of Gyantse extended from Ralung in the east to Lhatse in the west and Pari in the south.

Gyantse became the main center for Tibet's wool trade with India and the border countries of Nepal, Bhutan, and Sikkim, since it was suitably located at the junction of the trade routes from Lhasa and the east, Shigatse and the west, and India and the south. Nine major monasteries were built in the vicinity of the town.

In 1904 the town became the focal point of the British expedition to Tibet under Colonel Francis Younghusband. The British approached Tibet by the trade route leading to Gyantse and close to the town a battle took place in which several hundred Tibetans were shot dead by the superior British firepower. After storming the castle, Younghusband and his troops billeted here for a month before proceeding to Lhasa. The ensuing agreement reached between the British and the Tibetans resulted in a British trade agent's being stationed at Gyantse. The British also opened a small school here.

Until recently Gyantse was the third largest town in Tibet, after Lhasa and Shigatse. But because a sprawling Chinese new town has only recently begun to grow up around it, it has since been overtaken by other places. It is situated in a crescent of hills that rise up out of the wide valley that surrounds it. Nestling at the foot of this natural amphitheater are the closely packed whitewashed houses and narrow, wind-ing streets of the old town, along the western side of which a new, straight main road has been built, leading to the main entrance of the monastery complex. The town is dominated by a high, barren peak, along whose ridge sprout the forbidding walls and turrets of the castle.

The Kumbum and Pelkor Chöde Monastery are at the far end of the town. The area in which they are located is surrounded by a high wall that runs along the ridge of the hill behind and around to the front of the remaining religious buildings, thus effectively sealing off the monastic section from the town itself. Although this area seems rather bare today, it used to contain a complex of sixteen monasteries. Nine of these monasteries, including the Norbu Ganden Monastery founded by Tsong-khapa's disciple Khedrup Je, belonged to the Geluk order, four were Sakya, and three were affiliated with the Bu order, a small tradition established by Butön Rinpoche, the founder of Zhalu Monastery (see chapter 26.) Now only two remain: a large, deteriorating Sakya monastery in the courtyard in front of the Kumbum, where many of the monks now live, and Riting Monastery, a small Bu monastery on the hillside behind Pelkor Chöde. The high-walled structure up by the ramparts is where on ceremonial occasions a large tangka would be displayed.

The opposite end of town is dominated by the castle (*dzong*), the foundations of which were laid by Pelden Zangpo in

1365. It is open all day and can be visited for a small fee. The path leads you through a huge gateway and brings you to a number of deserted, gloomy buildings with dark rooms and mazelike corridors. There is a temple about halfway up to the top. Although it is in poor repair, some attempt at restoration has begun: three new Buddha images have been installed in the main chapel downstairs, murals of Avalokiteshvara and Padmasambhava have been crudely repainted, and two white stupas stand by the doorway. In the upper story there are no statues but some interesting, though badly damaged, murals remain, especially the three large mandalas of Guhyasamaja, Kalachakra, and Samvara on the back wall. In two of the smaller buildings higher up you can also find rooms with traces of religious murals. From the uppermost turret there is an unrivaled view of the town and Kumbum. In a cleft in the hills immediately behind the town are visible the extensive remains of Ritrö (Hermitage) Monastery, where monks would go for solitary retreat.

PELKOR CHÖDE MONASTERY
History

Work on Pelkor Chöde Monastery was started by Rabten Kunzang in 1418, under the spiritual guidance of Tsongkhapa's disciple Khedrup Je, and was completed seven years later in 1425. It has been remarkably well preserved, and many of the statues and paintings inside date back to the time of its founding. Although the shrines are predominantly Sakya, the monastery was traditionally unaffiliated, being used as a common assembly place for the monks from all the nearby monasteries. At present it is looked after by Gelukpa monks.

The Site

The Ground Floor

The first room on the left before you enter the assembly hall is the **Protector Chapel**. The three huge figures in this blackened room are barely visible because of the mountains of offering scarves draped over them. The main protector is the principal Sakya guardian, Guru Gönpo. To the left is the goddess of concentration, Ekajati, and to the right Pelden Lhamo. But apart from Pelden Lhamo's mule, little else can be made out. Tantric tangkas, gold lines traced on a black background, hang on the walls, depicting Dharmaraja, Yamantaka, Pelden Lhamo, and Vaishravana. The murals show the fearful entourage of Guru Gönpo. Antique weapons, chain mail, and masks are attached to the pillars.

There is little of note in the **assembly hall** itself. The woven tangkas that hang in rows from the ceiling around the skylight were commissioned from Hangchou in China in the early part of this century by the previous Panchen Lama.

The **main chapel** is at the back of the assembly hall. Before entering it you can see on the left a mural of Tsongkhapa and his two chief disciples, and on the right a mural of Atisha, Drom Tönpa, and Ngog Legpa'i Sherab, beyond which is a large statue of Maitreya. The gilded copper image of Shakyamuni was built in 1420 following the same proportions as the main image in Bodh Gaya. Avalokiteshvara is to the left and Manjushri to the right. Further to the left is Dipamkara, the Buddha of the Past, and further to the right Maitreya, the Buddha of the Future. Sixteen standing bodhisattvas are around the walls, representing the Eight Great Sons and, in female aspect, the Eight Great Daughters. Also on the left is a Medicine Buddha mandala. You can walk along an inner circumambulation path around the chapel, but the murals there are in poor condition. It is just possible to make out the forms of the thousand buddhas of the present eon.

To the left of the main chapel is **Dorje Ying Lhakhang**, dedicated to the Vajradhatu cycle of an important text of the yoga tantras, and consecrated in 1422. The subtlety and gracefulness of expression revealed through the craftsmanship of the main lacquered figures in this shrine are exceptional. The central buddha is a four-headed aspect of Vairochana, and along the back wall sit the other four Dhyani Buddhas: Ratnasambhava, Akshobhya, Amitabha, and Amoghasiddhi. Between the five Dhyani Buddhas sit their respective consorts. The twenty-eight smaller figures in alcoves around the back walls are deities associated with the practice of the tantric

deity Sarvavid. A gigantic scripture, bound in wooden covers and written in gold ink on black paper, lies to the right of the altar. It is a copy of the *Eight-Thousand-Verse Perfection of Wisdom Discourse.*

To the right of the assembly hall is a **Maitreya Chapel**. When Rabten Kunzang built this chapel, it was called the Chapel of the Religious Kings. The large statue of Maitreya, inside which are enshrined the remains of Rabten Kunzang, was probably added in the seventeenth century. The other figures along the walls date back to 1423. From the left they are: Atisha, Kamalashila, Padmasambhava, Shan-tarakshita, the triad of Manjushri, Avalokiteshvara and Vajrapani, the Kashmiri pandit Shakya Shri, and the three great Tibetan kings Songtsen Gampo, Trisong Detsen, and Ralpachen. A painting of Avalokiteshvara in the Newari style is on the wall, and a large embroidered tangka that formerly would have been displayed outside on special occasions is in a long box on the floor.

A small room to the right of the Maitreya chapel contains a large Vimala stupa, which enshrines the remains of Rabten Kunzang's mother, surrounded by shelves bearing an edition of the Kangyur. The smallish statues are (from the left): Amitabha, Shakyamuni, Khedrup Je, the Panchen Lama Chökyi Gyeltsen, and the Fifth Dalai Lama.

The Upper Story

There are five chapels on the upper story, all of which are worth visiting. We shall start from the first chapel on the left as you climb up to the roof from the main entrance, and go around clockwise.

We begin with the **Samvara Chapel**. The most striking feature of this chapel is the impressive three-dimensional gold and bronze mandala of Samvara erected by Khedrup Je himself. This has pride of place in the center of the room. It represents the sixty-two-deity mandala of Samvara belonging to the tradition of that tantra that traces itself back to the Indian mahasiddha Luipa. Khedrup Je's personal vajra and bell are supposedly kept in the monastery by the abbot, but it is not possible to see them.

However, the gilded mandala draws attention (and daylight) away from the exceptionally fine figures of the Sakya *lam-dre* lineage lined along the side and back walls. "Lam-dre" means "the path and its fruit," referring to the teachings received from the Indian mahasiddha Virupa that describe the stages along the path to enlightenment, combining both the sutric and tantric elements. All the statues are lacquered and probably made of clay. Like the five Dhyani Buddhas downstairs and the Sixteen Arhats across the way, they are of exceptional quality, perhaps even made by the same artist. Vajradhara is the central figure in the line, seated in the middle of the back wall. To the left sit the Indian teachers, concluding with the thirteen Sakya holders of the lineage up to the founder of the monastery Rabten

Kunzang. The mural on the wall to the left by the doorway depicts Pakpa in conversation with the Mongolian emperor Kublai Khan who, in 1260, appointed him as the temporal and spiritual head of Tibet. Another painting of Pakpa is nearby, surrounded by various scenes from his life. All around the upper part of the side and back walls are very well executed paintings of the eighty-four Indian mahasiddhas.

Next is a **Maitreya Chapel**. The main figure of Maitreya is accompanied by a number of smaller bronzes, some of which may be Nepalese or Indian in origin. There are stupas, buddhas, and tantric deities as well as lamas from the Bu, Sakya, and Geluk traditions. The most highly revered image on the altar is the small figure of Tara in the middle, buried beneath offering scarves. The chapel also contains a Victory stupa, an edition of the Kangyur written in gold ink, and some tangkas, one of which is an old Nyingma painting of the peaceful and wrathful deities depicted in *The Tibetan Book of the Dead*.

The chapel at the center back of the upper story is a shrine dedicated to **Tsongkhapa**. Two Buddhas are seated to the left of the central figure of Tsongkhapa. To the right, in descending size, are the Seventh Dalai Lama, a Buddha, Butön Rinpoche (with white hair), Sakya Pandita, and Padmasambhava. To the far right are images of the lamas of the Sakya *lam-dre* lineage. The murals in this chapel are very fine and must have been commissioned sometime during the reign of the Thirteenth Dalai Lama, a portrait of whom adorns one wall. The longevity triad of Amitayus, Tara, and Vijaya is shown on another wall, surrounded by numerous small images of Amitayus. The back wall depicts the Buddha with various scenes showing his twelve major deeds. The mantras of Manjushri, Avalokiteshvara, and Vajrapani are written above the door.

Directly opposite the Samvara chapel is a **Chapel of the Sixteen Arhats**. Again the lacquered, clay images of these sixteen saints are quite exceptional. Two small attendants stand to the side of each figure, while behind them are picturesque little cliffs with grottoes, stupas, and monks. Unfortunately, these slightly smaller-than-life-size statues are screened off by metal grilles. To the left, in front of the first arhats, is a set of five statues known as the Five Families of Manjushri. The central figure of these five is a fine image of Manjushri seated on a lion. The four surrounding figures depict four earthly representatives of the bodhisattva of wisdom who served as kings of China, Mongolia, India, and Tibet. The Four Guardian Kings protect the chapel.

The Uppermost Story

The **Zhelye Tse Chapel** is the sole shrine on this floor. "Zhelye Tse" means "peak of the celestial mansion," an apt name for the most tantric chapel in the monastery, which caps the profusion of deities housed in the shrines below. There is a single, newish-looking altar in the center of this rather bare and spacious room. One has the impression that it once contained rather more than it does now. The central image on the altar is Jowo Shakyamuni, with Maitreya to the left and Manjushri to the right. Above sit Tsongkhapa and his two chief disciples. Below are Amitayus, Padma-sambhava, and Tara, and further to the right Amitayus, Sitatapatra, and a peculiar little statue of Padma-sambhava. The masterpieces of this chapel, though, are the awesome eight-foot-diameter mandalas of the principal tantric deities of the Sakya tradition depicted along all three walls. Although they are sealed off by a wooden barrier, the caretaker-monk will let you go closer if you ask. The mandalas are all from the class of the supreme yoga tantra. The central mandala (immediately behind the altar) is that of Kalachakra. Among those to the left are the mandalas of Guhyasamaja, Samvara, and Yaman-taka. To the right are three of Hevajra as well as of different aspects of Guhyasamaja and Samvara. Formerly this chapel housed many volumes of the collected writings of the main Sakya lamas.

GYANTSE KUMBUM
History

In July 1427 Rabten Kunzang embarked on his most ambitious project, the construction of the Kumbum (or Tashi Gomang Chöten), which was probably completed in 1439. (The gilded copper

roofing and the final consecration ceremonies, however, were not completed
until 1474.) It survives today as one of
the most magnificent buildings in Tibet.
Gold-capped, it greets you with two
bewitching eyes painted high on its
upper wall. The term *kumbum* means
"having 100,000 images" and refers to
a particular style of stupa construction in
which chapels are housed in ascending
symmetrical stories. The Gyantse
Kumbum is probably the most famous of
all the kumbum-style stupas in Tibet.

Of the statues and murals that inhabit
its seventy chapels, Tucci wrote: "Now
peaceful, now terrific, [they] seem to jump
up alive before your eyes, to crowd on
your subconscious so as to haunt your
dreams as well. You would think that the
painters have by some wizardry conjured
up living forces and driven them into their
work, and that these could float out of the
walls, force their way into your soul and
take possession of it by a magic spell."
Many of these paintings are the work of
fifteenth-century Newari (Nepalese)
craftsmen, many of whom came from an
expatriate community at Lhatse. They are
among some of the best-preserved examples of that style to have survived in Tibet.

While most of the minor monastic
buildings around it are now destroyed,
the Kumbum has withstood all the bat-
tles and revolutions that have taken
place since its construction. Although
many of the statues were somewhat
defaced during the 1960s, they remain
fairly intact. Some have been restored
with rather garish gloss paints. The

innermost contents of the stupa—the
relics and so forth enshrined in its
core—were largely untouched during
the Cultural Revolution.

The Site

Before entering the great stupa itself, it is
worth visiting the small mani temple
between the Pelkor Chöde and the
Kumbum. This was preserved during the
Cultural Revolution because of the presence of a revered Mongolian lama who
lived there. The fine, detailed murals
depict Odiyana, the Pure Land of
Padmasambhava, and a thousand-
armed Avalokiteshvara, and may possibly date back to the fifteenth century.

The description of the Kumbum will follow the plan of the stupa on the following
pages. The descriptions are based on
field notes made in 1986 and 1994, the
brief Tibetan text pasted to the wall of
each chapel, and Franco Ricca and
Erberto Lo Bue's magnificent work *The
Great Stupa of Gyantse* (Serindia, 1993).

The First and Second Stories

The first floor of the Kumbum contains no
chapels. Climb the stairs in the southeast
corner (to your right as you enter) to
reach the chapels on the second floor.

Shakyamuni Chapel (1)

This is the first chapel you visit. It faces
you as you climb to the top of the stairs
after entering the Kumbum through the
main doorway. Buddha Shakyamuni is
shown seated in the posture of "turning
the Wheel of Dharma." At his sides his

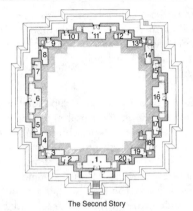

The Second Story

two chief arhat disciples, Shariputra and Maudgalyayana, are gracefully depicted. To the far left and right are two of the Eight Medicine Buddhas. Padmasambhava is also visible on the left. As with many of the larger statues in the Kumbum, the writhing animals and gods who populate the "halo" behind the Buddha are exceptionally well made.

Marichi (Özer Chenma) Chapel (2)

The female deity Özer Chenma (She Who Radiates Light) is the principal figure here. Three slightly different aspects of her are painted on the walls, surrounded by about one hundred minor deities. An Enlightenment Stupa containing a two-armed version of Marichi is also found in this shrine.

Bhutadamara Vajrapani (Jung Dul) Chapel (3)

A form of Vajrapani peculiar to the action (charya) tantras is the main figure here. Three painted images showing dif-

ferent aspects of him are on the walls, surrounded by numerous minor deities from the same tantric cycle.

Bhurkumkuta (Dag Je) Chapel (4)

"Dag Je" means "purifying" and refers to the main deity here, a smoky-colored Bhrukumkuta (He Who Purifies by Fire), with six arms and three heads. In front of him stand two dakini attendants. The ten wrathful ones and sixty-four diamond angels (dorje po-nya) are depicted in the murals.

Sitatapatra (Dok Je) Chapel (5)

"Dok Je" means "dispelling," and refers to the main deity here, a three-headed, six-armed seated Sitatapatra in the aspect of She Who Dispels Planetary Influences. She is attended by four wrathful female deities, Aparajita, Mahachanda, Mahajvala, and Mahakala. Five more images of her are painted around the walls.

Sukhavati Chapel (6)

"Sukhavati" means "land of bliss" and is the name of the Pure Land in the west presided over by the Buddha Amitabha. A giant seated statue of the red Amitayus is the central image. Two attendant bodhisattvas, a white Avalokiteshvara and a yellow Mahastamaprahapta, stand to his sides. Two other unidentified bodhisattvas, facing inward and seated on remarkably constructed lotus thrones, are beside them. Colorful paintings of the Pure Land are found on the left-hand and right-hand walls. The

Thirty-Five Buddhas of Confession are also depicted.

Parnashabari (Lo Gyunma) Chapel (7)

Lo Gyunma (She Who Is Dressed in Leaves) is the first of several deities described by Ricca and Lo Bue as appearing in the *Collection of Tantric Rites* (*Trubtab Gyatsa*), a basic Sakya liturgical work that assembles a number of different *sadhanas*, each used as a guide for the practice of a particular deity. This obscure female deity, an aspect of Pelden Lhamo, is the main figure in this chapel. She is yellow, with six arms and three heads, and kneels in a strange posture, with her left leg buckled beneath her. She wears a belt of fresh leaves at her waist. Two wrathful attendant deities stand beside her. The mural shows three more aspects of her in the company of numerous minor figures.

Hayagriva Chapel (8)

A red, two-armed form of Hayagriva as found in the *Collection of Tantric Rites* is the main image. Two smaller attendants stand at his sides. Murals of Hayagriva adorn the walls, as do two paintings of Avalokiteshvara and about eighty minor figures.

Achala Chapel (9)

Also from the *Collection of Tantric Rites,* this statue of the black, wrathful Achala (Immovable One) stands accompanied by two smaller deities. One white and two blue forms of Achala surrounded by twenty-two minor figures are painted on the walls.

Grahamatrika (Za Yum) Chapel (10)

"Za Yum" means "Mother of the Planets." She is depicted as a white female deity with six arms and three heads, sitting cross-legged and with her hands in the gesture of teaching the Dharma. The bodhisattvas Avalokiteshvara and Maitreya stand to her sides. Most of the murals are badly faded and in poor condition. The triad of Manjushri, Avalokiteshvara, and Vajrapani can be made out above the door.

Dipamkara Chapel (11)

Dipamkara, the Buddha of the Past, is shown here in a large, very delicately sculpted form, reminding one of a Thai Buddha image. His right hand is raised in the gesture of fearlessness. Four bodhisattvas, two standing and two seated, accompany him. Approximately two hundred smaller Buddhas and deities adorn the walls.

Vasudhara (Nor Gyunma) Chapel (12)

Another figure from the *Collection of Tantric Rites*, the female deity Vasudhara is depicted in a beautiful peaceful form with her left hand in the gesture of fearlessness and her right hand in the gesture of granting boons. She is surrounded by four female attendants, all displaying the same hand gestures. On the wall opposite the deity is a painting of her in a strange pose, holding a smaller figure of Vaishravana on her lap. The murals also show about fifty other deities, some with elephant heads.

Vyagravahana Mahakala (Tak Zhön) Chapel (13)

"Tak Zhön" means "Riding a Tiger" and refers to this two-armed form of Mahakala holding a skull cup in each hand. The very faded murals appear to depict a variety of wrathful tantric deities, vultures, skeletons, other aspects of Mahakala, and tantric symbols.

Mahabala (Tobpoche) Chapel (14)

This four-armed form of Mahabala (One of Great Strength) is red and holds a large stick in one of his arms. He is accompanied by smaller statues of Padmapani and Vajrapani. The back wall features a mandala of Trilokyavijaya (Conqueror of the Three Worlds) with four heads and eight arms. Most of the deities in this chapel appear in the *Collection of Tantric Rites*. The lamas depicted on the walls are probably from the Sakya tradition.

Dhvajagra (Gyeltsen Tsemo) Chapel (15)

This fierce reddish brown, standing female deity with four arms and three heads is accompanied by two smaller attendant figures. The murals are in fair condition, and one can make out a painting of Gyeltsen Tsemo, above whom sit Atisha and Drom Tönpa. A fine red dakini can also be discerned.

Tushita (Maitreya) Chapel (16)

A large seated image of Maitreya is the central figure, accompanied, as in the other chapels of the cardinal directions, by two standing and two seated bodhisattvas. Tushita, like Sukhavati (6), is a Pure Land. It is the place where Maitreya, the future Buddha, now resides prior to his appearance in this world. Thus in three of the four cardinal chapels we have seen the Buddhas of the Three Times: Shakyamuni, Dipamkara, and Maitreya.

Vaishravana Chapel (17)

A rather peaceful, solitary figure of Vaishravana, the god of wealth, is seated here on a lion. He holds a victory banner and a jewel-vomiting mongoose. This newly painted statue stands in contrast to the two old murals of the deity on the walls.

Four Guardian Kings Chapel (18)

The four familiar kings stand by the wall of this room, which serves more as the entry to the upper stories of the Kumbum than a chapel.

From here you climb up a series of dark, uneven staircases, which lead you to the upper floors. Although this is the route taken by pilgrims on their visit to the Kumbum, we shall continue with descriptions of the two remaining chapels on this floor before proceeding to the chapels above.

Panjara Mahakala (Guru Gönpo) Chapel (19)

This is the protector chapel of the Kumbum. It is dedicated to the principal

Sakya protector Guru Gönpo, who is accompanied here by two local protectors. The walls are black, with several gruesome paintings on them.

Vijaya Chapel (20)

A striking white Victory stupa stands at the far end of this small room. Inside the stupa is a statue of the six-armed female deity Vijaya ("Victory"). Her two main arms are in the gesture of teaching the Dharma. Two golden bodhisattvas stand on lotuses to each side, while two goddesses hover in the sky above.

The Third Story

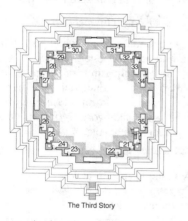

The Third Story

Manjughosha Chapel (21)

The statue is a form of Manjushri, the bodhisattva of wisdom, "who roars like a lion." He sits on a lion, his two hands in the gesture of teaching the Dharma. The familiar icons of a sword and book rest on lotuses that grow from his hands.

Murals of the historical Buddha and the Sixteen Arhats adorn the walls.

Avalokiteshvara Chapel (22)

A fine, Indian style, four-armed Avalokiteshvara is the main image, with two bodhisattvas, Shadakshari and Manidharin, in attendance. A beautiful multi-armed Avalokiteshvara mural is on the wall.

Amitayus Chapel (23)

A figure of Amitayus is the main image with smaller statues of the same buddha to the left and right, all holding vases of nectar with flowers. Each statue represents different aspect of Amitayus. The murals are also of different forms of Amitayus.

Tara Chapel (24)

A Green Tara with two standing, four-armed bodhisattvas to her sides is the central figure here. On the side wall is another Tara called She Who Completely Fulfills the Purpose of Beings. She is yellow and has eight heads and sixteen arms. The Twenty-One Taras and the Eight Taras Who Liberate One from Fear are painted around the walls.

Simhanada (Sengge Dra) Chapel (25)

This white, three-eyed female deity, seated on a lion, is called She Who Roars Like a Lion. Her right hand is in the boon-granting gesture and holds the stem of a red lotus that supports a sword. She is accompanied by Manjushri and Vajrapani.

Murals in the room depict Shakyamuni and Avalokiteshvara.

Avalokiteshvara Amoghapasha (Don Zhag) Chapel (26)

Another chapel dedicated to a lesser-known form of Avalokiteshvara with a silver body and a golden face. He is surrounded by four bodhisattvas: Bhrikuti, Hayagriva, Ekajati, and Shadakshari. The room also contains murals of Vairochana and Shakyamuni.

Black Hayagriva Chapel (27)

This wrathful aspect of Hayagriva is standing on two corpses with wrathful attendants to each side. The murals likewise depict aspects of Hayagriva.

Kurukulla Chapel (28)

Here is an aspect of the wrathful deity Kurukulla called The One Who Was Born from Tara (Tarodbhava Kurukulla). She is red, has four arms, and sits in the lotus posture. She holds a bow and arrow in her two main hands. Murals depicting other forms of Kurukulla are around the walls in this room.

Jamyang Gyelpo'i Rolpa Chapel (29)

This shrine is dedicated to an aspect of Manjushri called The Playful King. Other forms of Manjushri are depicted in the murals.

Vajravidarana (Namjom) Chapel (30)

Namjom, literally "destroyer," looks similar to Vajrapani. He is blue in color, carries a double vajra and a bell, tram-ples on two corpses, and is accompanied by two female attendants, Sarasvati and Vajratara.

Vimaloshnisha (Drime) Chapel (31)

The main statue here is an esoteric form of Shakyamuni known as Mahamuni. It is a yellow, cross-legged deity with eight arms and four attendant bodhisattvas. This deity is also known as Drime, or Stainless One.

White Tara Chapel (32)

A single, elegant White Tara with four attendants resides here. Other forms of White Tara are painted on the walls.

Samantabhadra Chapel (33)

The bodhisattva Samantabhadra is seated in a relaxed posture on an elephant in the teaching mudra, flanked by Maitreya and Padmapani. Fine murals of the Buddha, in an unusual relaxed pose, Avalokiteshvara, Manjushri, and Vajrapani are of note.

Vajrapani Chapel (34)

A shrine to a form of Vajrapani called Drozang (Good Rebirth), with images of Vajrapani on the walls.

Akshobhya (Mitrukpa) Chapel (35)

Akshobhya as a green/blue bodhisattva sits here with a vajra in the palm of one hand and the other hand in the earth-touching mudra. There are four attendants.

A vestibule dedicated to the "five god-

desses," images of whom are painted around the walls, leads to the next story.

The Fourth Story

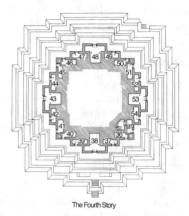

The Fourth Story

Jvalanala (Metar Barwa) Chapel (36)

"Metar Barwa," literally means the "one who burns like fire." He is a blue deity, slightly wrathful, with a vajra in one hand, accompanied by two female attendants. Murals of the same deity are on the wall. Vajrayaksha, a deity holding what appear to be animal tusks, is painted on the left-hand wall.

Vajrasattva Chapel (37)

A simple Vajrasattva is enshrined here, with the unusual feature of the vajra being poised on his fingertip of his right hand. His left hand holds a bell. The two accompanying deities are Dorje Kurikula and Dorje Drenma. A fine image of Vairochana is painted on the wall that faces the main image.

Amitayus Chapel (38)

This chapel contains a large seated image of the buddha Amitayus, a figure here connected with the Vajradhatu mandala of the yoga tantras. This room also contains paintings of a number of mandalas all related to the Palchok cycle of sadhanas.

Three Jewels Chapel (39)

The Three Jewels are represented here as follows: the Buddha Jewel as Vajrasattva; the Dharma Jewel as Avalokiteshvara; and the Sangha Jewel as Akashagarbha.

Wrathful Jvalanalarka Chapel (40)

This wrathful female deity matches the male deity in Chapel 36. She is orange in color, with a double vajra balanced on her finger and a bell in her left hand. Her mandala and other related paintings adorn the walls.

Perfection of Wisdom Chapel (41)

The central figure is a golden, four-armed image of the deity Prajnaparamita, the "Great Mother," who symbolizes the Perfection of Wisdom. Beautiful and unusual paintings of Ratnasambhava, Vairochana, and Akshobhya are on the walls.

Four-Headed Vairochana Chapel (42)

This image of the Dhyani Buddha Vairochana has four heads and two hands and is flanked by Vajrasattva and Vajraraga. About his right shoulder is Butön of Zhalu Monastery. Paintings of

Vajrasattva and all five Dhyani Buddhas are on the walls.

Ratnasambhava Chapel (43)

The central image is of the Dhyani Buddha Ratnasambhava, along with similar murals to those in the preceding chapels.

Six-Headed Manjushri Chapel (44)

An unusual image of a white Manjushri with six heads and two attendants, Vajrasurya and Vajrasattva, is the central figure here. The chapel also contains a mural of a Vairochana mandala and an image of Amitabha on a peacock throne.

Bodhicitta Chapel (45)

The central deity in this shrine dedicated to the altruistic resolve to attain enlightenment is the simple white deity Bodhicitta Vajra. Vajradharma and Vajravada are to the left and right.

Vajrapani (Chidak Jompa) Chapel (46)

This is dedicated to a form of Vajrapani whose name means "the one who destroys the lord of death," a simple, seated golden bodhisattva with two attendants. Vajrapani holds a vajra and a bell. The room also contains murals of Vajrahumkara and two other forms of Vajrapani.

Shakyasimgha (Ngensong Chöpa) Chapel (47)

This is dedicated to a deity whose name means "the one who acts in the lower

realms." This is Shakyasimha (Lion of the Shakya Clan), who is the orange bodhisattva in the center accompanied by the standing bodhisattvas Vajrasattva and Samantabhadra. The chapel also contains murals depicting a wrathful and a peaceful form of Prajnaparamita.

Amoghasiddhi Chapel (48)

A seated statue of the green Dhyani Buddha Amoghasiddhi with two attendants is found here, matching the Dhyani Buddhas in the other cardinal-direction chapels.

Sarvavid Chapel (49)

A silver, four-headed form of Vairochana in the meditation posture with two standing bodhisattva attendants is the main figure here.

Amitayus Chapel (50)

A simple red form of the buddha of longevity, bearing a vase of the nectar of immortality in his hands. The wrathful deity painted on the right and left is Dorje Humdze, the "one who emits the syllable HUM."

Buddha Dharmadhararaja (Sanggye Chözin Gyelpo) Chapel (51)

The central figure is a green, simple buddha called the King of Those Who Uphold the Dharma. Images of Vairochana adorn the walls.

Buddhavishvarupa Chapel (52)

The main figure is a red bodhisattva called the Form of the Various Buddhas, in meditation posture with his hands in the gesture of teaching the Dharma. He is flanked by two standing attendants. Images of Vairochana are on the walls.

Akshobhya Chapel (53)

In keeping with the other cardinal-direction chapels, this eastern chapel houses an image of the blue Dhyani Buddha Akshobhya. Numerous mandalas and deities adorn the walls.

Buddhasurya (Rinchen Rig) Chapel (54)

The principal figure here is called Buddhasurya (Sun Buddha), a yellow figure holding a mouth with bared teeth. Perhaps this is the patron deity of dentistry.

To reach the next story one enters a vestibule dedicated to the eight stupas, which are depicted on the walls. There are no statues.

The Fifth Story

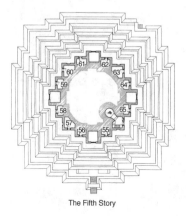

The Fifth Story

Kadampa Chapel (55)

The main images are of the Kadampa triad of Atisha (center), Drom Tönpa (left), and Nagtso Lotsawa. To their left is the Kadampa master, Geshe Potowa, and to their right the Kadampa master, Geshe Chengawa. Other important figures from the Kadampa tradition are painted around the walls.

Butön Chapel (56)

This is a shrine to the teachers of the lesser-known Bu lineage of Zhalu Monastery. The main image is of the founder of the school, Butön himself. To the right is Tuktse Lotsawa, to the left Kuzhang Dorje.

Lam-dre Chapel (57)

This chapel on the corner of the floor is dedicated to the teachings of the "Path and Its Fruit" (*lam-dre*) belonging to the Sakya school. The central, black figure is the Indian mahasiddha Virupa, from whom these teachings originated. To his sides are seated two of the early Sakya masters, Kunga Nyingpo (left) and Sonam Tsemo (right). On the far left is the siddha Gantipa and to the far right the powerful thirteenth-century hierarch Pakpa.

Asanga Chapel (58)

Statues of three monks are found here, the central one being the Indian pandit Asanga. Portraits of Asanga and the later commentator Haribhadra are depicted on the walls. All the monks here are renowned as experts on the doctrine of the Perfection of Wisdom.

Pacifying Chapel (59)

This chapel is dedicated to the Indian master Padampa Sanggye, who introduced to Tibet the doctrines of *zhije* (pacifying) and *chöd* (cutting). To the right is his female disciple, the Tibetan yogini Machik Labdrön.

Kagyupa Chapel (60)

The Indian mahasiddha Tilopa is the central figure in this chapel dedicated to the Kagyu tradition. On the right are Naropa and Gampopa, and on the left Marpa and Milarepa. Images of other Kagyu teachers are found around the walls.

Knowledge Holders' Chapel (61)

The central figure here is the portly Dolpopa Sherab Gyeltsen, founder of the controversial Jonangpa school, which was suppressed by the Fifth Dalai Lama in the seventeenth century. To the left is Bodong Chokle Namgyel, founder of Samding Monastery. All the teachers here are renowned for their teachings on the Kalachakra Tantra.

Chapel of the Dharma Kings (62)

This shrine celebrates the great kings of the Yarlung Empire, who unified Tibet and introduced Buddhism. Songtsen Gampo, Trisong Detsen, and Tri Ralpachen are the three main figures.

Translators' Chapel (63)

The main image in this shrine dedicated to the translators who first made the Buddhist teachings available in the Tibetan language is the great abbot Shantarakshita. To the immediate right and left are Padmasambhava and Kamalashila, and to the far right and left the Tibetan translators Loden Sherab and Rinchen Zangpo.

Padmasambhava Chapel (64)

An image of the Guru with his two consorts Yeshe Tsogyel and Mandarava is the main figure here.

Lineage of the Wise Chapel (65)

The main figure is the Kashmiri pandit Shakya Shri. Beside him are Jangchub Pelzangpo and Jamyang Rinchen Gyeltsen, who performed the first consecration of the Pelkor Chöde.

A vestibule with murals of the wrathful protectors of the ten directions leads to the cylindrical section of the stupa known as the Bumpa (vase).

The Bumpa

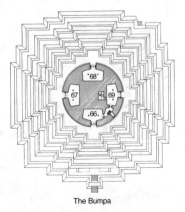

The Bumpa

Around the entrance to each of the four chapels on this level is some colorful stucco work depicting various animals and divine beings. From here the view over the town and castle is excellent.

Bodh Gaya Chapel (66)

A beautifully ornamented seated figure of Shakyamuni is the main image in this first chapel of the Bumpa. A white Avalokiteshvara and a golden Maitreya stand to his sides. Around the walls, enclosed in artificial grottoes, are the Sixteen Arhats. The Buddhas of the Ten Directions sit above them at a slightly higher level. As in each of the four chapels on this floor, the walls are covered with extraordinary mandalas, varying in size from eight feet to two feet in diameter. They probably represent tantric cycles practiced in the Sakya tradition.

Shakyamuni Chapel (67)

This large seated figure of the Buddha as Shakyasimha, "Lion of the Shakyas," is flanked by two bodhisattvas, one white and one gold. Ten superb, large mandalas belonging to the charya tantras are spread over the walls, with many smaller mandalas in between them.

Prajnaparamita Chapel (68)

"Prajnaparamita" means "perfection of wisdom," a quality of the enlightened mind here personified in the form of a female deity. She has four arms, the upper two holding a scripture and a vajra, the lower two showing the gesture of turning the Wheel of Dharma. A red bodhisattva stands to each side. Again, the murals are an intricate profusion of mandalas.

Vairochana Chapel (69)

A single bronze statue of the buddha Vairochana (the Illuminator) sits in this less ornate chamber. Metal grilles seal off sections of the chapel. Here, somewhat concealed at the back, is the staircase that leads up to the last chapel, at the pinnacle (harmika) of the Kumbum.

The Pinnacle

As you climb up even more steep and dark staircases to reach the top of the Kumbum, you pass walls covered with paintings of the main wrathful deities of the supreme yoga tantra. The first level is devoted to the "father" tantras, the second level to the "mother" tantras. The predominance of Hevajra and Samvara indicate the strong influence of the Sakya school, the Tibetan Buddhist order under whose spiritual guidance the Kumbum was designed. Other deities depicted on the two small landings where you can pause on your ascent are Yamantaka, Vajrayogini, Kalachakra, and many lesser-known dakinis. Lamas from the lineages of these tantric teachings are also shown.

Vajradhara Chapel (70)

The main image in this small, circular room in the pinnacle of the Kumbum is the tantric aspect of Shakyamuni, Buddha Vajradhara. A bronze statue of him on the altar is flanked by the bodhisattvas Avalokiteshvara and Manjushri. Another smaller Vajradhara is attached to the central pillar that supports the ceiling. The two rows of figures painted on the walls are the mythical kings of Shambhala.

GARU-LA NUNNERY

This recently reconstructed nunnery is situated on a low crest (the Garu-la) to the north of the northernmost ramparts of the wall surrounding the monastic complex of Gyantse. It is reached by driving out of the old town, going around the castle, then swinging back toward the monastic complex.

The ruins of a nunnery called Rinchen Khang, dating back to the time of the Empire, can be seen about a kilometer from the site of the present nunnery, on the crest of a foothill to the north-north-east. It used to house seventy nuns but was destroyed during the Cultural Revolution. The reason for the change in location is as follows. Sometime in the latter part of the nineteenth century a monk called Gelong Obar wanted to build a stupa and asked a lama where the best place would be. The lama answered cryptically: "The elephant will tell you." Three years later the Panchen Lama received an elephant as a gift from India, which he kept near Gyantse. One day the animal escaped and ran into the nearby hills, where he rolled on the ground and bellowed three times. Gelong Obar realized that this was where he should build his stupa (although it was not actually erected until his death in 1903).

Although the original stupa was destroyed during the Cultural Revolution, it was rebuilt in 1986 and the nunnery gradually erected beside it. The main image in the assembly hall is an eleven-headed, eight-armed Avalokiteshvara, flanked by Manjushri and Vajrapani. Although the thirty nuns here are of the Geluk tradition, the images of Tangtong Gyelpo and Milarepa in the assembly hall and the statue of Padmasambhava in the main stupa indicate a nonsectarian emphasis. The nuns are under the direction of an abbot from Pelkor Chöde. Beside the main stupa are two smaller stupas, one dedicated to world peace with an image of Shakyamuni, the other a Victory stupa. In the cliff face behind the nunnery a number of reconstructed hermitages are visible, one of which was where Gelong Obar himself meditated. A sky burial site can also be seen from here.

26
ZHALU & DRONGTSE MONASTERIES

The fertile Nyang Valley stretches between the towns of Gyantse and Shigatse, which are separated by a two-hour drive. Historically and artistically the most important monastery in this area is Zhalu, 19 km (12 mi) southeast of Shigatse. For a detailed study of the history and art of Zhalu, see Chapter Four of Roberto Vitali's excellent Early Temples of Central Tibet (*Serindia, 1990*).

We will also visit the sizable Drongtse Monastery, 23 km (14 mi) west of Gyantse.

ZHALU MONASTERY

The turnoff to Zhalu is on the Gyantse-Shigatse road, 19 km before Shigatse. The monastery is 5 km (3 mi) south of the main road, its distinctive green tiled roof just visible from the turnoff. While most of the monastery is open to the public, you may need a special government permit to visit the Segoma (or Kangyur) chapel and the Gosum chapel on the ground floor, and the east chapel on the upper floor. Since these chapels may not have any electric light, you should make sure to bring a flashlight to view the artwork.

History

Zhalu was founded in the eleventh century by a Sakya/Kagyu lama named Chetsun Sherab Jungne, who had promised to build a temple at the place where an arrow fired by his teacher Lotön Dorje would land. The first building on this site was modeled on the plan of an Indian Buddhist *vihara* (monastery). In the early fourteenth century, during the Mongol-sponsored rule of Tibet under Sakya lamas, Zhalu was largely remodeled. This work was carried out by Drakpa Gyeltsen, the leading lay figure of the family that supported the monastery, in the Newari/Yüan style. The murals of the Segoma (Kangyur) and Gosum chapels are the most striking examples of this style to have survived. They were painted by artists from the Yüan court trained in the school of the Newari master artist Aniko. Zhalu is thus unusual in that it preserves a combination of Indian, Nepalese, and Chinese stylistic features.

In addition to the main temple, on the hillside to the west was a section of the monastery called the Ripuk (mountain cave), a retreat center probably built during the eleventh century. It is here that Atisha spent some months in Zhalu in 1045 while on his way from Western to Central Tibet. Among the ruins on the hillside is a small pool associated with him, perhaps marking the spot where he retrieved twelve texts that had supposedly found their way there after being deposited in a lake in India. These would have been the twelve texts previously enshrined in Tangboche Monastery in the Chonggye Valley (see chapter 22). During the Cultural Revolution the Ripuk was reduced to ruins but now has a new assembly hall and four monks in residence

From the fourteenth century onward, Zhalu became the center of the small but influential order, the Butön or Zhalu Luk, founded by its most famous abbot, Butön Rinchen Drup (1312–1364).

Butön was brilliant scholar who played an important role in bringing Tibetan Buddhism to a state of full maturity. He was responsible for organizing the diverse scriptures that had been translated from Sanskrit in the preceding centuries into a coherent whole. Although the Kangyur, the translated discourses of the historical Buddha, had largely been put into order, the Tengyur, the far more numerous translations of the commentaries written by the later Indian masters, was still in disarray. Butön's contribution was to gather all these texts together, classify them, and write them down in a single series of volumes. That these volumes amounted to 227 thick tomes and that Butön wrote them all out by hand indicate both the amazing powers of mental synthesis and the sheer strength of dedication he must have possessed. Until the Cultural Revolution these handwritten volumes as well as his metal pen were kept in Zhalu. The Red Guards destroyed them all. He also composed a history of Buddhism in India and Tibet, a text that is still used today and has been translated into English. His own collected writings on subjects such as the Perfection of Wisdom and the Kalachakra Tantra amounted to a further twenty-six vol-

umes, the handwritten originals of which were kept in his personal residence nearby until they too were destroyed during the Cultural Revolution.

Butön lived in Zhalu for most of his life. He spent much time in the Ripuk section of the monastery where the original twenty-six volumes of his writings were kept. Through his immediate disciples Butön's influence extended to Tsongkhapa, who was seven years old when Butön died. Tsongkhapa held Butön in high esteem and studied at Zhalu with his successors.

Traditionally, the monks would spend the five summer months on the hillside and the seven winter months in the large temple complex in the valley. Once there were 350 monks in Zhalu; in 1994 there were 63. Seven elderly monks serve as teachers and attempt to pass on the teachings of the Butön tradition to the others. Since 1985 the monastery underwent a slow process of restoration under the direction of the "Cultural Repair Committee" of the government in Lhasa. In 1994 funding had ceased and the monastery was in desperate need of support to complete the considerable work still needed to be done.

The Site

About 500 meters before you reach the monastery, you will see the newly constructed **Delek Genkyong Chapel** off the road to the right. This shrine is dedicated to the protectress of Zhalu, Dorje Rabdenma. A gate leads into a pleasant garden. On the right is a worn stone basin in which Sakya Pandita supposedly shaved his head prior to receiving monastic ordination from the Kashmiri pandit Shakya Shri at the beginning of the thirteenth century. Dorje Rabdenma is the wrathful red deity housed in the recess above the altar in the small shrine to the right of the anteroom. A painting of Loden Dorje Wangchuk, the founder of this chapel, is on the left-hand wall. The chapel on the upper story is dedicated to Buddha Vairochana.

The Main Zhalu Monastery (The Serkhang)

The entrance to the monastery itself leads into a large, unkempt courtyard. The green-tiled roof of Zhalu reflects the artistic style of thirteenth-century Yüan China and contrasts vividly with the more usual design of Tibetan temple roofs. The **assembly hall** is entered through a door at the far right-hand corner of the courtyard. The room looks drab and underused. The ceiling is in poor repair and the murals are faded and damaged, though more through the ravages of time than deliberate desecration. During the Cultural Revolution the hall was used as a warehouse, and its murals suffered simply from having things stacked against them. The main image on the front altar is Shakyamuni, with an appliqué tangka of Butön behind him. The buddhas of the past and future sit to either side of him. Two bronze images of Padmapani are attached to pillars in front of them. The **main chapel** off the assembly hall is dedicated to Hayagriva,

but the main image is that of Vairochana. Hayagriva is to the left as you enter, with Vajrapani to the right.

The locked doorway, covered with a grille, on the left of the assembly hall leads to the **Segoma** (or Kangyur) **Chapel**. Inside, above the wreckage of texts and statuary on the floor, you are greeted with a huge mural of the five Dhyani Buddhas on the rear wall. This dates back to the early fourteenth century and (together with its sister image in the Gosum chapel) is surely one of the finest surviving pieces of artwork in Central Tibet. Its colors may have faded slightly, but it is otherwise in excellent condition. From left to right the Buddhas are: Ratnasambhava, Akshobhya, Vairochana, Amitabha, and Amoghasiddhi. The smaller images above, below, and in between the main figures are exquisitely crafted representations of minor divinities, bodhisattvas, siddhas, and pandits. To the far right is a somewhat archaic set of the eight auspicious symbols. Guarding the doorway on the front wall is a kneeling, white Achala and, on the other side, a similar blue, sword-bearing deity. Above the door is a mandala of Akshobhya.

The closed doorway on the right of the assembly hall leads to the **Gosum** (Three-Door) **Chapel**. This chapel contains artwork of a similar style, age, and subject matter as the Segoma chapel. It too is cluttered with dusty texts and broken statues. The five Dhyani Buddhas here have a slightly more sensuous appearance but otherwise are much the same. The only surviving mural on the left-hand wall is of the founder of Zhalu, Chetsun Sherab Jungne.

The only other chapel on the ground floor of Zhalu is the **Protector Chapel** at the very front of the assembly hall, facing the courtyard—whence it can be entered. While some newly made clay images of Mahakala, Pelden Lhamo, Vajrapani, Vaishravana, and Avalokiteshvara Karsapani have been made for this room, it was in very poor repair in 1994, still awaiting restoration.

The Upper Story

On the upper story, reached by steps to the right of the entrance of the assembly hall, are the four directional chapels (North, South, East, and West), which contain most of the remaining religious and artistic artifacts of Zhalu. All four chapels were once famous for their rare murals of mandalas from the yoga tantras, the third class of tantra. Today only those in the south chapel are well preserved. The mandalas one usually sees elsewhere in Tibet belong to the supreme yoga tantras, the fourth class, and the one most commonly practiced.

The West Chapel

The most revered image in the west chapel is that of Avalokiteshvara, called the Indian Jowo because it was brought to Tibet from Bodh Gaya in 1027 by the founder of the monastery, Chetsun Sherab Jungne. In front of it is a smaller stone statue called the Zhalu Jowo, which is actually two images: Avalokiteshvara on the front and a figure of

Yamantaka carved on the back (which you cannot see). The most prominent statue (in front of a pillar on the left), though, is one of a gaunt, austere-looking Butön Rinpoche, in front of whom is a very fine old Kalachakra. The small chair on the altar is for transporting a Jowo statue around the village at the new year. A conch shell in a glass case also dates back to the time of Butön, endowed, as usual, with mysterious properties such as being able to sound without human agency and possessing a naturally formed Tibetan letter "A" inside. A black stone with a perfectly formed OM MANI PADME HUM mantra standing out of it in white stone provides another puzzle. To the right of the main altar is an Indian vase filled with water which is distributed every twelve years as a blessing. Also to the right are images of Vajrasattva and Avalokiteshvara said to date back to the Empire period.

The North Chapel

The main feature of this chapel are the murals of fifty-two mandalas of the Vairochana cycle, which are too badly damaged to identify. A number of statues are arranged around the room, the main and largest one being of Butön. The smaller statues are of other incarnations of Butön as well as lamas from Zhalu, including a portly image of the Zhalu translator Chökyong Zangpo. Some of the surviving statues of the thirteen deities of a three-dimensional Akshobhya mandala are also here.

Around the walls are some finely carved wooden book covers, supposedly dating back to the time of Butön and possibly protecting the scriptures he edited and wrote.

The Amitayus Chapel

This small shrine is entered through a door between the north and east chapels. It is dedicated to the bodhisattva Amitayus, a large statue of whom is in the center of the altar, and six hundred newly pressed clay statues of whom line the walls. An Amitayus mandala is on the left wall, above which are Amitabha and two images of Butön.

The East Chapel (also known as the Butön Chapel)

A doorway leads to a spacious inner circumambulation passage with badly damaged and barely recognizable murals, the best preserved of which is one of the Fifth Dalai Lama at the end of the first corridor. The murals of yoga tantra mandalas inside the chapel are likewise in very poor repair and not identifiable. In 1994 the chapel was only used as a storeroom for masks, woodblocks, decorative motifs, and so on.

The South Chapel

In the entrance hall of this chapel are three murals. One is an astrological map designed by Butön to show the correlations between the movement of the planets and the days of the year. The one to the left of the doorway shows the stages of concentration one must ascend in order to attain mental quiescence. The picture to the right of the door shows details of the monastic rule, reminding the monks how to dress and behave and under what circumstances they can relax the rule.

Today only the south chapel contains well-preserved examples of these images. The original mandalas were traced onto the wall of this chapel in the fourteenth century, but the large ones that you see on the back wall were repainted in the late nineteenth century. Those on the side and front walls, however, have not been restored. From the left, the mandalas belong to the yoga tantra cycles of Peljor, Doying, Tsemo, and Kamsum Namgyel. These four mandalas are about four meters (twelve feet) in diameter and are extremely well painted, showing the artist's great precision and delicate sense of color. The remaining mandalas in the chapel are in poorer condition and belong to the minor deities in the Peljor cycle (within which there are four divisions and twenty-eight subdivisions).

Seated in front of the Tsemo mandala is Butön Rinpoche with copies of the twenty-six volumes of his collected works beside him. To the left sits his chief disciple Rinchen Namgyel and, about six statues further to the left, the portly figure of the Zhalu translator Dharmabhadra (a Tibetan with an Indian name). A fine statue of Kalachakra, made at the time of Butön, is to the right of the texts along with two Kadam stupas that may be of Indian origin. Other figures depict

Amitayus, Shakyamuni, and Tara.

DRONGTSE MONASTERY

About 3 km (2 mi) west of Gyantse is a tall hill covered in ruins to the north. This is what remains of Tsechen Monastery, founded in 1366 by Pelden Zangpo of Gyantse as one of the largest and most prestigious monasteries of the day. Pelden Zangpo died here in 1370, before the construction was complete. Five years later Tsongkhapa studied in the monastery with his Sakya teacher Rendawa. In 1881 Sarat Chandra Das wrote: "Our attention was attracted by the Tsechen Monastery, the entire northeastern slope of a hill being closely covered by its whitewashed houses, so that it looked like a great castle of towering height." However, it was used as a fortress against the British in 1904 and was badly damaged. When Tucci visited in 1937 it already lay in ruins. Reconstruction has been under way since 1987, and currently a few novices and monks live there. Drongtse Monastery is 23 km (14 mi) west of Gyantse, perched on the southern hillside of the valley. From the village of Drongtse you can either walk up a steep path or drive up a winding road to the monastery.

History

While Tsongkhapa was staying at Tsechen Monastery he met a small boy named Rinchen Gyatso, the son of a prosperous and devoted family in the nearby village of Drongtse. Tsongkhapa prophesied that in the future the boy would build a monastery above his home. Many years elapsed and the boy grew into a young man who became a recluse. He would spend most of his time away from towns and villages, living in the mountains like Milarepa. One day, however, he had a vision of the deity Tara, who told him that now it was time to leave his retreat and build a monastery. So he returned to his home village and started work on what was to be known as the Drongtse Monastery.

The monastery was erected on the hillside above the village of Drongtse in 1442. It consisted of a main assembly hall and two colleges, one specializing in the study of philosophy and the other in tantric rituals. It eventually became a subtemple of Tashilhunpo Monastery in Shigatse under the jurisdiction of the Panchen Lamas. Sarat Chandra Das stayed here in 1881 and gives a good description of life in the monastery at that time (see his *Journey to Lhasa and Central Tibet*).

During the Cultural Revolution it was completely destroyed. In 1986, largely through the efforts of Lobsang Senge Gyeltsen, the incarnate lama of the monastery, who then held a post in the religious affairs department of the government in Lhasa, it was granted sufficient funds to start restoration. Work proceeded rapidly, and in three months the main assembly hall was rebuilt in stone, wood, and mortar. The villagers retrieved some of the original pillars, which they had stored since the destruction, and returned them. Although the lama now spends most of his time in China, twenty-seven monks live here (in contrast to seventy before the Cultural Revolution).

The Site

When you arrive at the front of the monastery, the first thing you see is a small stupalike structure marked with the syllable "Kye!" ("Hey!"), to attract the attention of the local protector deity to whom the shrine is dedicated.

The steep steps on the left of the courtyard lead to the **assembly hall**. The large tangka on the left as you come in shows the founder of the monastery, Rinchen Gyatso, together with his second and third reincarnations. At the front of the room are three thrones: one on the left for the Dalai Lama and one on the right for the Panchen Lama, in front of which is one for the lama of the monastery. Between the two main thrones a door leads to the **main chapel**, which houses the monastery's original Shakyamuni statue, which was damaged during the Cultural Revolution but salvaged and restored. It is believed that this statue was made by an Indian artisan who appeared at Drongtse following the prayers of the founder for a craftsman to build a Buddha image as fine as that in the Jokhang. Beside him are statues of Maitreya and Manjushri, which did not originally belong to the monastery but were returned to Tibet from China. To the left of the hall is a **Protector Chapel** with a long altar on

which are images of Dharmaraja, Mahakala, and Yamantaka. Next to Yamantaka is Tunze Lhamo, the special protectress of Drongtse. A door to the right of the hall leads to a **Kangyur Chapel**, housing the Buddhist canon and a statue of the Buddha.

There are a number of rooms on the upper story of the assembly hall, one of which is a shrine to Tsongkhapa, whose statue is surrounded by a number of older images. There is also a tangka showing the monastery as it was before its destruction.

27

YUNGDRUNG LING & MENRI MONASTERIES: BÖN MONASTERIES ON THE TSANGPO

Yungdrung Ling is clearly visible across the Tsangpo from the metalled road that connects Lhasa and Shigatse. To reach the monastery, you must cross the Tsangpo at the Daktsuga ferry, then follow the main road north for 1.5 km (1 mi), and turn right up a dirt road that leads to the Oyuk Valley. The monastery is located on a wide shelf above the prosperous village of Ralep. We will also visit Menri Monastery, a more inaccessible retreat some kilometers by foot from Yungdrung Ling.

YUNGDRUNG LING

Because of the degree to which the native animist-shamanist Bön religion has been transformed by its long association with and dominance by Buddhism, it is hard to distinguish a modern Bön temple from a Buddhist one. The only overt difference is the fact that pilgrims circumambulate the shrines counterclockwise rather than clockwise. Apart from the telltale reverse swastika, iconographic differences are only discernible to a specialist. Recently, the Dalai Lama has even begun to speak of Bön as the fifth school of the Dharma in Tibet. On the other hand, the primitive spirit of Bön is perhaps best preserved not in an official Bön establishment, but in some of the eerie protector chapels of even the most orthodox Buddhist monasteries.

While Yungdrung Ling is the largest monastery of the Bön tradition in Tsang and Central Tibet today, the oldest functioning center of Bön in Tsang (possibly in the whole of Tibet), is said to be Kyikhur Rizhing Monastery in the county of Gyantse. Shentsang Rigyel Monastery, in the village of Tarding, Domay county, is also said to be active. Further west in Ngari, on the shore of Lake Paiku in Saga county, is Lhapuk Monastery. There are also active Bön monasteries far to the north on the Jangtang in Nagtsung district around the turquoise lake of Dangra.

Yungdrung Ling was founded by Kyabgön Dawa Gyeltsen, a former abbot of Menri Monastery, in the mid-nineteenth century. Judging by the extensive ruins, it must once have been of considerable size. It was razed during the Cultural Revolution. Today seven buildings and a stupa have been rebuilt and sixty monks have returned to live here. Numerous apricot trees still abound on the fertile shelf on which the monastery is built.

The main chapel is called the **Tongdröl Chapel**, which contains the stupa enshrining the remains of the monastery's founder Dawa Gyeltsen, to the right of which is a throne for the Panchen Lama. Mandalas are painted on the side walls while on the rear wall are images of Tönpa Shenrab, the mythical, quasi-divine founder of Bön, who serves a similar function in Bön as Shakyamuni does in Buddhism. On the upper floor are the abbot's quarters. The adjoining chapel to the right is called the **Hall of the Radiant Relics of the Lord** and houses another stupa (perhaps also with relics of the founder), this time made of wood, and a thousand small images of Shenrab. To the left of these two chapels is the current **assembly hall**, with eighteen images of Shenrab on the altar. In front of it a much larger assembly hall is under construction, whose altar will be dedicated to Dawa Gyeltsen. Side chapels will contain copies of the Bön canon, divided (like the Buddhist Kangyur and Tengyur) into original discourses of Shenrab and later commentaries. In front of the new assembly hall is a **Mani Chapel**, with a huge prayer wheel covered with the mantra OM MAHRI MUYE SALE DU (the Bön version of OM MANI PADME HUM). To either side of this chapel are monks' quarters, the one on the left being an **Amdo Khangtsen**, for students from Amdo, where Bön flourishes to a greater extent than in Central Tibet. At the eastern extremity of this complex is the **Taklhi Stupa** and a series of prayer wheels.

MENRI MONASTERY

One of the oldest surviving Bön monasteries in Tsang is **Menri**, a four- to five-hour walk from Topgyel Shung, the main village in the valley. This can most easily be reached by the coracle ferry about 35 km (22 mi) west of the Daktsuga ferry. By foot from Yungdrung Ling, continue along the northern bank of the river after the ferry until you reach Topgyel Shung. There is no vehicular access to Menri.

From Topgyel Shung one follows the river upstream to the village of Kamba. Nearby, on the eastern slopes of the valley are the ruins of **Yeru Ensa**, the first Bön monastery proper to have been established in Tibet. It was founded by Druchen Yungdrung Lama toward the end of the eleventh century but was destroyed by a flood in 1386.

Continue up the valley until you reach the village of Ruchen, where, next to the nonfunctioning Chensel Monastery, a trail leaves the main valley and leads to the Kangnyak Pass. The remote and lofty monastery of Menri can be seen from the pass and easily reached. It was founded by a lama named Sherab Gyeltsen nineteen years after Yeru Ensa was destroyed. The current abbot, Tsultrim Nyima Tashi, returned to Tibet in the mid-1980s to rebuild Menri after spending many years in north India where the monastery was relocated in Solan, Himachal Pradesh, the current residence of the thirty-second head of the monastery, Lungtok Tenpa'i Nyima.

Before reaching the monastery one passes prayer wheels being turned by a stream and a shrine called the **Tungra Khang** with three stupas on top. At the base of the main monastic building is a spring that drips forth *nyam-me drup-chu* (unequaled realization water), associated with the founder of the monastery. The low-ceilinged **assembly hall** has few images of note. A chapel beside it, however, contains the reliquaries of both Sherab Gyeltsen, the founder, and the twenty-fifth head of the monastery, Sonam Lodrö. A protector chapel dedicated to the protectress Sipa'i Gyelmo (similar to Pelden Lhamo) can be entered from here, but only if you are a Bön monk who has taken vows to worship this protector. Pilgrims are generally not allowed into the protector chapels of Bön monasteries. On the upper story is a chapel filled with scriptures of the Bön canon, among which is a life-size statue of Tönpa Shenrab. The chapel next door has two well-crafted life-size bronzes, one of the founder, the other of Shenlha Okar, a bodhisattva-like figure. There are also a hundred smaller statues of Shenrab. On the roof level are the quarters of the absent head of Menri. Some distance below this main building a Tsenyi Dratsang (philosophy college) is under construction.

28
SHIGATSE & TASHILHUNPO

Shigatse, the capital of Tsang province, is 395 km (247 mi) west of Lhasa via Gyantse and 307 km (192 mi) west of Lhasa via the metalled road along the Tsangpo. The daily bus service from Lhasa follows the latter route. This chapter will cover the town of Shigatse itself as well as the Panchen Lama's monastery of Tashilhunpo.

SHIGATSE

Aristocratic ladies of Shigatse, 1938

For centuries tension has existed between Lhasa, the capital of U, and Shigatse, the capital of Tsang. After the collapse of the Pamotrupa dynasty in 1481, the center of political power in Tibet shifted from the Yarlung Valley region to Tsang, first to Rinpung (east of Shigatse) and then, in 1565, to Shigatse itself (at that time called Samdrup Tse).

The Shigatse Dzong (castle), 1938

The town became the base of the powerful king of Tsang, who, allied with the Karmapas at Tsurpu, sought to gain control over the whole of Tibet. In 1610 the king's authority was tenuously extended to Central Tibet, but was still resisted by the powerful Geluk school and their patrons. The conflict culminated in 1642 in the defeat of the Tsang king by the principal Geluk patron, the Mongol Gushri Khan, and the enthronement of the Fifth Dalai Lama in the vanquished king's capital.

Shortly after the Great Fifth assumed power, he officially declared his teacher to be an incarnation of Buddha Amitabha and entitled him as the Panchen Lama. From that point on the authority of the Panchen tended to outweigh that of the district governor (*dzongpön*), appointed from Lhasa, who resided in the defeated king's castle in the town.

Because of its proximity to India, Shigatse was one of the first towns in Tibet to be visited by Westerners. In January 1628 the first two missionaries to reach Tsang, the Portuguese Jesuits Cacella and Cabral, arrived in Shigatse, where they were granted an audience with the king of Tsang, whom Cabral described as "a young man of twenty-two, of a fair complexion, in good health and, above all, very religious and generous towards the poor." Shigatse, he continued, "is at the foot of a mountain on whose top lies a fortress. The construction of the fort is after the plan of those in Portugal, the only thing wanting is artillery. The insides of the houses are gilded and painted, and the wing containing the king's apartments is really worth seeing. Hangings are much used in all his rooms, the plainer ones being of Chinese damask, but the others are equal to the very best in Portugal."

The last district governor to live in the castle was met by Giuseppe Tucci in 1948. Tucci, however, describes the building as an "old, massive, frowning Chinese fortress." His impression of the inside likewise differed from Cabral's: "The governor inhabited a wing, a few rooms which he had filled with Chinese household furniture, throwing together sacred and profane things as it was usual in Tibetan houses." Today only the bases of the ramparts of the fortress described by Cabral and Tucci are visible, the rest having been destroyed after the 1959 uprising.

Today Shigatse has a poor reputation among travelers to Tibet, justifiably based on the singularly unattractive sprawl of functional Chinese buildings that constitute the modern town. This impression has led visitors to ignore the delightful warren of alleys and townhouses of the old quarter, which is situat-ed between Tashilhunpo and the ruins of the fort, behind the market.

Shigatse has a population of about 40,000 and after Lhasa is the second largest town in Tibet. It possesses a bank, a post office, a public security office, and a department store. The open market lacks the charm of others in Tibet but offers a fairly wide range of items old and new.

TASHILHUNPO MONASTERY

Tashilhunpo, the seat of the Panchen Lama, is located on the western edge of modern Shigatse. In former days it was situated about 2 km outside the smaller old town. Although an obligatory stop on most tour groups, apart from the Maitreya chapel (1) and the assembly hall (20), it is somewhat disappointing, especially if you have just spent one or two days wandering around Sera and Drepung. If you have limited time in Shigatse, we would recommend only a short visit to the monastery, followed by a walk around the circumambulation path and the old town. The entire monastery is open only in the morning. In the afternoon it is possible to visit only the Maitreya chapel, and the tombs of the Panchen Lamas.

History

Tashilhunpo Monastery was founded in 1447 by Gendun Drup, a disciple of Tsongkhapa's, who was subsequently recognized as the First Dalai Lama. Gendun Drup was entombed in Tashilhunpo, one of two Dalai Lamas (the other was the Sixth) whose remains are not enshrined in Lhasa.

Shortly after his assumption of power, the Fifth Dalai Lama declared his teacher, Losang Chökyi Gyeltsen, then abbot of Tashilhunpo Monastery, to be a manifestation of Buddha Amitabha and the fourth in a line of incarnate lamas starting with Khedrup Je, one of Tsongkhapa's two chief disciples. Since the abbot of Tashilhunpo was already referred to by the title Panchen ("great scholar"), these incarnate lamas were called the Panchen Lamas. Losang Chökyi Gyeltsen thus became the fourth Panchen Lama. But in humbly proclaiming his teacher to be an incarnation of Buddha Amitabha (that is a buddha as opposed to a mere bodhisattva like Avalokiteshvara, of whom the Dalai Lama was an incarnation), he opened the way for trouble.

In 1728 the Manchu emperor bestowed Losang Yeshe, the Fifth Panchen Lama, with sovereignty over the entire province of Tsang. Although this was seen by both Tibetan parties at the time as a nominal gesture, it marked the beginning of a continuing Chinese attempt to divide the Geluk church by playing the two lamas against each other. Over time the Panchen Lama became the chief spiritual and temporal authority of Tsang. The greater the estrangement from Lhasa, the more absolute his power became.

In 1774 a young Scotsman named George Bogle was sent to Tibet to establish contact with the Sixth Panchen Lama, Pelden Yeshe, as the result of a letter sent by the Panchen to the British Governor of Bengal. This was the first official contact between the British and the Tibetans and apparently was conducted independently of the Lhasa government. Bogle became good friends with the Panchen Lama and even married a noble lady from his court, but the relationship between the two men was unable to mature since both died prematurely only a few years later. Descendants of Bogle and his Tibetan wife may still be found in Scotland.

Toward the end of the eighteenth century, in 1792, the monastery was pillaged by an invading Gurkha army from Nepal that had to be repelled by a Chinese force summoned to Tibet by the Dalai Lama's government. Although as part of reparations the Gurkhas agreed to return the valuables, it is possible that some pieces never found their way back.

In 1916 Alexandra David-Neel, the indomitable French traveler and writer, surreptitiously visited Tashilhunpo from Sikkim and spent some months in the company of the Panchen and other lamas. Frederick Fletcher, the first Western European to become a Tibetan Buddhist monk, was ordained as a novice at Tashilhunpo in 1922. Part of a three-man British Buddhist expedition to Tibet, he and his companions were forced to leave the country the following year.

In 1922 the powerful Thirteenth Dalai Lama, in attempting to bring Tashilhunpo back under the jurisdiction of

Lhasa, caused the Ninth Panchen Lama to flee to China, where he spent the remaining years of his life. His successor, the Tenth Panchen Lama, was born in 1938 in Amdo close to the Chinese border, and he remained in the hands of the Chinese until his death in 1989. The question of who has the right to recognize the new reincarnation of the Panchen Lama came to a head in 1995 when two Panchen Lamas were proclaimed: one who was chosen by the Dalai Lama and one chosen by the Chinese. Sadly, this conflict has led to the disappearance of the boy who was chosen by the Dalai Lama, leading some to call him the world's youngest political prisoner (see p.48). Pictures of the Chinese-chosen Eleventh Panchen Lama abound in Tashilhunpo, evidence of the Chinese government's unusual degree of control in the monastery.

THE PANCHEN LAMAS

1.	Khedrup Je	1385–1483
2–3.	Dates not known	
4.	Losang Chökyi Gyeltsen	1570–1662
5.	Losang Yeshe	1663–1737
6.	Pelden Yeshe	1738–1780
7.	Tenpai Nyima	1781–1853
8.	Tenpai Wangchuk	1854–1882
9.	Chökyi Nyima	1883–1937
10.	Chökyi Gyeltsen	1938–1989
11.	Gendun Chökyi Nyima	1990–
11a.	Gainchain Norbu	1990–

Because of the Tenth Panchen Lama's role in the Chinese administration, Tashilhunpo suffered relatively minor damage during the Cultural Revolution—despite the fact that the Panchen was out of favor and almost certainly imprisoned during that period.

The Site

Architecturally, Tashilhunpo presents a wonderful sight: a line of imposing red buildings of varying height crowned with gleaming, golden rooftops. Before them is a sprawling mass of single-story white monastic dwellings. A high wall surrounds the complex, and at the northeastern corner rises a mighty white wall on which a giant tangka was ceremoniously displayed on special occasions. Surrounding the monastery is a circumambulation route, along which are prayer wheels, carved rock inscriptions, and the occasional small shrine.

Extensive building was done during the time of the Fifth Dalai Lama and his teacher the Fourth Panchen. Further additions were made by the next two Panchen Lamas and also the Ninth. Between them, the Fourth and Fifth Panchen Lamas supplied the monastery with eight thousand religious images. While suffering relatively little intentional damage during the Cultural Revolution, many buildings nonetheless fell into disrepair due to inadequate maintenance. There used to be five (by some accounts six) colleges (*dratsang*) in the monastery. Now there are only two: a Philosophy College and a Tantric College. At its height Tashilhunpo is said to have housed up to 4,000 monks; at present there are 780, a fairly high proportion of whom are elderly.

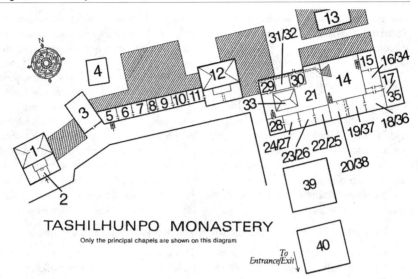

TASHILHUNPO MONASTERY

Only the principal chapels are shown on this diagram

To
Entrance/Exit

Although Tashilhunpo impresses one with the size and number of images in its chapels, there are relatively few statues or paintings of particular note. Many of the chapels are designed on a similar plan, and after a while it becomes hard to remember one from the other. The altars in the chapels are usually three to four levels of stepped shelves packed with numerous small bronzes surrounding a larger bronze figure.

The Maitreya Chapel (1)

This high building at the far left of the monastery was erected in 1914 by Chökyi Nyima, the Ninth Panchen Lama. The Maitreya chapel itself is several stories high and contains one single, enormous seated image of Maitreya, which reaches to the roof. The figure is coated with gold and impresses not merely by its huge size but also by the delicacy of the workmanship and the sublimity of its facial expression. A thousand images of Maitreya are painted in gold outline on the surrounding red walls. High on the left wall Tsongkhapa and his two chief disciples are depicted, and just before you leave the chapel, after circumambulating the metal base of the main image, you pass paintings of the Geluk yidams Guhyasamaja, Samvara, and Yamantaka. Next to them, also high up, are the Kadampa triad of Atisha, Drom Tönpa, and Ngog Legpa'i Sherab. Unfortunately, it is not possible to climb the higher stories to view the Maitreya statue from other angles.

There is one other chapel in this compound: on the first story facing the entrance to the Maitreya chapel, is a **Tushita Chapel** (2) containing one thousand small statues of Tsongkhapa, also built by the Ninth Panchen Lama.

The Victory Chapel (3)

The Victory Chapel is now used as a school for the monks to study philosophy and is often closed to the public. If you get a chance to go in, the central figures are huge gold images of Tsongkhapa and his two disciples. Tall figures of the bodhisattvas Maitreya and Manjushri stand to either side.

The Tomb of the Tenth Panchen Lama (4)

To the right of the Victory Chapel are steps and a path leading to the newly constructed tomb of the Tenth Panchen Lama. The formal name of this golden, bejeweled edifice is the Serdung Sisum Namgyel (The Golden Tomb That Conquers the Three Worlds).

This huge, elaborately decorated building was completed in October 1993. The Chinese government donated 500 kilograms (1,100 pounds) of gold for use in the construction of the tomb. While the highly detailed and colorful painting, which covers every square inch of wall and ceiling space, reflects the fine quality of craftsmanship still alive in Tibet today, it reflects a predominance of technical expertise over the sensitivity and religious feeling that imbues many older works. A lifelike replica of the embalmed body of the Tenth Panchen is enshrined in the front of the tomb.

In the ceiling immediately above the stupa is the mandala of Kalachakra. The surrounding walls are covered with the thousand buddhas of this eon (each painted with real gold paint), superimposed on which are Sitatapatra (left wall), a thousand-armed Avalokiteshvara (rear wall), and the Buddha (right wall). Higher up on the walls are painted the founders of all the major traditions of Tibetan Buddhism. High on the left-hand and right-hand walls the Ninth and Tenth Panchen Lamas face each other. Protectors cover the front wall as you enter.

The Panchen Lama's Palace

The main, residential section of the palace is the high white building that rises behind the long red front wall containing a series of seven connected chapels. It is not possible to visit the interior of the actual palace.

The first is called the **Chinese Chapel** (5) because of its decorative Chinese-style altar built by the Sixth Panchen Lama, Pelden Yeshe, in honor of his disciple Ch'ien-lung, the Manchu emperor, a painted image of whom is on the altar. Vajradhara, clasping a vajra in each hand, is the central figure on the altar. Other statues include Amitayus, the Medicine Buddha, Tsongkhapa, Vajrasattva, and Tara. To the left of the altar are hundreds of small statues behind a wire grille. Tangkas of the Sixteen Arhats hang on the walls.

The next room is the **Lhen Dzom Zim Puk** (6), the chamber in which the Panchen Lama would receive the official

Chinese representative, the Amban. Two thrones of equal height dominate this room, the one on the left being used by the Panchen Lama. A series of seventeen of the woven Hangchou tangkas that were commissioned by the Ninth Panchen Lama and are seen everywhere in Tashilhunpo, hang around the room. The seventeen tangkas show seventeen incarnations of the Panchen Lamas, although the last Panchen was usually considered the tenth, that is, the tenth in line after Khedrup Je. When seventeen are spoken of, the seven incarnations prior to Khedrup Je are counted, including five Indian masters, starting with Subhuti, a disciple of the historical Buddha, and two Tibetan masters, one of whom is Sakya Pandita.

The next room is an **Amitayus Chapel** (7), with a statue of this Buddha of Limitless Life on the left as you enter. The other two larger figures are Shakyamuni and Manjushri. Between the main images are many smaller bronzes. Editions of the Kangyur and Tengyur are also kept here. Note the exquisite Chinese brocade on the ceiling and the series of yellow cloth tangkas printed with a detailed woodblock from Nartang.

You must climb down a few stairs to reach the next chapel. At their top is a landing and on the left a small **Shrine to Dzegya Chökyong** (8), the red, wrathful, standing deity who is the special protector of Tashilhunpo.

A **Tushita Chapel** (9) is next. Tsongkhapa and his two disciples are the central figures. Avalokiteshvara, Tara, Shakyamuni, and numerous other buddhas, bodhisattvas, and deities line the shelves of the long altar.

Since there is no image in the next chapel, it is called the **Synoptic (Kundu) Chapel** (10). It houses a multitude of buddhas, bodhisattvas, and deities but none of particular note.

This long line of chapels ends with a **Tara Chapel** (11). The central figure of Tara is accompanied by two female bodhisattva attendants and surrounded by her twenty-one major manifestations.

The Tomb of the Fourth Panchen Lama (12)

This tall red building crowned by a golden roof is, with the Maitreya Chapel, the most prominent structure in Tashilhunpo and can be reached by an inner flight of stairs leading from the Tara chapel (11) or, alternatively, by a front entrance. It houses a large silver stupa in which is the intact, embalmed body of Chökyi Gyeltsen, the Fourth Panchen Lama. A small statue of the lama can be made out in a rainbow-enclosed niche in the stupa. An unusual triad of Avalokiteshvara, Amitayus, and Vajrapani are shown in fine statues before the stupa. As you circumambulate the stupa you can just make out the images of the thousand buddhas of this eon in the faded mural around the high walls.

The Kelsang Temple

This, the largest and most intricate complex in Tashilhunpo, is to the far right of the main set of buildings. Upon leaving the tomb of the Fourth Panchen Lama, turn left and continue along the base of the high red wall until you reach a passageway on the left. If you follow this dark, stone alley, you will emerge on the flagstones of the inner courtyard (14) of the Kelsang Temple. Images of the thousand buddhas of this eon are painted around the walls of the courtyard. Beneath each of these fresh, radiant figures is a small text with a verse describing each buddha.

The complex of buildings consists of two sections of different periods located on two separate levels. The older part, on the lowest level, consists of the assembly hall (20), which dates back to the fifteenth century when the monastery was founded. The rest of the temple more or less surrounds the assembly hall and consists of buildings that were added in the seventeenth century by the Fourth Panchen Lama. These include two floors of subsidiary chapels surrounding the courtyard on the east and south sides and two floors of chapels flanking the assembly hall on the south and the north.

In visiting this complex, we shall follow the somewhat circuitous route taken by most Tibetan pilgrims. We will begin with the chapels on the lower level of the L-shaped, two-storied complex to the east and south of the courtyard, proceeding then to descend a level to visit the assembly hall. Next, we emerge from the assembly hall to visit the chapels flanking it on south and the north. Finally, we return to the east side of the courtyard to visit the upper level of the L-shaped complex.

First Floor of the East and South Chapels

The first chapel you enter on the lower level of the building on the east side of the courtyard is a **Jokhang** (15) dedicated to Shakyamuni. The youthful form of the Buddha here is surrounded by a thousand smaller Buddhas, each dressed in a yellow cloth.

Next door to it is the **Silver Tomb Chapel** (16), a small room that houses two silver stupas in niches among all the Buddha images that fill the shrine. The main figure here is Vajradhara.

The **printing room** (17) is entered through a corridor to the left. It is a larger room lined with shelves containing the woodblocks of a complete edition of the Kangyur and several texts of the Tengyur. Monks can often be seen at work printing, usually for the benefit of passing visitors.

Another **Shakyamuni Chapel** (18) follows. The main image of the Buddha is surrounded by a thousand smaller figures. The paintings on the wall depict a form of Samvara with a white-colored consort and Pelden Yeshe, the Sixth Panchen Lama.

Next door is a **Tara Chapel** (19), in which a larger figure of Tara is surrounded by a mass of smaller bronzes. Copies of the seventeen Hangchou tangkas showing incarnations of the Panchen Lamas hang from the walls.

The final chapel in this section is a **Tushita Chapel** (20). Two sets of statues of Tsongkhapa and his two chief disciples are on the altar accompanied by various Buddha figures, Taras, and other deities.

Assembly Hall (20)

Exiting the East and South Chapels, you descend a level to reach the **assembly hall** (20), which was built at the time of Gendun Drup and is one of the oldest and most atmospheric buildings in Tashilhunpo. The giant, undecorated pillars are worn with centuries of bodily contact; on four of the main ones, facing south, are mounted fine golden statues of Vijaya, Tara, Sitatapatra and Avalokiteshvara. In contrast to the main Geluk monasteries in Lhasa, the rows of cushions on which the monks sit are raised about two feet from the ground, giving you the feeling that you are caught in a maze of knee-high corridors. The center of the room is occupied by the massive throne of the Panchen Lama. Woven Hangchou tangkas hang on the walls.

Two other chapels can be entered from the assembly hall. The larger of the two is dedicated to Shakyamuni. Shariputra and Maudgalyayana stand to his sides and the Eight Great Bodhisattvas are around the walls. High on the two pillars facing the doorway are Gendun Drup, the founder of the monastery, and Chökyi Gyeltsen, the Fourth Panchen Lama. Two images of seated Manjushris are immediately beneath them. A small statue of one of the Panchen Lamas is seated in a glass case on a pillar to the right and a standing Tara on a pillar to the left. The smaller chapel next door is a dark and rather dismal shrine to Tara. Three large images of the bodhisattva, which reputedly date back to the time of Gendun Drup in the fourteenth century, are seated in the center of the room. Unfortunately, they lack the soft, feminine quality usually associated with Tara. The murals have been erased, probably by time.

South Flanking Chapels

Ascending again to the ground floor level, you next enter the row of chapels that flank the assembly hall on the south side. Beginning with the chapels on the ground floor, you first visit the **Chapel of Great Joy** (22). The main image is a Kadam stupa. Numerous smaller stupas and statues of the Buddha line the shelves around it. A beautiful embroidered tangka of Yamantaka hangs on the wall.

Next door is a **Chinese Chapel** (23) housing a Jowo Shakyamuni. To either side of him are the Sixteen Arhats and, slightly in front, a statue of the Ninth Panchen Lama. As usual, the shelves are packed with many smaller images.

The final room on this floor is the **Precious Chapel** (24), which enshrines a heavily bedecked, standing Maitreya. Other prominent figures are Vajradhara, Avalokiteshvara, and Tara.

Continue up a flight of stairs to the next story, immediately above the three previous chapels. Here, you can visit four rooms, beginning with a **Tara Chapel** (25). The main figure is a standing Tara (Ngumi Drolma) said to have been brought to Tibet from India in the twelfth century. She is surrounded by numerous buddhas and bodhisattvas. In the rear right-hand corner is a statue of Pelden Lhamo, beside which is a very old mural of the protectress.

The **Pandrup Chapel** (26) follows. This shrine is dedicated to the Fourth Panchen Lama, a statue of whom sits with great dignity in the center of the altar. To the left is a beautiful image of Sitatapatra and to the right a thousand-armed Avalokiteshvara. A number of small, lithe standing Buddhas line the shelves. Two exquisite and apparently very old circular images of Tara and Manjushri surrounded by concentric rings of mantras and texts in tiny script are painted on the wall.

The next room is the **Chapel of Gadong Maitreya** (27). It contains a tall, noble Maitreya statue that was commissioned by the Fourth Panchen Lama and is surrounded by many minor figures. Tangkas hang from the walls.

In the end room of this row is the **Chapel of Miscellaneous Lamas** (28). Tsongkhapa and his two disciples are the most prominent and easily recognizable figures. Numerous other Geluk lamas surround them.

North Flanking Chapels

To reach the chapels to the north of the assembly hall, it is necessary to descend again to the first floor of the south flanking chapels and go to the back of the complex. The first chapel is a **Protector Chapel** (29). There are no statues in this room, only painted murals of the protectors Dharmaraja and Pelden Lhamo.

Further along is a **Maitreya Chapel** (30), founded by the Sixth Panchen Lama. This large room allows you to see a wonderful statue of the Maitreya seated on the ground floor of the assembly hall below, his head and shoulders rising into this chapel. To the left is a standing image of Manjushri and to the right, Avalokiteshvara. Both of these finely made deities are said to have been sculpted by the Sixth Panchen Lama himself.

Next take a flight of stairs up again to visit a strange **Shakyamuni Chapel** (31) in which the Buddha, in the pristine company of Shariputra, Maudgalyayana, and the Sixteen Arhats, sits in the midst of many macabre tantric hangings and motifs including two long, stuffed snakes. To the right is a small shrine to Pelden Lhamo. The monk who showed us around explained that these two apparently incompatible aspects of Buddhism, which in most monasteries are enshrined separately, are mixed here to emphasize the unity of sutra and tantra taught in the Tibetan Buddhist tradition.

Returning downstairs, you reach the **Chapel in Which You Can See the Face** (32), from which you can look down again into the main chapel adjacent to the assembly hall (20) and clearly see the face of the Jowo Shakyamuni there. Tangkas of the Six Ornaments and the Two Supreme Philosophers of India are on the walls, along with a beautiful modern painting of Amitabha. The large statue to the left of the window is of the Third Panchen Lama. On the right is a small mandala of the Medicine Buddha beneath a roofed canopy. On the altar is a black stone with the perfectly formed letters of OM MANI PADME HUM protruding from it in white, similar to the one in Zhalu Monastery.

If you are not lost by now, go upstairs again to visit one of the most sacred shrines in Tashilhunpo. This is the **Tongwa Dönden Chapel** (33), in which is enshrined the stupa containing the relics of the First Dalai Lama, Gendun Drup, the founder of the monastery. The tombs of the Second and Third Panchen Lamas are also found here. Two other stupas in the room contain the remains of two former abbots: Samdrup Yeshe and Lungrig Gyatso.

Second Floor of the East and South Chapels

To complete the visit to the Kelsang Temple you leave the assembly hall the way you came in, cross the open courtyard and climb to the second story of the building opposite. There are five chapels on this level. The first is an **Amitayus Chapel** (34) with three main statues of Amitayus. To the left of the central figure is a Tara and to the right a somewhat unusual seated form of Samvara with consort. A number of cymbals are placed along the altar.

The **Kangyur Chapel** (35) next

door seems to be directly above the Printing Room (17) on the floor below. Copies of the Buddhist sutras line the walls of this room, and cushions and reading tables are placed in rows on the floor. Each morning the room is filled with monks reciting the texts aloud. Images of the Buddha with Shariputra and Maudgalyayana are enshrined on an altar in one wall and a statue of Amitabha in another. The ubiquitous Hangchou tangkas depicting the Panchen Lamas hang from the walls.

The next room is a **Sukhavati Chapel** (36) and the main figure is Amitabha, the buddha who rules over the Pure Land of Sukhavati (Dewachen). To the left is Manjushri and to the right Maitreya. Numerous smaller buddhas and bodhisattvas fill the shelves around.

Another Pure Land is celebrated in the adjacent room, a **Tushita (Ganden) Chapel** (37). The main figure is that of Tsongkhapa. To the right are medium-size images of the Eighth and Sixth Panchen Lamas. The other statues depict the teachers of the Stages on the Path to Enlightenment (Lam-rim) lineage, including both Indian masters and their Tibetan successors. To the left of Tsongkhapa is a statue of the Fifth Dalai Lama. Whereas in Lhasa this would barely merit a mention, it seems to be the only image of a ruling Dalai Lama in the whole of Tashilhunpo. One might have expected at least some other images of the Fifth Dalai Lama, if only since it was he who inaugurated the line of Panchen Lamas. One cannot help wondering whether this absence betokens the rivalry that has periodically soured relations between the two leaders.

The final chapel is a **Tara Chapel** (38). A small standing Tara is in the center of the room, surrounded by numerous other seated and standing buddhas and bodhisattvas. Some of these are images of exceptionally high quality. A somewhat defaced but recently restored mural of the twelve major deeds of the Buddha adorns the walls.

The Tomb of the Fifth to Ninth Panchen Lamas (13)

Immediately behind the Kelsang Temple, overlooking the courtyard below, is the **Tashi Namgyel Temple** (13), constructed from 1986 to 1989 by the Tenth Panchen Lama to house the stupa of his predecessors from the Fifth to the Ninth. It is strikingly similar in design to the tomb of the Tenth Panchen (4). A statue of the Ninth Panchen Lama is visible in the huge silver and gold stupa, while the remains of all five Panchens are enshrined inside. Several mandalas are painted on the ceiling, including those of Kalachakra, Guhyasamaja, Samvara, Yamantaka, Sarvavid and Hevajra. High on the left wall is a symbolic representation of Shambhala. Around the walls are found images of the founding figures of all the major Tibetan Buddhist traditions.

The Tantric College (39)

To reach the Tantric College you leave the Kelsang Temple by the passageway that goes under the chapels at the front of the complex, then turn right and shortly after take a left down the main alley, which leads downhill to the main entrance of the monastery. Only recently has this quadrangle of buildings been converted into the Tantric College; previously it was a monastic residential area (*khangtsen*). There is only one chapel open to visitors. This is on the first floor and is the room the monks use for their daily services and assemblies. There are only a few images here; Tsongkhapa and his two disciples and the Fourth Panchen Lama are the main figures. The throne used by the tantric abbot and the Panchen Lama is prominently placed in the center of the room. Next to it is a Yamantaka mandala beneath a small roofed canopy. Images of some of the protectors can also be seen. Rows of peculiar high cushions used by the monks cover the floor.

The Philosophy College (40)

The Philosophy (Tsenyi) College is also a converted monastic residential area. The assembly hall on the ground floor has statues of six lamas beside the entrance to the main chapel at the rear. The three figures to the left resemble but are not Tsongkhapa and his two chief disciples; the central figure is Tsongkhapa, Gendun Drup is on the left, and the Fourth Panchen Lama on the right. The other three figures, to the right of the doorway, are the Tashilhunpo lamas who composed the philosophy textbooks studied in the monastery. The main chapel, reached through the doorway, houses a seated Buddha with Shariputra and Maudgalyayana. The Sixteen Arhats and the Eight Great Bodhisattvas are also on display. In front of the Buddha sits the Ninth Panchen Lama.

Upstairs are three protector chapels. The one on the far left is closed. The middle chapel contains no statues and its walls are covered with hangings and drapes concealing, perhaps, murals of wrathful protectors. A small doorway in the right-hand wall leads you into the third chapel, a small shrine to Tashilhunpo's special protector Dzegya Chökyong, the red, standing wrathful deity already seen in the Shrine to Dzegya Chökyong (8).

29

NARTANG & NGOR MONASTERIES

In this chapter we will visit three monasteries that are found south of Shigatse on the way to Sakya. The Kadampa monastery of Nartang was once renowned for housing one of the most important printing presses in Tibet, while the Sakya monastery of Ngor was, after Sakya itself, the next most important monastery of that school. We will also cover the Geluk monastery of Gangchen. All three suffered badly at the hands of the Red Guards, and most of what you see today has been reconstructed in the last ten years.

NARTANG MONASTERY

About 15 km (9 mi) to the southwest of Shigatse along the main highway to Sakya a sign directs you through a cluster of houses to Nartang Monastery, founded in 1153 by Tumtön Lodrö Drakpa, a disciple of the Kadampa master Drom Tönpa. The Kadam school subsequently divided into the scriptural (*zhungpa*) and oral (*dam ngagpa*) branches. Nartang adhered to the scriptural branch, of which Reting is the only other monastery to have survived. It became a Geluk monastery during the rise of the Fifth Panchen Lama, Losang Yeshe. During the same period the woodblock carving of the famous "Nartang" edition of the Buddhist canon

was undertaken. The task took twelve years and was not completed until five years after the death of the Panchen Lama in 1742.

Both the extent of the current ruins and the oral testimony of the handful of monks now living here suggest that before the rise of the Fifth Dalai Lama, Nartang may have been home to several thousand monks. It seems that as the nearby Tashilhunpo Monastery increased in power and prestige, monks who might otherwise have come to Nartang chose to go there. There were also few famous lamas associated with Nartang in recent centuries. In 1959 there were 165 monks living there, but by 1965 only thirty. At that point the thirty-five chapels, assembly halls, and printing house of Nartang were systematically torn down in the space of two weeks. As was often the case, this destruction was performed by local people under the supervision of gun-toting Red Guards.

This formerly noble monastery still stands largely in ruins, its high, crumbling mud-brick walls visible behind the roadside village. In the last few years two of the former monks have returned and have recruited fifteen novices. The government has said it will not allow more than twenty-five. A donation of 10,000 RMB from the late Panchen Lama allowed two buildings to be erected, one of which serves as an **assembly hall**. The main images on the altar are those of Tsongkhapa and his two chief disciples. There is also a throne for

67. Yamdrok Yumtso, the Turquoise Lake

68. On the road to Gyantse near Yamdrok Yumtso

69. The Gyantse Kumbum

70. Shakyamuni statue at Pelkor Chöde

71. Buddha Amitabha in the Sukhavati Chapel at the Gyantse Kumbum

72. Varapani mural at the Gyantse Kumbum

73. Sitapatra statue at the Gyantse Kumbum

74. Statue of Manjushri at the Gyantse Kumbum

75. Statue detail within the Chörten at Gyantse

76. View of the Gyantse from between the fort and the Kumbum

77. Tangka seller in Gyantse

78. Horses and prayer wheels outside of the Gyantse Kumbum

79. Zhalu Monastery

80. Tashilhunpo Monastery

81. Monks performing the "black hat dance" at Tashilhunpo

82. A nomad family visits Tashilhunpo Monastery

83. "Black hat" dance at Tashilhunpo

84. The main assembly hall at Sakya Monastery

85. Statue of Sakya Pandita at Sakya Monastery

86. Statue of Kunga Nyingpo at Sakya Monastery

87. The Southern Monastery at Sakya

the Panchen Lama and a new edition of the Buddhist canon. Stone carvings of the Sixteen Arhats are displayed to the right and left of the altar. Another 10,000 RMB donation, half of which is from the government, is allowing a larger assembly hall to be constructed, at which time the current one will become a chapel to the Sixteen Arhats.

A walk into the hills behind Nartang brings you to **Jangchen Ritrö**, a hermitage where several Kadampa lamas spent time in meditation.

NGOR MONASTERY

Ngor is situated in the foothills to the east of the Shigatse-Sakya highway. Around 2 km (just over a mile) past Nartang, at kilometer marker 4919, turn left on a dirt road in the direction of Migchu Xian. Before reaching Migchu, turn left again along a meandering route that takes you to the base of the hills, 7 km (4 mi) from the highway. Follow a wide river bed a further 7 km to the village below the monastery. A steep and precipitous access road takes you to Ngor itself. It is also possible to walk from Zhalu to Ngor. This is a good ten- to twelve-hour hike over two passes—a grueling day's walk. There is also a footpath between Nartang and Ngor which takes between four and five hours.

Ngor Monastery (or Ngor Evam Chöden) was founded in 1429 by Ngorchen Kunga Zangpo (1382–1444), the scholarly monk who established the Ngor suborder of the Sakya. After the monastery at Sakya itself, it is the second most important center of the school. Ngor was renowned for both its library and its Nepalese-inspired school of painting. Previously 500 monks lived among the five *labrangs* (residences of reincarnate lamas) and eighteen *khangtsens* (regional houses). Once a year a complete series of lectures would be held here on the Sakya teaching of *lam-dre* (the path and its fruit) which would have been attended by up to two thousand monks.

Ngor was totally destroyed during the Cultural Revolution, and its three reincarnate lamas fled into exile abroad. Since 1985 extensive rebuilding has been under way, aided by a grant of 150,000 RMB from the government. Twenty-five monks currently live here, of whom only five or so are qualified to teach. While still largely in ruins, two buildings, a courtyard, and a row of eleven covered stupas were restored in 1994.

As you enter the **assembly hall**, you can see in the portico some fine modern wall paintings by an artist from Nangchen in Kham depicting the Wheel of Life and a stylized image of the Buddhist cosmology. Unlike much repainted temple art, which tends to be technically proficient but uninspired, this artist's work stands out in seeking to qualify the traditional style with a contemporary sensibility to line and color. Inside the hall is a large throne with a statue of Kunga Zangpo, the founder of Ngor, a mural of whom is painted to the left of the Buddha and the Sixteen Arhats on the left wall. There are also murals of the five great founding lamas of the Sakya lineage. The main image on the altar is the Buddha, to the right of whom is Kunga Zangpo. The Kangyur is enshrined to the left, the Tengyur to the right. On the right hand wall the twelve deeds of the Buddha are depicted.

There are three chapels on the upper story, the central chapel again being dedicated to the Buddha and Kunga Zangpo. Between these two statues is a smaller Buddha that was previously the main image in the destroyed Denma Khangtsen. On both sides of the altar are shelves in which the surviving treasures of the monastery are kept. On the left is an old bronze Tara, above whom are old bronzes of lamas of the *lam-dre* lineage. Also enshrined here are what are believed to be the egg of a dragon and the horns of a sea monster. Of interest is the begging bowl of Pakpa, which the lama is said to have placed in the hands of the Jowo image at Ngor. Unfortunately, this image was destroyed during the Cultural Revolution, but a local villager spotted the bowl being used for feeding animals and subsequently returned it. A water vase belonging to Kunga Zangpo as well as the conch shell and old wooden beam that used to assemble the monks also survive. On the far right is a gong, believed to have been brought back from China by Pakpa. The cabinet on the left contains statues of the three "red protectors" of the Sakyapa: the dakini Rigjema (center) with the elephant-headed Tsoltang, and Dögyel.

To either side of the main chapel are protector shrines. To the left is the **West Chapel**, dedicated to the three principal Sakya protectors: Guru Gönpo (center), Pelgon (left), and Pelden Lhamo (right). The room is decorated with extraordinarily vivid and energetic murals painted by the artist from Kham who did the Wheel of Life. An ancient statue of Guru Gönpo is in a cabinet to the far left. To the right is the **East Chapel**, with the same three protectors but much larger in scale. Behind them is a very ornate relief carving. The fine murals here are painted by an artist from Derge, also in Kham. At the front of the upper story is another chapel used to conduct monastic ceremonies.

The one other restored building at Ngor is the **Khangsar Lhabrang**, below and to the right of the Assembly Hall. I was unable to visit it.

GANGCHEN MONASTERY

32 km (20 mi) to the southwest of Shigatse along the main highway is the restored Geluk monastery of Gangchen. A sign directs you to a village about 2 km north of the road, behind which is the monastery. It was founded sometime in the fifteenth century by a monk called Panchen Zangpo Tashi, a large statue of whom dominates the renovated assembly hall. Before 1959 up to 300 monks are said to have lived here, which is borne out by the extensive ruins behind the present site. The high wall on the hill to the left of the monastery was used to

display tangkas on the second day of the
sixth lunar month. Twenty-nine monks
currently live here. Of particular note is
the small pond in front of the monastery,
which is regarded as sacred to the protectress Pelden Lhamo; in its water visions
have been said to appear. A small
lukhang (naga chapel) stands nearby.

30
SAKYA

Sakya is 161 km (100 mi) to the south-west of Shigatse, along the upper reach-es of the small, fertile valley carved out by the Trom River. The highest pass between Shigatse and Sakya is the Tso-la (117 km or 73 mi from Shigatse, at the 5014 km marker). When coming from Shigatse, the turning for Sakya is 15 km (9 mi) from the pass. You turn left and drive 21 km (13 mi) up the valley until you come to the small town of Sakya, dominated by the massive struc-ture of the Southern Monastery. There are two small, rudimentary guesthouses in the town, in the roads around the Southern Monastery. The Southern Monastery is usually only open in the mornings. There is an entrance charge and photography is strictly controlled.

History

Sakya Monastery, the center of the Sakya order of Tibetan Buddhism, was founded in 1073 by Könchok Gyelpo of the powerful Khön family. Probably in retrospect, descendants of the Khön lin-eage created a myth of the distant, divine origins of this family, beginning with the descent from the sky of the three "Brothers of Luminosity." Nonetheless, the influential position of this family can be reliably traced back to the times of the early kings of Tibet, when Khön Palpoche appears as a minister of King Trisong Detsen. At the same time, a son of Palpoche called Lu'i Wangpo was a disciple of Padmasambhava and one of the seven "examined men" who, having been tested by Shantarakshita, were chosen to be the first Tibetans ordained as Buddhist monks.

Könchok Gyelpo, who lived during the latter half of the eleventh century, is regarded as the progenitor (in a quite literal sense) of the Sakya order. As a young man he became a monk and studied with the famous Tibetan mystic and translator Drokmi. Drokmi was also a teacher of Marpa, a founder of the Kagyu school, and a devotee of the Hevajra Tantra, which he translated from Sanskrit into Tibetan. It is because of Drokmi that Hevajra figures so greatly in the Sakya tradition and is prominently depicted in Sakya monasteries. Later in life, in accordance with a prophecy, Könchok Gyelpo disrobed, married, and in 1092 fathered Kunga Nyingpo (or Sachen, the Great Sakyapa).

Although Könchok Gyelpo is credited with the founding of Sakya Monastery, it was his son Kunga Nyingpo who, through his reputation as a scholar, meditator, and powerful leader, firmly established the place as the spiritual center of a newly founded Tibetan Buddhist order. Kunga Nyingpo also started construction of the Northern Monastery, a complex of buildings along the north bank of the Trom River by a peculiar patch of tawny hillside, which gave the order the name Sakya, or "tawny ground." He was posthumous-ly recognized as a manifestation of

Avalokiteshvara.

Kunga Nyingpo had four sons, two of whom, Sonam Tsemo and Drakpa Gyeltsen, became renowned monks in the Sakya tradition. Another, Kunga Bar, was also a monk but died young while studying in India. The fourth remained a layman and continued the family line. To this day, the Sakya hierarchy has remained very much a family affair. Unlike most of the other Tibetan orders, it does not rely greatly on the recognition of incarnate lamas to provide it with spiritual leaders. Instead, its hierarchy is continued through a system of heredity, the mantle of the heads of the order passing from father to son. A celibate monastic order is also preserved but is subordinate to the nonordained line of leaders.

One of the greatest Sakya lamas was Kunga Gyeltsen, better known simply as Sakya Pandita, who was to usher in the most glorious epoch of the dynasty's history. He was the grandson of Kunga Nyingpo and ordained as a monk. Revered as one of the greatest lamas of his generation, he was also recognized as a worthwhile ally by the Mongols, who were the dominant political force in Central Asia and China at that time. In 1244 the Mongolian prince Godan Khan summoned him to his court, and after a three-year journey in the company of two young nephews, Sakya Pandita arrived in Mongolia in 1247. He stayed there for the remaining four years of his life, during which time he taught Buddhism to and established a close relationship with the prince. After the death of both Sakya Pandita and Godan Khan in the same year, their relationship bore further fruit under their respective successors. Sakya Pandita's nephew, Pakpa, became the personal spiritual teacher of Godan Khan's heir Kublai Khan. The Khan heaped many rewards upon Pakpa, culminating in 1264, after Kublai had become the "great Khan" of the entire Mongol Empire, with Pakpa's being granted virtual sovereignty over Tibet as its "imperial preceptor." Sakya thus became the de facto capital of Tibet, and it continued to be ruled from there for nearly a century.

Pakpa died in Sakya in 1280 after a peripatetic life divided between stays in Mongolia, China, and Tibet. Power remained in the hands of the Sakyapa although other Buddhist orders vied with it for the backing of the Mongols. In 1290 the Sakya army destroyed Drigung Monastery to end that order's political ambitions. However, internal feuding and the collapse of the Mongolian Yüan dynasty in China allowed another powerful Tibetan family, the Pamotrupa, to gain control of the country in 1354.

Although Sakya never again achieved national prominence, it was still a quasi-autonomous "principality" in 1959. The line of religious teachers flourished, creating two main subsects, the Ngor and Tsar traditions, in the fifteenth century.

The Site: The Northern Monastery

To the north of the river, there used to be 108 chapels contained in the monastic

The Northern Monastery at Sakya, c. 1935

complex that stretched along the hillside. These have been largely destroyed or converted into homes. So far only two chapels have been restored, the most important of these being the **Labrang Shar** (Eastern Residence), the site of the very first monastic building in Sakya, reconstruction on which began in 1987.

On the ground floor are two rooms. The one on the far right is Kunga Nyingpo's *drup-chu* (attainment water) shrine, a low room with a wooden trapdoor that leads to a damp chamber with a muddy pool from a spring in the rock. Pilgrims collect and drink this water, which is believed to impart blessing. Next door is the *drup-puk* (attainment cave) shrine, where Kunga Nyingpo had the vision of Manjushri in which he received the core Sakya teaching of Parting from the Four Attachments. To honor this, statues of Kunga Nyingpo and Manjushri are encased behind glass in a cavelike section at the rear of the room.

The main chapel on the first floor is dedicated to the Twenty-One Taras, encased around the room. On the next story, the room of Kunga Nyingpo has been restored as it was originally. This also served as the private quarters of the great Sakya hierarchs Pakpa, Drakpa Gyeltsen, and Sonam Tsemo. Behind the throne is a fine appliqué tangka of Tara. An edition of the Kangyur is beautifully enshrined around the room. The forecourt from which you view the room contains two rows of painted statues of the lamas of the *lam-dre* lineage. On the top floor is a protector shrine with a life-size image of Guru Gönpo, beside whom are Pelgon and Pelden Lhamo.

To the west of the Labrang Shar is a small, square red building called the **Vijaya Chapel**, which was founded some nine hundred years ago by the translator Bari and restored in 1981. It houses the restored Victory stupa that was originally enshrined here by Bari and is said to contain relics of the historical Buddha. A portrait of the white-haired translator is on the left-hand pillar, and one of Kunga Nyingpo on the right-hand pillar. The small white stupa above the main one contains the relics of Kunga Nyingpo's mother.

Higher on the hillside is a large white

stupa reconstructed on the site of an original twelfth-century stupa to house the remains of Kunga Nyingpo.

A small footpath leads from the Labrang Shar eastward along the hillside to the **Rinchen Gang Labrang**, rebuilt in 1988 and now home to twenty-five nuns. The greater-than-life-size statues on the rear wall are (from the left): Pakpa, Drakpa Gyeltsen, Kunga Nyingpo, Virupa, Sonam Tsemo, Sakya Pandita, and Sonam Gyeltsen.

Another nunnery has recently been opened 5 km (3 mi) from the Friendship Highway on the road to Sakya.

The Southern Monastery

This complex of buildings is surrounded by a huge, thick square wall, with turrets at the four corners and a pathway on the top. The central monastic building inside is also square and enclosed between four high, windowless walls. Painted around these walls, about two meters (six feet) from the ground, is a continuous yellow and white band. At the rear of the complex are seven single-story, newly built monastic residential buildings. Before 1959 around 700 monks lived at Sakya; the government has now placed a limit of 150.

You enter through a tall gateway in the eastern wall and arrive in a courtyard facing the entrance of the large, reddish central building. To the right is a building that used to serve as the *kashag* (seat of local government) of Sakya.

The Puntsok Palace (1)

The Puntsok Palace is entered through the first doorway on the left when you reach the inner courtyard. It is on the second story. This palace is the residence of Dagchen Rinpoche, one of the two principal lamas of the Sakya school, now in exile in Seattle. The only room you can visit is a spacious, high-ceilinged chapel with exquisite statues lining two of the walls. The figure you encounter first nearest the door is White Tara. Next to her are two statues of Amitayus, one of Sakya Pandita, and one of Vijaya. This brings you to the main and most ornate statue, Manjushri, who is seated on a slightly higher throne.

Continuing along the back wall you then pass two stupas containing the relics of prominent Sakya lamas before

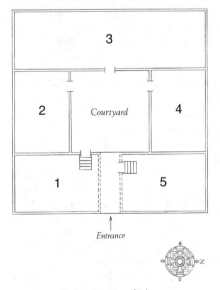

Southern Monastery of Sakya

reaching a most imposing figure of Kunga Nyingpo, which dates back to the founding of the monastery. In front of him is a small statue of Tangtong Gyelpo. The wall on the right shows murals of the longevity triad of Amitayus, Tara, and Vijaya, surrounded by smaller identical images covering the entire wall.

The Manjushri Chapel (2)

Entered from the left (south) of the courtyard, this high, spacious, rectangular chapel is overlooked by two principal figures. To the left is a fine Jowo Shakyamuni and, to the right, Manjushri. Both statues were designed by Sakya Pandita. An edition of the Tengyur is stored between the two images, and to the left are shelves with the Kangyur. The faded murals on the far left wall depict some of the Sakya tantric deities, the predominant one being Hevajra. The murals on the back wall show the longevity triad of Amitayus, Tara, and Vijaya, the Medicine Buddha, two versions of Shakyamuni, and Maitreya. Set in the right-hand wall are a mass of glass cases in which are housed several thousand small bronze statues around a central figure of Tara. Another Tara and the Protector of the West are in separate glass cases in front. The five principal Sakya protectors are painted around the doorway. In the center of the room is a glass case with a Hevajra sand mandala, made in the seventh month of each year.

The Great Assembly Hall (3)

This magnificent hall, built by Pakpa himself in the thirteenth century, is situated directly ahead of you as you enter the courtyard. To the left of the doorway are painted Achala and Brahma and to the right Hayagriva and Indra, thus ensuring both mundane and supramundane protection. Forty huge tree trunks converted into pillars support the roof of this immense hall, and rows of high cushions for the monks line the floor. Four of them are associated with miraculous events. The one plastered with coins on the right as you enter, for example, is believed to have bled black blood when it was cut down. Scenes from the Buddha's former lives as recounted in the *Paksam Trishing* are depicted in the murals covering the thick front wall.

The statues that dominate the room are mainly huge bronze Buddhas set against elaborate, wide bronze haloes. Not only is the style of the Buddhas unique, but they also serve the unusual purpose of being reliquaries for the remains of prominent lamas and rulers from Sakya.

The first Buddha along the left-hand wall contains the relics of Shakya Zangpo, Pakpa's first regent, who ruled from Sakya in Pakpa's absence, and who is remembered for having carried out one of the first censuses in Tibet. Next to this statue are a smaller Buddha, Avalokiteshvara, the reliquary of a minister, and finally a small Padmasambhava.

The first giant Buddha along the back

wall contains some of the relics of Sakya Pandita. This is followed by a stupa that houses the remains of Ngawang Tutob Wangchuk, the previous throne holder and father of the Sakya hierarch who now lives in Seattle. The central and largest Buddha contains some relics of the founder of the Southern Monastery, Pakpa himself (half of Pakpa's remains were taken to Mongolia, the rest enshrined in Sakya). Several important Sakya lamas sit in front of this Buddha: Kunga Nyingpo, in a red hat, is to the left; Sakya Pandita is immediately in front. After statues of the longevity triad of Amitayus, Tara, and Vijaya are three magnificent thrones reserved for the heads of the Sakya order. The next large Buddha contains more relics of Sakya Pandita, followed by the Sakya triad of the Three White Ones—Kunga Nyingpo and his two ordained sons, Sonam Tsemo and Drakpa Gyeltsen. Next are statues of the "Unburnable" Manjushri (so called because during a fire that ravaged the temple, this statue was untouched) and a seated Maitreya, the latter housing relics of the Sakya lama Pe Jungma. The remains of the Sakya Imperial Preceptor Dharmapala, a nephew of Pakpa who ruled from 1279 to 1286, are enshrined in the beautiful, adjacent figure of Vajradhara. The stupa that follows is called the Heart Stupa. It contains miscellaneous relics of Sakya lamas dating back to the foundation of the monastery. A Buddha with relics of Pakpa's minister Aklen, a statue of Manjushri with relics of Lama Dukhor (a

disciple of Sakya Pandita), a stupa, and a final Buddha complete the impressive series of figures on this long altar.

Also of note are the thirty-seven small deities from the Sarvavid tantric cycle lined along the base of the Buddhas to the right of the central figure, and the glass cases lined along the base of the entire altar containing cups and other porcelain objects of the Yüan period from China accumulated by ruling lamas during Sakya dynasty.

The right-hand wall starts with a Buddha in which are contained the relics of another of Pakpa's ministers, Kungawa Rinchen Pel. Also on this wall is a Buddha containing the relics of Mati Panchen, the lama who taught Tsongkhapa the Sakya tantric tradition, and the "Ara!" Buddha who is reputed to have cried in pain as the roof of the temple collapsed on him at one point. Numerous small statues of tantric deities and lamas are clustered along a dark altar, above which is a mural depicting the four aspects of Hevajra and the Five Great Ones: Kunga Nyingpo (center), Sonam Tsemo, Drakpa Gyeltsen, Sakya Pandita, and Pakpa.

At the front left-hand corner of the hall is a small doorway made of wood and wire, leading to the long, dark passageway behind the statues, where numerous handwritten copies of the Kangyur are enshrined from floor to ceiling along the left and back walls. These texts were placed here by Pakpa. During the Cultural Revolution they were concealed underground. At the far end, against the right wall is displayed behind glass a copy of the *Eight-Thousand-Verse Perfection of Wisdom Discourse*. This section is not generally open.

The Chapel of the Silver Stupas (4)

This chapel is named after the eleven tall silver reliquaries that line it and contain the remains of the eleven Imperial Preceptors, or throne holders, of Sakya who ruled during the Mongol era of the thirteenth century. On the wall behind the stupas are large paintings of the five Dhyani Buddhas. Above the head of each Buddha is a smaller figure of the one of the Five Great Ones of the Sakya order. By the left-hand wall are shelves filled with copies of the Buddhist canon and the collected writings of major Sakya scholars. Behind them is an unusual depiction of the triad of Manjushri, Avalokiteshvara, and Vajrapani (Rigsum Gonpo): the three bodhisattvas are shown standing, with Vajrapani in a peaceful rather than a wrathful aspect. Of particular note is the sand mandala of Hevajra on permanent display on the left of the room.

Five more stupas are found in a small chapel that is reached through a door in the back wall. An interesting image here is that of Sakya Pandita in conversation with Manjushri, of whom Sakya Pandita is considered to be a manifestation. Around the walls are paintings of mandalas. Those of the front wall belong to the *charya* tantric cycles of Vairochana and Amitayus (right) and the supreme yoga tantric cycles of Guhyasamaja and

Samvara (left). None is in particularly good condition.

Tara Palace (5)

Drakshul Trinle Rinchen, a Throne-Holder at Tara Palace, c. 1935

Like the Puntsok Palace on the opposite side of the corridor, the Tara Palace is on the second story; you reach it by a flight of stairs that leads off from a doorway in the entrance corridor. It, too, is part of the residence of one of the two chief Sakya lamas, the present incumbent, Sakya Trizin, being in exile in northern India. This majestic chapel contains five stupas of different heights, the largest of which contains the relics of the father of Sakya Trizin. Superb murals cover the walls. On the left are scenes from the life of Padmasambhava. The chapel is also called the Tenth-Day Chapel, the date in the lunar month when *pujas* are offered in honor of Padmasambhava. On the opposite wall is the longevity triad of Amitayus, Tara, and Vijaya, surrounded by smaller images of each deity. The front wall shows various Sakya lamas and protectors.

The Library

Between the Puntsok and Tara Palaces,
directly above the entranceway to the
central courtyard, is a long, shabby
room that houses the most valuable texts
preserved at Sakya. The walls are lined
with shelves containing bound Tibetan
volumes of the writings of the great
Sakya lamas; metal cabinets hold a
number of Sanskrit palm-leaf manu-
scripts from the time of the founding of
the monastery. Two hundred sixty-two
Sanskrit texts were removed by the
Chinese and taken to Beijing, leaving
only those texts of which there was more
than one copy at Sakya. In 1994 they
were reportedly back in Lhasa, due to be
returned shortly. One needs to have a
special permit to visit this room.

31
PUNTSOKLING MONASTERY & THE JONANG KUMBUM

West of Shigatse on the south bank of the Tsangpo at the confluence of the Raga River are the physical remains of the historical center of the controversial Jonangpa school of Tibetan Buddhism. By vehicle, the site is most easily accessible by turning northwest off the Friendship Highway at Zilung 81 km from Shigatse and then following the dirt road for another 30 km along the southern bank of the Tsangpo. Alternatively, you can connect with the same dirt road from the Lhatse Dzong, the old town of Lhatse, situated 5 km east of the new town on the highway. From Lhatse Dzong, it is a slow but spectacular drive of some 60 km.

History

The Jonangpa school is best known for its philosophical doctrine of ultimate truth, known as *shen-tong*, "other-emptiness" (in contrast to the *rang-tong* "self-emptiness" doctrine taught by Nagarjuna, Chandrakirti, and others in India and later by many leading teachers in Tibet). Briefly stated, the Jonangpas asserted that emptiness, in dispelling the illusive relative truths of the world, reveals an ineffable transcendent absolute reality with positive attributes. The *rang-tong* view,

on the other hand, claimed that emptiness is merely the elimination of falsely imagined projections upon the relative truths of the world and does not imply anything else. While such distinctions may strike us today as theological hair-splitting, in Tibet they became (and still are) crucial issues of faith. The most rigorous opponent of the *shen-tong* position was Tsongkhapa, founder of the Geluk school.

It seems that the *shen-tong* view was first promulgated as early as the eleventh century by a teacher named Yumo Mikyö Dorje. A follower of his thought named Kunpang Tukje Tsöntru (1243–1313) founded a monastery at Jonang in the thirteenth century, on the plan of Shambhala. But it was a former Sakya monk named Dolpopa Sherab Gyeltsen (1292–1361), a student of a disciple of the founder, who articulated the philosophy in its mature form and through whose writings it became widely known. In 1327 Sherab Gyeltsen founded the great Jonang Kumbum, called the Tongdröl Chenmo.

The last great representative of this school was the lama Taranata Kunga Nyingpo (1575–1634), a renowned historian of Buddhism and a noted scholar of both the Kalachakra Tantra and Jonangpa philosophy. In 1614 he built the Tagten Puntsokling Monastery at Jonang, after which he departed for Mongolia, where he spent the remaining twenty years of his life. In 1635, a year after his death, a son was born to the powerful ruler of Mongolia, Teshutu Khan (a descendant of Genghis), and recognized as the reincarnation of Taranata. The khan titled his son the Jetsundampa Khutuktu (Revered Living Buddha) of Urga (modern Ulan Bator), whose reincarnation continued to be recognized and gained increasing political power until the Communist takeover in the 1930s.

After the Fifth Dalai Lama assumed power in 1642, the Jonangpas suffered severe persecution and repression. Their texts at Jonang were confiscated and proscribed, and Taranata's Tagten Puntsokling (Eternal Place of Munificence) became a Geluk monastery called Ganden Puntsokling, (Ganden's Place of Munificence). Ironically, in 1649 Teshutu Khan sent Taranata's incarnation to study Buddhism in Tibet under the guidance of the usurpers of his former monastery, the Dalai and Panchen Lamas. Henceforth, the Jetsundampa Khutuktus belonged to the Geluk school, their main monastery in Urga also called Ganden.

Although officially proscribed, the Jonangpa *shen-tong* philosophy continued to be influential in Tibet, especially among Kagyu and Rime lamas, until 1959. Likewise, Taranata's historical writings and his commentaries on Kalachakra have remained important works even in the Geluk school. And while the Jonangpa school ceased to exist in Central Tibet, it nonetheless survived in the remote province of Amdo, where, notably in Ngaba (Aba) prefecture, several of its monasteries continue to thrive to this day.

The Site

Compared to the wide, multibraided river at Shigatse, the Tsangpo upstream at Jonang is just a narrow, deep, fast-flowing channel. Access to the north bank is made via one of the few (there are said to be three more further upstream: at Chung Riwoche, Pending, and Tasucha) surviving iron bridges across the Tsangpo built by the fifteenth-century genius Tangtong Gyelpo. While reputed to be the original, it is hard to tell whether it is a later replacement. It consists of two iron chains attached to pylons on the banks. Each hand-forged chain link is about 20 cm (8 in) long and worn smooth from long use. Suspended from the chains is a net of chicken wire enmeshing a single wooden plank, across which the locals dash back and forth. Ironically, a modern Chinese bridge beside it has fallen into disrepair.

Ruins of the Puntsokling Monastery

The original site of Puntsokling is reputedly on a conical hill covered with ruins on the northern bank of the river beside the iron bridge. It was subsequently rebuilt at the more accessible site on the southern bank, where it lies today, still largely in ruins. Before the Cultural Revolution, there were sixteen temples. Now there are five, with one more under construction. Fortunately, the largest building, the **assembly hall**, was preserved and converted to other uses. Some of the murals in the hall are still intact. The altar reflects the monastery's Geluk past, with statues of both

Tsongkhapa and the Fourth (that is, the first recognized) Panchen Lama. Connected to the rear of the assembly hall is the **Tsuklhakang** (cathedral). To the left of the entrance is a statue of Taranata, the founder of the monastery, and on the right a shrine to Pelden Lhamo. While a couple of Jowo Shakyamuni statues remain in the hall, all the images on the front altar have yet to be replaced. The murals were also badly defaced and have now been painted over. On the upper story are two protector chapels and a gallery with well-preserved murals of scenes from the Buddha's former lives.

JONANG KUMBUM

The Jonang Kumbum and the ruins of the original Jonang Monastery are situated about 5 km down a side valley running south of Puntsokling. The Kumbum is built on a shelf on the western side of this valley, facing, on the east side, the ruins of **Lingshar Nunnery**, now reduced to a single building inhabited by eleven nuns.

Dolpopa Sherab Gyeltsen named his seven-level Kumbum Tongdröl Chenmo, which means "the great mother on seeing whom one is liberated." Although not as intricate as the Kumbum at Gyantse, it was built more than a hundred years earlier and may well be the first structure of its kind to have been erected in Tibet. Although badly damaged during the Cultural Revolution, the Kumbum is now undergoing extensive restoration.

One enters the Kumbum by the south-ern gateway into an inner circumambulation passage around the base. None of the four directional chapels on the ground floor has yet been restored. They are dedicated to Amitabha (south), Maitreya (north), and Avalokiteshvara (east). No one was able to specify to whom the western chapel is dedicated; it currently serves as a repository for *tsa-tsas* (stamped clay images). Smaller, unrestored chapels are also situated in the intermediate directions. On the second floor, on the south side, is a chapel to the founder, Sherab Gyeltsen. A statue of the lama and his two chief disciples sit facing his meditation cave in the rock face opposite. On the third floor is a faded mural of Amitayus and two chapels, the statues for which have yet to be installed. The eastern chapel on the third floor is dedicated to Padmasambhava, and next to it a chapel with remains of original murals. The southern chapel on this level is dedicated to the Buddhas of the Three Times. Since the surviving murals include the Thirteenth Dalai Lama and the Ninth Panchen Lama, they probably date to the early years of this century. Photos of the present Dalai Lama and the recently deceased Tenth Panchen Lama are found to either side of Shakyamuni, the Buddha of the present time. The neighboring chapel is dedicated to Tara. The fourth floor is consecrated to a Buddhist doctrine much studied and practiced by the Jonangpas, that of the Kalachakra Tantra, with statues of the twenty-five kalki, the spiritual kings of Shambhala.

As you climb to the fifth floor, you leave the mandala plan of the lower floors and enter a cylindrical section, which consists of a circumambulation passage. On the inner wall are newly made statues in niches. These include Songtsen Gampo, Padmasambhava, Tangtong Gyelpo, and Dolpopa Sherab Gyeltsen's teacher Khetsun Yönten Gyatso. The outer wall of the passage is decorated with freshly painted red and gold buddhas, probably the thousand buddhas of this "fortunate" eon. The sixth floor is a smaller cylindrical section, still to be restored. It is planned to enshrine images of important Jonangpa lamas in niches around its walls. The final seventh level is that at which the eyes of the Kumbum will be painted. It consists of a single square chapel, with the "heart axis" of the Kumbum in the center. About twenty-four old bronzes are enshrined in cases to either side of the axis. Above this room is a cylindrical brass section enshrining one hundred volumes of scripture.

Around the area of the Kumbum are the remains of the former **Jonang Monastery**. One can see where an assembly hall, a lama's residence, a protector chapel, a philosophy college, and a meditation hall called Dewachen once stood. Only a part of Dewachen and a small temple at the college have been rebuilt. The monks hope next to restore the assembly hall.

Above the monastery are a number of retreat caves in the rock wall. In addition to that of Sherab Gyeltsen, another cave of note is reputedly where Padmasambhava meditated while staying in this area.

32

LHATSE, SHEKAR, TINGRI, & NYELAM PELGYE LING

This chapter covers the route that you would be most likely to take when leaving Tibet overland to Nepal. We will pass through the towns of Lhatse, Shekar, Tingri, Nyelam, and Zhangmu (Khasa), describing the places of interest on the way. South of Sakya the landscape becomes increasingly barren and vast, with less and less evidence of monastic Buddhist influence. The road offers views of Mount Everest and crosses one of the highest motorable passes in the world before descending abruptly into the lush valleys of the southern Himalaya.

LHATSE

150 km (94 mi) from Shigatse the Friendship Highway takes you into the drab, modern town of Lhatse on the bank of the Tsangpo. Lhatse Dzong, the old town of Lhatse, is about 15 km (9 mi) east of the new town (two dirt roads leave the highway between kilometer markers 5048 and 5050). The castle (*dzong*) of this once important regional center previously rose from the prominent rock that stands above the old Tibetan houses of the village.

Below the rock is the sizable monastery of **Lhatse Chöde**, founded at the

time of the Fifth Dalai Lama. This three-story structure, with an imposing courtyard, was turned into a granary during the Cultural Revolution and thus spared destruction. Although the statuary was removed, some of the higher murals date from early times. The main shrine in the assembly hall is a three-dimensional mandala of the Medicine Buddha. A rear chapel on the ground floor is dedicated to Shakyamuni, the elaborate halo around whom is one of the few old objects preserved here. There are numerous chapels on the upper floors, dedicated to Tsongkhapa and his two main disciples, Vairochana, Dorje Drakden (Pehar), Tara, the Fifth Dalai Lama, and others. Sixty monks lived here in 1994 under the direction of the reincarnate lama of the monastery, now a thirty-year-old monk. Some monks have gone to the reestablished Sera Monastery in South India to study. It is also the home monastery of Geshe Tengye, a lama resident in France.

The most significant historical site at Lhatse Dzong is the small meditation cave of the Indian siddha Gayadhara, located in the northern face of the prominent rock.

From Lhatse Dzong a small road takes you through a gorge of the Tsangpo to the wide, beautiful valley of the river that continues to Jonang.

SHEKAR

The town of Shekar is 90 km (56 mi) west of Lhatse on the Friendship Highway. 30 km beyond Lhatse you cross the Gyatso-la (or Lakpa-la) Pass (5,220 m or 17,200 ft), on the descent from which you have the first view of Everest and the Himalayan range.

Shekar Dzong, literally, "white crystal castle," was traditionally the provincial capital for the wider area of Tingri. The governor lived in the castle on the summit of the steep hill that rises above the old Tibetan part of town. Shekar Dzong has now become the Chinese administrative center for this part of Tibet and is sometimes referred to as New Tingri. In recent years a scattered complex of official, modern buildings has grown up about a mile from the old town. Despite its small population and remoteness, it is used as starting point for expeditions to the Mount Everest base camp and visits to Rongbuk Monastery.

If you walk from the new town through the cluster of old Tibetan houses at the base of the hill, you will reach a small temple called **Shekar Chöde**, or simply Shekar Monastery, which was founded in 1266 by a Sakya lama named Sindeu Rinchen. "Sindeu" is Chinese name that he was given during one of his visits to China. Although originally Sakya, it later became a Geluk monastery affiliated with Sera Monastery in Lhasa. Formerly it covered a wide area at this point midway between the village and the castle, housing up to three hundred monks. It was completely destroyed during the Cultural Revolution, and reconstruction began in the early 1980s. The sole chapel to have been rebuilt contains nothing remarkable. The main images are those of Tsongkhapa and his two chief disciples. Above them sit Vajradhara and a small Padmasambhava in a glass case. Several smaller bronzes recently donated by Sera are also on the altar. However, the construction is somewhat unusual in that there are two curved flights of stairs that join at the back of the main room, at an upper-level shrine, thus giving a circular effect to the shape of the room.

From the monastery you can gaze up at the ruins of the castle, which cling to the very steep, shale-covered mountainside. The castle itself, partially intact, is balanced incredibly on the very summit, which can be reached only by going around to the back of the mountain once you are about a third of the way up. From here you can see Mount Everest.

Rongbuk Monastery, considered to be the highest monastery in the world, can be reached from a turnoff at the 5150 kilometer marker, 10 km beyond the checkpoint. It is a grueling ride of about 60 km (37 mi) to the partially restored monastery below the Everest base camp. Rongbuk Monastery was founded only in the early years of this century.

TINGRI

The town of Tingri is a cluster of low buildings in a wide plain 70 km (44 mi) from Shekar. On clear days, it offers spectacular views of the Everest massif. Historically, the area is known for its connection with the eleventh-century

Indian master Padampa Sanggye, the teacher of the Tibetan yogini Machik Labdrön. Poverty and remoteness have reduced Buddhism in this area to a system similar to that in Nepal called *serkhyim* (yellow householders), whereby certain laymen assume priestly duties in small chapels at appointed times in the calendar but otherwise work with the villagers tending the livestock and fields. One such chapel south of the village, called Tingri Langkor, was originally the residence of Padampa Sanggye.

As you drive out of Tingri toward the border, you will see many dramatic ruins scattered along the valley floor. Judging by their size, there must once have been a larger and more prosperous population in this area. Ninety km (56 mi) from Tingri the road reaches the Nyalam Tong-la pass (5214 m or 17,000 ft), which offers a stunning view of the Himalayan range.

MILAREPA'S CAVE: NYELAM PELGYE LING

50 km (31 mi) beyond the Nyelam Tong-la pass lies the village of Shongang, below which is one of the four major caves of Milarepa.

Milarepa, probably the most widely revered Tibetan Buddhist yogi, never founded any monasteries or centers of practice. His life was an itinerant one that led him from one remote area to another throughout Central Southern Tibet. For most of his adult life he lived in caves, surviving on whatever he was

offered by local villagers or grew nearby. He was known and loved for the songs he composed and sang to the people, which poetically and succinctly expressed his insights into the truths of Buddhism.

As a young man he was robbed of his inheritance by a wicked uncle. In order to seek revenge for his now destitute mother, he studied the arts of black magic, in whose methods he become sufficiently adept to cause his uncle's house to collapse, killing all those inside. Eventually, remorse for his misdeeds led him to the Buddhist teacher Marpa, a farmer in the Lhodrak region of Southern Tibet. To atone for his murders and prove his sincerity, he was ordered to build single-handedly a series of stone towers. One of these, the final, nine-story tower called the Sekargutok, still survives in Lhodrak today.

Marpa then gave him religious instruction and initiated him into the secrets of the tantras. For several years he stayed with his teacher and practiced meditation under his guidance, until he was finally told to leave and continue his training in the solitude of the mountains. His yogic training enabled him to endure and transform the hardships of the elements.

Milarepa attracted a growing number of disciples, who would live around him and listen to his teachings. The best known of these were Gampopa, through whom the Kagya lineage was established in a definitive form, and Rechungpa. He died after being poisoned by rival teachers jealous of his achievement and popularity.

The small temple of **Nyelam Pelgye Ling** is located below the impoverished village and overlooks a valley, at the end of which the soaring peaks of the Himalayas rise into the sky. "Pelgye Ling" (Place of Increase and Expansion) was the name Milarepa himself suggested for this temple, which was to be erected around a cave where he and Rechungpa had meditated but which was not built until after his death. At first it belonged to the Kagyu school, but it was taken over by the Gelukpa at the time of the Fifth Dalai Lama. Once the surrounding buildings housed seventy monks; in 1994 there were eight, affiliated with Sera Me College in Lhasa. The original temple was destroyed during the Cultural Revolution, but in 1983 on the same site a new building was erected with the help of Nepalese supporters and craftsmen.

The main chapel contains an image of Padmasambhava and several protectors. Some of the smaller images are old and were donated by Sera Me. The principal shrine, however, is the **Namkha Ding Cave**, which is entered through a doorway to the left of the foyer to the chapel. "Namkha Ding," the name Milarepa gave this cave, means "hovering in space." Before going into the cave itself you will see on the ground a curious impression in the rock. This mark, blackened with the pious fingers and hands of Tibetan pilgrims, is said to have been made by Milarepa's buttocks, thigh, and foot as he sat in meditation. Next to it is

another impression, the hoofprint of Pelden Lhamo's mule, which appeared after Milarepa once received a vision of the protectress. The tiny, low-ceilinged cave lies beneath a large overhanging rock, which has been prevented from falling to the ground by a smaller rock resembling and serving as a pillar. Legend relates how Milarepa held the overhanging rock aloft with his mystical powers (the monks will show you his handprints in the rock, made while he accomplished this feat), while Rechungpa moved the smaller rock into position. On the upper side of this main rock you can see where Milarepa used to keep his bowl and barley flour (*tsampa*). There is now a statue of him in the place where he used to meditate. This statue and those of Tsongkhapa and his two chief disciples were rescued from the original site; the statue of Pelden Lhamo and the other images lining the altar are new.

NYELAM AND ZHANGMU (KHASA)

10 km (6 mi) from Milarepa's cave the road swings round a bend and you behold the modern clutter of buildings of Nyelam spreading across the hillside before you. The town contains nothing of note. In the last years it has grown considerably as a trading and forestry center and now provides a choice of simple restaurants and hotels.

From Nyelam you descend steeply into the dramatic Pochu Gorge that winds down a road above a tumultuous river through lush forest. After the barren vistas of Tibet, this is a welcome return to greenery and oxygen-rich air. It is well worth walking at least part of the 30 kilometers (19 mi) to the border. A hotel has been built halfway down and might one day offer facilities for hiking in the nearby hills.

Zhangmu, or Khasa in Tibetan, is a hodgepodge of buildings teetering on a precipitous hillside. It has all the characteristics of those towns whose only justification is to lie on an arbitrary line drawn by bureaucrats to separate one country from another. It is inhabited by a mix of Tibetans, Nepalese, and Chinese, vying with each other for a share in the lucrative dealings that flourish in such shadowy climates of exchange. There is no reason to be here except to enter or leave Tibet.

PART FOUR

NGARI—WESTERN TIBET

by Brian Beresford and Sean Jones

MOUNT KAILASH REGION
Western Tibet

Scale:

Key:
- 〰️ River
- ⋯ Kailas/Manasarovar Parikrama Route
- ● Village
- 🛆 Lake
- ═ Road
- 🏯 Monastery in poor condition
- ◎ Town
- ▲ Mountain

To Shiquanhe

Baer

To Töling (Zada) & Tsaparang

Sources of the Indus

Tirthapuri Menjir

Dri-ra Puk Drölma Pass (5670m)

Sutlej

Nyenri ▲ Kailas (6714m)

Zutrul Puk

Darchen

Barga ▲ Bönri (5995m)

Chiu

Huore

Tseti *Manasarovar*

Seralung

Rakshas Tal

Gosul

Truzo

Source of the Brahmaputra

Gurla Mandhata (7728m) ▲

India

Lipu Lek Pass Purang

Kojinath

Karnali

N

30

Nepal

81

33
MOUNT KAILASH

For most people, a trip to Western Tibet is virtually synonymous with a visit to Mount Kailash. The power of this strange, domed peak has gripped the imagination of the people of India and Tibet since time immemorial, with the result that it has long been one of Asia's most important (and remote) pilgrimage destinations. More recently, Mount Kailash's reputation as a sacred mountain as well as a place of natural beauty has begun to lure travelers and pilgrims from around the world. Beginning in 1984, when the Chinese authorities first opened Tibet to the outside world, Western visitors (the first since Lama Govinda in 1949) have begun to make their way into the area in trucks, land cruisers, and even on horseback and by foot. Today, it is still extremely difficult to reach the region, and the obstacles that people meet in trying to get here are frequently attributed to the sacred power of the mountain itself, which allows only those with sufficient spiritual preparation to gain a glimpse of its magical presence.

Mount Kailash is remarkable in that four of the largest rivers in Asia have their sources within 100 km (62 miles) of it: the Indus flowing to the north, the Brahmaputra to the east, the Sutlej to the west, and the Karnali (leading to the Ganges) to the south. As a mountain in this part of the world it is not particularly high, a mere 6,714 m (22,027 ft), yet it is striking in the way it rises above the surrounding range and remains perpetually snow-capped. The stunning image of this white peak against the clear blue sky helps to explain the mountain's name in Tibetan, Gang Rinpoche, or Jewel of Snow.

Traditional Buddhist cosmology has often connected Kailash with Mount Meru, the great mythological mountain that forms the axis of our world system. As the center of this world system, Mount Meru is often visualized surrounded by the various continents and adorned with the sun and moon and then offered to the buddhas and bodhisattvas as a mandala. In addition to Buddhists (who regard Kailash as the abode of Samvara), Hindus, Jains, and Bönpo practitioners all hold Mount Kailash to be sacred. Hindus most frequently see the mountain as the abode of Shiva and his divine entourage. A well-known Sanskrit lyrical poem from the fifth century, *The Cloud Messenger* by Kalidasa, pays tribute to the mountain and its surroundings through a message sent by an exiled denizen of Kailash to his wife via a passing cloud.

The Jains, whose own faith was founded at the time of the Buddha in India, regard Kailash as the place where the first Jain saint gained emancipation. Followers of the Bön tradition in Tibet worship the mountain as the spiritual center of the ancient country of Shang-shung and as the place where their founder, Shenrab, descended to the earth from the sky. Because of these and other religious associations, Hindu, Buddhist, Jain, and Bön ascetics and pilgrims have been drawn to the mountain for thousands of years. Once they arrive, they gaze upon it, circumambulate it, and sometimes settle down to practice austerities and meditation. The eleventh-century Tibetan Buddhist saint Milarepa is said to have resided there for eleven years. Padmasambhava is also associated with the mountain, particularly the valley on the western side, where he stayed in a cave.

CIRCUMAMBULATION (KORA) OF KAILASH

It is the goal of every pilgrim to Kailash to walk at least once around the base of the sacred mountain. This act of circumambulation, or *kora* in Tibetan and *parikrama* in Sanskrit, is considered to hold great powers of purification for the pilgrim. Some say that by completing the route just once, a person can purify the effects of all the negative actions of the present lifetime. Of course, the degree of purification can be increased by further trips around the mountain, with the most merit accrued to those who perform prostrations along the entire length of the circumambulation route.

Even if you do not plan to prostrate around the mountain, however, it is still necessary to be properly equipped and prepared before undertaking the arduous trek around the mountain. A waterproof and windproof jacket, strong shoes, sleeping bag, ground sheet, tent, stove, fuel, cooking pot, water bottle, and sufficient food for at least three days are all essential. Rain, hail, and even snow storms can be common, especially from June to September. It is generally not possible to complete the circuit before April or after October as the high Drölma Pass is blocked by snow. Binoculars and copies of *The Sacred Mountain* by John Snelling will greatly enhance your perception and appreciation of what you see and experience on your trip around the mountain. Lama Govinda's book, *The Way of the White Clouds*, should not be relied upon as a guide, although it does make interesting reading either before or after your journey.

Although many hardy Tibetan pilgrims complete the 51-km long (32 mi) circumambulation route in one day, less robust pilgrims should definitely take a slower pace, as should visitors who wish to contemplate the scenic beauty and absorb the various subtle moods and ever-changing atmosphere of the mountain. Even if one walks fairly quickly, the circumambulation can easily take two full days, with one overnight stay at Dri-ra Puk. (The Tibetan one-dayers leave at 4 A.M. and arrive back at midnight.) A three-day itinerary enables you to enjoy the trek at a relatively relaxed pace, with stopovers at Dri-ra Puk and Zutrul Puk. Our description of the route follows the three-day plan. Four- to five-day itineraries allow you to stop when and where you wish and to take a few side detours. Some of these detours are located on the so-called inner route (*nangkor*) and are considered best visited only after one has already circumambulated the mountain on the main, or outer, route twelve times or more!

The route around Mount Kailash takes you past a number of small monasteries. Most of these were badly damaged or even destroyed during the Cultural Revolution and were later rebuilt during the 1980s. Also along the route are sites connected with the great saints and other figures of Buddhism, Hinduism, Jainism, and Bön. The landscape is strewn with footprints and handprints in the rock, said to have been left there by meditation masters and buddhas, and many of the natural formations on and around Kailash have come to be associated with the ritual implements and other attributes of such great beings. Mount Kailash also sports many other extraordinary formations: on the peaks and ridges are needles, points, and protuberances, some of which are said to be stupas.

The staging point for the circumambulation is the sheep-trading station and tent town of **Darchen**, situated 6 km (4 mi) off the main Shiquanhe-Purang road, north of Barga, nestling at the foothills of Kailash. For details on how to arrange your trip as far as Darchen, see the chapter on Travel in Central and Western Tibet. Darchen itself holds little of interest, although there is a small Kagyu monastery in poor repair. A small bazaar has sprung up consisting of several dozen makeshift shops and stalls run by itinerant Khampa and nomad traders and a good variety of

basic supplies is available, as well as the usual religious artifacts and ethnic jewelry. There are also foodstalls, tea shops with pool tables, and marvelous views of Ghurla Mandhata to the south. Two new tourist and pilgrim hotels have been built, one owned by the police department with about ten rooms, the other a tourist company hotel with about eighteen rooms. You can also arrange for yaks or other pack animals to carry your gear in Darchen if necessary. Many people set out on the kora from Darchen itself, but it is not uncommon for people to continue in vehicles to Tarpoche and start the actual trek around the mountain from there.

Day One: Darchen to Dri-ra Puk

In order to begin your trip around Mount Kailash, you first head west from Darchen, skirting the base of the foothills rising up to your right from the plain. Make sure to leave early in the morning. After a couple of hours you come to a pile of mani stones with prayer flags. Here you turn northward into the valley that runs along the western side of the mountain, down which flows the Lhachu, or "divine river." A little further on you will see a tall flagpole streaming with prayer flags in the middle of a wide, grassy valley. This is **Tarpoche**, the site where local nomads and pilgrims gather to celebrate the important Buddhist festival of Sakadawa, or the Buddha's enlightenment day, on the full-moon day of May or June. Pass through the Kangnyi Chöten (the "two-legged" stupa), signaling the entry into the kora and the purification of negative karma. The views of Kailash from this spot on a clear day may well be the best you will see on the whole circuit. There are also good camping spots nearby if you choose to hang out here for an extra day.

From here, instead of heading straight down to the river, even better views can be obtained by climbing for a while up to the east side of the valley and skirting the base of the mountain, before coming down to the valley bottom on your left. If you take this trail, you will have the added advantage of being able to visit the **Site of the Five-Hundred Arhats**, a long, flat ledge covered in huge mani flagstones and said to be a place where the Buddha came with five hundred disciples flying through the air from India. Near this site, one can also find the cave of Naro Bönchung, the famous Bönpo master who was Milarepa's rival. At the entrance to the cave you can see Milarepa's footprint, which he left there during a competition with Naro Bönchung.

Returning to the main trail, descend and travel along the east bank of the river heading north of Tarpoche. After another half an hour or so, you will come to a bridge leading to the rebuilt **Chugu Monastery**, located on the west bank of the river. On the east bank, the path passes by the destroyed stumps of a line of large stupas near the river. Just before the path reaches Chugu there are hundreds of mani stones and, on a cliff above the stupas, the hard-to-spot

Pemapuk, a cave associated with the historical Buddha, in which it is possible to stay. If you have time, cross the bridge to visit the monastery itself, which is associated with the Drukpa Kagyu school. The main assembly hall contains a self-originated white marble statue called Chugu Rinpoche, which is a form of Shakyamuni Buddha. Just below the monastery is the **Langchen Bepuk**, the "Hidden Elephant Cave" where Padmasambhava is said to have meditated when he visited the region.

You can continue northward from here on either side of the Lhaschu. The views of the mountain are generally better from the western bank. On both sides of the river there is good, grassy camping ground to be found. Otherwise, return to the east bank of the Lhachu and proceed further up the valley. Towering above you on the left you will see three sharp peaks, which are associated with the longevity triad of Amitayus, White Tara, and Vijaya. The Tara peak to the south is remarkable for the peculiar stupalike formations that protrude from it. A bit farther up the valley on the right-hand side, you will see a squat domed outcrop of rock, which is known as Padmasambhava's Torma. As you approach it, it appears as one wing of a huge, sweeping arc of rock face. Hindu pilgrims consider this rock outcrop to be an embodiment of Hanuman, the monkey-god and disciple of Rama.

The valley now widens out and starts to curve around the east. Marmots have made this area their territory, showing little fear and sharing the paddocks with the nomads. There is a large boulder here with a carving of and offering dedicated to the protector Mahakala. Depending on the time of day, you may wish to make your camp here and continue on to Dri-ra Puk in the morning. If you decide to push ahead you will require another one to two hours before you reach the area north of the mountain, with its pleasant green terrain and, across the river, **Dri-ra Puk Monastery**. Continue along the south side of the river close to the path for another half hour to reach the newly constructed bridge to Dri-ra Puk. Once you have safely crossed the river you can camp near the monastery or stay in the Indian pilgrim's rest house (if there is room).

Dri-ra Puk faces southward straight up a narrow valley, at the end of which looms the impressive northern face of Kailash itself, a vertical wall of six thousand feet. Like Chugu, Dri-ra Puk Monastery is associated with the Drukpa Kagyu sect. The monastery traces its origins back to the thirteenth century, when the great meditation master Gotsangpa practiced in a cave there. The name of the monastery means "cave of the female yak horn," and it derives its name from the fact that a dakini in the form of a female yak, or *dri*, is said to have led Gotsangpa to the cave during a severe rainstorm. Imprints from the dri's horn can be seen on the walls of the cave.

Although you may be tempted to make a detour up the valley opposite Dri-ra Puk to the edge of the moraine at the north face, you should do so only if you have ample time (allow at least three hours) and the weather is clear. You should also be aware that from a traditional perspective, this side trip is considered inauspicious unless you have already made twelve full circumambulations of Kailash on the outer circuit. Whether you make the trek or not, you can still enjoy the spectacular view of the north face of Kailash surrounded by three other peaks. These three peaks are associated with the bodhisattvas Manjushri, Avalokiteshvara, and Vajrapani, the triad known as the Protectors of the Three Realms. Manjushri is to the west of the valley looking up to Kailash, Avalokitesvara and Vajrapani to the east.

Day Two: Dri-ra Puk to Zutrul Puk

Cross the Lhachu River over the bridge again and head southeast to begin the steady and physically taxing climb toward the highest point on the kora route: the **Drölma (Tara) Pass** (5,670 m; 18,420 ft). Half way up to the pass is the Vajrayogini Burial Ground, a place where the bodies of Tibetan pilgrims who die while visiting Kailash are still deposited. Tibetan pilgrims who do not die leave a piece of clothing, a lock of hair, or another personal item at this site. The idea is that the pilgrim can symbolically replicate the moment of death here in the cremation ground, thus preparing for the moment of his or her actual death. Some pilgrims even lie down, visualizing their own death and subsequent rebirth. To the left of the path and above the burial ground is the Vajrayogini peak, on which devout pilgrims have piled countless small heaps of stones. There is also said to be a footprint of Milarepa in a rock above the burial ground.

The trail beyond the burial ground contains many significant sites that can be difficult to identify without the aid of an experienced pilgrim. Many of these sites involve crawling through narrow passages among the rocks, tasting the earth, and collecting stones and water. These items that are collected from the circumambulation route are considered to have extensive medicinal and spiritual powers. For example, one of the streams that crosses the trail not long before the pass is said to have the ability to purify the negative karma that comes from slaughtering animals. Pilgrims search the bottom of the stream bed for small black "pills" that are held to be powerful medicine.

Before reaching the pass itself, you will see a small lake; from here you turn right to struggle up the last slope to the pass. Because of the altitude the ascent of the pass is the most arduous stretch of the circuit around Kailash. The air becomes increasingly thin as you climb, and it is important not to overexert yourself. Make sure to rest frequently and to walk slowly.

The pass itself is broad and contains a large cairn in the middle. From the midst of the piled-up rocks rises a pole, attached to which are numerous prayer flags. One also finds clothing, hair, and other personal mementos on and around the rock pile. Many pilgrims will stop and make ritual offerings on the pass, praying to the bodhisattva Tara for help on their path. The atmosphere is generally one of great gaity and celebration. Tibetan pilgrims call out their exuberant verbal offering to the local mountain deities: *ki ki so so lha gyalo!*

Shortly after the Drölma Pass, to the south of the path is another very small lake, the **Tukje Tso**, "Compassion Lake" (called Gauri Kund by the Indians). It takes half an hour to climb down to it from the path. The scenery around the lake is particularly dramatic, with soaring cliffs rising a thousand feet up from the turquoise or frozen water. Indian pilgrims often make a detour to this lake to perform their ritual ablutions, even though the water is extremely cold. After the lake there is a steep descent of several thousand feet down a rock "staircase." At the bottom of the staircase you meet the eastern valley. This begins with a stretch of marshy boulder-strewn terrain, where it is easy to make the serious mistake of crossing the river by a stone causeway toward which the path at one point leads. Instead, make sure to keep on the west bank of the river, hugging the mountain itself. At this point, depending on the amount of daylight left, you should decide either to make camp here or to proceed to **Zutrul Puk**.

Although some maps may suggest otherwise, the eastern stretch of the route from the base of the staircase of Zutrul Puk, though fairly level and straight, is a good five-hour walk. Hence, the entire stretch from Dri-ra Puk to Zutrul Puk can take up to ten or twelve hours to complete. Once you arrive at Zutrul Puk, you should make camp immediately and explore the monastery and caves the next morning. As at Dri-ra Puk, there is an Indian pilgrim's rest house, as well as ample room for tents.

Day Three: Zutrul Puk to Darchen

Zutrul Puk (Miracle Cave) is where part of the magic contest between Milarepa and Naro Bönchung took place. Having displayed his superior magical powers at Lake Manasarovar and other points around Kailash, Milarepa suggested to his opponent that they build a shelter against the rain that had started to fall. Mila split a stone to use for the roof, but it was too heavy for Naro Bönchung to lift. So Milarepa maneuvered it into place himself, leaving impressions of his hands and head in the rock as he did so. These imprints are still visible in the roof of Zutrul Puk today.

Further contests took place between the two, the final and decisive one being the race to the summit of Kailash on the day of the full moon. Early in the morning Milarepa's disciples saw the Bön priest riding through the sky toward Kailash on his drum. Milarepa was unconcerned and patiently waited for the first ray of sunlight, which he miraculously alighted to reach the summit in a fraction of a second. According to the Buddhist accounts of this story, Naro Bönchung was humiliated and conceded defeat. As a gesture of his compassion, Milarepa stated that the Bön followers could continue circumambulating the mountain in their traditional, counter-clockwise fashion and bestowed upon them Bönri mountain, between Barga and Huore, so that they might have a place from which they could see Kailash.

The small monastery of Zutrul Puk is currently looked after by a monk of the Drukpa Kagyu order. The building was renovated after the Cultural Revolution, and the monastery itself now surrounds the cave. Photography is strictly forbidden inside the cave. The main image in the cave is a bronze statue of Milarepa, said to be crafted by the master himself. You can enter the cave and even sit there for a while, although you will need a flashlight if you want to take a closer look at things.

Around the monastery are a vast collection of mani stones and huge piles of rock with mantras and scriptures carved into them. There are also the remains of several large stupas. Above it are a number of small caves where hermits used to live. Now they are only occasionally used by nomads and pilgrims and when empty can be used as shelters for the night. Below Zutrul Puk, at the bottom of the valley, are some fine examples of mani walls. If you have time, you can visit the beautiful waterfall in a small side valley to the south of the monastery.

It is a leisurely four- to six-hour walk

from Zatrul Puk back to the starting point of Darchen. Continue to the end of the eastern valley, then turn westward across the edge of the plain, passing many huge mani walls, until you arrive at Darchen.

Either before or after completing the circumambulation, it is possible to make a short but outstanding excursion from Darchen into the center of the Kailash massif. By proceeding uphill due north over the foothills from Darchen for about two hours, you will reach the small monastery of **Gyangtra**. This has been rebuilt by monks of the Drigung Kagyu order, to which sect the monastery has traditionally belonged. The largest of the monasteries around Mount Kailash, it is located high on the wall of a natural amphitheater. Descending west to the bottom of the amphitheater, you follow a path that takes you to the ruins of **Seralung Monastery**. Although all pilgrims are allowed to proceed this far into the massif, to go any closer to the mountain you must first have qualified by completing twelve circumambulations by the route described above. If you are thus qualified to continue north from here, you will finally reach the moraines that lead to the base of the south face of Kailash. To cross this terrain can be dangerous for those who are inexperienced or ill equipped. Originally there were thirteen stupas erected at this spot, containing the relics of great lamas from Drigung Monastery in Central Tibet (see chapter 15). They are now being slowly rebuilt. Tso Kapala, a complex of two

tiny lakes, is somewhere off this route but is difficult to locate. Those with less time are strongly encouraged at least to climb up onto the western ridge behind Darchen. It takes only a couple of hours to walk to the tops of these hills, from where there is an utterly spectacular view of the great south face of Kailash and the plains below Darchen, with the lakes of Manasarovar and Rakshas Tal lying at the base of Mount Gurla Mandhata.

South of Mount Kailash, across the great plain of Barga at the base of Mount Gurla Mandhata, are the two lakes Manasarovar (Mapam Yumtso) and Rakshas Tal (Lhanag Tso). They are among the highest bodies of fresh water in the world, with Manasarovar at 4,558 m (14,954 ft) and Rakshas Tal about 15 m (50 ft) lower. The two lakes are connected by a channel called Ganga Chu which, although it flows in various degrees of volume, occasionally becomes totally dry. Traditionally, it is believed that ample water flowing in this channel augurs well for the Tibetan people, and the years of drought in the 1980s for the channel were taken as a bad sign for the country. More recently the channel has begun to flow again, but it is unclear whether there has been any corresponding shift in the fortunes of the Tibetan people.

Manasarovar is the larger of the two lakes and is considered by both Buddhists and Hindus to be much holier than Rakshas Tal. Hindus regard Manasarovar as the mental creation of the god Brahma, especially made so that pilgrims to Kailash would have a place to perform their ablutions. In 1948, some of Mahatma Gandhi's ashes were carried here from India and scattered on the lake. Buddhists believe that Queen Maya, the Buddha's mother, was carried here by the gods and washed prior to conceiving the Buddha in her womb. The lake is considered to have pure, healing waters and to represent the forces of sun, light, and victory (the Tibetan name for the lake means "unconquerable"). The lake is traditionally circumambulated as part of the Kailash pilgrimage. There are eight Buddhist monasteries on the shores of the lake.

In contrast to Manasarovar, the smaller lake Rakshas Tal is usually ignored by pilgrims, who compare it to the moon and the forces of darkness. Others associate Rakshas Tal, "the demon lake," with Mahakala, a wrathful protector. Unlike the healing waters of Manasarovar, the waters of Rakshas Tal are said to be poisonous. The association of Manasarovar with the sun and of Rakshas Tal with the moon is also linked to the respective shapes of the two lakes, with Manasarovar more closely resembling the full orb of the sun while Rakshas Tal resembles a half moon. As if to support such characterizations, the mood at the lake is frequently overcast and dull. Whereas there are many monasteries at the larger lake, Rakshas Tal has only one.

Before you set out to circumambulate Manasarovar, it is vitally necessary to have sufficient supplies. You must make sure to have food for four to five days, since it is generally not possible to buy any along the way. In the summer make sure to bring a surgical mask as well as insect repellent to protect yourself against the swarms of flies and mosquitoes that can plague the trekker at various points. The walk itself is longer than that around Kailash, but it is completely flat.

The starting point for the circumambulation of Manasarovar is the village of **Huore** (near the site where Bönri Monastery used to be). To reach Huore, you leave Darchen and go to Barga, a small settlement of three compounds and a military post, at the junction of the road connecting Shiquanhe and Purang with the so-called southern route to Central Tibet. The old site of Barga is a few kilometers away from the present, Chinese-built town. From New Barga you continue east along the southern route for a further 28 km (17 mi), passing to your left the snow-capped mountain Bönri (5,995 m or 19,668 ft) said to have been given by Milarepa to his vanquished Bön opponent in the magic contest that took place at Kailash (see p. 275). The only regular transport between Darchen and Huore is the Indian pilgrim bus, which leaves once every four days during the pilgrimage season. It is also possible to hitch a ride on a truck or jeep.

At Huore you can stay the night at a smallguest house before starting off for the lake itself the following morning. From Huore you can also hire horses to ride or carry your baggage around the lake. The body of water you see to the south of Huore is not Manasarovar but a small independent lake. Make sure to keep it to your right as you cross the

deserted landscape, heading southwest to Manasarovar. When you first reach the northeast shore of the lake, there is a short stretch where peculiar egg-shaped balls of weed and Karmapa stones, (small pieces of highly polished jet) can be found. Both objects are venerated by Tibetans as precious relics.

From here you head south for about three hours until you reach **Seralung Monastery**. The original Seralung Monastery, which housed up to one hundred monks, was located a couple of kilometers up the valley from the lake. It was destroyed during the Cultural Revolution, but in the early 1980s a modest temple was rebuilt at its present site on the lakeside. Seralung is traditionally a Drigung Kagyu monastery, at present cared for by monks of the Geluk order, with a married Nyingma *ngag-pa* lama acting as caretaker. It has a single shrine room. If you feel like sleeping here, it may be possible to stay either in the kitchen or in tents nearby. At the lakeside by the monastery one can find layers of five-colored sand—black, red, gold, green and silver—which is also venerated by the Tibetans.

From Seralung it is a seven-hour walk to **Trugo Monastery** on the southern shore of the lake. Most pilgrims walk from Huore to Trugo in one day. Trugo has also been rebuilt on the lakeside instead of its original site, at a place where both Ra Lotsawa and Atisha spent time in meditation. Atisha is also associated with Yer-ngo Monastery, the ruins of which are 4 km (2.5 mi) east of

88. Mount Kailash from the circumambulation route

89. Mount Kailash

90. The Kangnyi Chörten on the Kailash circumambulation route

91. Mount Kailash and pilgrims

92. Pilgrims circumambulating Mount Kailash

93. Tirthapuri Hot Springs

94. Mani stones and yak horns

95. White Tara mural at Tsaparang

96. The remains at the monastic buildings at Toling

97. Nomad boy in Western Tibet

98. Chiu Monastery with Mount Kailash in the background

Trugo. The long walk down the eastern shore takes you through diverse and beautiful landscapes, often cutting through areas of desert instead of following the shoreline. All along the southern shore of the lake Kailash can be seen clearly to the north. You can picnic at the Ta-ge River, where there was a footbridge. (The footbridge was washed away in 1995 and until it is rebuilt the river must be forded, a task that could prove difficult unless you have a horse to carry you across.) Several kilometers up this river are hot spring and geysers. There is a government-built Pilgrim's Guest House at Trugo, where you can spend the night for a small fee. Trugo is an excellent place to stay for a few days as it is isolated, peaceful, and friendly, and the views and sunsets are often spectacular. There are plenty of idyllic walks to take, and the monastery itself is a trading crossroad with regular arrivals and departures of caravans of loaded yaks heading off in various directions. Trugo is also a trading point for Tibetan nomads, who come down from the northern plains (Jangtang) to sell wool and salt to Nepalese traders. Many Nepalese Hindus from northwest Nepal also come here to bathe and perform ablutions in the lake, but these pilgrims rarely continue to Kailash. Behind the monastery is the great mountain, Gurla Mandhata.

The next stretch of the circumambulation entails a full day's walk from Trugo to **Tseti Lake** on the western shore. As you turn around the southwest corner of

Manasarovar, you will notice that this is the nesting place for many wild geese that migrate to the region. Also near this corner is a cairn made up of several peculiarly shaped rocks, upon which Tibetans make offerings of scarves, sweets, and *chang*. This act of devotion is done to recall the time that a spirit visited the tantric adept who was living at the spot and transformed cakes of brown sugar into these rocks (which explains their strange shape). A couple of hours further around the shore you will pass by some tall cliffs in which are several blackened caves. A small monastery, **Gosul Gompa**, has been rebuilt on top of the cliffs. A climb up affords a magnificent view of the entire lake. From here you can peer down into the clear blue water and see giant fish swimming in its depths. Unfortunately, Kailash itself is obscured from this point, even though it is visible directly before you along most of the western shore.

The only building at Tseti is a rest house, where it is possible to spend the night, although there are no cooking facilities. From here, it is possible to meet the pilgrim's bus, or you can try your luck hitchhiking on the road nearby, either back to Purang or on to Darchen and Shiquanhe.

If you decide to continue on the pilgrimage, you walk another two hours or so to **Chiu Monastery** at the northwest corner of the lake. This small monastery is on a hill and marks the place where Padmasambhava spent the last seven days of his life on this earth.

You can visit the cave where he is said to have meditated. Chiu Monastery is also the point where the Ganga Chu, the channel connecting the two lakes, passes. Hot springs are found nearby, a short distance down the channel. They are great for washing your hair!

The northern shore of the lake is not usually covered as part of the circumambulation because of marshes and cliffs that prevent one from approaching the shoreline. The cliffs themselves contain meditation caves where ascetics from the various religious traditions have spent time in meditation. One can only traverse the marshy section in winter when the ground is frozen.

Pilgrims must now make their way back to either Darchen via Barga or Purang. From Chiu Monastery you can walk to Barga in about four hours, or hitch a ride with a truck on the nearby road. From Barga it should be possible, though not necessarily easy, to arrange transport back to Shiquanhe. You would probably have more success at Darchen. It is 104 km (65 mi) from Chiu to Purang, which has to be hitched unless you have prearranged transport. Remember that hitching in Tibet means stopping a truck and negotiating with the driver how much you will pay for the journey. Because there is no public transport, all travelers, including Tibetans, pay for lifts. During the summer months the Indian pilgrims' bus picks up groups of Indians here every few days and takes them to Darchen and then back to Purang. If seats are available, it may take other passengers for a charge.

TIRTHAPURI

The only other point of pilgrimage considered essential to the traveler in the Kailash region is Tirthapuri, located on the Sutlej River. The traditional order of the pilgrimage is first to circumambulate Manasarovar, then Kailash, and then to go to Tirthapuri. While some may reverse the order of the first two sites, Tirthapuri is almost always the final stop. Perhaps this has something to do with the soothing waters of the shallow hot springs, where weary travelers can relax, soak their feet, and contemplate the adventures they have undergone.

Tirthaputi is best known for being a sacred place of Padmasambhava and his consort Yeshe Tsogyel. The monastery, which was formerly connected with Hemis Monastery in Ladakh, was completely destroyed during the Cultural Revolution and rebuilt in the 1980s. Behind the monastery is a cave where Padmasambhava and Yeshe Tsogyel both meditated and a granite rock with their embedded footprints. The hot springs are surrounded by pink and white limestone terraces, which make a favorite picnic spot for Tibetans. Small pure opaque calcium balls are found among the terraces; search carefully, for these small beads are considered to be powerful medicine. Ravens and rainbows abound in this magical spot.

Tirthapuri can also be visited as part

of a journey to or from the kingdom of Guge, or as part of a return journey to Shiquanhe. To reach it turn southwest off the main road at Menjir (also called Mensi) and continue for 13 km (8 miles). Despite the excuses your driver may make to avoid going there, be assured that it is an easy, quick, and enjoyable side trip. It is also a good place to camp for a night. From Tirthapuri to Toling is approximately one long day of driving, so consider spending an extra night here and enjoy.

35
GUGE: TOLING & TSAPARANG

After the breakup of the Yarlung dynasty in central Tibet following the assassination of Langdarma in 842, the entire country was divided into small regions under the control of one or another local prince or lord. One of Langdarma's sons, Ö Sung, retreated from the central part of the country and established a small state in Western Tibet, in the upper Sutlej Valley, called Guge. Nothing much is known of the early history of Guge, but it came into prominence with the ascendency of King Korde, who is better known as Lha Lama Yeshe Ö, the name the king took in later life as a Buddhist monk. Yeshe Ö was a key figure in the second period of the dissemination of Buddhism in Tibet. Around 970 he sent the gifted young monk Rinchen Zangpo to India to study Buddhist philosophy. Rinchen Zangpo spent a total of seventeen years in India and became possibly the greatest Tibetan translator of Sanskrit scriptures. He was responsible for the invitation of a number of Indian scholars to Tibet and the construction of over one hundred monasteries in Western Tibet. Towards the end of his life King Yeshe Ö was captured and held for ransom by a rampaging Turkic army. His grandnephew Jangchub Ö, also a Buddhist monk-ruler, raised the gold for Yeshe Ö's release but was told by his great-uncle to use it instead to invite the renowned Indian master Atisha to Tibet. In this way Yeshe Ö sacrificed himself for the sake of Atisha coming to Tibet.

In 1042 Atisha, already sixty years old, arrived in Guge. He stayed for three years at Toling, the capital of Guge at that time, giving teachings and composing his most famous work, *The Lamp for the Path to Enlightenment*. He also met the eighty-five-year-old Rinchen Zangpo, who had founded two of the main temples at Toling, and exhorted him to spend his remaining years in solitary mediation. From Guge, Atisha made his way to central Tibet, where he taught extensively before dying in 1054.

The kingdom of Guge with its two main centers of Toling and Tsaparang continued to prosper for another five hundred years or so. Tsaparang in particular was once was a thriving city, located on a major trade route with links to India, Central Tibet, and Central Asia. A war with the king of Ladakh in the 1680s, combined with a drop in the local water table, resulted in the final demise of the city, which has remained mostly abandoned until now. The smaller city of Toling remained active as a religious center until the 1960s, although the political power of Guge was greatly reduced since the fall of Tsaparang. Despite the inevitable desecration that subsequently took place during the Cultural Revolution, several buildings and temples remain, and many works of art are still preserved in both sites. Today a few farming families still live in the formerly prosperous valley, eking out a living from the dry, eroded soil.

Guge is a two-day journey by jeep or truck from either Purang or Shiquanhe, and a one-day journey from Tirthapuri. There is no public transport to Guge. During the wet season (June to August) the road can become completely impassable and no driver will agree to take you. If you are coming from Purang, it is best to break the journey at Tirthapuri, camping there overnight. The next day you continue for about 40 km (25 mi), crossing a high pass, to Baer. At Baer you turn left onto the newly built road, which takes you the remaining 180 km (112 mi) to **Zada**, the new Chinese name for Toling. About three hours after leaving Baer and crossing the two passes that lead into the northern plateau above the upper Sutlej basin, you reach an elevated section of the road from which can be had one of the most spectacular views of the Himalayan range possible: a wide arc of mountains stretching hundreds of miles from the Dhaulagiri/Annapurna mass in the southeast to the Karakoram peaks in the northwest. The focal point of this extraordinary landscape is Mount Nanda Devi, directly south of your vantage point. The distance to Zada from Shiquanhe is about 100 km (62 mi) less than from Purang, but it would still be an arduous one-day drive.

TOLING

Formerly there were six main temples at Toling, which operated as a monastery until 1966. Three of these buildings, the Golden Temple, the Neten Lhakhang, and the Tongyu Lhakhang, have been completely destroyed. The Yeshe Ö Chapel, which was built in the form of a three-dimensional mandala, is badly damaged. The assembly hall, also called the Red Temple, still survives, as does the frequently closed White Temple.

The **Yeshe Ö Chapel** (which Lama Govinda refers to in *The Way of the White Clouds* as the Golden Temple) was perhaps the most significant building at Toling. Situated at the center of the complex, this ancient structure was built on the plan of a three-dimensional mandala. A large statue, possibly of Vairochana, sat in the middle of the building, with subsidiary statues lining the walls in all directions. The chapel was utterly destroyed during the cultural revolution, and today one needs a powerful imagination to envision its former glory. Only the remains of the building's structure and a few surviving statues are visible among the rubble.

The Red Temple, where both Rinchen Zangpo and Atisha worked and lived, is the main assembly hall at Toling. Although normally closed and inactive as a place of worship, it has been partially restored and was reconsecrated for worship. The extensive murals, which show similarities to Newari art, probably date from the fifteenth century. Traces of the older Kashmiri style, dating back to the eleventh and twelfth centuries, can also be discerned. Previously, the extremely fine workmanship of many of these murals was partly obscured by a layer of grime and mud, but much of the dirt has now been cleaned away. Nonetheless, a powerful flashlight is an indispensable item in these dim interiors.

Next door, the **White Temple** (now the color of the earth) is frequently closed, although it is worth trying to get the caretaker to open it. Here the scene before you is one of extraordinary contrast. All the paintings along the left-hand wall have been badly damaged by water seepage. They depict life-size images of the main male peaceful tantric meditational deities. Those along the right-hand wall, however, are in immaculate condition and represent a corresponding selection of female deities such as Vijaya, Tara, Sarasvati, and Prajnaparamita. The deities are seated within landscapes, palaces, and superbly executed scenes of life in the world. Their colors seem as fresh as when they were painted, possibly around three or four hundred years ago. Major figures of the Drigung Kagyu are also featured, as is the founder of the Gelukpa order, Tsongkhapa, dating these murals to the fifteenth century at the earliest.

Other points of interest include the citadel of Toling, now just ruined walls and caves, which can be reached by climbing to the top of the cliff behind the town up a dangerous staircase and precipitous tunnel. From this vantage point you get a superb view of the immediate Sutlej Valley as far west as Tsaparang. Also worth seeing is the large stupa

attributed to King Yeshe Ö on the far bank of the small stream southwest of the Tibetan village.

TSAPARANG

The older of the two ancient capitals of Guge, **Tsaparang**, is a one-hour journey (26 km or 16 mi) by jeep down winding roads, west of Toling (Zada). It is best to put aside an entire day to explore the area. For the most part, all that remains of the abandoned city is a mall of ruins and crumbling walls. But within the city there are five surviving temples, four in the main part around the lower ramparts of the deserted town, and one on top of the citadel in the midst of the ruins of the ancient summer palace of the kings.

In the lower complex of buildings, the **White Temple** contains some of the earliest examples of Tibetan Buddhist tantric art, probably about one thousand years old. The paintings have been executed in a dynamic, less-stylized manner than most later works and clearly show an affinity to Indian and Kashmiri art. Although the statues on the pedestals have been badly damaged, the incredibly detailed murals remain intact. The roof panels too present a magnificent array of classical decorative motifs. The inside of this temple, and other sites at Tsaparang, was photographed by Li Gotami and Lama Govinda on their trip to the area in 1949.

Directly above the White Temple is the **Red Temple**. This also abounds with very well preserved examples of tantric images, though of a later period, depicting the five Dhyani Buddhas, the Eight Great Bodhisattvas, and some protectors. The statues in this temple have all been recently destroyed. Near the Red Temple is the smaller **Yamantaka Temple**. Previously this housed a statue of the wrathful, bull-headed deity, but sadly it too has been destroyed. However, there remain on the walls gold images on a black background of Guhyasamaja, Samvara, Hevajra, Tsongkhapa, Maitreya, Tara, and several protectors. The fourth temple in this part of Tsaparang is a small building below the White Temple near the entrance dedicated, it seems, to Tsongkhapa, and hence later in date. It contains rather more seriously damaged paintings, stylistically similar to those in the Yamantaka temple.

To reach the actual citadel of the kings, an impregnable fortress above the city, you have to climb via a tunnel and staircase, up through the center of the pinnacle to a small plateau on the top of the sheer cliffs that rise above the ruins below. The eroded walls of the king's summer palace and temple complexes stand starkly against the sky. In the middle of these ruins is another red-walled temple, the **Demchok Mandala**. This once contained a three-dimensional mandala of Samvara (Demchok), which has now been smashed to rubble. The murals, however, have hardly been damaged at all and are exceptionally beautiful. On the front wall are depicted two forms of the protector Mahakala and the dakinis of the mandala; on the left-hand wall, the five forms of Samvara; on the back wall, five aspects of Guhyasamaja; and on the right-hand wall, five forms of Hevajra. Being the chapel of the king, they must have been painted by the greatest craftsmen of the age and are possibly five hundred years old. The ceiling, panels, and carved beams are also covered with finely painted patterns and motifs, likewise in excellent condition.

The king's winter palace is also in the citadel. This is a complex of rooms, chambers, and passageways carved deep down into the very heart of the mountain. Take care as you descend the very steep staircases into this area.

To visit the temples in Tsaparang you generally must pay a fairly hefty fee. You must also leave your camera with the attendant at the main gate: photography is strictly prohibited for Chinese as well as other foreign tourists. To take pictures it is necessary to obtain a special permit from Beijing, usually available only at an extremely high price. The exorbitant rates for photography and the even higher rates for video are an indication of the high regard in which these works of early Buddhist art are held by the authorities.

PART FIVE
TRAVEL IN CENTRAL & WESTERN TIBET

BASIC INFORMATION FOR THE VISITOR

The first point to make is that by the time you read this (or any other) book about travel in Tibet, the details may already be out of date. The remoteness of Tibet, the relative newness of its "tourist industry," and the heavy-handed policies of the Chinese Communist government in the region all contribute to a situation in which rapid and unpredictable changes in regulations, prices, routes, and accommodation are inevitable. Even within a period of hours or days, different people may have considerably different experiences in the same place. Depending on their own approach to the situation or the whims and moods of the people they are dealing with, they may end up paying different prices, following a different route, being allowed to see different things, staying in a different place, and eating different quality food.

The lesson, then, is this: if you travel to Tibet (even with an officially organized tour), do not expect things to conform to your preconceived notions of what the journey will or should be like or to information read in books. Otherwise, frustration is virtually guaranteed. To enjoy Tibet it is necessary to be as open-minded and tolerant of "inefficiency" (that is, things being done in a way other than that to which you are accustomed) as possible.

Package and Individually Organized Tours

Many, if not most, travelers to Tibet elect to go there as part of an organized tour. Basically, there are two types of tours. The first is the well-known package tour whereby you enter and exit the country with the group. Such trips are generally fairly expensive and provide relatively limited freedom for the traveler. For many travelers, however, the package tour is the only feasible way to go to Tibet. This is particularly true if you do not want to carry a backpack everywhere you go and if you are wary of having to negotiate checkpoints and permits on your own. When booking your package tour, make sure that the trip includes ample time in Tibet itself. A two-week trip to China that includes a short side trip to Lhasa will not even provide enough time to get used to the altitude. A full two weeks in Tibet itself is really the minimum that will allow you to acclimatize and see just a few of the wonders of the "roof of the world." More time would be even better, as you can easily spend one or even two weeks exploring Lhasa and its environs. Remember that the best package tours are the ones that give you the most free time.

Package tours can be arranged through agencies with connections to the permit-granting authorities in Tibet. In order to gain permission to operate in Tibet, Chinese government regulations require that tour companies hire an officially approved guide. In Tibet, many of the so-called "local guides" are not

Tibetan but Chinese, and almost all of them have received special "training" in Beijing. The actual depth of their knowledge regarding history may be scanty, and some guides are downright apathetic and biased, repeating only the official party-line version of Tibetan history and culture. Some of the guides available through Lhasa-based companies are Tibetan, and although they do not generally have the freedom to express an overtly nonparty line, they are usually more open-minded than the typical guide contracted through CITS (the government-run state travel agency, China International Travel Service). In addition, your package tour company may contract to bring along a Western scholar of Tibet or Tibetan Buddhism.

The second type of tour is the individually arranged tour. This type of tour has developed in the past few years as a way for backpackers and other seemingly "independent" travelers to legally visit Central and Western Tibet. Although some of the cities in Central and Western Tibet (including Lhasa) have been defined as "open cities"—meaning that you do not need a special permit beyond your visa to visit them—the routes between these cities are still restricted. Travelers who arrive in Lhasa independent of an organized tour will find that their options for travel in Central Tibet are limited. Many areas require a permit, and failure to produce a permit at checkpoints can result in a fine or even in having your visa revoked (with one week to leave the country). To

obtain a permit, therefore, you need to form a small "tour" of your own. This can be done through one of the approved Lhasa agencies (consult a travel agent in the West or in Nepal for a list). The catch, of course, is the additional requirement of hiring a vehicle and a guide. These companies can obtain permits, vehicles, tents, and occasionally even visa extensions (for a price).

To organize your own tour, it helps to have four to five people to defray the considerable costs of the overland transport. The bulletin boards at most of the backpacker hotels in Lhasa display notices of tour groups forming to share the price of various excursions. These may be relatively short tours to places like Samye or they may be headed to such far away pilgrimage spots as Mount Kailash. If you choose to organize your own tour through a Lhasa company, be sure to write a small contract specifying cost and itinerary, and be certain that the company signs it. Note also that the vehicles generally belong to the drivers, not the companies, and thus any contract drawn up between tourists and the company should be shown to (and translated for) the driver. Getting such documents beforehand tends to minimize disputes and additional fees en route. This form of travel, while requiring considerably more effort to organize than the package tour, can in fact be wonderful as you can design your own trip and optimize your time.

Individual Travel

Genuinely independent travel is difficult

to achieve and generally consists of traveling on the limited public transportation, hitchhiking, or walking. Public transportation consists mainly of buses, many of which can be difficult for foreigners to board without permits. The one exception is for the buses in the Lhasa area, which depart from near the Jokhang and take you to outlying regions such as Tsurpu Monastery. Truck drivers tend to be hesitant to take Westerners as they can be fined (or in extreme cases, lose their licenses) at checkpoints. Without a doubt walking affords the most freedom. In many ways walking from place to place is the most pleasant anyhow, as the camping and hiking are sublime, and the nomads encountered nearly everywhere are hospitable and kind (but beware of their dogs). If you have plenty of time, a good sleeping bag, a tent, a stove, and a blossoming sense of adventure, you can go almost anywhere. Technical mountain climbing, on the other hand, can be difficult. Many journeys should not be attempted by those inexperienced with mountains.

For remoter regions you can try traveling on trucks. These can be picked up either at truck stops in the towns or by hitchhiking. This can be a very slow and unreliable way of traveling but to get to some destinations you may have no choice. You will often have to stand in the back of an open truck, squeezed in with numerous Tibetans, for hours on end. It is therefore important to be equipped with warm clothing and a dust

mask. The cost of traveling by truck is very low. Even when hitchhiking, however, you should be prepared to pay something to the driver.

Mountain bikes are another possibility. Several people have brought them to Lhasa by plane and cycled out to the Nepalese border. Others have come from even further afield. People have been reported carrying kayaks into the country and a French team has even hang-glided over Lhasa.

Visas and Permits

If you travel to Tibet with a package tour, then the arrangements for the necessary visas and permits will be taken care of by the agency organizing the trip. For individuals who are organizing their own tours, the process of obtaining visas and permits will give you your first taste of the vagaries of Chinese bureaucracy. Permits can usually be arranged once you arrive in Lhasa, but visas should be obtained before you set out for the Land of Snows. In some cases the visa is effective as of the date of issue, so be careful not to get it too far in advance.

Chinese embassies worldwide can issue visas for the People's Republic of China. Individual visas are valid for stays one, two, or three months. It is very rare that the embassy in Kathmandu will issue individual visas (if they do it will most likely stipulate Shanghai as the only possible point of entry), but New Delhi may be a good bet. If you plan to cross into Tibet through Nepal, therefore, you should secure your Chinese visa before you arrive in Kathmandu. Bangkok has a reputation for granting lengthy visas (up to three months). Visa extensions (to a maximum of six months) can be procured rather easily at Public Security Bureau (*Gong An Ju* in Chinese) offices in much of China, but Tibet is another story. Sometimes Lhasa travel agencies can extend your visa if you join a tour, but the bottom line is that non-package tour travelers will have a much more challenging time trying to obtain a visa for China if the obvious destination is Tibet.

In addition to a regular visa for China, you need to get special permits, called Aliens' Travel Permits (ATP) to visit many regions in Tibet. If you wish to obtain these permits before your arrival in Tibet you need to work with a travel agency that has links to one of the approved agencies in Lhasa. Inside China or Tibet, you can apply for the permits at the local Public Security Bureau. The permits are valid for particular regions, and they list the towns and sites that you will be allowed to visit. They cannot be changed after they have been issued, so make sure that you give the full details of your requested travel itinerary when applying for the permit. Another type of permit, a military permit is required for travel to more sensitive spots. The big mystery is determining which places are open and which are not. This tends to fluctuate, so talk to other travelers.

The bureaucracy embedded in the Chinese system can be massively frustrating. For good training, see *The Castle* by Franz Kafka. Patience and perpetual calm smiles will open many doors for you. Logic, alas, often will not. Showing the anger and agitation that you may be feeling will certainly be counterproductive. Generally if you act innocent, ignorant, enthusiastic, and insanely patient, you will learn that the system can actually function.

Customs

Foreigners these days are generally not subjected to more than perfunctory baggage checks both upon entering and leaving Tibet and China. Be careful though to conceal anything that may be interpreted as "harmful to the State Security of the People's Republic of China," such as Dalai Lama pictures (officially outlawed in 1996), Tibetan national flags, and so on. When you enter the country you will be asked to fill in a form declaring whatever valuables (cameras, tape recorders, watches) you are bringing in. The customs officials are quite strict about checking this form when you leave the country to make sure you have not mislaid anything en route. You may have difficulty bringing out objects such as statues, paintings, and jewelry that were made before 1959 and are therefore classified as part of the "Chinese Cultural Heritage." Make sure to keep receipts from all purchases and be prepared to show them if necessary.

Currency

The Chinese currency, known as the Renminbi (RMB), is used in Tibet. In

Chinese, the RMB unit is called the yüan but is also referred to by its common name: the *kuai*. The kuai can be further divided into ten *mao* (or *jiao*), or 100 *fen*. In recent years the exchange rate has hovered around 8 yüan to the U.S. dollar. The Foreign Exchange Currency (FEC) that previously had been specially designated for foreigners has (thankfully) been discontinued.

In Lhasa and Shigatse, major foreign currencies in either cash or traveler's checks can be changed into RMB at the Bank of China, the only bank authorized to make transactions with foreigners. Hotels are sometimes also authorized to change money. When traveling off the beaten track make sure to take sufficient cash in RMB. At present, black market money changers in Tibet are only occasionally interested in exchanging U.S. dollars for RMB and their rate is rarely better than at the bank.

Credit cards are accepted at only a handful of places in Tibet. Do not expect to be able to use them. Some foreigners have been able to receive cash advances on their credit cards at the Bank of China, yet others have been refused with no apparent explanation. It could well be determined by the mood of the teller. Again, don't count on this option. Do not have money sent to the Bank of China in Lhasa unless you plan to have your visa extended. It may take up to a month to arrive.

Postal and Telegraphic Services

The post to and from Lhasa can be amazingly efficient. Packages and letters sent from Lhasa to foreign countries vary in the amount of time it takes them to reach their destination, yet they seem to always make it. Receiving mail in Lhasa is a bit more sketchy. The poste restante drawer at the Main Post Office has been known to be emptied into the trash every few months. If you know approximately when you will be in Lhasa, your can have mail sent to: Poste Restante, Main Post Office, Lhasa, China. Another option is to have mail sent to your hotel in Lhasa. Again, beware of sending politically sensitive messages, particularly to your Tibetan friends in Tibet.

International telephone calls can be made from Lhasa from either the Telecommunications Office on Dzuk Trun Lam or your hotel. The lines can be remarkably clear. International calls cost around 35-50 yüan per minute, so having someone call you back can be considerably cheaper (for you, perhaps not for the other party). It is also possible to send or receive faxes at some locations. Do not expect to be able to make international calls from areas outside of the major cities.

Weather

Tibet is *not* as cold as most people imagine. Even in winter, it is unpleasantly cold only during the night. Rather than the cold, the most characteristic feature of Central Tibetan weather is dryness. There is very little rain except during a couple of months in the summer. Snow settles only above 5,000 m (16,500 ft).

Snow in Lhasa usually does not last more than a few hours. There is generally very little precipitation and a great deal of direct, strong sunlight. Whether you travel to Tibet in winter or summer, you will definitely notice a significant drop in the temperature very shortly after the sun has set. The days, on the other hand, can be quite hot.

The weather patterns are seasonal and regular. The spring comes late, with blossoms not appearing until mid- to late April. But by March the cold edge of winter has already gone and as it gets closer to summer, the weather gets progressively hotter and the atmosphere dustier. When combined with winds, which can be strong, very unpleasant dust storms can occur. The rains come in July and August and can occasionally cause flooding and mudslides. The autumn is clear and it gradually gets colder until December, when the first chill of winter can be felt. Although winter is cold and rather bleak, it is also extremely clear and bright. During winter, travel is made more difficult because passes are blocked by snow. On the other hand, there are far fewer tourists present, and if you go to Lhasa during the period of the Tibetan New Year (Losar) you can witness the great influx of Tibetan pilgrims there. Western Tibet is much drier and Eastern Tibet is more similar to the wetter Chinese weather patterns.

Health

Compared to the Indian subcontinent and to China, Tibet is a relatively disease-free place. No vaccinations are required in order to travel to Tibet but it can still be wise to consider immunization against hepatitis, meningitis, typhoid, tetanus, and rabies. Anti-malaria medication is not necessary in Central and Western Tibet, but it may be indicated for parts of Eastern Tibet and Nepal. Check with your doctor before your departure for the latest health reports for the areas that you will be visiting. It is also recommended that you have a full physical exam before your departure. Pregnant women and people with a history of heart, lung, or blood diseases are usually advised not to travel the high altitudes of Central and Western Tibet.

The relative lack of disease in Tibet is due primarily to the dry and sunny atmosphere and to the small concentrations of people. Nonetheless, most Tibetans have little conception of hygiene so there is always the danger of bacterial or viral infection from dirty kitchen utensils and so on. Periodic stomach upsets resulting in diarrhea and mild food poisoning are not rare. Be discerning about where you eat, and always avoid uncooked or undercooked meat or fish. Beware also of food that has been left in the open air where it may have been exposed to dust and flies. Beware of water that has not been purified and avoid ice in softdrinks (since it is probably not made with filtered water). In the event of mild diarrhea, replenish your fluids and salts through a rehydration powder. If necessary, you can make your own preparation with one teaspoon of salt and four tablespoons of sugar mixed into a liter of purified water. More severe types of diarrhea (dysentery) require strong medications; see a doctor for an analysis of the problem.

Respiratory problems such as colds, flu, and vicious sore throats are particularly common, so bring along your favorite remedies. Dehydration, sun stroke, and sunburn can all take you by surprise. By far the most dangerous potential health problem, however, is altitude sickness (see section immediately below). This disease can be deadly, so make sure you are well informed about its symptoms and treatments and be on the lookout for early warning signs. For the lesser problem of rabies, see the section on dogs.

Altitude Sickness

Almost everyone who travels to Central or Western Tibet will suffer from the effects of altitude. Although Lhasa is one of the lowest places in Central Tibet, it is still 4,000 m (13,000 ft) above sea level. How greatly one is affected by altitude varies from person to person and depends in part on how gradually one has made the ascent into Tibet. Obviously, acclimatization is much more difficult if you fly in than if you drive in. It also tends to strike people who overexert themselves in the first few days above 3,000 m (9,800 ft).

The so-called "early mountain sickness" usually develops during the first two or three days at high altitude. Its symptoms include headache, nausea, loss of appetite, sleeplessness, and difficulty breathing. People will be affected in different ways and not all the symptoms need to be present. If you experience some or all of the symptoms, you definitely should not go any higher until they have disappeared. To be safe, it is best to plan for three days of relatively reduced activity upon first arriving in Central Tibet (this is assuming that you are flying in). Headache medication, avoidance of alcohol, cigarettes, and heavy food, and direct intake of oxygen can help alleviate these symptoms. The drug Acetazolamide (also known as Diamox) is often used nowadays both preventatively (in cases of quick ascent) and as a treatment for mild symptoms of altitude sickness. Most people experience no side effects with this drug, and it has the added advantage that it does not mask more serious developments of illness. Before your trip to Tibet, you should consider obtaining a course of Acetazolamide from your doctor. Even without any drugs, most people get over the initial symptoms quite soon but it usually takes six weeks for a complete adaptation to occur.

The so-called early mountain sickness can sometimes develop into acute mountain sickness, which may involve the life-threatening conditions of pulmonary or cerebral edema—waterlogged lungs or brain. These are serious occurrences that can result in death if not treated immediately. They are liable to occur only if the symptoms of early mountain sickness are ignored and you continue to ascend. The symptoms of pulmonary edema are as follows: weakness, tiredness, shortness of breath, increased respiratory and heart rates, dry cough at first followed by cough with watery or bloody sputum later, noisy and bubbly breathing, congested chest, and dark blue fingernails and lips. If pulmonary edema is diagnosed (not all symptoms need to be present), you must descend to a lower altitude immediately. If the symptoms develop while you are in Lhasa, go straight to the hospital. Form there it is probable that you will be flown out of the country, either to Chengdu or to Nepal.

The symptoms of cerebral edema are extreme tiredness, vomiting, severe headaches, difficulty in walking, abnormal speech and behavior, drowsiness, and unconsciousness. If cerebral edema is diagnosed (again not all of the symptoms need be present), you must descend immediately and stay down. Descent should not be delayed for any reason and someone should accompany the patient. No medication is a substitute for descent. If in Lhasa, go straight to a hospital, from where descent by air will be arranged.

Although early mountain sickness is common, pulmonary and cerebral edema (acute mountain sickness) are not. The greatest risk is for those with heart or lung diseases. It is advisable that before leaving for Tibet such persons, the elderly and people with chronic illnesses consult their doctor.

What to Bring

Strong, resistant clothing and sturdy walking shoes or boots are essential. Windproof, insulated jackets, thermal underwear, gloves, hats, and wool socks are all necessary for trekking, traveling on trucks, and in winter. In all seasons, bring at least one set of light clothes. In addition, you should have a hat that can protect you from the sun, some light rain gear, and a cotton face mask to protect your lungs against the dust.

Dark glasses, suntan lotion, lip salve, a water flask and mug, a good penknife (with bottle opener, can opener, screwdriver, and scissors), toilet paper (can be bought in Tibet), insect repellent, and a powerful flashlight (with batteries) are all indispensable. Trekkers should also have a compass, binoculars, a tent, a means of purifying water (iodine or a filter), rope, a camping stove, matches, fuel, and cooking utensils.

A sleeping bag is useful but not essential unless you are trekking or traveling through remote country. Hotels and guesthouses generally provide thick, warm quilts. Budget travelers might also wish to bring along soap, a towel, plastic sheeting to ward off bed bugs, and a sturdy lock and chain.

Naturally you will need to have your passport and other essential documents. It is also a good idea to make photocopies of these and pack them in your luggage while carrying the originals in a money belt on your person. Extra passport photos can come in handy (and are often essential) when requesting visas, permits, and visa extensions.

Basic first aid equipment includes bandages, antiseptic solution, aspirin or other headache medicine, lozenges for sore throats, antacid tablets, rehydration powders, and medication for altitude sickness (see section on Health). You should also bring personal hygienic supplies such as toothbrush, toothpaste, tampons, solution for cleaning contact lenses, and contraceptives. It is also worthwhile to take a supply of multivitamins or at least vitamin C.

Concentrated and dried foods that are rich in vitamins and protein are the most valuable dietary supplements you can bring with you. Instant coffee, tea bags, and powdered soups are also good to have. They can always be used with the hot water provided in all guesthouses and hotels. Powdered milk is available in Lhasa (see section on Food).

As gifts for Tibetans, color photos of Tibetan Buddhist religious figures, particularly of the Dalai Lama, are cherished. Remember, however, that photographs of the Dalai Lama are now explicitly outlawed and those of the Tibetan choice of the Panchen Lama are decidedly inflammatory in the eyes of the authorities. If you choose to bring such photos with you, be very careful both when entering the country and when giving them out. Only give them to Tibetans in private settings when you are sure that there are no spies around.

White silk *kata* scarves are great items to have on hand at all times in Tibet. They can be used as honorific offerings at monasteries throughout the country (simply bow your head and place the scarf around the neck or across the lap of the statue you are honoring). When greeting a lama, bow your head and hold the kata with both hands slightly raised in front of you. Depending on the situation, the lama may keep the kata, or he or she may return it to you as a blessing by placing it around your neck. Katas are also traditionally given as a form of offering congratulations or to a departing friend; in these cases it is acceptable to place the kata around your friend's neck. You can get katas in the Barkor and in Tibetan markets in Kathmandu.

As more and more tourists travel to Tibet, the problem of children begging for gifts has been exacerbated. Giving lots of candy and ball-point pens to kids, often to draw them into photographic range, tourists unwittingly encourage a beggar-mentality among the already beleaguered and often impoverished Tibetans. Rather than giving lots of gifts, some tourists have brought along plastic bottles of soap bubbles with which they can entertain and delight young children. Another possibility is to bring along a Polaroid camera, allowing you to give the gift of a photograph on the spot.

Accommodation

Only in Lhasa, Gyantse, Shigatse, and Tsetang is there anything remotely resembling Western hotel accommodation. If you travel as part of a package tour to Central Tibet, it is quite possible that you will never spend a night any-where other than these four cities. As an individual traveler, on the other hand, you may well find yourself spending many of your nights in either Tibetan-style or Chinese-style guesthouses, which usually charge between 10 and 20 RMB for a bed. The quality of these places varies considerably but at the very least you will be provided with enough quilts, a vacuum flask of hot water, and a wash basin. When traveling further afield you can stay in truck stops, or you can camp. Where there are no truck stops the local people will sometimes take you in for the night.

In most cities and towns in Central and Western Tibet you will find that there are really only one or two options for accommodation. The one exception is Lhasa, where there are a variety of hotels and guesthouses aimed both at the tourist and the business communities. For many years, the extremely expensive Lhasa Holiday Inn, located at the west-ern edge of the city near the Norbu-lingka, hosted most of the package tour groups. After considerable international pressure and a boycott on Holiday Inn, the company pulled out of Central Tibet in 1997. Undoubtedly some other large hotel chain will move in to fill the gap. Although the smaller guesthouses come and go, some of the more highly recom-mended budget spots include the Banak Shol Hotel, the Snowlands Hotel, the Yak Hotel, the Pentoch Hotel, and the Kyire Hotel. More expensive with better quality rooms and service are the Sunlight Hotel

and the Himalaya Hotel. All of these hotels are located within walking dis-tance of the Jokhang Cathedral and the Barkor.

Food

Tibet is not noted for its cuisine. The food tends to be coarse, heavy, and rather bland. Since the Chinese occupation wheat, rice, and vegetables have become more common, but outside Lhasa these are often hard to find. The standard Tibetan dish in restaurants is *thukpa*, a noodle and meat soup with a sprinkling of vegetables. Occasionally *momo* (meat dumplings) and hard-boiled eggs can also be found. The chili sauce on the table in most restaurants helps these dishes considerably.

In the countryside the staple diet con-sists of *tsampa* (roasted barley flour), butter, tea, curd, dried cheese, and meat. Local fruit is rarely available. Eating tsampa can be a bit of a chal-lenge. The general technique is to pour a bit of hot buttered tea into your bowl of tsampa and then kneed the flour into lit-tle balls of dough, call *pak*. Tibetans learn how to make pak at an early age, and will probably find it amusing to see you with clumps of flour all over your hands and face.

In most towns with a Chinese presence (this includes the major cities of Lhasa, Gyantse, Shigatse, and Testang) you will find restaurants with Chinese food. This rarely resembles the food that one gets in Chinese restaurants in the West. It is char-acteristically very greasy (cooked in pork fat) and frequently unappetizing.

The restaurants in the towns will rarely serve you traditional Tibetan butter tea or *chang*, barley beer. The standard drinks are weak sweet tea or cans or bottles of beer. It is rare to find soft drinks outside of large towns, but the Chinese "sports" drink Janlibao is a nice combination of honey and orange soda. In the countryside you will be served the more traditional drinks (when served the traditional Tibetan salted butter tea it helps to think of it as a broth rather than tea) or plain Chinese tea. It is not advisable to drink the water unless it comes from a spring or has been boiled or purified.

Lhasa now stocks a fairly wide range of canned and bottled food from China. These include meats, fish, green vegetables, preserved food, and jams. Powdered milk (even 'Kerrygold' from Ireland!) can be purchased quite cheaply. Imported fruits and vegetables, nuts, and dried fruits are also available in the market in Lhasa. It is a good idea to stock up on these items before you head out to other regions of Tibet.

Photography

Tibet offers wonderful opportunities for the photographer, but it is still necessary to be equipped with not only the equipment but also the right attitude.

To maintain cordial relations between foreign visitors and Tibetans it is most important to respect the local customs, regulations (however annoying) and people's feelings. Always try to put yourself in the place of the person you would like to photograph. How would you feel if Asian tourists constantly tried to photograph you while you were out shopping? Worse still, how would you feel if a group of strangers tried to photograph your grandmother's funeral? Tibetans are no less disturbed by the invasion of their privacy than anyone else. So either ask permission to take someone's photograph or at least take such shots discreetly with a telephoto lens.

Many Tibetans have heard of Polaroid cameras and expect that if you ask to take their picture, you will be able to produce an instant photograph of them. Thus always make it clear whether or not you will be able to do this. Others will ask you to send a copy of the picture to them by post. Elderly people and many women will refuse outright to be photographed. Although we might consider their reasons superstitious, they have every right to have their wishes respected. Some believe, for example, that a photograph of them left on earth after their death will somehow bind a part of them to this world.

In most monasteries and temples the monks will ask you to pay to take photographs. The charge is often as high as 20 RMB or more per chapel. This is a regulation imposed on the monasteries by the Chinese. Many of the monks selected to enforce this rule seem to have been chosen for their officious bent of mind and get very upset if they catch you trying to snap something secretly. Others, however, will go out of their way to spite the Chinese by breaking the regulation and will keep watch at the door while you take your pictures. In some instances, photography will be forbidden at any price.

Film supplies in Lhasa are unreliable, so it is best to bring with you all the film you need. The very strong sunlight makes film above 100 ASA impractical. But the dark shadows require at least 100 ASA to expose without flash. If you have two camera bodies you can get around this by loading one with 25 ASA film for bright outdoor shots and the other with a higher speed film for shadow shots and interiors. I used 100 ASA film with a single camera for all occasions and that quite satisfactorily met my needs.

A flashgun and tripod are extremely useful. Skylight filters are essential and a polarizing filter can produce some stunning results. Because of the dust make sure to bring a good case for your camera and a lens brush.

Dogs

Tibetans are one of few Asian peoples who are genuinely fond of dogs. In the towns they are kept as pets and in the country as protection against wild animals and thieves. The streets and monasteries abound with half-wild mongrels that are surprisingly well cared for and generally good-natured. However you must always be careful of the occasional dog with a penchant for human calves and ankles. Be especially wary when walking through back streets or visiting Tibetan homes. Before entering a court-yard or house, first inquire if there are any dogs (kyee). In the countryside the danger of dogs is greater and it is advisable to always carry a stick or stone to ward them off. Most dogs will retreat merely by being threatened by an upraised arm.

If you are bitten there is apparently little danger of rabies. Nonetheless, in Lhasa at least, Tibetans receive inoculation against this disease every October. Otherwise no treatment is available for a case of suspected rabies for those not inoculated. The only solution is either to rely on traditional Tibetan medicine or to leave the country by air (I would advise the latter). It may be worth considering inoculation before leaving for Tibet.

GETTING TO CENTRAL & WESTERN TIBET

GETTING TO LHASA

There are currently several ways to get to Tibet. If you are with a package tour group, the journey will be arranged for you. As an individual you can try one of a number routes, some of which are straightforward, others more difficult. The two main options for mode of transportation are by air and overland. Air travel is considerably easier and affords stunning views from the airplane windows. The disadvantages are that you do not get to see the stunning landscapes on your way to Central Tibet, and your risk of mountain sickness is much higher. Overland travel is challenging, both in terms of the physical rigors and the bureaucracy involved. Many routes require special permits. If you choose to travel without these, remember that you can face arrest.

By Air — Chengdu to Lhasa

The easiest, quickest and most expensive way is to fly in. At present the only city in China with a regular service to Central Tibet is Chengdu, the capital of the western province of Sichuan. There are rumors that flights from Kunming and from Hong Kong may be instigated soon, but so far these rumors have not proven true. Chengdu can be reached by a direct flight from Hong Kong or by rail or air from other major cities in China such as Shanghai or Beijing. Kunming, the capital of Yunnan province south of Sichuan can be reached from various places in southeast Asia. Kunming is a beautiful train ride away from Chengdu.

From Chengdu there are daily flights to the Gonkar airport (also called the Lhasa airport) which depart at 7 A.M. In the summer, the height of the tourist season in Tibet, flights leave from Chengdu twice a day. The problem is procuring a plane ticket. Generally China Southwest Airlines will not sell you a ticket unless you have a permit for Tibet and are part of an organized tour. Depending on the political mood of the moment, it is occasionally possible to arrange a nominal mini-tour. This may simply entail paying the price of the plane ticket, the permit, and airport transportation from Gonkar airport to Lhasa. There are a number of tour companies in Chengdu that can arrange this. The safer procedure is generally to purchase your ticket in Hong Kong, before you even arrive in Chengdu.

Chengdu itself is an interesting city with many places to stay. Prices vary, from the fancy Jinjiang hotel to the clean but not cheap Jiaotong Fandian. Be sure to leave early for the airport, either on the 5:30 bus or by taxi. If you are staying in Chengdu for the day you should visit the **Wen Shu Yuan Monastery**, located between the Jinjiang Hotel and the Railway Station. This complex is an active city temple with several chapels, gardens, and a delightful vegetarian restaurant and traditional tea shop run by the monks. It can be reached by bus, four stops north of the Jinjiang (act the conductress to tell you when to get off).

There are two major airlines in China. CAAC (China Airlines) and China Southwest Airlines. Take China Southwest if at all possible. The acronym CAAC is often jokingly said to stand for 'Cancel At Any Cost.' This airline is notorious for suddenly declaring that your flight has been canceled, the usual reason being "bad weather." Such heavy cloud cover usually turns out to be nothing more than a hazy bureaucratic smokescreen. Informed sources explain that CAAC habitually cancels flights if they are not full enough to cover their costs and then wait until they are.

The flight from Chengdu to Lhasa takes an hour and a half and proceeds over Kham, the eastern Tibetan province now partly incorporated into the Chinese province of Sichuan. As the sun rises on the morning flight you are greeted with the spectacular sight of massive white mountain ranges extending to the horizon in all directions. For the best views, try to get a seat on the left side of the airplane. The highest peak of one of the first ranges you see to the south is the Munya Gongkar, which stands at 8,200 m (26,900 ft). Traversing these mountains further to the west are three of the largest rivers in Asia—the Yangtse, the Mekong, and the Salween—all of which have their sources in the high plateau of North Central Tibet (the Jangtang). Having flown over these valleys, the plane heads for the Brahmaputra Valley, along the banks of which is the Gongkar Airport.

It is 110 km (68 mi) from the airport to Lhasa. The road connecting the two takes two hours by bus. You ride along the banks of the Brahmaputra, passing Gongkar Monastery before reaching the bend in the river where you cross the bridge leading to the last 60 km (37 mi) of road running along the Kyichu River to Lhasa. The small temple that stands alone in the sand to the left of the road about 25 km (15.5 mi) before the city is the Drolma Temple of Netang, where Atisha spent the last years of his life (see chapter 17).

The first glimpse of Lhasa is of two tiny hillocks protruding from the vast valley basin to the north. On the hillock to the left you can just make out the white of the Potala. As you approach the more built up area around Lhasa you pass Drepung Monastery on your left. The airport bus should drop you off somewhere in the middle of town, from where it is possible to catch a ride by another bus or rickshaw to your hotel. Remember to take it slow at first as you acclimatize.

By Air — Kathmandu to Lhasa

Flights operate from April to November across the Himalaya, weather permitting. This spectacular flight begins by heading east then makes a remarkable bend just east of Mount Everest and crosses over onto the plateau for a quick descent to Gonkar Airport. As with the

Chengdu–Lhasa flight, try to secure a window seat on the left side of the airplane.

Again, in order to book a ticket it is usually necessary to join an expensive tour. There are scores of travel agencies in Kathmandu that can arrange this for you. If you do book through Kathmandu agencies, the Chinese embassy will arrange a limited visa for you, usually only valid for the amount of time of the official tour. Be wary, because if you already have, for example, a two-month Chinese visa, the embassy may well alter your visa, effectively reissuing it for only the length of the tour. Tours arranged from Nepal tend to be more "official" than those organized from Chengdu. Extending visas is possible in Lhasa, yet extremely unpredictable and never cheap.

Overland — Chengdu to Lhasa

An alternative way of reaching Lhasa from Chengdu is to take a bus or a truck. This is a grueling journey of at least twelve days that takes you through the spectacular mountains of Kham to Derge, where the still intact monastery contains the woodblocks of the most authoritative edition of the Buddhist canon in Tibet. From Derge you continue to Chamdo, the third largest town in Tibet (after Lhasa and Shigatse). The main monastery there is the Jampa Ling Temple, founded during the fifteenth century by a disciple of Tsongkhapa. After leaving Chamdo you enter the region of Kongpo before reaching

Central Tibet and Lhasa.

A less traveled route runs south from Chengdu via Litang, Batang, Markam, and Nyingchi to Lhasa (or Tsetang). This overland journey is dazzlingly beautiful, absolutely satisfying, and exceptionally difficult. Plan on one to two weeks for the trip. Most of the area from Batang, at the far western border of Sichuan, to Nyingchi (called Bayi in Chinese) east of Lhasa is off-limits to foreigners without special permits. Without these, your only option is to hitch, which is becoming more and more difficult as the authorities turn up the pressure on truck drivers. There are numerous checkpoints (particularly an ultra-nasty one outside Bayi) which can ruin your journey (and your day). You can face multiple fines, arrest, and may be turned back. Truck drivers will sometimes let you out before checkpoints so that you can try to walk around the authorities, so be prepared to hike and camp. This area is beautiful yet rugged. Temperatures can drop well below freezing at night, so bring lots of warm clothes and food.

Overland — Kunming to Lhasa

From Kunming, travel northwest through Dali, the Naxi town of Lijiang, through the ethnically Tibetan frontier towns of Zhongdian and Deqen to the border of Yunnan and Tibet. From here your progress is illegal and thus occasionally it can be exasperating trying to successfully flag down a passing truck. When you do, continue west on the route outlined in the Chengdu to Lhasa section.

This route is even more interesting and difficult than the Chengdu to Lhasa road.

Overland — Golmund to Lhasa

The other principal overland route from China to Tibet is from the city of Lanzhou, a large industrial town to the north of Chengdu in the province of Gansu. Lanzhou can be reached by air or rail from most major cities in China. It is located on the western border of China and Amdo, the northeast region of Tibet.

If you pass through Lanzhou, you should definitely visit **Labrang Monastery**. This can be reached by an eight hour bus ride to Xiahe, the town near the monastery. The bus leaves Lanzhou at 6:30 each morning. This large, impressive and still active complex was founded in 1709 by Jamyang Zhepa, a renowned abbot of Drepung Monastery, who in the last years of his life returned to his home province and founded this monastery, whose full name is Labrang Tashi Khyil. There are a couple of cheap Chinese hotels near where the buses leave you, or you can stay at the mock Tibetan Guest House on the far side of the monastery.

From Lanzhou you can take a train to Xining, the capital of the neighboring province to the east, Qinghai, which now includes the Tibetan province of Amdo. 25 km (15 mi) to the southwest of Xining is the famous Tibetan monastery of **Kumbum** (full name: Kumbum Jampa Ling; in Chinese, Taer Si). A regular bus service from Xining leaves you in Huangzhong, about 1 km (.6 mi) from the monastery. Kumbum was built in 1588 by Özer Gyatso in accordance with the wishes of the third Dalai Lama, Sonam Gyatso, to honor the place where the founder of the Gelukpa order, Tsongkhapa, was born. The present Dalai Lama, Tenzin Gyatso, was also born near this monastery, in 1935. The monastery grew into a sizable complex with four colleges, including a medical college and a college dedicated to the study of the Kalachakra, and many chapels and stupas. It was a center of study for both Tibetan and Mongolian monks. It is still active, with several hundred monks in residence. The monastery is also renowned for its exquisite butter sculptures. It is sometimes possible to stay in the traditional guesthouse within the monastery itself.

From Xining you can take either a morning or evening train to Golmund in Central Qinghai, passing by the northern shore of Lake Kokonor. Depending on the kind of train, this journey takes between thirteen and twenty-two hours. From Golmund a thirty-hour (if you are lucky) bus ride through mountainous regions and open, barren country will bring you to Lhasa. Try to take the modern Japanese bus, and always try to sit as close as possible to the front of the bus. Prices vary, and the ticket sellers will doubtless give you the run-around. You may be told that Tibet is closed, and you need to buy a ridiculously expensive permit. Just stay relaxed and persistent. Be sure to bring plenty of warm clothes and plenty of food.

Overland — Kathmandu to Lhasa

The overland journey from Kathmandu to Lhasa is extraordinary by any measure. You climb through the lush valleys of the Himalayan foothills to reach the barren plateau of Central Tibet in the course of a single day. (The entire trip from Kathmandu to Lhasa takes at least three days.) The only problem is that individual travel on this route is not yet officially approved. Despite this fact, it is still possible to get to Tibet this way even if you are not part of a tour. You must be prepared for the possibility, however, that you will be forced to turn back. To be on the safe side, overland tours from Kathmandu to Tibet can be arranged at many agencies in Nepal.

The road from Nepal takes you first to Zhangmu, which lies at the border of Nepal and Tibet. Public buses leave daily from Kathmandu. If you are an individual traveler and have a valid Chinese visa, it is sometimes possible to simply walk across at the border, depending on the political climate and the mood of the Chinese border authorities. If you are accustomed to the ways of South Asia, be aware that it is absolutely *never* a good idea to try to bribe Chinese border officials. You might want to alert the Nepalese border officials at Kodari (the last town in Nepal) of the possibility that you might be back in a few hours.

Once you get stamped in at the border checkpoint in Zhangmu, if you are not on a tour, go directly to the PSB (Public Security Bureau) and buy a permit. This office is easy to miss. It is on your right on the main road before you reach the first hairpin turn. This permit may help you more than you first believe, as you will likely be stopped and checked en route to Lhasa. From the border, try to arrange a ride, or begin walking and hitching. You may well find empty vehicles at the border, their drivers having deposited groups departing from Tibet and willing now to take you (for a price that can be considerably cheaper than going in the other direction) back to Lhasa. It is, at record breaking speed in the fastest of Landcruisers, a long day ride from the border to Lhasa. The road takes you through Lhatse and then Shigatse before continuing on to Lhasa. Most people break the trip at Shigatse.

You should also be aware due to the Chinese government's naive belief that the time on the face of the clock somehow indicates the unity of a country, Tibet (like all of China) operates on Beijing time. This means that the clock in Tibet is set three hours later than the clock in Nepal. (It also means that the sun only rises at about 9 A.M. even in the summer.) You should take this into consideration when planning your overland journey from Kathmandu to Central Tibet. Either leave Kathmandu on the earliest possible bus to Kodari or spend a night near the border. Because of the time change, it is difficult to make it to the Chinese border checkpoint in Zhangmu by 5 P.M. when it closes. Be sure to factor at least a half hour into your plans for a truck ride (be sure to haggle over the price) from the border proper (the Friendship Bridge) to the border checkpoint, located up the mountain in Zhangmu. If you do not make it in time the officials will take your passport, let you stay in a Zhangmu hotel, and fine you the next day for staying in the People's Republic of China without having your visa validated.

Overland — Kashgar to Lhasa

The final and most adventurous overland route into Tibet is through Pakistan and the Kunjirab Pass, the highest road in the world, which traverses the magnificent Karakoram mountains. Officially opened on May 1, 1986, this border can be crossed from May to November. From Pakistan you enter the province of Xinjiang, in the far north-west of the Chinese empire. The road takes you northeast to the city of Kashgar, from where the Silk Road leads you into China proper.

The Pakistan–China border has been opened to encourage trade between the two countries and to allow Chinese Muslims from Xinjiang to reach Pakistan, from where they can make the pilgrimage to Mecca. It has *not* been opened to allow Western travelers to enter Tibet. At present foreigners are almost always turned back at the checkpoint in Yecheng, 250 km (155 mi) south of Kashgar. The only real chance that you have of getting through the checkpoint is to hire, for an exorbitant rate, a Landcruiser from Kashgar or Yecheng to Shiqunahe. It is an arduous three day drive on very bad roads, and the road is only open for a few days each month. Once you have hired a Landcruiser and drivers, however, this can effectively serve as your "travel permit." Given that you may pay up to US$2,000 for the ride, it is a very expensive travel permit indeed. Even after you manage get past the officials at Yecheng, you will still face considerable difficulties in reaching Tibet.

Assuming you can find transport and avoid being turned back, the road will take you to the main Chinese outpost in Western Tibet, Shiquanhe. The main Xinjiang-Tibet highway continues east from here through Chagtsaka, Gertse, and Tsochen to Raga and then on to Lhatse. However it is worthwhile to go south from Shiquanhe to Baer, where you can turn off into the ancient Tibetan kingdom of Guge. Further south from Baer is Purang, another ancient kingdom of Western Tibet. From the town of Purang you can go to Barga, where you are only a few kilometers south of the sacred Mount Kailash and two holy lakes of Manasarover and Rakshas Tal (see chapters 33 and 34). The southern route from Purang to Lhatse and Central Tibet is little traveled and it is best to return to Shiquanhe and take the northern route via Gertse and Tsochen to Lhatse. From Lhatse you are only a half-day's drive from Shigatse. For details of travel in this area see the section just below on travel to Western Tibet.

If you find yourself in Kashgar and

unable to proceed to Tibet via Kailash, then your only alternative is to continue by bus to Urumqi. From Urumqi you can travel to Golmund via the delightful **Dunhuang Caves**, which contain some of the finest examples of Central Asian Buddhist art. See the section entitled Overland—Golmund to Lhasa for more details on the Golmund to Lhasa journey.

GETTING TO WESTERN TIBET
Overland — Kathmandu to Mount Kailash

There are numerous agencies in Kathmandu that can arrange for your overland trip to Mount Kailash on a full package tour basis. Some of these agencies have a franchise arrangement with the Chinese government. This advantage of this kind of package tour is that all of your permits as well as food, fuel, and other necessities will be taken care of for you. The disadvantage to this kind of tour is, as always, its greater expense coupled with the relative lack of freedom to change your itinerary once you arrive.

It is almost impossible to arrange your own trip to Mount Kailash overland from Kathmandu. For arranging your own tour, it is best to proceed first to Lhasa. If you do travel directly from Kathmandu to Western Tibet, you will most likely proceed through Zhangmu to Lhatse. From Lhatse you will have a choice between the so-called northern and southern routes. These are described in the section called Overland—Lhasa to Mount Kailash immediately below.

Overland—Lhasa to Mount Kailash

Individual travel west to Kailash can be quite difficult as truck drivers are extremely reluctant to take hitchers due to the rigorous checkpoints west of Shigatse. It is therefore recommended that you arrange a tour once you reach Lhasa. To defray costs, you may want to hook up with other travelers at one of the budget hotels (see section on Accommodation above). This is definitely the cheapest option. In arranging your tour, keep in mind the advice given in the section on Package and Individually Organized Tours above. Remember, also, the Mount Kailash is located in one of the most remote areas of Tibet, and supplies are not easily obtained en route. In addition to your Landcruiser or other similar vehicle, you will probably have to hire a truck to carry your fuel (there are no petrol pumps along the way).

Basically, there are two routes from Lhasa to Western Tibet: the northern route and the southern route. Although the northern route is longer, the roads are better as it traverses the relatively drier great northern plain, or Jangtang. The southern route is extraordinarily beautiful, but it is much wetter and drivers are generally reluctant to take it in the wetter summer months. Since it is also closed for much of the winter, this effectively means that you should count on taking the southern route only in May and early June and again in October and November. For both routes, you must proceed from Lhasa through

Shigatse to Lhatse, along the road that leads eventually to Nepal.

For both routes, continue on past Lhatse for 6 km (3.7 mi) to where the road forks. Take the northern fork on your right (the southern fork takes you to Nepal) and continue on this road for another 2 km (1.2 mi). You will then come to a ferry crossing (a bridge should be completed soon) which you should take to cross the Brahmaputra. After crossing the river, head for the town of Raga, where the northern and southern routes part ways. For the southern route, continue on this road through Saga, Zhongpa, and Paryang. Continue across the Maryum Pass (5151 m; 16,900 ft) and on to Barga (from which you can easily reach Darchen, the starting point for the Mount Kailash circumambulation route).

For the northern route, turn north at Raga and continue on through Tsochen, Gertse, and Chagtsaka. You may find that you wish to spend a night in each of these towns, although it is possible to travel the entire distance from Tsochen to Chagtsaka in a single day. This road will eventually take you to Shiquanhe (also known as Ali), an administrative outpost built at the confluence of the Indus and the Gar Rivers. Here you can stock up on canned and dried foods, among other items.

From Shiquanhe you can drive to Barga and Mount Kailash in one long day, taking the road that passes through Menjir (or Montser) near Tirthapuri. If you take the northern route, you may wish to visit the ancient kingdom of Guge before undertaking your trek around Mount Kailash.

Overland—Kashgar to Mount Kailash

For details on this extremely challenging route (in terms of both physical and political conditions) see the section entitled Overland—Kashgar to Lhasa.

LEAVING TIBET

Any of the above routes can be chosen to leave Tibet. It is generally easier to leave the country than to enter it and transport from Lhasa in any direction can be arranged without difficulty. If you plan to leave by going overland to Pakistan or Nepal it is essential that you have an exit permit from the PSB (Public Security Bureau). The Xinjiang route via Shiquanhe to Kashgar and Pakistan is less problematic when leaving. If you do go this way it is necessary to have your Pakistan visa (people from most Western countries do not need one, but check anyway) before you arrive in Tibet. Lhasa has no Pakistani consulate. Nepalese visas can be obtained in Lhasa at the Nepalese consulate, near the Norbulingka. Nepalese visas can also be purchased for cash dollars at the border. Have passport photos with you.

Probably the most popular and easiest way of visiting Central Tibet is to fly in from Chengdu and leave overland through Nepal (or vice versa). This has the advantages of being relatively quick and allows you to visit nearly all the major historical sites in Central Tibet and Tsang. Many people these days are also choosing air travel for both directions of the trip—often flying in from Chengdu and out to Kathmandu. If you do fly in to Central Tibet, make sure that you take precautions against early mountain sickness (see above).

It is necessary to book your flight out of Lhasa several days in advance, especially in summer. This can be a rather laborious procedure since, in good Chinese bureaucratic fashion, you cannot actually buy the ticket until two days before the flight. This usually means lining up twice (once to book, once to pay). With sufficient advance warning, the airline office in Lhasa can also book your onward flight from Chengdu to Guangzhou, Beijing, or another destination in China. To be on the safe side, give yourself a day's layover in Chengdu in case "bad weather" prevents your plane from leaving Lhasa on schedule.

At present it is also possible to take a bus from Lhasa to the Nepalese border. The bus leaves twice a month, on the 2nd and 22nd. Busses from Lhasa to Shigatse leave daily. Group minibusses or Landcruisers to the border are also easily arranged from Lhasa. Busses also depart daily to Golmud and Xining. Purchasing bus tickets east to Chamdo is basically impossible, but hitching east to Sichuan is far easier than the reverse. Hitching from Kailash to Kashgar is nearly impossible. Few trucks ply this route. In addition, the road is massively

rugged and the rapid and extreme ascents and descents claim many lives annually due to the quick onset of altitude sickness.

There are three bus stations in Lhasa. An old one, just up the road from the CAAC office, has become generally obsolete. There are two new bus stations—one is south of the Norbulingka on the Tsang Gyu Nub Lam and the other is one block east of the post office. For all journeys out of Lhasa it is necessary to buy tickets two to three days in advance. Before departure, make sure that your luggage is securely fastened on the roof. Bring food and water in a small day pack, and some kind of cushioning for the ride. If possible, take a Japanese-built vehicle as these are more comfortable. Talk to other foreign travelers for the latest details.

It is also possible, as always, to hire your own jeep or Landcruiser. Various routes are possible. Most of them are described (in reverse, of course) in the sections on Getting to Lhasa and Getting to Western Tibet.

ICONOGRAPHICAL GUIDE

Drawings and Text by Robert Beer

It is impossible to depict here all the deities you will see in Tibet because they are far too numerous. We have chosen the most commonly seen buddhas, bodhisattvas, tantric deities, historical figures, and protectors in the hope that the following drawings and descriptions will help you recognize them as statues or paintings. The symbolic significance of the various deities and their postures and implements can be given only in the broadest outline. Full understanding would require much deeper study with qualified teachers. Most of the names are given in Sanskrit with their Tibetan equivalents in parentheses. Where no equivalent is given, the name is Tibetan. The colors mentioned below are those traditionally used in paintings and on statues.

1 Shakyamuni

Shakyamuni (Tib. Shakya Tubpa) (1)

Shakyamuni is the historical Buddha Gautama, who lived in India about 500 B.C.E. and was the founder of Buddhism. He is shown sitting in the full lotus posture on the discs of sun and moon, which are on a lotus blossom supported by a lion throne. His body is gold in color, he wears the three robes of a monk, his hair is dark blue, and the golden emblem of enlightenment rises above the protuberance on his head. In his left hand he holds the blue iron begging bowl of a monk, while his right hand touches the earth in the "earth witness" gesture, invoking the earth as a witness to his realization.

Maitreya (Tib. Jampa) (2)

Maitreya is the bodhisattva who will be the next Buddha to appear in this world. He is shown here as a buddha seated in the "western" posture, with his feet resting on a moon disc and a lotus. His hands are held to his heart in the gesture of teaching, or "turning the Wheel of Dharma." Maitreya may also be depicted as a bodhisattva with a yellow body, wearing the clothing and ornaments of a bodhisattva and holding the stems of two lotus blossoms that bear his emblems: a vase and a Dharma Wheel. He can be

Amitabha, the "Buddha of Infinite Light" is one of the five Dhyani Buddhas, the personifications of the five buddha energies. He represents the lotus energy, which transmutes passion into spiritual purity. His family of emanations includes Avalokiteshvara. He is the buddha of the Pure Land of the West called Sukhavati or "Happy Place" (Dewachen). He is red in color, wears the monastic robes of a buddha, and with his hands in the meditation gesture holds a begging bowl. He is sometimes shown seated on a peacock throne.

The Medicine Buddha (Skt. Baishajyaguru; Tib. Sanggye Menlha) (4)

The Medicine Buddha is the buddha of

2. Maitreya

shown seated either in the full lotus posture or with his legs extended down to the floor. Maitreya may also be recognized by a white or golden stupa in his hair.

Amitabha (Tib. Öpagme) (3)

4. The Medicine Buddha

3. Amitabha

healing, invoked to care for the sick. He wears the monastic robes of a buddha and sits on a lotus blossom upon a lion throne. His body is dark blue and he holds an iron bowl in his left hand containing the medicinal plant *arura*. He may also hold a stem of the arura plant in his right hand. A set of eight Medicine Buddhas are often depicted in the company of Shakyamuni.

Four-Armed Avalokiteshvara (Tib. Chenrezi Chak-zhi) (5)

5. Four-Armed Avalokiteshvara

Avalokiteshvara, the bodhisattva of compassion, sits in the full lotus posture on sun and moon discs supported by a lotus blossom. His body is white and he wears the five silk robes and jeweled ornaments of a bodhisattva. Two of his hands hold a wish-fulfilling gem to his heart and the other two hold a crystal rosary and the blue flower of compassion. Avalokiteshvara has many forms, but he can often be identified by a green/gray

deer skin draped over his left shoulder.

Thousand-Armed Avalokiteshvara (Tib.Chenrezi Chak-tong Chen-tong)(6)

6. Thousand-Armed Avalokiteshvara

The bodhisattva Avalokiteshvara once took a vow to save all beings from suffering, but when he realized the magnitude of his task his head exploded into countless pieces. His body was then reassembled by the Buddha Amitabha and the bodhisattva Vajrapani into a much more powerful form with eleven heads and a thousand arms. Each of his hands has an eye in the center of the palm, symbolizing the union of wisdom (eye) and skillful means (hand). His body is white and he stands on a moon disc and a lotus flower. He has eight main hands, the first two of which hold a wish-fulfilling gem; the next five hold a lotus, bow and arrow, vase, rosary, and wheel. The eighth is held in the open-palmed gesture of generosity. He has three rows of three faces colored red, white, and green, symbolizing the three principal aspects of buddhahood. Above these nine heads are the blue wrathful face of Vajrapani and the red face of Amitabha.

Manjushri (Tib. Jampelyang) (7)

7. Manjushri

Manjushri, the bodhisattva of wisdom, is shown as a beautiful youth with a golden yellow complexion. In his right hand he holds aloft the flaming sword of wisdom, which cuts through ignorance. His left hand holds the stem of a lotus blossom bearing a *Perfection of Wisdom* scripture. The sword and the scripture are the emblems of Manjushri and he is sometimes symbolically indicated by means of them alone. He is often depicted in a triad of three protectors (*rigsum gonpo*) along with Avalokiteshvara and Vajrapani, symbolizing the compassion (Avalokiteshvara), wisdom (Manjushri), and power (Vajrapani) of buddhahood.

Vajrapani (Tib. Chana Dorje)(8)

8. Vajrapani

Vajrapani is the bodhisattva of energy and power. Here he is represented in his wrathful aspect, standing on a sun disc and wielding a vajra his right hand. His body is dark blue in color and he wears a tiger skin around his waist and a snake around his neck. In his peaceful aspect Vajrapani is represented as a dark blue bodhisattva holding a lotus flower on which rest his principal symbol, the vajra.

Green Tara (Tib. Drölma Jang) (9)

Green Tara, the "Green Savioress," is the patron female bodhisattva of Tibet and represents the motherly aspect of compassion. Her body is green and she sits in the royal posture on a moon disc and lotus flower, her right leg extended with its foot resting on a small lotus blossom. Her two hands hold the blue lotuses of compassion. Sometimes there may be

9. *Green Tara*

Amitayus is the buddha of longevity. His body is red and he wears the clothing and ornaments of a celestial buddha. His hands rest in his lap in the meditation gesture, and in them he holds a golden vase containing the nectar of immortality and a sprig of the myrobalan plant (bell fruit). Amitayus is invoked for long life, health, and happiness, and is often depicted in a trinity together with White Tara and Vijaya.

White Tara (Tib. Drölkar) (11)

11. *White Tara*

an image of Amitabha in her tiara. It is said that she has taken a vow to attain buddhahood in a female form. She is known for her ability to save her devotees from dangerous situations such as famines and floods.

Amitayus (Tib. Tsepame) (10)

White Tara represents the fertile aspect of compassion. Her body is white and she sits in the full lotus posture on moon and sun discs upon a lotus flower. In her left hand she holds the stem of the blue lotus of compassion, while her right hand makes the gesture of generosity. White Tara may be easily recognized by her seven eyes: three in her face, two in the palms of her hands, and two in the soles of her feet. She was born from a

10. *Amitayus*

tear of compassion that fell from the eye of Avalokiteshvara.

Vijaya (Tib. Namgyelma) (12)

12. *Vijaya*

13. *Vajrasattva*

Vijaya is a bodhisattva-goddess of longevity, often represented in a triad with Amitayus and White Tara. She has eight arms and three faces and is seated in the full lotus posture upon a lotus throne. Her body is white, her right face is blue, and her left face yellow. She holds a double vajra, a hook, a snare, a bow, an arrow, an image of the buddha, and a vase containing the nectar of immortality. Her two other hands display the gestures of generosity and fearlessness. Her image is often shown on Victory (vijaya) stupas.

Vajrasattva (Tib. Dorje Sempa) (13)

Vajrasattva is the bodhisattva of purification and thus personifies the purity of the awareness of ultimate reality. He is also known as the primordial Buddha of all mandalas since he is a reflection of all buddha qualities. He is white in color and wears the robes and ornaments of a bodhisattva. He has one face, two arms, and his hands hold a vajra to his heart and a bell to his left hip. Sometimes Vajrasattva is represented in the form and aspect of Vajradhara.

Vajradhara (Tib. Dorje Chang) (14)

14. *Vajradhara*

Vajradhara is the tantric manifestation of Shakyamuni Buddha and, for the Kagyu order, the primordial Buddha. He is dark blue in color and sits in the full lotus posture on moon and sun discs upon a lotus and lion throne. He has one head and two arms, which are crossed at his heart holding a vajra and a bell, symbolizing the enlightened union of bliss and emptiness. He is often depicted embracing his consort, who is also dark blue and holds a skull cup and a curved knife.

Yamantaka (or Vajrabhairava; Tib. Dorje Jigje) (15)

15. Yamantaka

Yamantaka, the "Destroyer of Death" is a wrathful manifestation of Manjushri. He belongs to the supreme yoga tantra division of the Vajrayana and is a special protector of the Geluk order. He has nine heads, thirty-four arms, and sixteen legs. His main head is that of a buffalo

and his uppermost head is that of Manjushri. His body is dark blue, he wears bone ornaments, and around his neck hangs a garland of fifty-one freshly severed human heads. He holds a skull cup and a curved flaying knife in front of him, and stretches an elephant skin across his back. His other hands are outstretched holding various symbolic implements. Underfoot he tramples upon eight Hindu deities, eight mammals, and eight birds. He is shown here as a single figure but is often depicted with his consort Rolangma in the *yab-yum* posture.

Samvara (or Chakrasamvara; Tib: Demchok) (16)

16. Samvara

Samvara also belongs to the supreme yoga tantra division of the Vajrayana. He is usually represented in his twelve-armed form embracing his consort Vajravarahi (Tib. Dorje Pagmo). Together they symbolize the union of bliss and emptiness. His body is dark blue, he wears a tiger skin around his waist, and holds an elephant skin across his back. He wears bone ornaments, a tiara of skulls, and a necklace of fifty-one freshly severed heads. He has four faces colored yellow, blue, green, and red. In his hands he holds a vajra and bell, a skull cup, a snare, the head of Brahma, a tantric staff, an elephant knife, a flaying knife, a trident, and a drum. He is surrounded by a halo of flames and stands on a sun disc trampling the Hindu god Bhairava and his consort. His consort, Vajravarahi, is red and has two arms and one face. She holds a skull cup and curved knife. In his two-armed form Samvara has only one face and embraces his consort with crossed arms holding a vajra and a bell.

17. Vajrayogini

Vajrayogini (Tib. Dorje Naljorma or Naro Kachoma) (17)

Vajrayogini personifies the female wisdom energy of emptiness. Here she is depicted in the form of "Naropa's dakini." She is red in color and stands on a sun disc crushing underfoot the Hindu god Bhairava and his consort. She is naked and wears bone ornaments, tiara and skirt, and a necklace of fifty-one skulls. She holds a curved knife in her right hand and a skull cup of blood in her left. A tantric staff rests on her left shoulder symbolizing the essence of bliss. Vajrayogini can also be depicted

standing in the "bow and arrow" posture dancing upon a corpse. Another form is that of Vajravarahi, the "adamantine sow," where she has a small pig's head above her right ear.

Guhyasamaja (Tib. Sangdu) (18)

18. Guhyasamaja

Guhyasamaja also belongs to the supreme yoga tantra. He has three faces and six arms and sits in full lotus posture on a moon disc upon a lotus throne. His body and central face are dark blue, his right face is white and his left face red. He embraces a light blue consort who also has three faces and six arms. They both carry the same emblems: a vajra, bell, sword, jewel, wheel, and lotus.

Hevajra (Tib. Kye Dorje) (19)

19. *Hevajra*

Hevajra is another important supreme yoga tantra deity and is particularly practiced in the Sakya order. He is dark blue in color with eight faces, sixteen arms, and four legs. He embraces his consort Nairatmya (Tib. Dagmema) and together they dance on four lesser deities, who symbolize the four demonic

forces. Hevajra wears bone ornaments, a tiara of five skulls, and a necklace of fifty-one severed heads. In each of his sixteen hands he holds a skull cup. The skull cups in the right hands contain eight animals and those in the left hands eight Hindu gods. His consort is also dark blue. She has one face and two arms, and holds a skull cup and a curved knife. She wears bone ornaments, a tiara of five skulls, and a necklace of fifty-one freshly severed heads. They are encircled by flames and dance in the "bow and arrow" posture on a sun disc resting on a sixteen-petaled lotus. Hevajra may also be portrayed in a two-armed form.

Kalachakra (Tib. Dukor) (20)

20. *Kalachakra*

Kalachakra, the "Wheel of Time," is the most complex of all the supreme yoga tantra deities. He has four faces, twenty-four arms, and two legs. He wears a tiger skin around his waist, golden ornaments, vajra earrings, bracelets, belt, and necklace. His torso and central face are dark blue or black, his right face is red, and the two left faces are white and yellow. His right leg is red and his left leg is white. His two feet trample on the Hindu deities Ananga and Rudra and their respective consorts. Kalachakra's eight lower arms are dark blue or black; the eight middle arms are red; and the eight upper arms are white. Each hand holds a symbolic tantric implement. Using his two principal arms, he embraces his consort Vishvamati and holds a vajra and bell. She is golden in color with four faces, eight arms, and two legs. Together they stand on four discs symbolizing the astrological planets of the sun, moon, Rahu, and Kalagni. Kalachakra is sometimes depicted in simple two-armed form.

Hayagriva (Tib. Tamdrin) (21)

Hayagriva, the "Horse-necked One," is a wrathful emanation of Avalokiteshvara. He has several forms, and functions as both powerful protector who destroys evil spirits and a tutelary deity (*yidam*) in tantric practice. He is represented here as a yidam, with three faces, six arms, and four legs. His body is red, his right face is white, and his left face is green. He wears a tiger skin around his waist, a tiara of five skulls, and a necklace of fifty-one

21. *Hayagriva*

freshly severed heads. Across his back are an elephant skin, a human skin, and the unfurled wings of a large mythical bird called a *garuda*. He holds a lotus, a skull cup, a snare, a sword, an ax, and a club. He embraces a blue consort who wears a leopard skin and holds a skull cup and lotus. Together they stand on a sun disc and trample underfoot male and female corpses. Hayagriva can most easily be identified by the one or three horse heads that protrude from the top of his head.

Songtsen Gampo (22)

Songtsen Gampo, the king who unified Tibet in the seventh century and introduced Buddhism, is considered to be a manifestation of Avalokiteshvara. He is depicted with a white or flesh-colored

22. *Songtsen Gampo*

23. *Trisong Detsen*

complexion, seated on a throne, wearing the royal attire of a king. He is usually represented holding a wheel and a lotus flower. On his head he wears a white turban, which is folded around an image of a red Amitabha Buddha. He is often accompanied by his Chinese queen Wen Cheng (to his left) and his Nepalese queen Bhrikuti (to his right).

Trisong Detsen (23)

Trisong Detsen, the second great religious king of Tibet, who ruled during the eighth century, is represented in a form similar to that of Songtsen Gampo, but without the image of Amitabha in his turban. He is a manifestation of Manjushri, the bodhisattva of wisdom, and holds lotus flowers that bear the emblems of Manjushri, the sword and the *Perfection of Wisdom* scripture. Songtsen Gampo, Trisong Detsen, and Ralpachen are often portrayed in a trini-

ty as the three great religious kings of Tibet.

Padmasambhava (Tib: Pema Jungne or Guru Rinpoche) (24)

24. *Padmasambhava*

Padmasambhava, the "Lotus Born One" was the Indian tantric master invited to Tibet by King Trisong Detsen in the eighth century to remove the obstacles to the spread of Buddhism. He is usually represented wearing royal robes and seated on a lotus blossom that rises from a lake, his right foot resting on a smaller lotus blossom. His body is flesh-colored and his face has a stern and regal expression. His right hand holds a vajra and his left hand a skull cup containing a vase of the nectar of immortality. He carries a tantric staff (*khatvanga*) surmounted with a trident in the fold of his left arm. He wears the folded red hat of the Nyingma order, of which he is the founder. There are eight principle forms of Padmasambhava and these are often found together in a single chapel or set of tangkas.

Milarepa (25)

Milarepa was a founding figure of the Kagyu order and a greatly loved saint throughout Tibet. He is usually depicted sitting on a yogi's antelope skin in a cave. He wears a single white cotton robe and a red meditation belt around his body. His skin is either flesh-colored or has a light green hue on account of the years he spent eating only nettle soup. His left hand holds a skull cup and his right hand presses his ear forward in the attitude of singing his songs of realization.

Atisha (or Dipamkara Shrijnana; Tib. Jowo-je) (26)

26. Atisha

Atisha, the Indian Buddhist master who helped revive Buddhism in Tibet in the eleventh century, is depicted with a gold or flesh-colored body seated on a lotus throne in the full lotus posture with his two hands in the gesture of teaching. He

25. Milarepa

wears the robes of a monk with a blue under-jerkin, and a red hat. He can be identified easily by the stupa and basket of scriptures placed beside him.

Tsongkhapa (or Je Rinpoche) (27)

27. *Tsongkhapa*

Tsongkhapa, the fourteenth-century reformer of Tibetan Buddhism and founder of the Geluk order, is considered to be a manifestation of Manjushri. His body is either golden or flesh-colored. He wears the robes of a monk and a yellow hat. His two hands are in the gesture of teaching and hold the stems of two lotus blossoms that bear a sword and a *Perfection of Wisdom* scripture, the emblems of Manjushri. He is often depicted in a triad with his two chief disciples, Gyeltsab Je (to his right) and Khedrup Je (to his left).

The Fifth Dalai Lama (28)

Among the fourteen incarnations of the

28. *The Dalai Lama*

Dalai Lama, here we show the Great Fifth Dalai Lama, Lobsang Gyatso (1617–1682), who built the Potala Palace and established the system of government that lasted until 1959. He is seated on a cushioned throne, wearing monastic robes and a yellow hat. He holds a Dharma Wheel and lotus flower and wears a ritual dagger (*purbu*) in his belt. All the Dalai Lamas are generally represented in a similar form but with variations in their hand gestures and the symbols they hold.

Pelden Lhamo (Skt. Shri Devi) (29)

Pelden Lhamo, the "Glorious Goddess," is one of the most important protectors of the Geluk order and the guardian of Lhasa. She is dark blue in color and has one face and two arms. In her right hand she holds a club and in her left a skull cup of blood. She wears a tiger

Vaishravana (Tib. Namtöse) (30)

30. *Vaishravana*

29. *Pelden Lhamo*

skin around her waist and a human skin over her shoulders. In her mouth she holds a corpse, and hanging from her earrings are a snake and a lion. Her hair streams upwards and she is shaded by a canopy of peacock feathers. The moon rests in her hair and the sun in her navel. Around her ankles she wears broken chains, and at her waist she carries a baton bound with a snake belt. She sits astride a mule on a cannibal skin saddle and rides across a sea of menstrual blood. The reins of the mule are snakes and a single eye is on the mule's rump. From her saddle hangs a skull, a skin bag of poisons, and two divination dice. She is usually attended by her two companions: the blue "lion-headed one" and the red "crocodile-headed one." She sometimes has four arms instead of two.

Vaishravana, also known as Kubera and Jambhala, is the Guardian King of the North and the Buddhist god of wealth. As the god of wealth he is shown here riding a white lion, which stands on a moon disc and a lotus. He is golden yellow in color and has a large, rounded body. In his right hand he holds a silk banner of victory and his left hand holds a mongoose that vomits jewels. The sun and moon are usually shown resting on his right and left shoulders.

The Four Guardian Kings (Skt. Lokapala; Tib. Chok-kyong) (31)

The Four Guardian Kings are the protectors the four cardinal directions and are almost always found at the entrance to monasteries and temples. They each have two hands and one face and are dressed in the ornate armor and clothing of a warrior king. They may be depicted either sitting of standing. Illustrated here

31. *One of the Four Guardian Kings*

is Dhritarashtra, the Guardian King of the East; he is white in color and plays a lute. Virupaksha, the King of the West, is red in color and holds a small stupa in his right hand and a serpent in his left. Virudhaka, the King of the South, is blue in color and carries a sword and scabbard. Vaishravana, the King of the North, is yellow in color and carries a banner of victory in his right hand and a mongoose that vomits jewels in his left (see above).

The Eight Auspicious Symbols (Skt. Astamangala; Tib. Tashi Tagye) (32)
(see following page for illustrations)

The Eight Auspicious Symbols, or Glorious Emblems, represent the offerings that were presented to Shakyamuni Buddha after he attained enlightenment. They may be shown either singly of grouped together to form a vase-shaped motif. They are as follows:

1. The White Conch Shell. It spirals to the right and is blown as a horn to announce the Buddha's enlightenment.

2. The Precious Parasol. The silk canopy that is held above the Buddhas and gives protection from all evil influences.

3. The Banner of Victory. The silk banner that proclaims victory of the Buddhist teachings over ignorance.

4. The Two Golden Fishes. They represent spiritual release from the ocean of samsara.

5. The Eight-Spoked Golden Wheel. This is also known as the Wheel of the Dharma and represents the Noble Eightfold Path of the Buddha's teaching.

6. The Knot of Eternity. This is also known as the Lucky Diagram and represents unending love and harmony.

7. The Lotus Flower. It represents spiritual purity and compassion.

8. The Vase of Great Treasures. It contains the spiritual jewels of enlightenment.

THE EIGHT AUSPICIOUS SYMBOLS

1.

2.

3.

4.

5.

6.

7.

8.

THE TIBETAN LANGUAGE

The Tibetan language belongs to a small independent language group called Tibeto-Burman. It bears no structural similarities with either of the main language groups of its neighbors, China and India. Apart from occasional words that have been borrowed from Chinese and mantras, which are recited in Sanskrit, it is an independent form of speech peculiar to the Tibetan people, from Amdo in northeastern Tibet to Ladakh to the west of Mount Kailash.

The written Tibetan script is alphabetic and consists of thirty letters. It was invented in the seventh century by Tönmi Sambhota, a minister of King Songtsen Gampo, who based it on an ancient Indian script used for writing Sanskrit. Certain letters can be placed above or below others to denote particular sounds and give spelling variations for words of the same sound but different meaning. Other letters can be used as prefixes and suffixes, some of which affect the sound and some of which do not (although the precise rules for these sound changes vary with the dialect). Most Tibetan words consist of either one or two syllables. There are only three main grammatical particles, each of which serves a number of functions. The word order of a simple sentence is generally 1) subject, 2) object, 3) verb. The verb must be placed at the end.

There are many variations of the Tibetan script. Three of the most common forms are: **U-chen**, capitalized letters, used in printed texts and on most signs; **U-me**, a more flowing cursive script often used in inscriptions and in formal letter writing; and **Kyu-yig**, the common cursive script used by Tibetans in non-formal letter writing and daily business. An example of each script is given below:

U-chen: བཀྲ་ཤིས་བདེ་ལེགས་ཕུན་སུམ་ཚོགས།

U-me: བཀྲ་ཤིས་བདེ་ལེགས་ཕུན་སུམ་ཚོགས།

Kyu-yig: བཀྲ་ཤིས་བདེ་ལེགས་ཕུན་སུམ་ཚོགས།

In addition to these scripts there are also ornamental scripts used for writing Sanskrit mantras. You will see these scripts on monastery walls throughout Tibet.

Like other Asian languages, Tibetan has a structure and system of pronunciation very different from our own. Since making yourself understood depends a great deal upon intonation and inflection, you may find it difficult and frustrating to get even the simplest words and phrases across. There are also many different regional dialects in Tibet and ways of pronouncing the same word can vary wildly. The pronunciation given here approximately follows the Lhasa dialect. Keep in mind that Tibetans generally do not raise the inflection of their voices when asking questions; if anything, the voice tends to drop at the end of a question.

Perhaps the most difficult sound for
foreigners to make at first is the sound
nga, which is found in many Tibetan
words and by itself means "I" or "me."
To practice making this sound, it may
help at first to repeat the phrase *sing
along* several times quickly. As you do
so, try to isolate the sound that you produce when you combine the final *ng* of
sing with the initial *a* of along. That is
that sound *nga*.

USEFUL WORDS & PHRASES

BASICS

Hello!	tashi deleg!	བཀྲ་ཤིས་བདེ་ལེགས།
How are you?	ku su depo yinbay?	སྐུ་གཟུགས་བདེ་པོ་ཡིན་པས།
I'm fine.	la yin, or nga depo yin	ལགས་ཡིན། or ང་བདེ་པོ་ཡིན།
goodbye (to person leaving)	kallay pay-ro nahng	ག་ལེར་ཕེབས་རོགས་གནང་།
goodbye (to person staying)	kallay shu-ro nahng	ག་ལེར་བཞུགས་རོགས་གནང་།
please	took jay zig	ཐུགས་རྗེ་གཟིགས།
thank you	took jay chay	ཐུགས་རྗེ་ཆེ།
no, thank you	la min took jay chay	ལགས་མིན། ཐུགས་རྗེ་ཆེ།
sorry	gonda	དགོངས་དག
okay? Is this allowed?	driggi raybay	འགྲིག་གི་རེད་པས།
it's okay/all right/allowed	driggi ray	འགྲིག་གི་རེད།
That's good!	day yakpo doo!	དེ་ཡག་པོ་འདུག
That's not good.	day yakpo mindoo	དེ་ཡག་པོ་མིན་འདུག
this	dee	འདི།
that	day, pagi	དེ། ཕ་གི།
What is this?	dee karray ray?	འདི་ག་རེ་རེད།
How much does it cost?	de-yi gong kadzö ray?	དེའི་གོང་ག་ཚོད་རེད།
	day-la gomo kadzö ray?	དེ་ལ་སྒོར་མོ་ག་ཚོད་རེད།
when?	kadoo?	ག་དུས།
where?	kabar?	ག་པར།
who?	soo?	སུ།
why?	karray yinna? karray chay nay?	ག་རེ་ཡིན་ནམ། ག་རེ་བྱས་ནས།
today	tay-ring	དེ་རིང་།
yesterday	kesang	ཁ་སང་།
tomorrow	sang-nyin	སང་ཉིན།
now	tah-da	ད་ལྟ།
I/me	nga	ང་།

you	kyerahng	ཁྱེད་རང་།
he	korahng (or kohng)	ཁོ་རང་། or ཁོང་།
she	morahng (or kohng)	མོ་རང་། or ཁོང་།
hot	tsa-po	ཚ་པོ།
cold	drang-mo	གྲང་མོ།
new	sar-pa	གསར་པ།
old	nying-pa	རྙིང་པ།
near	tah-nyay-bo	ཐག་ཉེ་པོ།
far	tah-ring-bo	ཐག་རིང་པོ།
difficult	kali kakbo	དཀའ་ལས་ཁག་པོ།
easy	lay labo	ལས་སླ་པོ།
big	chen bo	ཆེན་པོ།
little	choong-choong	ཆུང་ཆུང་།
much, many	mahng bo	མང་པོ།
little	nyoong nyoong	ཉུང་ཉུང་།
a few	kha shai	ཁ་ཤས།
mountain	rhee	རི།
pass	la	ལ།
road	lahm-ka	ལམ་ཀ།
park	ling-ka	གླིང་ཀ
rain	char-pa	ཆར་པ།
snow	gahng	གངས།
Where are you from?	kyerahng loong-ba kanay yin?	ཁྱེད་རང་ལུང་པ་ག་ནས་ཡིན།
I'm from England.	nga Inji nay ray	ང་ཨིན་ཇི་ཡུལ་ནས་ཡིན།
America	a-may-ri-ka, or (Chinese) may gwo	ཨ་མེ་རི་ཀ
Germany	jur-meni	ཇར་མ་ནི།
France	pa-rahn-see	ཕ་རན་སི།
Tibetan (person)	pö-mee	བོད་མི།
Chinese (person)	gya-mee	རྒྱ་མི།
Indian (person)	gya-kar-wa	རྒྱ་གར་པ།

What is your name?	kyerahng gi ming la karray ser gi yö?	ཁྱེད་རང་གི་མིང་ལ་ག་རེ་ཟེར་གྱི་ཡོད།
My name is...	ngay ming la. . . ser gi yö	ངའི་མིང་ལ་ .... ཟེར་གྱི་ཡོད།
Where is the toilet?	sahng-chö kabah yö ray?	གསང་སྤྱོད་ག་བར་ཡོད་རེད།
I'm ill.	nga naggi doo	ང་ན་གི་འདུག
Where is the hospital?	men-khang kabar yö ray?	སྨན་ཁང་ག་བར་ཡོད་རེད།
Is there a doctor?	em-chi doo gay?	ཨེམ་ཆི་འདུག་གས།
What is that called?	dee ming la karray ser gi ray?	འདིའི་མིང་ལ་ག་རེ་ཟེར་གྱི་རེད།

FAMILY MEMBERS

mother	ama-la	ཨ་མ་ལགས།
father	pa-la	པ་ལགས།
grandmother	momo-la	རྨོ་མོ་ལགས།
grandfather	powo-la	སྤོ་བོ་ལགས།
older sister	chen-mo or acha-la	གཅེན་མོ་ or ཨ་ཅག་ལགས།
older brother	chen-po or jo-la	གཅེན་པོ་ or ཇོ་ལགས།
younger brother	choong-po	གཅུང་པོ།
younger sister	choong-mo	གཅུང་མོ།
aunt (father's sister)	ani-la	ཨ་ནེ་ལགས།
aunt (mother's sister)	soomo-la	སུ་མོ་ལགས།
uncle (father's brother)	akoo-la	ཨ་ཁུ་ལགས།
uncle (mother's brother)	ashang-la	ཨ་ཞང་ལགས།

NUMBERS

one	chik	གཅིག
two	nyi	གཉིས།
three	soom	གསུམ།
four	shee	བཞི།
five	nga	ལྔ།
six	drook	དྲུག
seven	doon	བདུན།

eight	gyay	བརྒྱད།
nine	goo	དགུ།
ten	choo	བཅུ།
eleven	choo-chik	བཅུ་གཅིག
twelve	choo-nyi	བཅུ་གཉིས།
thirteen	chup-soom	བཅུ་གསུམ།
fourteen	chup-shee	བཅུ་བཞི།
fifteen	cho-nga	བཅོ་ལྔ།
sixteen	choo-drook	བཅུ་དྲུག
seventeen	chup-doon	བཅུ་བདུན།
eighteen	choap-gyay	བཅོ་བརྒྱད།
nineteen	choop-goo	བཅུ་དགུ།
twenty	nyi-shoo	ཉི་ཤུ།
thirty	soom-choo	སུམ་ཅུ།
forty	shib-choo	བཞི་བཅུ།
fifty	ngap-choo	ལྔ་བཅུ།
sixty	drook-choo	དྲུག་ཅུ།
seventy	doon-choo	བདུན་ཅུ།
eighty	gyay-choo	བརྒྱད་ཅུ།
ninety	goop-choo	དགུ་བཅུ།
one-hundred	(chik)gya or: gya tahm-pa	(གཅིག་)བརྒྱ། or བརྒྱ་ཐམ་པ།
two-hundred	nyi-gya	ཉི་བརྒྱ།
one thousand	(chik)tohng	(གཅིག་)སྟོང་།

COUNTING MONEY

The basic monetary unit in Tibet nowadays is the Chinese yüan. One yüan is broken into ten mao (or jiao) and one mao into ten fen.

yüan	gomo	སྒོར་མོ།
mao	mo-tsi	མོ་ཚེ།
fen	ping	ཕེང་།
one yüan	gomo chik	སྒོར་མོ་གཅིག

two yüan	gomo nyi	སྒོར་མོ་གཉིས།
two yüan and five mao	gomo nyi dang mo-tsi nga	སྒོར་མོ་གཉིས་དང་མོ་ཚི་ལྔ།
two yüan, five mao, and three fen	gomo nyi, mo-tsi nga dang ping soom	སྒོར་མོ་གཉིས་དང་མོ་ཚི་ལྔ་དང་པིང་གསུམ།

FOOD AND DRINK

restaurant	sa-khahng	ཟ་ཁང་།
Where is the/a restaurant?	sa-khahng kabar yö ray?	ཟ་ཁང་ག་པར་ཡོད་རེད།
food	khala	ཁ་ལག
Please give me some water.	nga-la choo nang-ro nang	ང་ལ་ཆུ་གནང་རོགས་གནང་།
hot water	choo tsa-po	ཆུ་ཚ་པོ།
tea	cha (or: söl-cha)	ཇ། or གསོལ་ཇ།
Tibetan tea	pö-cha	བོད་ཇ།
beer	piju (Chinese)	པེ་ཇུ།
Tibetan barley beer	chahng	ཆང་།
yogurt	sho	ཞོ།
bread	ballep	བག་ལེབ།
rice	dray	འབྲས།
butter	mar	མར།
milk	o-ma	འོ་མ།
meat	sha	ཤ།
egg	go-nga	སྒོ་ང་།
vegetables	tsel	ཚལ།
noodle soup	tookpa	ཐུག་པ།
dumplings	mo-mo	མོག་མོག
salt	tsa	ཚྭ།
pepper (chili)	see-pen	སེ་པན།
This is delicious.	dee shimbo doo	འདི་ཞིམ་པོ་འདུག
I don't want this.	dee mo-go	འདི་མི་དགོས།
I don't eat meat.	nga sha sagi may	ང་ཤ་ཟ་གི་མེད།

VISITING MONASTERIES

monastery	gompa	དགོན་པ།
(monastic) college	dra-tsang	གྲྭ་ཚང་།
house (within a college)	khahng-tsen	ཁང་ཚན།
temple	lha-khahng	ལྷ་ཁང་།
chapel	lha-khahng	ལྷ་ཁང་།
protector chapel	gön-khahng	མགོན་ཁང་།
monk	trapa	གྲྭ་པ།
nun	ani	ཨ་ནེ།
deity	lha	ལྷ།
What is this deity called?	lha dee-yi tsen karray ray?	ལྷ་འདིའི་མཚན་ག་རེ་རེད།
Can I go in here?	dee-yi nang la dro choggi repay?	འདིའི་ནང་ལ་འགྲོ་ཆོག་གི་རེད་པས།
Can I go upstairs?	togka-la dro choggi repay?	ཐོག་ཁ་ལ་འགྲོ་ཆོག་གི་རེད་པས།
Can I take a photograph?	par gyap choggi repay?	དཔར་བརྒྱབ་ཆོག་གི་རེད་པས།
What religious order is this?	chö-luk karray ray?	ཆོས་ལུགས་ག་རེ་རེད།
How many monks are here?	trapa ka-dzö yö ray?	འདིར་གྲྭ་པ་ག་ཚོད་ཡོད་རེད།
I am a Buddhist.	nga nang-pa yin	ང་ནང་པ་ཡིན།
I am on pilgrimage.	nga nekor-la drogi yö	ང་གནས་སྐོར་ལ་འགྲོ་གི་ཡོད།

Getting Around

Where is the hotel?	drön-khahng kabar yö ray?	མགྲོན་ཁང་ག་པར་ཡོད་རེད།
Can I stay here?	deer day choggi rebay?	འདིར་སྡོད་ཆོག་གི་རེད་པས།
How much is a bed?	nyel-tri ray la gomo ka-dzö ray?	ཉལ་ཁྲི་རེ་ལ་སྒོར་མོ་ག་ཚོད་རེད།
That's too expensive.	day gohng chay-traggi doo	དེ་གོང་ཆེ་དྲག་གི་འདུག
Where are you going?	(kyerahng)kabar drogi yin?	ཁྱེད་རང་ག་པར་འགྲོ་གི་ཡིན།
I'm going to Lhasa.	nga Lhasa la drogi yin	ང་ལྷ་ས་ལ་འགྲོ་གི་ཡིན།
Where is the bus station?	mimang chi-chö lang-kor	མི་དམངས་སྤྱི་སྤྱོད་རླངས་འཁོར་འབབ་
	pap-sug kabah yö ray?	ཚུགས་ག་པར་ཡོད་རེད།

English	Transliteration	Tibetan

When does the bus leave? mimang chi-chö lang-kor kadoo drogi ray? མི་དམངས་ཀྱི་སྤྱོད་ནྲངས་འཁོར་ག་ དུས་འགྲོ་གི་རེད།

Can I rent a vehicle? lang-kor la-gyu yö rebay? ནྲངས་འཁོར་ག་རྒྱུ་ཡོད་རེད་པས།

How much is it per kilometer? gong-li chik la gomo ka-dzö ray? ཀཎ་ལི་གཅིག་ལ་སྒོར་མོ་ག་ཚོད་རེད།

I want a Japanese vehicle. reebeen lang-kor go gi doo རེ་པིན་ནྲངས་འཁོར་དགོས་ཀྱི་འདུག

Are there any dogs here? dee-bar kyeeyö rebay? འདི་བར་ཁྱི་ཡོད་རེད་པས།

Do the dogs bite? kyee gee so gyap gi repay? ཁྱིས་སོ་རྒྱག་གི་རེད་པས།

GLOSSARY

A

Achala (Tib. Miyowa) "The Immovable One," a wrathful protector.

Akshobhya (Tib. Mikyöba) "The Unshakable One," one of the five Dhyani Buddhas; sometimes a name given to statues of Shakyamuni.

Amban The representative of the Manchurian imperial government of China who was appointed to oversee the Dalai Lama's government in Lhasa. The post was created in 1727 and abolished by the Thirteenth Dalai Lama in 1913.

Amdo The northeastern region of Tibet bordering on China and eastern Turkestan. It has now been incorporated into Qinghai and Gansu provinces.

Amitabha (Tib. Öpagme) "The One of Infinite Light," one of the five Dhyani Buddhas; the buddha who reigns in the Pure Land of Sukhavati. See the Iconographical Guide.

Amitayus (Tib. Tsepagme) "The One of Infinite Life," the bodhisattva who personifies the power of longevity. See the Iconographical Guide.

Arhat A person who has attained enlightenment through the practice of the Hinayana.

Asanga (Tib. Togme) The fourth-century Indian Buddhist philosopher who founded the Cittamatra or Mind Only system of thought.

Atisha (Tib. Jowoje) An Indian Buddhist master (982–1054) who came to Tibet in 1042 to help in the revival of Buddhism. His main disciple was Drom Tönpa. He died in Netang Drölma Lhakhang. See the Iconographical Guide.

Avalokiteshvara (Tib. Chenrezi) The bodhisattva who personifies compassion. See the Iconographical Guide.

B

Bardo The intermediate state between death and rebirth where beings wander while looking for a place to be reborn.

Bhrikuti (Tib. Trisun) The Nepalese wife of King Songtsen Gampo.

Bodhicitta (Tib. jangsem) The "mind of enlightenment" or the altruistic intention to attain enlightenment for the sake of all beings. A hallmark of Mahayana practitioners.

Bodhisattva (Tib. jangchub sempa) A person intent upon realizing enlightenment for the welfare of others; one who is on the way to becoming a buddha on the Mahayana or "universal vehicle." A personification of a particular quality of enlightenment.

Bön The pre-Buddhist religion of Tibet.

Buddhas of the Three Times The buddha of the past, Dipamkara; the buddha of the present age, Shakyamuni; and the buddha of the future, Maitreya.

Butön A great Tibetan Buddhist scholar (1312–1364) who organized the Tibetan Buddhist canon into its present form. He was based at Zhalu Monastery near Shigatse.

C

Chakpori "The Iron Mountain," one of the four holy mountains in Central Tibet; it is situated opposite the Potala Palace in Lhasa. Formerly the site of the Tibetan Medical College, which was destroyed in 1959. Presently crowned with a radio mast.

Chakrasamavara See *Samvara*.

Cham dances. Religious dances performed by monks wearing ornate costumes at various festivals throughout the year.

Charaya Tantra The second of the four divisions of the Buddhist tantras.

Chenrezi See *Avalokiteshvara*.

Ch'ien-lung (1735–1796) Emperor of the Chinese Manchu dynasty who drove the invading Gurkhas out of Tibet in 1792.

Chöd The "cutting" practice initiated by Machik Labdrön in which one visualizes cutting one's body into pieces and then feeding them to hungry ghosts and other beings in need of sustenance.

Chökyi Gyeltsen (1570–1662) A teacher of the Fifth Dalai Lama who was declared to be the Fourth Panchen Lama. The textbook writer of Sera Monastery.

Chuwo Ri One of the four holy mountains of Central Tibet. It is on the southern bank of the Brahmaputra at Chaksam, at the confluence with the Kyichu.

D

Dakini (Tib. khandroma) A female deity who personifies the wisdom of enlightenment.

Dalai Lama One in a series of incarnate lamas, the first of whom was Gendun Drup, the nephew and disciple of Tsongkhapa. The Dalai Lamas ruled Tibet from the time of Losang Gyatso, the Fifth Dalai Lama. The present Dalai Lama is the fourteenth in the succession. Recognized as manifestations of Avalokiteshvara.

Deity (Tib. lha, Skt. deva) This term is mainly used to refer to the tantric personifications of enlightenment with whom the practitioner identifies in meditation.

Demoness-Subduing Temples Thirteen temples in different parts of Tibet, including the Jokhang, which were built during the time of Songtsen Gampo to subdue a demoness who was perceived in the from of the land by the king's Nepalese wife, Bhrikuti.

Desi Sanggye Gyatso (1652–1705) The regent of the Fifth Dalai Lama and a renowned physician and scholar.

Dharma (Tib. chö) The teachings of the Buddhist tradition as a whole.

Dharmakaya The "reality body" or "truth body" of a buddha. This is the ultimate reality of the Buddha; it is the aspect of the Buddha that appears to the Buddha himself and to others who have reached enlightenment.

Dharmaraja (Tib. Chögyel) A wrathful, bull-headed protector particularly worshipped in the Geluk order. Not to be confused with Yamantaka, Dharmaraja can be distinguished by his standing on a bull and a human corpse.

Dhyani Buddhas (Tib. Gyelwa rig nga) The five buddha types or "families." They are Vairochana, Ratnasambhava, Amitabha, Amoghasiddhi, and Akshobhya.

Dipamkara (Tib. Marmedze) The Buddha of the past.

Dorje Drakden Traditional protector deity and oracle consulted on all important matters of state.

Drakpa Gyeltsen (1147–1216) One of the five great masters of the Sakya order. The son of Kunga Nyingpo.

Dratsang A college within a monastery.

Drölma (Skt. Tara) The Tibetan name for the extremely popular female deity, Tara. Her main forms are white and green.

Drom Tönpa (1005–1064) The main Tibetan disciple of Atisha. The founder of the Kadam order and Reting Monastery.

Dzog-chen Literally the "Great Perfection"; a form of meditation practiced in the Nyingma and Kagyu schools that seeks a direct realization of the nature of the mind.

E

Ekajati (Tib. Tsechigma) "The lady of the single point," a wrathful female deity with one eye, one tooth, and so on who personifies mental concentration. A special protectress of Dzog-chen practitioners.

Eight Great Bodhisattvas Avalokiteshvara, Manjushri, Vajrapani, Maitreya, Samantabhadra, Akashagarbha, Kshitigarbha, and Sarvanivaranavishkambini.

Emptiness (Skt. shunyata, Tib. tongpanyi) The ultimate absence of independent self-existence, as taught in the Madhyamaka philosophy of Buddhism.

G

Gampopa (1079–1153) One of the chief disciples of Milarepa and a founding father of the Kagyu order. Also known as Dakpo Lhaje.

Gangpori One of the four holy mountains in Central Tibet. It is near Tsetang and is where Avalokiteshvara descended to Tibet in the form of a monkey to mate with a demoness and produce the first Tibetans.

Geluk "The virtuous order," the order of Tibetan Buddhism founded by Tsongkhapa and his disciples in the early fifteenth century. The "Yellow Hats."

Gendun Drup (1391–1475) A nephew and disciple of Tsongkhapa who founded Tashilhunpo monastery and was retrospectively named the First Dalai Lama.

Gendun Gyatso (1475–1542) The Second Dalai Lama.

Gönpo Guru A principal protector of the Sakya order.

Guardian Kings (Tib. chok kyong) The four kings of the four cardinal directions, who offer protection against harmful influences. They are found at the entrance of almost all temples and monasteries. They are Dhritarashta (east); Virupaksha (west), Virudhaka (south) and Vaishravana (north). See the Iconographical Guide.

Gushri Khan (1582–1655) The Mongolian emperor who installed the Fifth Dalai Lama as ruler of Tibet in 1642.

Guhyasamaja (Tib. Sangdu) A deity of the supreme yoga tantras. See the Iconographical Guide.

Gyeltsab Je (1364–1431) One of the principal disciples of Tsongkhapa and the second Throne Holder of Ganden.

H

Hayagriva (Tib. Tandrin) The "Horse Necked One," a wrathful protector and tantric deity. See the Iconographical Guide.

Hepori One of the four holy mountains of Central Tibet. It is located behind Samye Monastery.

Hevajra (Tib. Kye Dorje) A deity of the supreme yoga tantras especially revered in the Sakya order. See the Iconographical Guide.

Hinayana (Tib. tegmen) The so-called "individual vehicle" or "smaller vehicle" of Buddhism, in which one is concerned with one's own liberation alone.

J

Jamöchen Choje (1352–1435) Shakya Yeshe, the disciple of Tsongkhapa who founded Sera Monastery.

Jampel Gyatso (1758–1804) The Eighth Dalai Lama.

Jamyang Chöje (1397–1449) The disciple of Tsongkhapa who founded Drepung Monastery.

Jamyang Zhepa (1648–1721) A renowned scholar of Drepung Monastery who founded Labrang Monastery in Amdo.

Jangchub Gyeltsen (1302–1373) The leader of the Pamotrupa who overthrew the Sakya dynasty in 1354 and established himself as ruler of Tibet.

Jangtang The great northern plain of Tibet, inhabited mainly by nomads.

Jataka tales (Tib. kyerab) Stories of Buddha Shakyamuni's previous lives.

Jokhang The main cathedral in Lhasa that houses the Jowo image of Shakyamuni brought to Tibet by Wen Cheng, the Chinese wife of Songtsen Gampo, in the seventh century.

Jowo "Precious one," a name given to highly venerated statues of Shakyamuni Buddha.

K

Kadam The order of Tibetan Buddhism founded by Atisha and his followers in the eleventh century. The forerunner of the Geluk order.

Kagyu The order of Tibetan Buddhism founded in the eleventh century by Marpa, Milarepa, Gampopa, and their followers. It has many suborders.

Kalachakra (Tib. Dukor) The "Wheel of Time," one of the most complex of the supreme yoga tantras. It is associated with the mystical land of Shambhala. See the Iconographical Guide.

Kalki (Tib. rigden) The "spiritual president" of Shambhala. There are twenty-five of them, each of whom rules for one hundred years. We are now in the reign of the twenty-second kalki, Aniruddha (Tib. Magagpa) (1927–2027).

Kamalashila An Indian disciple of Shantarakshita who came to Tibet in the eighth century to debate with the Chinese master Hvasang Mahayana at Samye Monastery.

Kangyur "The Translation of the Word," the part of the Tibetan Buddhist canon that contains the discourses attributed to Buddha Shakyamuni.

Karmapa The line of incarnate lamas of the Karma Kagyu suborder within the Kagyu order who are based at Tsurpu Monastery near Lhasa. The First Karmapa, Dusum Khyenpa (1110–1193) was a disciple of Gampopa and the founder of Tsurpu. The Sixteenth Karmapa, Rigpai Dorje, died in Chicago in 1981. The Seventeenth Karmapa, Ugyen Tinley, resides in Tsurpu.

Kashyapa (Tib. Ösung) A buddha of the past.

Kelsang Gyatso (1708–1757) The Seventh Dalai Lama.

Kham The large eastern province of Tibet, now partially annexed to the Chinese provinces of Sichuan and Yunnan.

Khangtsen A house of a college (*dratsang*) in a Tibetan Buddhist monastery, which serves as the residential quarters of the monks. The members of a particular khangtsen usually all hail from the same region of Tibet.

Khedrup Je (1385-1438) A chief disciple of Tsongkhapa who became the third Throne Holder of Ganden and was retrospectively recognized as the First Panchen Lama.

Könchok Gyelpo (1034–1102) The founder of the Sakya order and father of Kunga Nyingpo.

Kshitigarbha (Tib. Sa'i Nyingpo) The "Essence of the Earth," one of the Eight Great Bodhisattvas.

Kunga Nyingpo (1092–1158) Also called Sachen, the son of Könchok Gyelpo and one of the five great masters of the Sakya order.

L

Labrang The hereditary wealth and dwellings of an incarnate lama (*tulku*).

Lama (Skt. guru) A religious teacher and guide, either male or female. Only a few monks and even fewer nuns are considered to be lamas.

Langdarma (803–842) The last king of the Yarlung dynasty, who persecuted Buddhism. Assassinated by a Buddhist monk, Lhalungpa Pelgyi Dorje.

Lhatotori (c. 347–467) The twenty-eighth king of the Yarlung dynasty, during whose reign Tibet had its first contact with Buddhism.

Longchenpa (1306–1363) A great scholar and mystic of the Nyingma order.

Losang Gyatso (1617–1682) The Great Fifth Dalai Lama, who started the rule of the Dalai Lamas and the construction of the Potala Palace.

Losar The Tibetan New Year, celebrated on the first day of the first lunar month (usually in February or early March).

M

Mahakala (Tib. Nagpo Chenpo) A wrathful protector and tantric deity.

Mahasiddha (Tib. drupchen) A realized adept of the tantric path. There are traditionally eighty-four Indian mahasiddhas.

Mahayana (Tib. tegchen) The "great vehicle" or "universal vehicle" of Buddhist practice, in which one is dedicated to the attainment of enlightenment for the welfare of others.

Maitreya (Tib. Jampa) The "Loving One" who is the buddha of the future. Also one of the Eight Great Bodhisattvas. See the Iconographical Guide.

Mandala (Tib. kyilkor) The divine abode of an enlightened being visualized during tantric practices. Represented two-dimensionally as a circular pattern.

Mandarava Padmasambhava's main Indian consort.

Manjushri (Tib. Jampelyang) The bodhisattva of wisdom. See the Iconographical Guide.

Mantra A series of Sanskrit syllables, sometimes but not always possessing a literal meaning, the utterance of which is thought to create particular effects in the mind of oneself or others.

Marpa (1012–1097) One of the founding figures of the Kagyu order. A translator who visited India and studied under the mahasiddha Naropa. Milarepa's lama.

Maudgalyayana One of the two chief arhat disciples of Buddha Shakyamuni.

Medicine Buddha (Tib. Sanggye Melha) The buddha of healing. See the Icono-

graphical Guide.

Milarepa (1040–1123) The great poet-saint of Tibet. The chief disciple of Marpa and teacher of Gampopa. A founding figure of the Kagyu order. See the Iconographical Guide.

Mönlam Festival A prayer festival inaugurated by Tsongkhapa in 1409. It takes place at the Jokhang in Lhasa after the new year celebrations of Losar. It was discontinued by the Chinese from 1959 to 1985.

Mudra Most commonly a hand gesture that indicates a particular attitude of a buddha or bodhisattva.

N

Naga (Tib. lu) A species of intelligent subaquatic being with snakelike features.

Nagarjuna (Tib. Lu Drup) The second-century C.E. Indian Buddhist philosopher who propounded the Madhyamaka philosophy of emptiness.

Naropa (1016–1100) The Indian scholar and mahasiddha who taught Marpa.

Ngog Legpa'i Sherab A renowned Tibetan translator who became the interpreter for and close disciple of Atisha.

Nirmanakaya The so-called "emanation body" of a buddha. This is the form of a buddha that is visible to ordinary sentient beings. The emanation body of

Shakyamuni is usually depicted wearing monk's robes. In Mahayana Buddhism, it is maintained that a buddha can emanate in any form that will help sentient beings.

Nyatri Tsenpo The somewhat mythical first king of Tibet, whose origins are traced back to the Indian descendants of King Bimbisara, a contemporary of the Buddha.

Nyingma The "ancient" order of Tibetan Buddhism, which traces its teaching back to the time of Padmasambhava and includes in its canon works and translations dating from the early period of the dissemination of Buddhism in Tibet.

P

Pabongka Rinpoche (1878–1941) An influential and powerful lama of the Geluk order, the teacher of the tutors of the present Dalai Lama.

Padmasambhava The eighth-century Indian tantric master invited to Tibet by King Trisong Detsen to clear away the influences obstructing the establishment of Buddhism. See the Iconographical Guide.

Pakpa (1235–1280) One of the five great masters of the Sakya order, who was appointed spiritual and temporal ruler of Tibet by Kublai Khan in 1260.

Paksam Trishing (Skt. Avadanakalpalata)

A work by the Indian Buddhist poet Ksemendra recounting some of the previous lives of the Buddha.

Pamotrupa (1110–1170) A disciple of Gampopa and an important lama of the Kaygu order who founded Densatil Monastery near Tsetang. Also the family name of the dynasty founded by Jangchub Gyeltsen that succeeded the Sakya dynasty.

Panchen Lama The head lama of Tashilhunpo monastery. A series of incarnate lamas, the first of whom was Tsongkhapa's disciple Khedrup Je, and the fourth of whom was Chökyi Gyeltsen, a teacher of the Fifth Dalai Lama. The identity of the present Panchen Lama is under dispute, with the Dalai Lama's choice being rejected by the Chinese authorities in favor of their own candidate. Traditionally recognized as a manifestation of Amitabha Buddha.

Pandit or *pandita* A Sanskrit term meaning "wise and learned person."

Parinirvana. The final passing away of a buddha.

Pelden Lhamo (Skt. Shri Devi) A wrathful protectress who is depicted riding a mule. See the Iconographical Guide.

Potala The winter palace of the Dalai Lamas in Lhasa built during the seventeenth century. Also the Pure Land of

Avalokiteshvara.

Prajnaparamita (Tib. sher chin) The "Perfection of Wisdom." A series of discourses given by Shakyamuni on the topic of emptiness. Also the name of the female deity who personifies wisdom.

Pure Land (Tib. dag shing) A nonsamsaric realm of existence created by the wisdom and compassion of a buddha or advanced bodhisattva, in which one can be reborn through the force of meditation and prayer.

R

Ralpachen (805–836) The last of the three great religious kings of Tibet (the other two being Songtsen Gampo and Trisong Detsen). Considered to be a manifestation of Vajrapani.

Ramoche The smaller of the two main cathedrals in Lhasa. Founded by Wen Cheng, the Chinese wife of Songtsen Gampo, in the seventh century.

Rechungpa (1084–1161) An important disciple of Milarepa and leading figure of the Kagyu order.

Rendawa The Sakya lama who was the main teacher of Tsongkhapa.

Rinchen Zangpo (958–1055) An important Tibetan translator from Western Tibet who was a contemporary of Atisha.

Rinpoche. A title of respect and reverence that means "Precious One." It is used mostly for *tulkus* and also great beings like Padmasambhava.

S

Sadhana (Tib. drub tab) Literally a "means" or a "method," a *sadhana* is a liturgical text used in tantric meditation.

Sakya "Tawny Earth," the name of the place where Könchok Gyelpo founded the first monastery of the Sakya order of Tibetan Buddhism in 1073.

Sakya Pandita (1182-1251) The title of Kunga Gyeltsen, one of the five great masters of the Sakya order.

Sambhogakaya The so-called "enjoyment body" of a buddha. This is the form of a buddha that is perceived by high level bodhisattvas. It is usually adorned with the royal ornaments associated with kings.

Samvara (Tib. Demchok) An important deity of the supreme yoga tantras. See the Iconographical Guide.

Samye The first monastery established in Tibet. It was founded by King Trisong Detsen, Shantarakshita, and Padmasambhava on the northern bank of the Brahmaputra near Tsetang in the eighth century.

Sangha The community of Buddhist practitioners; one of the "three jewels" of

Buddhism. Sometimes refers specifically to Buddhist monks and nuns.

Sarasvati (Tib. Yangchenma) "The Melodious Lady," the bodhisattva of music, poetry, and learning.

Self-originating images Images (usually statues, but also frequently impressions left in rocks) that are said to have arisen spontaneously, without human effort or design.

Seven Symbols of Royal Power These are seven objects that a great king, especially a Dharma king, must possess. They are the precious wheel, the precious jewel, the precious queen, the precious minister, the precious elephant, the precious horse, and the precious general.

Shakyamuni (Tib. Shakya Tubpa) The historical Buddha, Gautama, who lived in India around 500 B.C.E. See the Iconographical Guide.

Shambhala The mythical land associated with the Kalachakra tantra; it is thought to lie somewhere north of Tibet in Central Asia.

Shantarakshita (Tib. Shiwatso and Khenchen Bodhisattva) A great Indian philosopher and abbot invited to Tibet in the eighth century by King Trisong Detsen. He helped founded Samye and established the monastic order in Tibet.

Shariputra (Tib. Shari-pu) One of the chief arhat disciples of Shakyamuni.

Sitatapatra (Tib. Dugkarma) "The Lady with the White Parasol," a multi-headed and multi-armed deity.

Six Ornaments (Tib. gyen druk) Six of the most important Buddhist philosophers of ancient India: Nagarjuna, Aryadeva, Asanga, Vasubandhu, Dignaga, and Dharmakirti.

Sixteen Arhats (Tib. neten chu-druk) The sixteen principal saints who were the immediate disciples of Shakyamuni in the Hinayana tradition.

Sonam Gyatso (1543–1587) The Third Dalai Lama, the first of the line to be given the title Dalai Lama, which was bestowed on him by the Mongolian emperor Altan Khan.

Sonam Tsemo (1142–1182) One of the five Sakya masters, a son of Kunga Nyingpo and brother of Drakpa Gyeltsen.

Songtsen Gampo (617–649) The first of the religious kings of Tibet. He introduced Buddhism to the country, consolidated the Yarlung dynasty, and built the Jokhang. He is considered to be a manifestation of Avalokiteshvara.

Stupa (Tib. *chöten*) A reliquary for a buddha's remains. Stupas can also contain relics of great masters, texts, and other precious substances. Tibetans maintain that circumambulating a stupa in a clockwise direction produces great merit toward enlightenment.

Sukhavati (Tib. Dewachen) The Pure Land in the west, where the Buddha Amitabha resides.

Supreme yoga tantra (Tib. lame naljor gyu, Skt, mahanuttarayogatantra) The highest of the four classes of Buddhist tantras.

Sutra (Tib. do) A discourse attributed to Shakyamuni Buddha. Sometimes used to distinguish the exoteric teachings of the Buddha from the esoteric teachings of the tantras. The texts that make up the Kangyur.

T

Tangka Religious scroll painting.

Tangtong Gyelpo (1385–1509) Tibetan saint, doctor, engineer, and artist.

Tantra (Tib. gyu) A class of Buddhist scriptures that speak in a symbolic language and describe practices that involve mantra recitation, visualization of deities and mandalas, and yogic practices aimed at rechanneling the energies of the body and mind. There are four classes of tantra: kriya (action), charya (performance), yoga, and supreme yoga tantra.

Tara (Tib. Drölma) The female deity whose two primary peaceful forms are Green Tara and White Tara. See the Iconographical Guide.

Taranata (1575–1634) A Buddhist scholar of the short-lived Jonangpa school. A master of the Kalachakra tantra and a noted historian.

Tathagata An alternative name for a fully enlightened buddha. Literally it means "One who has Gone Thus."

Tengyur The "Translation of the Commentaries," the part of the Tibetan Buddhist canon that contains the Indian commentarial literature on the Buddha's discourses. See also *Kangyur*.

Tenzin Gyatso (1935–) The Fourteenth Dalai Lama. He now lives in exile in Dharamsala, North India.

Tertön A discoverer of texts hidden by Padmasambhava and others in the early years of Buddhism's dissemination in Tibet.

Thirty-Five Buddhas of Confession A group of thirty-five archetypal buddhas before whom the practice of confessing unwholesome deeds is performed. They are listed in the *Triskandha Sutra*.

Tibetan Book of the Dead (Tib. Bardo Tödröl) A text attributed to Padmasambhava in which the experiences and visions of the after-death state (*bardo*) are described. It is often read for the deceased during the forty-nine day period between death and rebirth.

Tönmi Sambhota A gifted minister of King Songtsen Gampo who devised the script and basic grammar of written Tibetan.

Torma A cake made from *tsampa*, butter, and sugar, which is used as an offering in religious ceremonies.

Trijang Rinpoche (1899–1981) The late junior tutor of the present Dalai Lama. One of the most renowned lamas of the Geluk order of this century.

Trisong Detsen (742–797) The second great religious king of Tibet. He is considered as a manifestation of Manjushri.

Tsampa Roasted barley flour. A Tibetan staple food.

Tsang The province of Tibet to the west of Lhasa. The capital is Shigatse.

Tsangyang Gyatso (1683–1706) The Sixth Dalai Lama.

Tsa-tsa. Small images made from pressing clay (often mixed with sacred substances and relics) into molds. Tsa-tsa are frequently made by the thousands and placed inside stupas.

Tsongkhapa (1357–1419) Also known as Losang Trakpa, the great reformer of Tibetan Buddhism who founded what came to be known as the Geluk order.

Tubten Gyatso (1876–1933) The Thirteenth Dalai Lama.

Tulku A reincarnate lama. A person who can control the rebirth process and who takes rebirth in a manner calculated to benefit sentient beings. This aspect of Buddhism appears to be unique to Tibet.

Tushita (Tib. Ganden) The name of the Pure Land where the future Buddha Maitreya presently resides.

Two Supreme Ones (Tib. chok nyi) Shakyaprabha and Gunaprabha, two Indian masters who wrote on the Buddhist monastic rule (*vinaya*). Usually represented together with the Six Ornaments.

V

Vairochana (Tib. Nampa Nangdze) "The Illuminating One"; one of the five Dhyani Buddhas.

Vaishravana (Tib. Namtose) The Buddhist god of wealth. The guardian king of the north. See the Iconographical Guide.

Vajrabhairava. See *Yamantaka.*

Vajradhara (Tib. Dorje Chang) The tantric form of Shakyamuni Buddha. See the Iconographical Guide.

Vajrapani (Tib. Chana Dorje) The bodhisattva who personifies the energy and power of the Buddha. See the Iconographical Guide.

Vajrasattva (Tib. Dorje Sempa) The bodhisattva who personifies the purity of enlightenment. See the Iconographical Guide.

Vajrayana (Tib. dorje tegpa) The "diamond vehicle" of tantric Buddhism. A division of Mahayana Buddhism.

Vajrayogini (Tib. Dorje Neljorma) A female tantric deity who represents the female energy of buddhahood. See the Iconographical Guide.

Vasubandhu (Tib. Yig Nyen) An Indian Buddhist scholar of the fourth century. A brother of Asanga.

Vijaya (Tib. Namgyelma) A female deity associated with longevity. See the Iconographical Guide.

W

Wen Cheng The Chinese wife of King Songtsen Gampo.

Y

Yab-yum Literally meaning "father-mother," this term refers to the depiction of male and female tantric deities in sexual union. In the yab-yum symbolism, the male deity represents compassion and the female deity represents wisdom.

Yamantaka (Tib. Dorje Jigje) The wrathful, bull-headed deity who is the tantric manifestation of Manjushri. Also known as Vajrabhairava. See the Iconographical Guide.

Yeshe Tsogyel The chief Tibetan consort of Padmasambhava, formerly a wife of King Trisong Detsen. A renowned tantric practitioner.

Yidam Tutelary deity; the particular tantric deity with whom a practitioner has a special affinity and whom he or she visualizes in meditation.

Yoga tantra (Tib. Neljor Gyu) The third of the four classes of the Buddhist tantras.

Yogi (Tib. nyal jor pa). A male advanced practitioner of tantric meditation.

Yogini (Tib. nyal jor ma). A female advanced practitioner of tantric meditation.

Yogurt Festival A joyous end of summer celebration held annually in Lhasa on the twenty-ninth day of the sixth lunar month.

Yutok Yönten Gonpo (729–854) A famous physician who founded the unique form of Tibetan medicine.

SUGGESTED READING

TRAVEL

Journey to Lhasa and Central Tibet. Sarat Chandra Das. New Delhi: Manjushri Publishing House, 1970 (reprint).

This is the journal that Sarat Chandra Das wrote describing his fourteen-month visit to Tibet in 1881 and 1882. Das, an Indian scholar and probably a British intelligence agent, proves to be a transparent observer who provides a clear and detailed picture of old Tibet, good and bad. He visited Tashilhunpo, Sakya, Gyantse, Lhasa, Samye, and Tsetang.

The Way of the White Clouds. Lama Anagarika Govinda. London: Rider, 1966.

This beautifully written book describes Lama Govinda's pilgrimage to Western Tibet in 1948. The account of the journey is enriched by the author's personal reflections on the spiritual path and the mystical teachings of Tibetan Buddhism.

To Lhasa and Beyond. Giuseppe Tucci. London: East-West Publications, 1985 (reprint).

This travelogue recounts the 1949 expedition to Central Tibet of Professor Tucci, one of this century's foremost Tibetologists. It covers Shigatse, Gyantse, Yerpa, Ganden, Samye, and the Yarlung and Chonggye Valleys.

Seven Years in Tibet. Heinrich Harrer. Translated from the German by Ewald Osers. New York: Viking Penguin, 1985.

This story of the escape from India from a British internment camp across the Himalayas into Western Tibet and the arduous journey to Lhasa is both a tribute to human endurance and a rare account of life amongst the Tibetan nobility during the final years of independence. Harrer became a tutor to the young Dalai Lama.

From Heaven Lake. Vikram Seth. London: Chatto and Windus, 1983.

The acclaimed novelist Vikram Seth describes the overland journey he made as a student in the summer of 1981 from China via Xinjiang, Gansu, Qinghai, Tibet, and Nepal to India. One of the very first post-Mao accounts of Tibet and Seth's first published work.

Inside the Treasure House. Catriona Bass. London: Gollancz, 1990.

A vivid and moving description of life in Lhasa and Central Tibet by one of the first Westerners to spend an extended period in the country after the liberalizations of the mid-1980s.

The Sacred Mountain. John Snelling. London: East-West Publications, 1983 (updated and expanded, 1989).

This is an informative and entertaining study of foreign travelers and pilgrims who have visited Mount Kailash in Western Tibet, from the first Jesuit missionaries in 1715 to latter day explorers Victor Chan, Bradley Rowe, Brian Beresford, and Sean Jones in the 1980s. An invaluable companion for anyone contemplating a trip to this part of Tibet.

HISTORY

Tibet: A Political History. Tsepon W.D. Shakapa. New York: Potala Publications, 1984.

This authoritative history of Tibet was authored by Tibet's Secretary of Finance from 1930–50. Written from an informed Tibetan perspective, it tells the story of Tibet from the times of the early kings until the Dalai Lama's exile in 1959.

A History of Modern Tibet, 1913–1951. Melvyn C. Goldstein. Berkeley: University of California Press, 1989.

This detailed study of the crucial years in Tibet's struggle to preserve its independence offers a nonpartisan and well-documented account of the political events that led to the invasion of Tibet by the Chinese PLA.

In Exile from the Land of Snows. John F. Avedon. London: Wisdom, 1985.

This acclaimed account of the Tibetan situation is one of the most readable currently available. It describes the historical and political background of the Dalai Lama's flight to India in 1959, the subsequent events that have taken place in Tibet under Chinese occupation, and the struggle the refugees have undergone to sustain their culture abroad.

A Cultural History of Tibet. David Snellgrove and Hugh Richardson. Boston: Shambhala, 1986.

This excellent though rather dense study explores all the principal features of Tibetan culture and provides a comprehensive view of the people, their religion, customs, literature, and history. It has many good photographs of old Tibet but the scholarly transliteration of Tibetan words may trouble non-specialists.

Civilised Shamans: Buddhism in Tibetan Societies. Geoffrey Samuel. Washington: Smithsonian Institute, 1993.

This encyclopedic, 700-page description of all aspects of Tibetan society and history in their relation to Buddhism takes a fresh and challenging look at the way old Tibet functioned.

TIBETAN BUDDHISM

The Door to Satisfaction. Lama Thubten Zopa Rinpoche. Boston: Wisdom, 1994.

A traditional and clear account of the basic teachings and practices of Tibetan Buddhism by one of the foremost lamas teaching in the West today.

Ceremonies of the Lhasa Year. Hugh Richardson. London: Serindia, 1993.

This fascinating eye-witness account of the ceremonies and festivals of old Lhasa starts with the New Year festival, Losar, and continues through all the months of the year. The narrative, in which many details of Tibetan religious practice and culture are explained, is accompanied by stunning black and white photographs from the 1930s and 1940s.

Cutting Through Spiritual Materialism. Chögyam Trungpa Rinpoche. Boston: Shambhala, 1973.

This popular introduction to Tibetan Buddhism is written in a clear and humorous style that makes traditional teachings accessible to a contemporary audience.

The Crystal and the Way of Light. Namkhai Norbu Rinpoche. London: Routledge, 1986.

This book combines autobiography with a clear exposition of the Dzogchen (Great Perfection) teachings of direct self-liberation.

The Wisdom of No Escape. Pema Chödrön. Boston: Shambhala, 1991.

An engaging and down-to-earth presentation of Buddhist practice as taught during a one-month intensive retreat by a senior Western nun.

Awakening the Buddha Within: Eight Steps to Enlightenment, Tibetan Wisdom for the Western World. Lama Surya Das. New York: Broadway Books, 1997.

A contemporary presentation of Tibetan Buddhist teachings and practices, illustrated with both traditional tales and anecdotes from the author's own time spent with Tibetan lamas in India and the West.

The Tibetan Book of the Dead. Guru Rinpoche according to Karma Lingpa. Translated by Francesca Fremantle and Chögyam Trungpa. Boston: Shambhala, 1975. (Other translations by Robert Thurman and Gyurme Dorje are also available.)

Although well-known, this book might be baffling for a beginner seeking an explanation of Tibetan Buddhism. It is nonetheless an evocative and inspiring text, which vividly describes the stages and visions believed to occur between death and rebirth.

The Words of My Perfect Teacher. Patrul Rinpoche. Translated by the Padmakara Translation Group. New York: Harper Collins, 1994.

This detailed and readable nineteenth-century text describes the stages on the Buddhist path to enlightenment by one of the most renowned teachers of the time.

TIBETAN MEDICINE

Health through Balance. Dr. Yeshe Donden. Ithaca: Snow Lion, 1986.

The Tibetan medical system is clearly explained in this collection of lectures presented to students at the University of Virginia by the former personal physician to the Dalai Lama.

BIOGRAPHY

Ama Adhe: The Voice that Remembers. Adhe Tapontsang as told to Joy Blakeslee. Boston: Wisdom, 1997.

After twenty-seven brutal years in Chinese prison camps, Adhe survived with extraordinary courage and dignity to tell this chilling story.

The Life of Milarepa. Translated by Lobsang P. Lhalungpa. Boston: Shambhala, 1986.

This autobiography of Tibet's most loved saint is a classic in its own country and readable and moving in translation.

Born in Tibet. Chögyam Trungpa Rinpoche. London: Unwin, 1987.

The vivid account of the life of a Tibetan incarnate lama who was born in Kham in 1939 and enthroned as the abbot of Surmang Monastery. Trungpa describes his training as a monk and his eventual flight to India.

Warriors of Tibet. Jamyang Norbu. Boston: Wisdom, 1987.

This is the story of a Tibetan Khampa warrior, Aten, and his people of Nyarong. Aten recalls his life as a child, the simple ways of the Khampas and the beauty of his homeland in Eastern Tibet.

Freedom in Exile. The Dalai Lama. London: Hodder and Stoughton, 1990.

This life of the present Dalai Lama in his own voice covers everything from his childhood in Lhasa to his receiving the Nobel Peace Prize. The book provides both a unique perspective on the tragedy of Tibet and personal reflections that illuminate the Dalai Lama's understanding and application of Buddhism.

INDEX

PHOTOGRAPHIC ACKNOWLEDG- MENTS

COLOR (by plate number)

Stephen Batchelor 33, 39, 50, 66, 71, 95, 96

Robin Bath 28, 75

Simon Chaput 2, 5, 9, 15, 17, 51

Ted Hallstrom 34

Sara Jolly 3, 6, 18, 21, 23, 35, 38, 40, 41, 43, 58, 60, 63, 67, 68, 78, 82, 87

Brian Kistler 10, 11, 14, 19, 22, 25, 26, 30, 46, 69, 70, 73, 74, 76, 77, 79, 80, 85, 88, 89, 90, 91, 92, 93, 94, 97, 98

Trey Nicholson 57

Hamid Sardar 13, 16, 20, 27, 29, 31, 32, 36, 48, 49, 52, 53, 54, 59, 61, 62, 64, 65, 72, 81, 83, 84, 86

Vernon Soni 1, 8, 24

Amina Tirana 4, 7, 12, 42, 44, 45, 47, 55, 56

BLACK AND WHITE (by page number)

Charles Allen 51

Hugh Richardson 2 (except for top), 12, 21, 22, 45, 46, 49, 50, 103, 130, 138, 144, 147, 152, 169, 185, 200, 233 (left and right)

F. Williamson, Esq, C.I.E., I.C.S., reproduced by kind permission of Mrs. Margaret D. Williamson 20, 205, 252, 256

FRONT COVER

Clockwise from the upper left corner: Kistler, Hallstrom, Sardar, Chaput, Sardar, Chaput, Tirana, Tirana, Tirana, Chaput, Sardar, Kistler (center)

BACK COVER

Clockwise from lower left corner: Sardar, Sardar, Kistler, Jolly, Nicholson, Beer (diagram), author photo courtesy of *Tricycle: The Buddhist Review*

ABOUT THE AUTHORS

Stephen Batchelor

Stephen Batchelor was born in Scotland and educated at Watford Grammar School and in Buddhist monasteries in India, Switzerland, and Korea. He has translated and written several books on Buddhism, including *A Guide to the Bodhisattva's Way of Life, Alone with Others, The Faith to Doubt, The Tibet Guide* (winner of the 1988 Thomas Cook Award), *The Awakening of the West* (joint-winner of the 1994 Tricycle Award), and most recently *Buddhism Without Beliefs*. He lectures and conducts meditation retreats worldwide, is a contributing editor to *Tricycle: the Buddhist Review*, and is Director of Studies at the Sharpham College for Buddhist Studies and Contemporary Enquiry, Devon, England.

Sean Jones

Sean Jones is a British traveler, based in Pakistan since 1967. He has lived and traveled extensively in the upper Indus Basin between Afghanistan and Nepal, and Northern India. He traveled independently in Tibet in 1985, 1986, 1988, and 1995, spending several months in Western Tibet in the course of two pilgrimages to Mount Kailash. In London he ran a travel business in the 1980's, helping to found there a number of Tibet- and Buddhist-related voluntary organizations. He now works as a trustee of one of these, the charitable development agency "Appropriate Technology for Tibetans" (ApTibeT), to facilitate sustainable development amongst the Tibetan community in exile.

Brian Beresford

Brian Beresford was born in Auckland, New Zealand in 1948. He traveled extensively through Asia in the early 70s and studied Tibetan Buddhism, its philosophy, language and culture in Dharamsala between 1972-78. He translated many Tibetan texts, and was an accomplished photographer and raconteur, being one of the first Westerners to reach the Mount Kailash region in 1986. He had a particular passion for Western Tibet, and led several pilgrimage groups to Mount Kailash. A man of many talents, he lived in London until his death in January 1997.

Robert Beer

Robert Beer was born in 1947. In the 60s he developed an interest in oriental art and symbolism. A self taught artist, he has practiced and studied Tibetan art since then. Between 1970 and 1975 he lived in India and Nepal, where he studied thangka painting and Indian music. At present he lives in London and is currently completing a manual on Tibetan art and symbolism.

OTHER BOOKS FROM WISDOM PUBLICATIONS

AMA ADHE:
THE VOICE THAT REMEMBERS
The Heroic Story of a Woman's Fight to Free Tibet

Adhe Tapontsang as told to Joy Blakeslee

This is the story of a woman's and her country's spiritual struggle for survival. Imprisoned for participating in the resistance to China's occupation of Tibet during the 1950's, Adhe Tapontsang spent 27 years in Chinese labor camps. She is one of the few who survived to tell the stories of torture, starvation, and degradation that countless Tibetans endured and continue to experience today. As the first full-length testimony of a Tibetan woman's prison camp experience, Ama Adhe is "the voice that remembers" for those who can no longer speak. Her personal story speaks powerfully of modern Tibet's tragic saga of occupation, genocide, and cultural destruction.

"A book that must be read"—Amnesty International

272 pp., 6 x 9, cloth, ISBN 0-86171-130-0, $19.95

DAUGHTER OF TIBET

Rinchen Dolma Taring

The moving personal story of a Tibetan woman raised in the closely-knit world of Tibetan nobility and her subsequent work for her people in exile.

324 pp., 5 1/4 x 8 1/2, paper, ISBN 0-86171-044-4, $18.95

THE TIBETAN ART OF PARENTING
From Before Conception Through Early Childhood

Anne Hubbell Maiden and Edie Farwell

"Provides a fascinating, invaluable context for understanding our desires for the best possible childbirth experiences. Well researched and clearly written." —Elizabeth Davis, C.P.M., author of Heart and Hands: A Midwife's Guide to Pregnancy and Birth

"The Tibetan Art of Parenting brings to those of us in the West a finely crafted distillation of centuries of Tibetan experience of reproduction and parenting from a circle-of-life perspective, including the spiritual dimension and what it means to be invested in life."—Robert A. Anderson, M.D., President, American Board of Holistic Medicine

208 pp., 6 x 9, paper, ISBN 0-86171-129-7 $16.95

TIBETAN BUDDHISM FROM THE GROUND UP
A Practical Approach for Modern Life

B. Alan Wallace

Here at last is an organized overview of the teachings of Tibetan Buddhism, beginning with the basic themes of the sutras—the general discourses of the Buddha—and continuing through the esoteric concepts and advanced practices of Tantra. This accessible, enjoyable work doesn't stop with theory and history but relates timeless spiritual principles to the pressing issues of modern life, both in terms of our daily experience and our uniquely Western world view.

"This book is user-friendly." —Mandala

228 pp., 6 X 9, paper, ISBN 0-86171-075-4, $14.00

THE WORLD OF TIBETAN BUDDHISM
An Overview of Its Philosophy and Practice

The Dalai Lama
Foreword by Richard Gere

With characteristic humility, His Holiness the Dalai Lama begins this landmark survey of the entire Buddhist path saying, "I think an overview of Tibetan Buddhism for the purpose of providing a comprehensive framework of the Buddhist path may prove helpful in deepening your understanding and practice."

224 pp., 6 x 9, cloth, ISBN 0-86171-100-9, $25.00; paper, ISBN 0-86171-097-5, $14.00

THE WARRIOR SONG OF KING GESAR

Douglas J. Penick
Introduction by Tulku Thondup Rinpoche

In his modern rendition of this ancient tale, Penick brings us the unbroken heritage of spiritual warriorship embodied by the life of the enlightened warrior-sage Gesar, King of Ling. Recreated by visionary bards of Central Asia for centuries, the Gesar story dramatizes the struggle to overcome the obstacles which prevent us all from finding true freedom. "...valuable and inspiring..."—*Shambhala Sun*

176 pp., 6 x 9, paper, ISBN 0-86171-113-0, $16.95

MEMOIRS OF A POLITICAL OFFICER'S WIFE IN TIBET, SIKKIM, AND BHUTAN

Margaret D. Williamson

A personal account of three Himalayan kingdoms between 1930 and 1935.

240 pp., 5 1/4 x 8 1/2, paper
ISBN 0-86171-056-8, $18.95

PORTRAIT OF A DALAI LAMA
The Life and Times of the Great Thirteenth

Charles Bell

The story of one of Tibet's greatest religious and political leaders as told by his English friend.

464 pp., 5 1/4 x 8 1/2, paper
ISBN 0-86171-055-X , $22.95

TIBET IS MY COUNTRY
The Autobiography of Thubten Jigme Norbu, Brother of the Dalai Lama, as Told to Heinrich Harrer (author of *Seven Years in Tibet*, the subject of a movie starring Brad Pitt)

Thubten Jigme Norbu

The Dalai Lama's brother recalls the details of his life.

276 pp., 5 1/4 x 8 1/2, paper
ISBN 0-86171-045-2, $16.95

WARRIORS OF TIBET
The Story of Aten and the Khampas' Fight for the Freedom of their Country

Jamyang Norbu

A heartfelt story of one man's struggle for Tibetan independence.

152 pp., 5 1/4 x 8 1/2, paper
ISBN 0-86171-050-9, $12.95

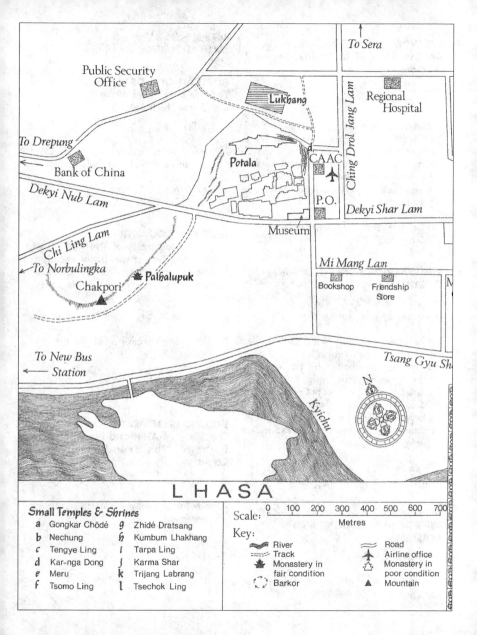

To Sera

Public Security
Office

Lukhang

Regional
Hospital

To Drepung

Bank of China

CAAC

Potala

P.O.

Dekyi Nub Lam

Dekyi Shar Lam

Chi Ling Lam

Museum

To Norbulingka

Mi Mang Lam

Palhalupuk

Bookshop

Friendship
Store

Chakpori

To New Bus
Station

Tsang Gyu Sh

Kyichu

N

LHASA

Small Temples & Shrines

a Gongkar Chödé   g Zhidé Dratsang
b Nechung   h Kumbum Lhakhang
c Tengye Ling   i Tarpa Ling
d Kar-nga Dong   j Karma Shar
e Meru   k Trijang Labrang
f Tsomo Ling   l Tsechok Ling

Scale: 0 100 200 300 400 500 600 700
Metres

Key:
〜 River
‑‑‑ Track
🛕 Monastery in fair condition
◌ Barkor

〜 Road
✈ Airline office
⛩ Monastery in poor condition
▲ Mountain

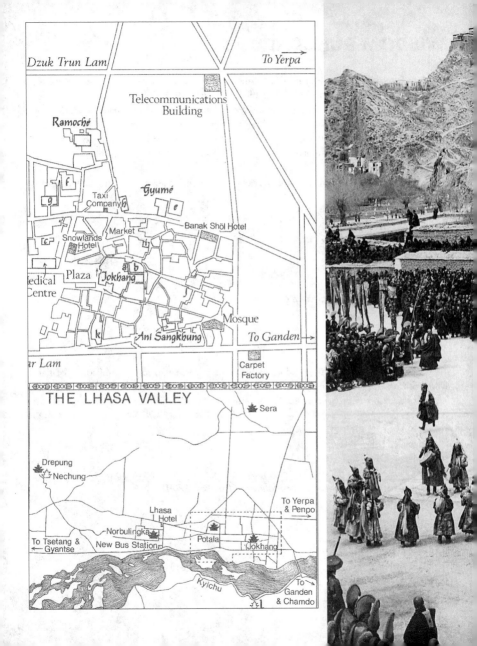

Dzuk Trun Lam

To Yerpa

Telecommunications Building

Ramoché

f

g

Taxi Company

Gyumé

h

e

Banak Shöl Hotel

Market

Snowlands Hotel

c

Medical Centre

Plaza

Jokhang

a b

j

Mosque

k

Ani Sangkhung

To Ganden

ar Lam

Carpet Factory

THE LHASA VALLEY

Sera

Drepung

Nechung

Lhasa Hotel

To Yerpa & Penpo

Norbulingka

New Bus Station

Potala

Jokhang

To Tsetang & Gyantse

To Ganden & Chamdo

Kyichu

WISDOM PUBLICATIONS

Wisdom Publications, a not-for-profit publisher, is dedicated to making available authentic Buddhist works for the benefit of all. We publish translations of the sutras and tantras, commentaries and teachings of past and contemporary Buddhist masters, and original works by the world's leading Buddhist scholars. We publish our titles with the appreciation of Buddhism as a living philosophy and with the special commitment to preserve and transmit important works from all the major Buddhist traditions.

If you would like more information or a copy of our mail-order catalogue, please contact us at:

Wisdom Publications
199 Elm Street
Somerville, Massachusetts 02144 USA
Telephone: (617) 776-7416
Fax: (617) 776-7841
E-mail: info@wisdompubs.org
Web Site: http://www.wisdompubs.org

THE WISDOM TRUST

As a not-for-profit publisher, Wisdom Publications is dedicated to the publication of fine Dharma books for the benefit of all sentient beings and dependent upon the kindness and generosity of sponsors in order to do so. If you would like to make a donation to Wisdom, please contact our Somerville office.

Thank you.

Wisdom Publications is a non-profit, charitable 501(c)(3) organization and a part of the Foundation for the Preservation of the Mahayana Tradition (FPMT).